UN Peacekeeping Doctrine in a New Era

This edited volume offers a thorough review of peacekeeping theory and reality in contemporary contexts, and aligns the two to help inform practice. Recent UN peacekeeping operations have challenged the traditional peacekeeping principles of consent, impartiality, and the minimum use of force. The pace and scope of these changes have now reached a tipping point, as the new mandates are fundamentally challenging the continued validity of the UN peacekeeping's core principles and identity.

In response the volume analyses the growing gap between these actual practices and existing UN peacekeeping doctrine, exploring how it undermines the effectiveness of UN operations, and endangers lives, arguing that a common doctrine is a critical starting point for effective multinational operations. In order to determine the degree to which this general principle applies to the current state of UN peacekeeping, this book:

- provides a review of conceptual and doctrinal developments in UN peacekeeping operations through a historical perspective;
- examines the debate related to peace operations doctrine and concepts among key member states;
- focuses on the actual practice of peacekeeping by conducting case studies of several UN peacekeeping missions in order to identify gaps between practice and doctrine;
- critically analyses gaps between emerging peacekeeping practice and existing doctrine; and
- recommends that the UN moves beyond the peacekeeping principles and doctrines of the past.

Combining empirical case-based studies on UN peace operations, with studies on the views and policies of key UN Security Council members that generate these mandates, and views of key contributors of UN peacekeepers, this volume will be of great use to policy-makers; UN officials and peace operations practitioners; and academics working on peace and conflict/security studies, international organizations, and conflict management.

Cedric de Coning is a Senior Research Fellow with the Peace and Conflict Research Group at the Norwegian Institute of International Affairs and is a Senior Advisor on Peacekeeping and Peacebuilding for ACCORD, South Africa.

Chiyuki Aoi is Professor of International Security and Strategic Studies, Graduate School of Public Policy (GraSPP), University of Tokyo, Japan.

John Karlsrud is Senior Research Fellow at the Norwegian Institute of International Affairs. He is an External Associate at the Centre for the Study of Globalisation and Regionalisation, University of Warwick, UK.

Global Institutions

Edited by Thomas G. Weiss
The CUNY Graduate Center, New York, USA
and Rorden Wilkinson
University of Sussex, Brighton, UK

About the series

The "Global Institutions Series" provides cutting-edge books about many aspects of what we know as "global governance." It emerges from our shared frustrations with the state of available knowledge—electronic and print-wise, for research and teaching—in the area. The series is designed as a resource for those interested in exploring issues of international organization and global governance. And since the first volumes appeared in 2005, we have taken significant strides toward filling conceptual gaps.

The series consists of three related "streams" distinguished by their blue, red, and green covers. The blue volumes, comprising the majority of the books in the series, provide user-friendly and short (usually no more than 50,000 words) but authoritative guides to major global and regional organizations, as well as key issues in the global governance of security, the environment, human rights, poverty, and humanitarian action among others. The books with red covers are designed to present original research and serve as extended and more specialized treatments of issues pertinent for advancing understanding about global governance. And the volumes with green covers—the most recent departure in the series—are comprehensive and accessible accounts of the major theoretical approaches to global governance and international organization.

The books in each of the streams are written by experts in the field, ranging from the most senior and respected authors to first-rate scholars at the beginning of their careers. In combination, the three components of the series—blue, red, and green—serve as key resources for faculty, students, and practitioners alike. The works in the blue and green streams have value as core and complementary readings in courses on, among other things, international organization, global governance, international law, international relations, and international political economy; the red volumes allow further reflection and investigation in these and related areas.

The books in the series also provide a segue to the foundation volume that offers the most comprehensive textbook treatment available dealing with all the major issues, approaches, institutions, and actors in contemporary global governance—our edited work *International Organization and Global Governance* (2014)—a volume to which many of the authors in the series have contributed essays.

Understanding global governance—past, present, and future—is far from a finished journey. The books in this series nonetheless represent significant steps toward a better way of conceiving contemporary problems and issues as well as, hopefully, doing something to improve world order. We value the feedback from our readers and their role in helping shape the on-going development of the series.

A complete list of titles appears at the end of this book. The most recent titles in the series are:

Global Environmental Institutions (2nd edition, 2017)
by Elizabeth R. DeSombre

Global Governance and Transnationalizing Capitalist Hegemony (2017)
by Ian Taylor

Human Rights and Humanitarian Intervention (2016)
edited by Elizabeth M. Bruch

The UN Peacebuilding Architecture (2016)
edited by Cedric de Coning and Eli Stamnes

Displacement, Development, and Climate Change (2016)
by Nina Hall

UN Security Council Reform (2016)
by Peter Nadin

International Organizations and Military Affairs (2016)
by Hylke Dijkstra

The International Committee of the Red Cross (2nd edition, 2016)
by David P. Forsythe and Barbara Ann J. Rieffer-Flanagan

UN Peacekeeping Doctrine in a New Era

Adapting to Stabilisation, Protection and New Threats

Edited by
Cedric de Coning, Chiyuki Aoi and John Karlsrud

Routledge
Taylor & Francis Group

LONDON AND NEW YORK

First published 2017
by Routledge
2 Park Square, Milton Park, Abingdon, Oxon OX14 4RN

and by Routledge
711 Third Avenue, New York, NY 10017

Routledge is an imprint of the Taylor & Francis Group, an informa business

British Library Cataloguing in Publication Data
A catalogue record for this book is available from the British Library

Library of Congress Cataloging in Publication Data
A catalog record for this book has been requested

ISBN: 978-1-138-22674-6 (hbk)
ISBN: 978-1-138-22675-3 (pbk)
ISBN: 978-1-315-39694-1 (ebk)

Typeset in Times New Roman
by Taylor & Francis Books

MIX
Paper from responsible sources
FSC
www.fsc.org   FSC® C013604

Printed and bound by CPI Group (UK) Ltd, Croydon, CR0 4YY

Contents

List of illustrations

Figure

Table

Contributors

Seun Abiola (Nigeria and UK) has served as Training Officer in the United Nations Department of Peacekeeping Operations (DPKO) in New York. As part of the Member States Support Team, she was the Project Manager for the revision of the United Nations Core Pre-deployment Training Materials for Peacekeeping Operations (CPTM), which is required mandatory training for all civilian, military, and police personnel. Previous to this, Seun was the Coordinator of the Peacekeeping Unit and the Head of the Training for Peace in Africa (TfP) Programme at the African Centre for the Constructive Resolution of Disputes (ACCORD), where she led research, policy development, and training initiatives in support of United Nations peacekeeping and African Union peace support operations. She was also a Researcher and Programme Officer at Prisoners' Rehabilitation and Welfare Action (PRAWA), where her work focused on justice and security sector reform in Nigeria, Kenya, Zambia, Rwanda, Burundi, and the Democratic Republic of Congo. She holds a Master's degree in Anthropology and (International) Development from the London School of Economics and Political Science (LSE), and a Bachelor's degree in Philosophy Politics and Economics from Oxford University.

Chiyuki Aoi (Japan) (co-editor) is Professor of International Security and Strategic Studies, Graduate School of Public Policy (GraSPP), University of Tokyo. She holds a Ph.D from Columbia University (USA). She has held various visiting research positions internationally, including Visiting Fellow at the Department of War Studies, King's College London (2008–9). Her main publications include *Legitimacy and the Use of Armed Force: Stability Missions in the Post-Cold War Era*, Routledge (Contemporary Security Studies Series), 2011; *Asia Pacific Nations in International Peace*

Support and Stability Missions, Palgrave (Asia Today Series), 2014 (Co-editor with Yee-Kuang Heng); "Japan and Stabilisation: Contributions and Preparedness," *RUSI Journal*, Vol. 156, No. 1 (February/March 2011), pp. 52–57; *Unintended Consequences of Peacekeeping Operations*, United Nations University Press, 2007 (Co-editor with Cedric de Coning and Ramesh Thakur). She previously held professional positions at the United Nations High Commissioner for Refugees (UNHCR) and the United Nations University (UNU).

Ian Bowers (Ireland) is an Assistant Professor at the Norwegian Institute for Defence Studies in Oslo. He holds a Ph.D. in War Studies from King's College London. His main research interests are Asian naval strategy and maritime security, South Korean security and foreign policy and military change. His most recent publications include "A Question of Balance: Warfighting and Naval Operations other than War" (with Jo Inge Bekkevold), in *International Order at Sea*, Till and Bekkevold (eds) (Palgrave, 2016); *Security, Strategy and Military Change in the 21st Century: Cross-Regional Perspectives*, co-edited with Jo Inge Bekkevold and Michael Raska, (Routledge, 2015) and "The Republic of Korea and Its Navy: Perceptions of Security and the Utility of Seapower," (*Journal of Strategic Studies*, 2014).

Maxim Bratersky (Russia) is a Professor in the Department of International Relations at the Higher School of Economics and Director of IMESS double-degree Master's Program at HSE. He graduated from Leningrad (now St. Petersburg) University with a degree in Oriental Languages and worked for several years as interpreter and translator, and published a book of translations of Hindi short stories. In 1987 he joined the Institute of US and Canada Studies of the Soviet Academy of Sciences and received his first doctorate in History of International Relations there. In 1993–2004 he worked at Stanford University, School of Social Sciences and Humanities as Director of Stanford's Moscow based program and taught as Visiting Professor there as well. In 2004 he joined the Higher School of Economics, and in 2005 defended his Habilitation in International Relations. He is the author of "What is What in International Relations" (co-authored*)* *Moscow, HSE, 2015* (forthcoming) (in Russian), "Russia and China in Eurasian Integration" (co-authored), Moscow, 2015 (in Russian), "Economic Instruments of Russian Foreign Policy" (2012) (in Russian), and "Economic Instruments of Foreign Policy and Political Risks", HSE, Moscow, 2010 (in Russian).

David Curran (UK) is a Research Fellow at the Centre for Trust, Peace and Social Relations, Coventry University, specializing in Peacekeeping, Peacebuilding, and Conflict Resolution. David's primary research investigates the role of conflict resolution in training programmes for military peacekeepers, which is the topic of his forthcoming monograph to be released in 2017 (with Springer Press). He has also published on the evolution of rapid-reaction peacekeeping and peacebuilding capabilities, as well as undertaking research into the United Kingdom's relationship with UN peacekeeping. David's recent publications include: "Perspectives on Peacekeeping and Atrocity Prevention—Expanding Stakeholders and Regional Arrangements" (co-editor, Springer, 2015); "Resonating, Rejecting, Reinterpreting: Mapping the Stabilisation Discourse in the United Nations Security Council, 2000–2014" (with Paul Holtom, *Stability Journal*, 2015); "Training for Peacekeeping: Towards Increased Understanding of Conflict Resolution" (*International Peacekeeping*, 2013); "The 'Bradford model' and the Contribution of Conflict Resolution to the Field of International Peacekeeping and Peacebuilding" (UOC *Journal of Conflictology*, 2012); "Cosmopolitan Peacekeeping and Peacebuilding in Sierra Leone: What Can Africa Contribute?" (with Tom Woodhouse *International Affairs*, 2007).

Cedric de Coning (South Africa) (co-editor) is a senior research fellow with the Peace and Conflict Research Group at the Norwegian Institute of International Affairs (NUPI) and he is also a Senior Advisor on Peacekeeping and Peacebuilding for ACCORD. He serves on the editorial boards of the journals Global Governance and Peacebuilding. Cedric has a Ph.D. in Applied Ethics from the Department of Philosophy at the University of Stellenbosch. Selected publications include: *The Future of African Peace Operations*, co-editor (Zed Books, 2016); *UN Peacebuilding: The First 10 Years*, co-editor (Routledge, 2016); *Complexity Thinking for Peacebuilding Practice and Evaluation*, co-editor (Palgrave, 2016); *The BRICS and Coexistence*, co-editor (Routledge, 2015) and *The Unintended Consequences of Peacekeeping*, co-editor (UNU Press, 2007).

Diana Felix da Costa (Portugal) is a Ph.D. candidate at the School of Oriental and African Studies (SOAS), University of London where she has also taught on issues of forced migration, and a research associate at the Norwegian Institute of International Affairs (NUPI). She conducted her Ph.D. fieldwork with the Murle people in Greater Pibor, South Sudan focusing on politics of identity, meanings of violence, and state-society relations. Other areas of interest include displacement strategies and social networks, the local political economy of peace and conflict, anthropology of aid, and local community-international aid relations. She has lived and conducted extended research in South Sudan and Timor-Leste as well as done shorter research visits to Chad, Haiti, and Mozambique. Recent publications include "The Ethics of Researching in Conflict: Personal Reflections from Greater Pibor and South Sudan" (*Journal of the Anthropological Society of Oxford*, 2016) and "United Nations Mission in South Sudan" (*Oxford Handbook of UN Peacekeeping Operations*, 2015).

William Flavin (USA) is the Assistant Director at the US Army Peacekeeping and Stability Operations Institute (PKSOI), located at the US Army War College in Carlisle, Pennsylvania. Before this assignment he was the head of the Doctrine and Education Division in PKSOI. Previously he was a senior foreign affairs analyst with Booz Allen and Hamilton on contract to assist the US Army Peacekeeping Institute for doctrine development with a focus on Peace and Stability Operations. From 1995 to 1999, he was a Colonel in the US Army serving as the Deputy Director of Special Operations for the Supreme Allied Commander Europe at the Supreme Headquarters, Allied Powers Europe. William Flavin has a BA in History from VMI and an MA in History from Emory University. He was a senior fellow at the Center for Strategic and International Studies (CSIS) and taught at the Army War College. He has published several monographs and articles in the field.

Ingvild Magnæs Gjelsvik (Norway) is a researcher in the Peace and Conflict Research Group at the Norwegian Institute of International Affairs (NUPI). Gjelsvik's main research interest are preventing and countering violent extremism, disengagement, and reintegration from violent groups. She has carried out research based on fieldwork in Somalia on piracy groups; al-Shabaab; and women, peace, and security, and has worked for UNDP Somalia. Gjelsvik is also working in the field of right-wing extremism at the Center for Research on Extremism (C-REX) at the University of Oslo and at the Norwegian Police University College. She is currently working in an EU-funded project on community policing in conflict and post conflict contexts.

Eduarda Hamann (Brazil) is the Coordinator of the Peacebuilding Program at the Igarapé Institute. Her main areas of interest include peacekeeping and peacebuilding, contemporary Brazilian foreign policy and South-South cooperation, among others. In the last decade, she was a consultant to a variety of institutions, such as the World Bank and Viva Rio, and taught in key Brazilian schools of international relations, such as PUC-Rio and Fundação Getúlio Vargas. Recent publications are on reforming the UN Security Council from a Brazilian perspective, Brazil's engagement in UN missions, "responsibility while protecting," civilian capacity, and related topics. Eduarda is a lawyer, and holds a Ph.D. in international affairs (major in international peace and security).

He Yin (China) is Associate Professor at the China Peacekeeping Police Training Center, where he has been teaching peacekeeping training courses for fifteen years. Mr. He holds a Ph.D. in international relations from the China Foreign Affairs University. From October 2001 to October 2002, he was an UN police officer in the United Nations peacekeeping mission in East Timor. From September 2006 to June 2007, he was a visiting scholar at the Silkroad Studies Program based in Uppsala University, Sweden. From February to June 2015, he was Fellow at the Harvard Weatherhead Center for International Affairs. His recent publications include "Norm Competition and Complementation: Peacebuilding as A Case" (*World Economics and Politics*, 2014, in Chinese); "UN Peacebuilding and Protection of Human Security" (*Journal of International Security Studies*, 2014, in Chinese), and "China's Changing Policy on UN Peacekeeping Operations" (Asia Paper, Institute for Security and Development Policy, 2007).

John Karlsrud (Norway) is Senior Research Fellow and Manager for the Training for Peace programme at the Norwegian Institute of International Affairs. He is an External Associate at the Centre for the Study of Globalisation and Regionalisation, University of Warwick, where he also earned his Ph.D. He is a member of the Editorial Boards of *Internasjonal Politikk* and *Contemporary Security Policy*, and he is also Editorial Advisor to *Global Peace Operations Review*, published by the Center on International Cooperation at New York University, where Karlsrud previously was a Visiting Fulbright Fellow. He has also been a Research Fellow at the International Peace Institute. Topics of particular interests are norm change, peacekeeping, peacebuilding, and humanitarian issues. Recently published books are *Norm Change in International Relations* (Routledge, 2016) and *The Future of African Peace Operations: From the Janjaweed to Boko Haram* (Zed Books, 2016, edited with Cedric de Coning and Linnéa Gelot). He has worked in Bosnia,

Chad, Palestine, and conducted field research and shorter missions to Haiti, Liberia, Mozambique, Serbia, Sierra Leone, South Sudan, and Ukraine.

Stian Kjeksrud (Norway) is a Senior Researcher at the Norwegian Defence Research Establishment (FFI) and a Ph.D. candidate at the University of Oslo. The thesis will explain variations in the utility of military force to protect civilians in contemporary UN peacekeeping operations in Africa. Recent publications include "Protecting Civilians: Comparing Organizational Approaches," with Ravndal, Stensland, Lotze, Weir and de Coning and "The Use of Force for Protecting Civilians" in *The Protection of Civilians in International Law,* Weller, Willmot and Mamyia (eds), Oxford University Press (November 2015), "The Future of UN Peacekeeping Operations," in *International Military Operations in the 21st Century,* Norheim-Martinsen and Nyhamar (eds), Routledge (2015). Kjeksrud also has served as a soldier and officer in several international operations, including Lebanon, Kosovo, Macedonia, and Afghanistan.

Alexander Lukin (Russia) is Director of the Center for East Asian and Shanghai Cooperation Organization Studies at Moscow State Institute of International Relations (MGIMO) University and Head of the Department of International Relations at National Research University Higher School of Economics and Director of the Center for East Asian and Shanghai Cooperation Organization Studies at Moscow State Institute of International Relations (MGIMO) University. He received his first degree from MGIMO University in 1984, a doctorate in politics from Oxford University in 1997 and a doctorate in history from Russian Diplomatic Academy in 2007. He is the author of *The Political Culture of the Russian Democrats* (Oxford University Press, 2000), *The Bear Watches the Dragon: Russia's Perceptions of China and the Evolution of Russian-Chinese Relations since the Eighteenth Century* (M.E. Sharpe, 2003), *Grasping Russia with Your Mind* (with Pavel Lukin, Ves' Mir, 2015, in Russian) as well as numerous articles and policy papers on international relations, Russian and Chinese politics.

Alexandra Novosseloff (France) is a Senior Visiting Fellow at the Center on International Cooperation of New York University. She is also a research associate at the Centre Thucydide, a research center of the University of Paris-Panthéon-Assas (Paris 2). She holds a Ph.D. in political science from that University. She is specialized in the field of international organizations and UN peacekeeping. She has also written extensively about border walls, crisis, and post-conflict situations. Among her recent publications are: "Demystifying Intelligence in UN Peace Operations: Toward an Organizational Doctrine" (with Olga Abilova, IPI, July 2016); *Le Conseil de sécurité, entre impuissance et toute puissance* (editor, 2016, Paris, CNRS editions); *Walls Dividing People* (with Frank Neisse, pictures and texts, La Documentation française, 2015, second edition); *La paix par la force? Pour une approche réaliste du maintien de la paix « robuste »* (co-editor with Jocelyn Coulon, 2011); *The History of the UN Military Staff Committee*, 2008.

Mateja Peter (Slovenia) is a Lecturer in the School of International Relations at St Andrews University and a Senior Research Fellow at the Norwegian Institute of International Affairs (NUPI). Dr Peter's research interests include global governance and international organisations, peace operations and peacebuilding, the politics of international law, and IR theory. She is interested in both theoretical and policy implications of the shift from short-term to sustained third-party engagements in contemporary interventions. Previously she held a transatlantic post-doctoral fellowship (TAPIR) at the United States Institute of Peace, the German Institute for International and Security Affairs, and the Norwegian Institute for Defence Studies. She received her Ph.D. from the University of Cambridge.

Chander Prakash (India) is Distinguished Fellow and Advisor UN Policy Research, United Service Institution of India (USI). Has over 40 years of distinguished active service including five years related to the UN peacekeeping operations in the field. He is the Former Force Commander of the United Nations Organization Mission in the Democratic Republic of Congo (MONUSCO) (August 2010–March 2013). Prior to that was the Head of the Indian Army's Peacekeeping Operations and on the Board of Directors at the Centre for United Nations Peacekeeping at New Delhi. Previously was the Indian Defence Advisor in Paris responsible for defence cooperation between India, France, EU and BENELUX countries. Has been the Senior Operations Officer in the United Nations Iran-Iraq Military Observers Group (UNIIMOG) in Iran (1986–7).

Thierry Tardy (France) is Senior Analyst at the European Union Institute for Security Studies (EUISS). He has researched and published extensively on military and civilian crisis management with a particular focus on the United Nations and the European Union, inter-institutional cooperation in security governance, security regionalism, and the EU Common Security and Defence Policy. His latest publications include the *Oxford Handbook on United Nations Peacekeeping Operations* (Oxford University Press, co-edited with J. Koops, N. MacQueen and P. Williams, July 2015), and "CSDP in action. What contribution to international security?", *Chaillot Paper* 134, EUISS, May 2015. He is a member of the editorial board of *International Peacekeeping*. He has taught at the Graduate Institute of International and Development Studies (IHEID) in Geneva as well as at the *Institut d'Etudes Politiques* in Paris. He runs a seminar on the EU Common Security and Defence Policy at the Sorbonne University and regularly lectures at the European Security and Defense College.

Lotte Vermeij (The Netherlands) is currently based in Bukavu, Democratic Republic of the Congo, as Chief of the Gender and Sexual Violence Advisory Section/Women Protection Advisor for the United Nations Organization Stabilization Mission in the Democratic Republic of the Congo (MONUSCO) in South Kivu. Previous to this, she was the Head of the Peace Capacities Programme at the Norwegian Institute of International Affairs (NUPI) and regularly facilitated peace operations training for UN and NATO personnel (military, police, and civilian). As a Senior Research Fellow at NUPI her research mainly focused on peacekeeping operations; peacebuilding; children and armed conflict; disarmament, demobilisation, and reintegration (DDR); conflict related sexual violence; civilian capacities; and child protection. She holds a Ph.D. degree in Disaster Studies from Wageningen University, the Netherlands, where she focused her research on child soldiers and African rebel groups. She has done extensive field work in DR Congo, Liberia, Mali, Mozambique, northern Uganda, Rwanda, and Sierra Leone.

Paul D. Williams (UK and USA) is Associate Professor in the Elliott School of International Affairs at the George Washington University, USA. Dr Williams is also a Non-Resident Senior Adviser at the International Peace Institute in New York where helps manage the "Providing for Peacekeeping Project." Between 2011–2014 he served as a Visiting Professor at the Institute for Peace and Security Studies at Addis Ababa University in Ethiopia. His books include *War and Conflict in Africa* (Polity, 2nd edn, 2016), *Providing Peacekeepers: The Politics, Challenges, and Future of UN Peacekeeping Contributions* (Oxford University Press, 2013); *The Oxford Handbook of United Nations Peacekeeping Operations* (Oxford University Press, 2015), *Understanding Peacekeeping* (Polity, 2nd ed., 2010), and *British Foreign Policy under New Labour* (Palgrave Macmillan, 2005).

Introduction

Addressing the emerging gap between concepts, doctrine, and practice in UN peacekeeping operations

Chiyuki Aoi, Cedric de Coning and John Karlsrud[1]

- **Defining the key terms**
- **Transformation and diversification of peace operations**
- **Development of UN peacekeeping doctrine: The preeminence of the Brahimi reform**
- **Emerging tensions**
- **Towards a new typology of peacekeeping**
- **Outline of the book**

Several recent United Nations (UN) peacekeeping operations, including those in the Central African Republic (CAR), the Democratic Republic of the Congo (DRC), Mali, South Sudan, and Sudan, have been given mandates that significantly challenge the traditional UN peacekeeping principles of consent, impartiality, and the limited use of force. In the DRC and in Mali the UN is supporting governments against insurgencies and violent extremists and in the CAR, Darfur, and South Sudan the UN is protecting civilians without an overarching peace agreement in place. These new mandates have positioned UN peacekeepers in situations where there are no clear parties to the conflict from whom they can seek consent. As a result, these peacekeepers have had to project more force, including undertaking offensive operations at times; engage in intelligence; and use weapon systems and tactics, including special forces, that are unprecedented in the UN's more than 60 years of peacekeeping history. The new security environment has pushed peace operations to the limit of what can be considered peacekeeping. As of 31 May 2016 the UN mission in Mali has endured 68 fatalities from improvised explosive devices (IEDs), mortar attacks, and other attacks by rebel and terrorist groups on its bases, troops, and contractor convoys.[2] Future missions may be deployed to similar environments in Libya, Syria, and Yemen. This accentuates the need for more reflection and guidance on how UN peacekeeping operations should respond to this new security environment.

This book analyzes the growing gap between these emerging practices and existing UN peacekeeping doctrine, exploring how it undermines the effectiveness of UN operations, and endangers lives. The contributors argue that this gap is widening, and demonstrate that it has broad-ranging strategic and practical consequences. The gap is caused by the expanding scope of UN peacekeeping mandates. When UN peacekeeping started it undertook ceasefire observation missions. These expanded, especially after the end of the Cold War, to missions that supported the implementation of comprehensive peace agreements. Since the late 1990s newer missions that are mandated to protect civilians have become the norm, and in some cases, such as Darfur and Chad, protection missions have been mandated without the usual entry-benchmark of a peace agreement. Most recently the UN has been mandated to protect governments against insurgencies and aggressors in the DRC and Mali, and in the CAR to stabilize a country where there was no peace settlement in sight. We argue that these latter missions have gone a step beyond the existing UN peacekeeping doctrine that is based on the core principles of consent, impartiality, and the limited use of force. Without a ceasefire or peace agreement there are no parties to the conflict that can consent to the mission—other than the government of the day; or to whom the UN can be impartial, and in the case of offensive operations the UN has clearly identified an aggressor, so there is no question of impartiality, and in these cases the UN has also gone beyond using limited force.

This study is the first book-length comprehensive attempt to identify and analyze this growing gap between emerging practice and the existing official UN peacekeeping doctrine, and as such fills a critical gap in the literature on peacekeeping. The existing UN peacekeeping literature tends to focus on operational and institutional reform issues but rarely on doctrines. This volume combines empirical case-based studies on UN peace operations, with studies on the views and policies of key UN Security Council members that generate these mandates, as well as the views of key contributors of UN peacekeepers. In this way we are able to relate practice to existing concepts and doctrines, as well as to the strategic thinking emerging from within the Security Council and major troop-contributing countries (TCCs) about the future directions in which UN peacekeeping may develop.

This study recognizes that doctrines in general, but the UN peacekeeping doctrine in particular, is an important tool to create a common understanding among a diverse body of UN member states about what

UN peacekeeping is (and is not). As such, it serves as the basis for preparing UN peacekeepers for a common task so that once deployed they are able to have a common approach or baseline that will enable greater interoperability. Doctrine is also crucial for guiding actions under uncertainties, as it provides decision-makers with a common set of principles to fall back on. We thus argue that a common doctrine is a critical starting point for effective multinational operations. The larger the gap between agreed doctrine and actual practice, the more room there will be for misunderstandings, misperceptions, disagreements, incoherence, lack of unity of purpose and lack of synergy. In order to determine the degree to which this general principle applies to the current state of UN peacekeeping, this book undertakes the following tasks:

- firstly, it provides a review of conceptual and doctrinal developments in UN peacekeeping operations through a historical perspective;
- secondly, it examines the debate related to peace operations doctrine and concepts among key member states—both those in the Security Council that generate the mandates and those that contribute the actual peacekeepers—with a view to identifying possible future directions and possibilities for reform based on their own experiences;
- thirdly, it focuses on the actual practice of peacekeeping by conducting case studies of several UN peacekeeping missions in order to identify gaps between practice and doctrine; and
- finally, it critically analyzes gaps between emerging peacekeeping practice and existing doctrine, with a view to proposing a new typology of peace operations that better fits the realities in the field. This book also presents recommendations for doctrine revision and reforms, as well as considering the institutional and operational implications of such reforms.

This study thus fills an important gap in the existing literature by taking a critical reappraisal of the doctrinal deficit in contemporary UN peacekeeping operations. The trend over the past two decades has been that most of the analytical focus has gone to the North Atlantic Treaty Organization (NATO) and other non-UN peace support, stabilization or counterinsurgency (COIN) operations, understandably with the missions in Afghanistan and Iraq proving difficult. This book is thus a rare attempt to reflect back into the challenges of UN peace operations, gaining in part from considerations made in these related operational and conceptual fields.

Defining the key terms

In this book, definitions of key terms are adapted from the UN usage as defined most of all in the Capstone Doctrine. The following terms from the Capstone are repeatedly used:

- *Peacekeeping* is a technique designed to preserve the peace, however fragile, where fighting has been halted, and to assist in implementing agreements achieved by the peacemakers. Over the years, peacekeeping has evolved from a primarily military model of observing ceasefires and the separation of forces after interstate wars, to incorporate a complex model of many elements—military, police and civilian—working together to help lay the foundations for sustainable peace.
- *Peace enforcement* involves the application, with the authorisation of the Security Council, of a range of coercive measures, including the use of military force. Such actions are authorised to restore international peace and security in situations where the Security Council has determined the existence of a threat to the peace, breach of the peace or act of aggression. The Security Council may utilise, where appropriate, regional organisations and agencies for enforcement action under its authority.
- *Peacebuilding* involves a range of measures targeted to reduce the risk of lapsing or relapsing into conflict by strengthening national capacities at all levels for conflict management, and to lay the foundation for sustainable peace and development. Peacebuilding is a complex, long-term process of creating the necessary conditions for sustainable peace. It works by addressing the deep-rooted, structural causes of violent conflict in a comprehensive manner. Peacebuilding measures address core issues that affect the functioning of society and the State, and seek to enhance the capacity of the State to effectively and legitimately carry out its core functions.[3]

There is no formally adopted definition of *stabilization* at the United Nations at the time of writing. Nor is there a doctrine covering this type of operation. The definition of *stabilization* used in this book hence is adopted from the UK concept, which provides for the most in-depth analysis available to date. The term applies to situations where there is no political settlement in place, indicating there is no basis, or at best a fragile basis for "consent" to deploy UN missions. The definition of stabilization, from the British Ministry of Defence "Security and Stabilisation" report, is as follows:

> *Stabilisation* is the process that supports states which are entering, enduring or emerging from conflict in order to: prevent or reduce violence; protect the population and key infrastructure; promote political processes and governance structures which lead to a political settlement that institutionalises non-violent contests for power; and prepares for sustainable social and economic development.[4]

Hence the term *stabilization* applies to the "process" that builds a political settlement and framework for a stable state, not to a concrete end-state. It is essentially a statebuilding construct, aiming to create conditions of "stable state" with abilities to ensure governance, security, and development, founded upon political settlement among key elites, the state (government), and the people. In this process, an integrated approach is the key.[5]

There have been significant debates as to the boundary of stabilization, especially as regards whether it includes both counterinsurgency and peace support at the same time. We note that while counterinsurgency can be part of a type of a stabilization in which a clear insurgency exists, not all stabilization will be identified as counterinsurgency, as it may not necessarily involve insurgency. Stabilization denotes, in more general terms, conditions accompanying a lack of stability, for example, lawlessness, the lack of state administration or government itself, or existence of significant level of state fragility, and/or widespread violence against or among the population. Stabilization is also not equivalent to peace support or peacebuilding, although there may be overlaps between these concepts, especially at the tactical level or over the long-term. Stabilization presupposes a lack of political solution to the conflict, while peace support and peacebuilding require such a solution (although consent to such solutions may fluctuate, or be treated as a "variable") as a starting point.

Counterinsurgency, likewise, is not part of UN terminology. In this study, we will also use the UK definition, namely:

> Those military, law enforcement, political, economic, psychological and civic actions taken to defeat insurgency, while addressing the root causes. Successful counterinsurgency requires a multi-faceted approach that addresses the political, economic, social, cultural and security dimensions of the unrest.[6]

Insurgency, on the other hand, is defined in the UK doctrine: "An organised, violent subversion used to effect or prevent political control, as a challenge to established authority."[7]

Counterinsurgency hence is an essentially political challenge, in response to efforts to disrupt political control and authority. Dealing with legitimate grievances is also essential. Response to insurgencies hence implies an integrated approach that combines diplomatic, development, and defense capabilities at all levels—strategic, operational, and tactical.

There have been important debates as to whether counterinsurgency and peacekeeping have some commonalities or overlapping tasks in some contexts, particularly as peacekeeping has come to be more robust and involve restoration of order and security—also a goal in counterinsurgency—in the post–Cold War era.[8] Doctrinally, too, concepts adopted by major governments in the early post–Cold War era, such as "low intensity operations" and "operations other than war" seemed to lump counterinsurgency and peacekeeping in the same category of operations. In the post-Cold War "war among the people," some saw mutual convergence of peacekeeping and counterinsurgency as the former came to involve robust and kinetic methods to implement mandates and the latter came to rely on a defensive approach.[9] Some also viewed peacebuilding as essentially political or politically motivated, whose effect could involve the countering of insurgency.[10]

Yet, this book starts from the recognition that even if in practice the boundary between peacekeeping and counterinsurgency seems blurred, it is essential to recognize that they are distinct. Brocades Zaalberg, having compared "broad" post–Cold War peacekeeping and population-centric counterinsurgency, and having found an increasing degree of convergence between the two, still concluded that they were different and needed to be kept separate, because counterinsurgency was not impartial.[11] This chapter concurs with this observation that the principle of impartiality should be the dividing line between peacekeeping—including its more "robust" variant—and counterinsurgency, which is a form of warfare with [designated] enemy insurgent groups. While stabilization could include counterinsurgency, the lack of political settlement distinguishes stabilization from peacekeeping and hence, peacekeeping is separate from both stabilization and counterinsurgency. It is the presumption of this volume that impartiality is the bedrock of peacekeeping, even if other peacekeeping principles such as minimum use of force and consent might be challenged. If, as explained below, a peacekeeping mandate involves protection of government from a recognized insurgency, then application of peacekeeping principles most likely creates complications.

Transformation and diversification of peace operations

The United States and other Western nations have devoted most of their security energy and attention to NATO-led counterinsurgency and stabilization operations in Afghanistan and Iraq over the past decade. Over the same period the United Nations deployed an average of 15 peacekeeping operations annually, and managed and supported the second-largest number of troops, next only to the United States during the same period. These operations varied significantly in type and scope. The UN continues to conduct traditional observer and limited peacekeeping missions on the border between India and Pakistan, and in Western Sahara, Cyprus, and the Middle-East. The UN also assisted nation-building in newly independent states in East Timor and South Sudan, and it embarked upon protection of civilians mandates in protracted conflicts in Darfur (together with the African Union), Chad/CAR, the DRC, and Côte d'Ivoire. In West Africa, the UN missions in Liberia and Sierra Leone helped to bring decades old conflicts to an end by aiding in the implementation of comprehensive peace agreements.

Some of these missions reached successful ends—the UN has recently withdrawn from East Timor, Burundi, and Sierra Leone—after contributing significantly to bringing these conflicts to an end, despite several lapses during the course of the peace process. A case in point is Liberia where the UN has started to draw down its forces, but where it had to reconsider the role of the mission after the outbreak of the Ebola pandemic in 2014.

Still others face ongoing turbulence. As a result of the review of peace operations conducted under the leadership of the Algerian special representative of the secretary-general, Ambassador Lakhdar Brahimi, and the ensuing reforms, the major peacekeeping failures of the early 1990s have not recurred over the past 15 years;[12] yet, some operations face new difficulties and challenges brought on by the nature of conflict today, as well as inadequacies of peacekeeping mandates, authority, and capabilities. For example, the UN Stabilization Mission in the Democratic Republic of the Congo (MONUSCO) entered its fifteenth year in 2015, and despite recent gains that are analyzed in this book, ongoing disturbances in the eastern region of the country ensure that the end of the mission is not yet in sight.

UN peacekeeping operations have significantly evolved over the more than 60 years that peacekeeping has been practiced by the organization, and it is possible to trace several historical developments that occurred over this period. One is the emergence of "multidimensional,"

:cebuilding, missions after the end of the Cold War, where strategic assumptions underlying the operations shifted from static ceasefire agreements to tasks related to transforming societies from war to peace, often under situations involving uncertainties.[13] At the end of the 1980s and into the 1990s, from El Salvador and Cambodia to the former Yugoslavia, Namibia, Angola, and Mozambique, the UN supported the implementation of comprehensive peace agreements that typically included organizing post-conflict elections; the disarmament, demobilization, and reintegration of former combatants; and supporting national reconciliation efforts. These operations were undertaken with the consent of the parties to the conflict.

Furthermore, in a significant development, the Security Council has repeatedly expressed readiness to sanction tougher measures in peacekeeping operations, should situations on the ground so demand, when peace processes or civilian lives are endangered. Although the mid-1990s saw a reduction in the readiness for the UN to use force, due largely to the debacle in Somalia, that lull proved temporary as the UN embarked on new large-scale peace operations mandated under Chapter VII of the UN Charter (which authorizes enforcement)—for instance, in East Timor and Sierra Leone (although the latter started as a Chapter VI operation). The Security Council insisted on staying in the West African states of Liberia, Sierra Leone, and Côte d'Ivoire, despite conflicts recurring in these countries during the first half of the 2000s. Other cases also involved Security Council tackling entrenched gangs (e.g., Cité de Soleil in Haiti), and to reinforce election results if necessary (as in Côte d'Ivoire in 2011).[14]

Furthermore, the Security Council has been ready to authorize the use of force to protect civilians in numerous missions.[15] In 1999, it adopted Resolution 1265 with a unanimous vote, followed subsequently by Resolutions 1296 (2000) and 1738 (2006) that emphasized the importance of protection of civilians in the context of peace operations. Protection of civilians mandates were given to UN missions in Lebanon, Sierra Leone, Haiti, Burundi, and Liberia, as well as Sudan, the DRC, Côte d'Ivoire, Chad/CAR, and most recently in South Sudan, Mali, and the CAR. These protection of civilians mandates challenge the UN's established concepts and principles in complex ways, as will be discussed below.

Most recently, the Security Council has also ventured into tasking UN peacekeeping operations with stabilization mandates. In 2013, the UN sent a Force Intervention Brigade (FIB) with essentially a peace enforcement mandate to eastern Congo. The UN also deployed a new 12,000-strong mission to Mali to stabilize its northern territory, initially under the condition of lacking a peace agreement, the existence of violent extremist and terrorist threats, and general destabilization, although since then the UN has tried to arbitrate an agreement. The UN also approved a new mission to stabilize the crisis in the CAR, and this mission took over from the African Union's International Support Mission to the Central African Republic (MISCA) on 15 September 2014.

In these more recent stabilization missions deployed to the CAR, Mali, and the DRC there is a trend of decentralizing authority: feeding intelligence into operations on local levels, using a combination of human and signals intelligence sources such as drones, and including special forces to support more conventional forces. These changes mirror the lessons learned by NATO member states from counter-insurgency operations in Afghanistan and Iraq.[16] In 2014 and 2015, the United States exerted significant pressure on member states to increase their pledges to UN peace operations, and during the General Assembly in 2015, President Barack Obama chaired a summit on UN peace operations that gathered about 50 heads of state and government, making concrete pledges that will strengthen the capabilities, effectiveness, and efficiency of UN peace operations.

These developments reflect an increased interest by Western member states in UN peace operations as their engagement in Afghanistan is tapering down. The engagement is increasing at strategic, operational, and tactical levels. At the Security Council, the pressure is increasing for reform, updating UN peacekeeping to reflect changes in modern warfare and technology. The push for more robust mandates, tactical intelligence units in Mali, and surveillance drones in the DRC could be evidence of this new engagement at the strategic level. At the operational and tactical levels, The Netherlands, Sweden, and other European countries have chosen to contribute troops to the All Sources Information Fusion Unit (ASIFU) in Mali, and The Netherlands has also deployed close to 100 tactical intelligence officers and four Apache attack helicopters. Bert Koenders, a Dutch politician and diplomat, was the head of the mission for the initial period.

With the large Dutch contingent and smaller contingents from Finland, France, Norway, Sweden, and the United Kingdom, the UN Multidimensional Integrated Stabilization Mission in Mali (MINUSMA) has a large participation of western troops in UN peace-keeping in Africa. For the Europeans it is likely that the mission has been a laboratory for including some of the lessons learned from network-centric warfare and counterinsurgency operations from Afghanistan, particularly taking into consideration the worsening situation in the north of Mali.[17] Introducing these concepts into the UN peace-keeping culture, however, will not be easy, partly because there is a lack of common understanding towards what stabilization and counter-insurgency entail in concept and practice across international and national agencies, as well as differing understandings of the role of the military in peacekeeping, stabilization, and counterinsurgency opera-tions. Across nations and agencies, furthermore, there are different methods and concepts for civil-military cooperation and integration.

However, it would be wrong to understand the recent trend towards stabilization mandates as only due to Western experiences in Afghanistan. Over the same period the African Union (AU) has had somewhat similar experiences in Somalia, Mali, and the CAR.[18] It was African countries that insisted on a more forceful approach to pacifying the rebels in the eastern DRC that resulted in the deployment of the FIB. And African countries have subsequently invoked the FIB example as a best practice that could be used in other trouble spots. For instance, the African Union has assessed the option of deploying an FIB in northern Mali, and the countries of the region have called for an FIB-type force to stabilize Juba after the violent breakdown of the ceasefire agreement in South Sudan in July 2016. The emergence of these new stabilization mandates thus came about as a result of a convergence of a number of developments, including the UN experience with protection of civilians mandates, the experiences of the African Union in Somalia and elsewhere, and the experiences of European countries in Afghanistan and Iraq.

As a result of these developments and pressures on the existing UN peacekeeping doctrine, the UN secretary-general in October 2014 nominated a high-level independent panel to review UN peace opera-tions. Led by the former president of Timor-Leste (East Timor), José Ramos-Horta, the panel submitted its report to the secretary-general in June 2015.[19] The secretary-general subsequently provided his own implementation report to the 2015 session of the General Assembly and Security Council.

The Ramos-Horta panel noted that UN peace operations have been increasingly called upon to deploy "in the midst of conflict as a crisis response tool to deter escalation, to contain conflict while protecting civilians and, at the same time, to attempt to restart or revive peace processes."[20] The panel referred to these as "conflict management" missions, and differentiated them from both ceasefire monitoring and peace implementation missions. The panel recognized, however, that the Security Council and the Secretariat have used the term *stabiliza-tion* for a number of missions, and it asked that the usage of this term by the UN be clarified.[21]

The panel also stated that "United Nations troops should not undertake military counter-terrorism operations,"[22] and that UN peace operations "are not suited to engage in military counter-terrorism operations. They lack the specific equipment, intelligence, logistics, capabilities and specialized military preparation required."[23] In a similar vein, the new US policy memorandum on UN peace operations, released on the same day that President Obama chaired the summit on UN peace operations during the General Assembly in 2015, also stated that the UN will not be able to take on "more forceful military interventions that need to be carried out in non-permissive environments by individual states or coalitions that possess the will and capacity to do so."[24]

However, some Western and also African states see a role for the UN in countering violent extremism and perhaps limited counter-terrorism operations going forward. Also the panel stressed that the UN needs to prepare itself to deal with the threat of violent extremism and should work with national and international civil society and other actors to counter violent extremism.[25] Traditional troop-contributing countries are more reluctant to deploy where UN peace operations are given the tasks of countering violent extremism and counter-terrorism.

As the panel observed, the United Nations has not yet formally defined the notion of stabilization in its official doctrine or terminology. Given these new developments at strategic, operational, and tactical levels, the pressure on the UN to explain what the stabilization concept means in the UN peacekeeping context, for example in the mandates and names of its missions in the CAR, the DRC, and Mali, is only going to increase. That is why the continued validity of the UN's current doctrinal posture and other core characteristics of UN peacekeeping is the subject of critical analysis in this book.

Development of UN peacekeeping doctrine: The preeminence of the Brahimi reform

The transformation and diversification of peacekeeping missions makes it an urgent task to re-assess the existing UN peacekeeping doctrine, represented by the UN Capstone Doctrine published by the UN Department of Peacekeeping Operations (DPKO) and Department of Field Support (DFS) in 2008. On the conceptual level, UN peacekeeping has been understood to rely upon consent, impartiality, and the limited use of force. The issuing of protection-oriented mandates since 1999, the Brahimi reform in 2000, the Capstone Doctrine of 2008, and the Ramos-Horta review in 2015 broadened the interpretation of these principles but did not question their continued validity.[26]

The 2008 Capstone Doctrine grew out of the 2000 Brahimi reforms. The doctrine was intended to confirm the basic principles of UN peacekeeping and to define the parameters of what constituted UN peacekeeping. It took stock of the ill-fated operations during the early 1990s—most notably Bosnia, Somalia and Rwanda—and the later large-scale operations in Sierra Leone and East Timor in the late 1990s. The Capstone Doctrine is the outcome of the attempt by the UN and its member states to bring UN peacekeeping back to its foundational principles of consent, limited use of force, and impartiality. However, important modifications were introduced in the use of force principle. In addition to the use of force in self-defense, the Capstone introduced the authority to use force to defend the mandate, and at the tactical-level use of force was now allowed to deal with "spoilers" of peace processes and for the protection of civilians.[27] Although the Brahimi reform entailed 56 specific recommendations covering both the field and headquarters, its central message was that the Security Council needed to be realistic in the sense that their mandates needed to be achievable, and that they needed to match the mandate with the resources and political will to back up the operations.[28]

Capstone had the following characteristics. First, it reaffirmed the centrality of consent in UN peace operations and made consent both the foundation of peacekeeping operations and the condition of their success.[29] Such an approach can be contrasted with the NATO and African Union concepts of "peace support operations" (PSOs) which treats consent as a variable.[30] The Capstone Doctrine stated that UN peacekeeping missions are to be deployed only with the consent of the main parties of the conflict, and as a result, these parties will guarantee the UN's role in supporting the implementation of peace processes. Consent also ensures the UN's political and physical freedom of action. The doctrine thus stated: "In the absence of such consent, a United Nations peacekeeping operation risks becoming a party to the conflict; and being drawn towards enforcement action, and away from its intrinsic role of keeping the peace."[31]

Secondly, Capstone made UN peacekeeping largely compatible with other international doctrines such as peace support operations. Specifically, it adopted a spectrum of operations comprising peace enforcement, peacekeeping, and peacebuilding, and situated UN peacekeeping in this spectrum. It stated that peace enforcement involves use of force at the strategic level, and is best left to member states to implement. In contrast, peacekeeping refers to activities conducted with the consent of the main parties to the conflict. The document identified two types of peacekeeping activities, traditional peacekeeping and multidimensional peacekeeping, involving military, police, and various civilian components engaged in mostly peacebuilding tasks associated with supporting the implementation of peace agreements.[32] Capstone specified where DPKO/DFS would be found in this spectrum, along with other UN agencies playing a significant part in peacebuilding.

Thirdly, it drew a sharp conceptual divide between peace enforcement and peacekeeping, perhaps in response to NATO and the African Union where these two concepts are merged into one operational concept of PSO.[33] Here, peace enforcement and peacekeeping are *not* in a continuum but they signify a qualitative divide where there is no overlap, normatively speaking. By contrast, many Western and African nations (and organizations such as NATO and the African Union) do not draw this qualitative division, even if they see differences in operational requirements.

As such, the Brahimi reform and the issuing of the Capstone Doctrine represent an attempt by the UN to draw a red line between what it is prepared to do in peace operations and what it cannot do—and should not be asked to do. This is both a normative stance and a realistic choice given the UN's capabilities. It essentially ties the organization to traditional peacekeeping operations and multidimensional peacekeeping missions with peacebuilding tasks, whose primary purpose is to support the implementation of a ceasefire or peace agreement, while maintaining a limited use of force—only as a last resort—approach, even where it is authorized under Chapter VII to use force. The utility of the Brahimi guidelines and the relevance of the Capstone Doctrine were proved in operations such as those in Timor-Leste, Sierra Leone, and Liberia, where implementation of peace agreements were the core tasks.

Protection of civilians also became a new focus as UN peacekeeping operations were allowed to become more "robust" in the field. While Capstone gave a rather ambivalent stance *vis-à-vis* protection of civilians mandates, which were treated as "a cross-cutting theme," without developing the doctrinal implications in full, the protection of civilians mandates given by the Security Council increasingly seem to add complexity to the core principles of peacekeeping (as discussed: consent, impartiality, and minimum use of force to defend the self and the mission). Whereas the doctrine seemed to imply that protection of civilians was a matter addressed by the provisions for robust peacekeeping in Capstone—i.e., the use of force only at the tactical level—the issue proved to be more complex when some peacekeeping missions were now being deployed into situations which lacked a viable peace agreement to begin with (such as in Darfur, and South Sudan most recently). The strategic implications of the possibility of UN peace-keepers having to use force against government security forces, were they to pose an imminent risk to civilians, were also never spelled out in the Capstone. The protection of civilians, hence, requires a more comprehensive doctrinal concept than currently available, given the complexity and diversity of operations involving such mandates. In addition, protection of civilians mandates also typically imply the need for stronger military capabilities, stronger leadership and more sophisticated information-processing tools to support crisis decision-making, and suitable preparation, as well as readiness on the side of the UN's member states to back up operations under uncertainties.

Emerging tensions

More recently, the pace and scope of these changes in emerging practice have now seemed to reach a tipping point as the new mandates in the eastern DRC, Mali, and the CAR are fundamentally challenging the continued validity of UN peacekeeping's core principles and identity.

The first of these emerging issues has to do with the use of force for offensive operations and the more advanced military assets such as special forces, attack helicopters, and intelligence units and technologies in peacekeeping contexts. As noted, UN doctrine writers and the broader doctrine community have been particularly concerned about the use of force aspect in UN peace operations. During the "traditional peacekeeping" period, when peacekeeping operations were mandated under Chapter VI, the principle was no use of force, except in self-defense. Subsequently, specific mandates gave specific missions the authority to use limited force, under Chapter VII, for instance to protect civilians in imminent threat of danger. The major contribution of the Brahimi reform process and the subsequent Capstone Doctrine was its assertion and recognition that when facing threats from spoilers to a peace process, the UN may use force at the tactical level, because self-defense can be interpreted to mean the "defense of the mission." In an attempt to avoid a situation where the UN would be drawn into a peace enforcement role, the Brahimi reform process determined that the use of force at the strategic level was a task that needed to be entrusted to member states.

While such an interpretation about the UN's approach to the use of force served the organization well when its peacekeeping tasks related to implementation of peace agreements with the consent of local counterparts, some contemporary UN missions, such as those in Mali,

Côte d'Ivoire, and the DRC, have had to adopt a much broader inter-pretation to the new robust approach to the use of force. In all these cases the actual mandates, rules of engagement, and practices of UN peacekeeping missions have gone beyond the limits intended in the Capstone. The reality is that in these missions the UN is now routinely using much more force than the existing doctrine implies. Most recently, with the deployment of the FIB in eastern DRC, with a "neutralize" and "disarm" mandate,[34] the argument that the robust use of force is only a tactical-level adjustment to the use of force principle can no longer be upheld. In this case a UN peacekeeping operation clearly undertook offensive operations and used deadly and over-whelming force to destroy the M23 rebels, as they were authorized to do by the Security Council. Doctrinally, Capstone incorporated tac-tical use of force by peacekeepers with the consent by host authorities, and this was confirmed in a concept note on robust peacekeeping in 2010, where it was clearly stated that:

> *Robust peacekeeping is not peace enforcement.* Robust peace-keeping is distinct from peace enforcement where use of force is at the strategic level and pursued often without the consent of the host nation and/or main parties to the conflict. The threat and use of force in robust peacekeeping is at the tactical level, limited in time and space, and aimed at countering or containing specific spoiler and residual or looming threat in a conflict or post-conflict environment. Large scale violence or one where the major parties are engaged in violent conflict is no longer a robust peacekeeping context. Robust missions are not configured or intended to address any systemic breakdown in a political process.[35]

The FIB mandate showed the willingness of the Security Council to test the limits of this principle. Similarly, the mandate for the UN Operation in Côte d'Ivoire (UNOCI) in 2011, leading to their using force to attack the compound of President Laurent Gbagbo—to sup-press the heavy weapons fire that originated from within the com-pound, which was harming the civilian population—showed the willingness of the Security Council to authorize UN peacekeeping operation to use force at the strategic level.

Despite these practical developments, however, the UN's doctrinal culture remained fundamentally reluctant to move beyond tactical level "robustness," as witnessed by the stark distinction made in the Cap-stone Doctrine between "peacekeeping" and "peace enforcement." As noted, Capstone maintained a clear distinction—for instance in comparison to NATO and the African Union that embraces the notion of peace enforcement—between peacekeeping and peace enforcement, but in Côte d'Ivoire, the DRC, Mali, and now the CAR, UN peacekeepers are mandated, and expected, to use levels of force that are unprecedented in UN peacekeeping missions.[36]

Closely related to this is the issue of consent in peace operations. Again, the Capstone, building on the Brahimi reform process, firmly states that the UN takes consent as the bedrock of its operations. Just as with the use of force, the post-Brahimi UN maintained a rather conservative approach to sovereignty, and it remained skeptical that it can manage effective peace operations when consent is absent. The UN's take on its own failures in Bosnia, Somalia, and Rwanda during the early 1990s was precisely that consent was the bedrock of effective peace operations. By contrast, in many contemporary missions the centrality of consent is more than questionable. For example, in the eastern DRC, Darfur, and Mali, the UN missions now operate in situations where armed groups are openly hostile to the UN presence, and where ambushes and attacks on UN personnel are common. In some cases, the armed groups were not part of the original peace agreement whilst in others there is no peace agreement in place. The consent of the parties to the conflict, then, cannot be assumed in these cases. In all these cases the UN operates with the agreement of the host state, but the principle of consent refers to consent from all the parties to the conflict. The existing doctrine's insistence on the centrality of consent offers little guidance under these new circumstances, and causes tensions with operational requirements, for instance regarding intelligence and the use of special forces.

In fact, the naming of some recent UN missions seems to reflect this contextual shift. In the DRC, the UN used the term stabilization when it changed the mandate and the name of the mission from the UN Mission in the Democratic Republic of the Congo (MONUC) to MONUSCO, to reflect that the main focus of the new mission was the stabilization of the eastern DRC. In Mali, the UN also introduced the term as part of the name of the mission, indicating that it is aware that in Mali a political solution is still missing and that the UN is operating in that political void to try to contribute to the general stabilization of the situation.

The use of the term follows the earlier examples of the NATO peace support mission in the Balkans (Stabilization Force, SFOR), as well as the UN mission in Haiti (UN Stabilization Mission in Haiti, MINUSTAH). So while the UN has at times used stabilization before, the naming of the Mali mission recently was significant as it revealed the

UN's increasing awareness of the prevailing lack of what has been previously considered a benchmark condition for the entry of a peace-keeping mission—strategic stability in the form of a peace agreement between the parties to the conflict. A similar situation prevails in the Central African Republic where the UN deployed its newest mission in September 2014.

Under these circumstances, the more relevant question that needs to be asked is what the operational requirements for the UN are in case consent cannot be assumed, the answer to which could have broad-ranging implications overlapping with other peace operations principles. Some argue that the UN does have consent in these missions in the form of an invitation by and agreement with the host government. Of course, any UN mission would require the agreement of the host government, otherwise it would be an invasion, but this kind of status of forces agreement is not what the principle of consent means. The principle of consent requires the parties to the conflict to agree to the role and presence of the UN peacekeeping mission. If only one party agrees, then we cannot refer to that one-sided agreement as consent.

The UN used this argument in Burundi in 2003 when the AU argued that the UN should take over the African Mission in Burundi (AMIB). At the time the government and one of the rebel groups had signed an agreement and the AU had deployed a force to help to implement it. Later a second rebel group signed the peace agreement, but the UN only agreed to take over the mission from the AU when the last and final rebel group had signed the agreement, on the basis that all the parties to the conflict needed to give consent prior to the UN deploying a peacekeeping operation. In the cases of Mali and the CAR, the best we can say is that the government of the day had agreed to the presence of the UN. And in some of the new cases one would have to acknowledge that consent is no longer required or desired, for instance where the Security Council has identified specific actors as aggressors, as in the case of the FIB in the DRC and with terrorist groups in northern Mali.

In these cases, consent is no longer a principle as the Security Council has authorized the peacekeeping operations to act against these actors, including by using force. So in the cases where we argue the new mandates have gone beyond the existing doctrine, consent is either not in place, and in these cases the missions thus do not meet the basic benchmark for a UN peacekeeping mission in the Capstone Doctrine, or the Security Council's mandate has made the principle of consent obsolete because it has authorized an enforcement action against identified aggressors, rather than a peacekeeping action.

Furthermore, the concept of impartiality, and its role as a core principle of UN peace operations, also needs to be reexamined. It contains two dimensions. On the one hand, in some cases, the UN may encounter a situation where either the lack of political will or capabilities might hinder its ability to implement key mandates, such as protection of civilians, in an impartial manner *vis-à-vis* local parties. For instance, it may act against armed groups to protect civilians but it may fail to act against government security forces for this purpose.

On the other hand, the UN may encounter a situation where it is forced to take the side of one of the parties to the conflict, normally the government of the day, beyond the boundaries of being impartial. In this case, the key question becomes whether the UN is capable of retaining impartiality when it is mandated to protect governments against insurgencies particularly viewed from the perspective of local parties.

For example, in the DRC and Mali the UN mission is defending the host state, and thus in reality the government, against an insurgency. In practice this means working closely with the security forces of the state, including, for instance in the DRC, undertaking joint operations against armed groups. From the perspective of the parties engaged in the insurgency, the UN is not impartial. It thus boils down to an interpretation as to whether the UN is dealing with a "legitimate" conflict among multiple parties where it should take an impartial role, or whether one or more of the parties have been identified by the Security Council as aggressors or are otherwise in breach of international peace and security, and in these latter cases the UN or member states are then authorized by the council to use force to implement its decisions—usually under Chapter VII. In principle, the UN is thus protecting the state institution (based upon assumptions related to the legitimacy of the government according to the state's constitution), as opposed to the specific political party in power. "The government of the day," thus refers to the fact that who forms the government may change, and the UN is not supporting the position of a particular political party to be in power, but rather the constitutional order. This distinction is meant to ensure that the UN maintains its impartiality— at least in principle. However, in practice a more complicated picture usually emerge regarding the UN's role in protecting the government of the day, especially when the legitimacy of the government is in question. For instance, some rebel groups, although not recognized by the international community, may have the support of local communities, and acting against the rebel group makes the UN partial in the eyes of these communities. In some cases, these associations may have ethnic or religious implications that may make some populations groups doubt the impartiality of the UN, even if they do not support the rebel group. One can also question whether the impartiality principle still makes sense if the UN is only impartial to one identifiable party. Impartiality, like consent, requires that there is more than one side involved. If there is only one party to which the UN can be impartial, it implies that the concept does not make sense in the context in which it is being attempted to be applied. So in the cases where we argue the new mandates have gone beyond the existing doctrine, impartiality is either not upheld, or in some cases impartiality is no longer a relevant concept.[37]

Below these core principles, many other operational concepts are in need of critical reappraisal, including for example, the protection of civilians. Despite various attempts to generate guidance, it remains a challenge to implement the protection of civilians concept because of the tension between the implied obligations, existing capacities, and the demands of conflicting doctrinal principles and guidelines.

Another concept that requires reevaluation is "local ownership." It has assumed much greater meaning than understood in 2008 and UN peacekeeping missions now need to devote much more effort than in the past to align their actions with those of the government, to serve the needs of local populations, and to work in support of local and regional security forces. In several missions the UN peacekeeping mandate is to support the local security forces to protect the state against insurgencies or to help manage local conflicts. These mandates and the actions that flow from them, and the capacity-building and training that the UN missions provide to local security forces as part of these mandates, create a very close link between the UN mission and the government of the day. This creates tensions between the actual realities of these missions and the impartiality, neutrality, and the use of force principles as outlined in the existing doctrine. On the one hand, UN peacekeepers are expected to be impartial and often required to facilitate dialogue between conflicting groups. On the other hand, they are mandated and tasked with supporting the government and the extension of state authority, challenging more traditional forms of authority and ownership.

In sum, the current situation necessitates a reevaluation of existing peacekeeping doctrine based upon a thorough analysis of *the mandates and operational activities* of key contemporary UN peacekeeping missions. Such a reevaluation should be aimed at identifying, among other things, the operational challenges of having to manage complex field missions without appropriate doctrinal guidance. Recommendations will be aimed at identifying gaps, and suggesting conceptual refinements, doctrinal adjustments, and/or diversification.

We anticipate that the result may suggest that the UN needs to move beyond the peacekeeping principles and doctrine of the past, and thus beyond the horizons set by the past peace operations reforms, including the prominent Brahimi report and the 2015 Ramos-Horta review, so that it can come to grips with the demands of the new challenges the UN is called upon to manage. If so, new questions arise about the identity and comparative advantage of UN peace operations, especially compared to those carried out by "coalitions of the willing" and regional organizations such as the African Union. As noted by the Ramos-Horta review, the UN needs to come to grips *conceptually* with some of the newer missions it has been conducting, most notably in the CAR, the eastern DRC, and Mali, where the UN has introduced the concept of stabilization missions.[38]

Towards a new typology of peacekeeping

Despite some active interest in peace operations, there is a lack of existing research that analyzes the complexities and diversities of contemporary UN peace operations and then links such analysis to doctrinal issues. Due to the lack of a focused study on UN peacekeeping doctrines, in addition, one is left without references when reviewing policies and actions of those states that contribute capacities to peacekeeping missions, as it remains unclear what capabilities are in demand in light of the nature and tasks of contemporary peace operations.

Hence this book provides for a review of the types of peace operations that the UN conducts today, and generates a new typology of UN peace operations, and these types of missions are then analyzed to assess the validity of existing UN peace operations doctrine. In this book, we propose the following typology of UN peacekeeping operations:

1 missions that support the implementation of ceasefire or peace agreements;
2 missions that support the formation of new states or new transitional administrations;
3 missions that have protection of civilians mandates in the absence of peace agreements; and
4 missions that protect governments or peace processes from insurgencies.

Existing peacekeeping typologies are either function-based (hence too numerous to be broken down as a typology),[39] or follow United Kingdom/NATO/AU conceptions of a spectrum of operations (ranging from traditional peacekeeping, peace support to peace enforcement),[40] and hence are not focusing on UN peacekeeping operations.

In contrast this book proposes a new typology based upon a review of the core principles of UN peacekeeping—consent, impartiality, and non-use of force—in relation to core peacekeeping mandates: implementation of peace agreements, assisting the formation of new states, and protection of governments and civilians from insurgents. These mandates will relate to peacekeeping principles in different ways, and hence form the backbone of our typology.

The first typology group, missions that support the implementation of ceasefire or peace agreements, is the one that is envisaged by the Capstone Doctrine, and is institutionally preferred by the UN. Cases in this category may include Liberia, Sierra Leone, and Burundi.

The second group, missions that support the formation of new states or administrations, entail an entirely different type of operation than the first. Here the cases would include South Sudan, Kosovo, and Timor-Leste. Whereas the implementation of the comprehensive peace agreement may include some aspects of state-building, the former takes place in contexts where an existing state experienced a lapse into violent conflict that requires a rebuilding of state institutions in the post-conflict phase. In contrast, in the latter cases, the conflicts has resulted in new states being formed that require new state institutions to be established, and in some cases may entail the UN having the mandate to administer the new territories until they become independent states or until their status has been clarified. In this category, the security environment surrounding the operation might be relatively permissive (such as in the later phases of East Timor) or non-permissive (such as in the early phases of Kosovo and in South Sudan), a factor which may affect the issue of consent and use of force. Once independence or self-government has been granted there is typically only one party, the government of the day that the UN is helping to establish through its state-building and extension of state-authority actions. This is likely to have implications for how the principles of consent and impartiality are understood and interpreted.

The third group refers to missions that have protection of civilians mandates in the absence of peace agreements. Cases here may include Darfur, Chad, the CAR, Haiti, and Côte d'Ivoire. Protection of civilians in the absence of peace agreements entails tasks that are not addressed in the Capstone Doctrine. Here there is no peace agreement and thus no formal consent of the parties to the conflict. The peacekeepers' attempt to protect civilians may bring them into tension with armed groups, bandits, ethnic militias, and even the government of the day.

Finally, the fourth group refers to missions that protect governments or peace process from insurgencies. Cases here would include the DRC and Mali. This may bring the peacekeeping mission closer to counterinsurgency, rather than envisaged robust peacekeeping, particularly as the mission becomes longer in duration. As noted above, it is the state that is protected by the peacekeeping mission, not the government of the day. However, in actual practice, many of the actions undertaken by the peacekeepers may entail counterinsurgency aspects, with peacekeepers either coordinating their actions with the government, or actually operating alongside and in support of the government forces. The positioning of the peacekeeping mission alongside the government gives the perception towards the locals that the peacekeepers are partial to the party in government, especially if it is associated with a specific ethnic, linguistic, or religious group in a contested body politic.

Of these four typology groups, three pose significant challenges to the existing peacekeeping principles and doctrine. We have identified significant gaps between the existing UN doctrine and the challenges posed by these actual mission experiences. It is the recognition of this book that such a doctrinal void is not sustainable, given the prevalence of cases belonging to the last three groups and the actual challenges these operations entail to the peril of lives of those involved. Better guidance of field operations relies upon relevant principles and guidelines. This book is a first attempt to engage in meaningful thinking and discussion about this fact.

In 2014, the secretary-general established a High-Level Independent Panel on Peace Operations under the leadership of José Ramos-Horta, and tasked it to undertake a wide-ranging review of UN peace operations, given the new realities and challenges addressed in this volume. The panel released its report in June 2015 and the General Assembly and the Security Council started to debate the panel's report in the fall.[41] If this review follows a similar pattern to the Brahimi reforms of the 2000s, that eventually resulted in the adoption of the new Capstone Doctrine in 2008, the Ramos-Horta report is likely to usher in a new period of reflection and renewal that will last several years, and this volume is intended to contribute to inform that debate.

Outline of the book

Through problematizing the central tenets of the Capstone Doctrine in the light of developments and practices in the field, this book aims to influence and enlighten ongoing debates on UN peacekeeping doctrines both at the UN and in major capitals. Strategic debates and concerns about the nature and characteristics of contemporary peacekeeping missions are also examined. The main contribution of this book to the literature of UN peacekeeping is that it offers the first comprehensive critical review of the existing UN peacekeeping doctrine, and then identifies directions for doctrinal modifications and revisions, including a proposal of a new typology of peacekeeping. As such this book offers a first thorough review of peacekeeping theory and reality in contemporary contexts, and attempts to align the two to help inform practice.

The book is divided into three parts, on UN peacekeeping debate, practice, and emerging issues, respectively. The first part analyzes the debate on doctrine at the strategic or political level, from the perspective of key UN member states. The states analyzed are the permanent members of the Security Council, as well as major TCCs and police-contributing countries (PCCs). These countries provide the bulk of peacekeepers and the resources for UN peacekeeping operations. Some are also permanent members of the Security Council, and some take the lead in drafting the resolutions that determine the actual mandates that UN peacekeeping missions have to implement. The aim is to understand the national positions that influence the formation of mandates at the level of the Security Council and how these decisions influence the actual practice of peacekeeping operations. These chapters outline the respective country's positions on peace operations doctrine, debates concerning peacekeeping principles, in particular in light of proliferation of other types of operations in the lower end of spectrum of operations, views towards the level of efficacy within UN peacekeeping missions in dealing with conflicts today, and what they think their own contributions are *vis-à-vis* UN peacekeeping, particularly as regards leading doctrine formation.

The second part of the book analyzes practice. It introduces and analyzes a new typology of UN peace operations that groups contemporary and recent missions into the previously mentioned four categories of cases:

1   missions that support comprehensive peace processes (Liberia, Sierra Leone, and Burundi);

2   missions that support the formation of new states or administrations (South Sudan, Kosovo, and Timor-Leste);
3   missions that have protection of civilians mandates in the absence of peace agreements (Darfur, Chad, the CAR, Haiti, and Côte d'Ivoire); and
4   missions that protect governments or peace processes from insurgencies (DRC and Mali).

Of these, the first category is omitted from the analysis of this book because this is a well-established UN practice and does not necessarily pose doctrinal questions. The case studies analyzed in the book hence focus on groups two to four. They focus on the nature of conflict and the type of UN intervention; operational mandate; performance (or practical challenges and difficulties in implementing the given mandate); lessons learned; and the evaluation of how these lessons are likely to affect existing UN doctrines, including lower level guidelines and procedures. The analysis here provides the basis of the new typology of UN peacekeeping that is proposed in the book.

The third part of the book explores emerging issues, synthesizes the findings, and makes recommendations about future developments in UN peacekeeping doctrine. The chapters on the use of naval assets in support of peacekeeping and related operations, and on new trends, such as the role emerging technologies play in UN peace operations, discuss their doctrinal implications. The concluding chapter of the book focuses on stabilization as an emerging issue for the UN both in practice and conceptually, building upon the analyses of policy debates and implications of newer types of peacekeeping operations.

In Part I, Flavin and Aoi's analysis in Chapter 1 embeds the evolution and key issues of US doctrine on peace operations within the broader spectrum of stability and other related concepts, highlighting the need for a doctrine that is more than a "guidance" but an enabler of national security strategy. The authors demonstrate how the principles of peace operations, especially pertaining to the use of force, are influenced by the US military's approach to use of force and, while noting the bedrock importance of the integrated approach in peace operations, they identify critical gaps in this aspect. They highlight further the US focus on improving the availability of trained personnel to take part in UN missions, including those capable of conducting robust operations.

In Chapter 2, Curran and Williams analyze the British doctrine for peace support. The United Kingdom, as a permanent member of the Security Council and a key architect of NATO PSOs, has influenced both UN peacekeeping practices and concepts, especially concerning consent, minimum use of force, and impartiality. The chapter further traces the shifts in the United Kingdom's political focus away from peacekeeping to stabilization in the last decade. It argues that while the "pragmatic approach" of the British to doctrine and peacekeeping participation/contribution has helped UN peace operations to become more robust and resilient, this in turn raises the question for the UN about how to develop/sustain its own capabilities as it starts deploying to more complex situations.

In Chapter 3, Novosseloff and Tardy analyze French policy and understanding towards UN peacekeeping concepts and approach. While France takes the UN as the world's legitimate security framework, it nonetheless also takes the view that the UN still has to adapt if it is to occupy a central place in the French approach to managing military crises. The French concept of peace operation is, moreover, characterized by a particular "warrior" approach where key military principles such as the freedom of action and the possibility of resort to coercion are applied to peacekeeping. The authors argue that the latter approach poses a difficult question about the role of force in peace operations, where political, economic, and other non-military dimensions take precedent over a narrowly focused security imperative.

In Chapter 4, He Yin analyzes the Chinese doctrine and approach to peace operations. While peace operations doctrine is less explicitly spelled out in China, he argues that its approach to UN peacekeeping operations has over time transformed from that of a recluse communist state to one that reflects the country's increasingly pragmatic involvement in UN peacekeeping, including formed police and infantry duties. He goes on to analyze how and to what extent China goes beyond traditional peacekeeping by interpreting and applying the core principles of peacekeeping, i.e., consent, impartiality, and non-use of force, including how China's position on the "responsibility to protect" concept (R2P) is linked to these principles.

In Chapter 5, Bratersky and Lukin analyze how Russia views UN peacekeeping, which increasingly operates with regional organizations and which, in Russia's view, is becoming a tool for great power interests. Such trends have resulted in a stance within Russia that is concerned more with the political consequences of a mission than its scope and scale. While supporting a new generation of peace operations such as Mali and South Sudan, Russia has to date developed a vision of peacekeeping operations that emphasizes the role of state actors in resolving conflict—as represented by its opposition to regime change by interventions (including peace operations) and operations by coalitions of the willing.

In Chapter 6, Abiola, de Coning, Hamann, and Prakash consider the views and perceptions of the large troop- and police-contributing countries (TPCCs). One observation they make is that the level of satisfaction with the current system is rather low. Asian and African countries are expected to take the highest risks when deploying troops to missions with mandates to protect civilians. However, they have limited or no access to the elaboration of the mandates they would have to implement. The issue that is causing the most serious tension among TPCCs, between the North and South and between the UN Secretariat and contributors, is differences in opinion and interpretation when it comes to the trend towards the more robust use of force in peacekeeping. Another observation is that there is a wider need for regular and substantive discussions on key peacekeeping issues, as well as mission-specific consultations with TPCCs. These dilemmas facing the large TPCCs reinforce the main argument of the book, namely that the tensions between peacekeeping doctrine and current praxis are undermining the overall effectiveness of UN peacekeeping.

In Part II, Chapter 7, Felix da Costa and Peter analyze three peacekeeping missions, East Timor, Kosovo, and South Sudan, with statebuilding mandates in all different contexts pertaining to history, international support, and existence or not of the Brahimi doctrine. They argue that these missions are essentially political, and with vast and often contradicting mandates, complexities emerge over time in missions' relations with the host government and other key actors with far-reaching consequences for peacekeeping principles, especially of consent, impartiality, and non-use of force. Furthermore, they examine the legitimacy and credibility of peacekeeping mission from the viewpoint of the local population, particularly when peacekeeping mandates are understood in overly technical-administrative terms.

In Chapter 8, Karlsrud and Gjelsvik argue that missions deployed to situations where there is no peace to keep, and with a limited or absent political mandate, are destined to fail the expectations of their masters, funders, and host populations, being Band-Aids for the international community without real capacity to fulfill their mandates. Furthermore, when UN peacekeeping missions are deployed with protection of civilians mandates but without the requisite resources, capabilities, and political support to back them up, there is a real risk that they can become a party to the conflict, and such missions may detract attention from the need to deal with fundamental and political questions, focusing instead on harder security issues and leading to a securitization of the situation.

In Chapter 9, Kjeksrud and Vermeij analyze the missions with mandates to protect civilians, governments, and peace processes from insurgency, taking up as cases the DRC and Mali. They argue that the recent deployments of the FIB as part of MONUSCO and MIN-USMA in Mali point to the need for the UN to revise its peacekeeping principles. Operating within states without peace to keep, with unreliable consent from a complex web of local parties, often protecting the governments against recognized insurgencies, the impartiality of these missions is "merely an illusion" with broad-ranging consequences also for the civilian dimensions of these operations. While increasing effectiveness, partiality makes peacekeeping missions riskier. These missions also indicate alterations in principles concerning consent and the use of force.

In Part III, the impact of some of the newly available techniques and technologies in the context of UN peacekeeping is discussed. In Chapter 10, Bowers offers a first thorough review of the use of naval, littoral, and riverine assets by the UN in peacekeeping contexts. Maritime mandates to date range from transport, patrol both on rivers and coasts, capacity building (of maritime forces of the host state), counter-piracy and illicit activities, and protection of civilians, to fire support and other assets suited to robust missions, such as the UN missions in the DRC and Mali. The flexibility of maritime assets would suit equally varied mission types and purposes of the UN, enabling flexible doctrinal considerations.

In Chapter 11, Karlsrud examines the potential of new technologies for UN peace operations, and argues that the digital revolution we are in the midst of is a paradigm shift at the level of the industrial revolution, creating new opportunities, but also new challenges. Karlsrud looks closer at issues such as crisis-mapping, big data, and surveillance drones—tools that UN peace operations should make use of to listen to local voices, alleviate suffering, protect civilians in need, and increase the protection of UN troops and civilians in the field. He also underscores that new tools require new capacities—for example, analysis capacity is crucial—it is not a layman task to analyze satellite pictures and synthetic aperture radar data. Finally, new technologies also create the need to update the doctrinal framework, enabling peace operations to engage more directly with host communities, and highlighting the need for popular and not only host state consent.

Finally, in the concluding Chapter 12, Aoi and de Coning analyze the UN's experience and practice in what might be termed *stabilization*, although it is not an officially defined term in the UN. The chapter further considers the concept and characteristics of stabilization in generic terms and adapts that to the UN context given the history of engagement by the organization in proximate practices to consider whether a standalone UN doctrine of stabilization is possible. The chapter concludes that given the practical problems that the UN peacekeeping currently faces in the lack of appropriate doctrines, as analyzed in all previous chapters, a proactive and forward-looking approach is warranted to create a standalone UN doctrine on stabilization, in addition to the existing UN doctrine on peacekeeping.

Notes

1 This book project was supported by Japan Society for the Promotion of Science (JSPS), Grants-in-aid for Scientific Research (KAKENHI), Grant no. JP24530175, and the Training for Peace programme at the Norwegian Institute of International Affairs.
2 UN, Peacekeeping, "(4a) Fatalities by Mission, Year and Incident Type, up to 30 June 2016," www.un.org/en/peacekeeping/fatalities/documents/stats_4a.pdf. The question of under what conditions future UN peacekeeping operations will be deployed is a crucial one. When Mali is excluded from the fatality count, UN peacekeeping is experiencing a historic low in the number of deaths per 1,000 of population. For more on fatality trends, see Jaïr Van der Lijn and Timo Smit, "Peacekeepers under Threat? Fatality Trends in UN Peace Operations," *SIPRI Policy Brief*, September 2015, 3.
3 DPKO/DFS, "United Nations Peacekeeping Operations: Principles and Guidelines" (so-called "Capstone Doctrine"), United Nations, New York, 2008, 18, www.un.org/en/peacekeeping/documents/capstone_eng.pdf.
4 UK Ministry of Defence, "Security and Stabilisation: The Military Contribution," *Joint Doctrine Publication* 3–40, November 2009, XI.
5 UK Stabilisation Unit (Foreign and Commonwealth Office, Ministry of Defence, and Department for International Development), "The UK Government's Approach to Stabilisation (2014)," May 2014, www.sclr.stabilisationunit.gov.uk/attachments/article/520/TheUKApproachtoStabilisationMay2014.pdf
6 UK Ministry of Defence, "British Army Field Manual," Vol. 1, Part 10: Countering Insurgency, October 2009, 1–6.
7 Ibid., 1–5.
8 See, for example, John Mackinlay, *Insurgency Archipilago* (London: Hurst, 2009), 68, who argued that lessons of countering insurgencies should have been more relevant than was then recognized.
9 Karsten Friis, "Peacekeeping and Counter-insurgency: Two of a Kind?" *International Peacekeeping* 17, no. 1 (2010): 49–66.
10 For example, Mandy Turner, "Peacebuilding as Counterinsurgency in the Occupied Palestinian Territory," *Review of International Studies* 41 (2015): 73–98.
11 Thijs Brocades Zaalberg, "Counterinsurgency and Peace Operations," in *Routledge Handbook on Insurgency and Counterinsurgency*, ed. Isabelle Duyvesteyn and Paul Rich (London: Routledge, 2014).

12 William Durch, *UN Peacekeeping, American Policy, and the Uncivil Wars of the 1990s* (Washington, DC: Henry Stimson Center Books, 1996).
13 The literature on peacebuilding is voluminous. See, for example, Susanna Campbell, David Chandler, and Meera Sabaratnam, *The Liberal Peace? The Problem and Practice of Peacebuilding* (New York: Zed Books, 2011); Edward Newman, Roland Paris, and Oliver Richmond, eds, *New Perspectives on Liberal Peacebuilding* (Tokyo: UN University Press, 2009); and Edward Newman and Roland Rich, eds, *The UN Role in Promoting Democracy: Between Ideals and Reality* (Tokyo: UN University Press, 2004).
14 Durch, *UN Peacekeeping*; Alex Bellamy, Paul Williams, and Stuart Griffin, *Understanding Peacekeeping* (Hoboken, N.J.: Wiley-Blackwell, 2004), and the 2010 second edition by Polity Press; Trevor Findlay, *Use of Force in UN Peace Operations* (Oxford: SIPRI Publications and Oxford University Press, 2003); and Alex Bellamy and Paul Williams, "The New Politics of Protection? Cote d'Ivoire, Libya and the Responsibility to Protect," *International Affairs* 87, no. 4 (2011): 825–50.
15 Benjamin de Carvalho and Ole Jacob Sending, eds, *The Protection of Civilians in UN Peace Operations: Concept, Implementation and Practice* (Baden-Baden: Nomos, 2012); Vesselin Popovski, Charles Sampford, and Angus Francis, eds, *Norms of Protection: Responsibility to Protect, Protection of Civilians and Their Interaction* (Tokyo: UN University Press, 2012)
16 Maren Leed, "What Battlefield Lessons Have We Learned from 12 Years of War?" in *Global Forecast 2014: U.S. Security Policy at Crossroads*, ed. Craig Cohen, Kathleen Hicks, Josiane Gabel (Washington, DC: Center for Strategic and International Studies, 2013); Elizabeth Young, "Decade of War: Enduring Lessons from a Decade of Operations," *Prism* 4, no. 2 (2013): 123–41.
17 Jean-Philippe Remy, "Anarchy and Death in Mali," *The New York Times*, 10 November 2013, www.nytimes.com/2013/11/11/opinion/anarchy-and-death-in-mali.html?src=recg&_r=0.
18 Cedric de Coning, Linnea Gelot, and John Karlsrud, *The Future of African Peace Operations: From Janjaweed to Boko Haram* (London: Zed Books, 2016).
19 UN, "Uniting Our Strengths for Peace: Politics, Partnerships and People," Report of the High-Level Independent Panel on Peace Operations, New York, 16 June 2015.
20 Ibid., 28.
21 Ibid., 29.
22 Ibid., 12.
23 Ibid., 45.
24 The White House, "United States Support to United Nations Peace Operations," 28 September 2015, www.defense.gov/Portals/1/Documents/pubs/2015peaceoperations.pdf.
25 UN, "Uniting our Strengths for Peace," 35.
26 Security Council Resolution 1265, UN doc. S/RES.1265, 17 September 1999; and DPKO/DFS, "United Nations Peacekeeping Operations."
27 John Stedman, "Spoiler Problem in Peace Processes," *International Security* 22, no. 2 (1997): 5–53.

28 DPKO/DFS, "United Nations Peacekeeping Operations," 51.
29 Ibid., 31–2.
30 NATO, "Peace Support Operation," doc. no. AJP-3.4.1, July 2001. See also the UK Ministry of Defence, Doctrine, Concepts and Development Centre, "Peace Support Operations," doc. no. JWP 3–50, 1998.
31 DPKO/DFS, "United Nations Peacekeeping Operations," 32.
32 Ibid., 22–3.
33 This characteristic is particularly relevant to the initial PSO construct. See UK Ministry of Defence, "Peace Support Operations." The UK PSO concept has since been revised to more closely reflect the UN definitions of peace enforcement and peacekeeping. See UK Ministry of Defence, Doctrine, Concepts and Development Centre, "Peacekeeping: An Evolving Role for Military Forces," Joint Doctrine Note 5/11, 2011.
34 Security Council Resolution 2098, UN doc. S/RES/2098, 28 March 2013, 7.
35 DPKO/DFS, "Draft DPKO/DFS Concept Note on Robust Peacekeeping," New York, 2010, 3. Emphasis in original.
36 The UN mission in Congo from 1960–64 is an exception in some respects, as the mission was engaged in combat with Katangese forces on the ground as well as conducting air attacks. See Walter Dorn and David Bell, "Intelligence and Peacekeeping: The UN Operation in the Congo 1960–1964," *International Peacekeeping* 2, no. 1 (1995): 11–33; and Jane Boulden, *Peace-Enforcement: The United Nations Experience in Congo, Somalia, and Bosnia* (Westport, Conn.: Praeger, 2001).
37 For a comprehensive study of these recent challenges to impartiality in UN peace operations, see Emily Paddon Rhoads, *Taking Sides in Peacekeeping: Impartiality and the Future of the United Nations* (Oxford: Oxford University Press, 2016).
38 UN, "Uniting our Strengths for Peace," 29.
39 William Durch, "Exit and Peace Support Operations," in *Exit Strategies and State Building*, ed. Richard Caplan (Oxford: Oxford University Press, 2012), 79–99.
40 Bellamy, Williams, and Griffin, *Understanding Peacekeeping* (2004 and 2010 editions).
41 UN, "Uniting our Strengths for Peace."

Part I

Doctrinal Debates

1 US military doctrine and the challenges of peace operations

William Flavin and Chiyuki Aoi

- US interests and peace operations: The policy context
- The origin and development of US peace operations doctrine: Convergence into "stability"
- Peacekeeping principles and the use of force
- US civil-military operations and UN civil-military coordination
- Emerging thematic focus
- Conclusion

Peace operations, counterinsurgency, and stability operations have not been a traditional focus of US military doctrine. Even though the majority of US military operations have fallen into those categories, the institutional preference has been toward conventional, large-scale, force-on-force operations such as those during World War II (WWII) or the Gulf War. The demands of the international situation, however, have forced the US military to address what it once termed "military operations other than war" (MOOTW). From Lebanon (1982–4) to Somalia (1992–5); from Haiti (1994–6) to the Balkans (1995–) to Iraq (1991/2003–) and Afghanistan (2001–), the US military has been engaged in operations "among the people" or what today might be termed "stabilization," requiring a much different approach from the conventional warfare of previous periods. As the term MOOTW indicated, these vastly different events, ranging from peace operations to counterinsurgency, were lumped together in the US doctrine as activities "outside warfare"—or something less political and less directly related to US interests than conventional warfare. However, in the mid-2000s, the adoption of the full-spectrum approach led to clarification of each operational theme belonging to that spectrum. The way doctrine was developed and evolved, moreover, reflected the US policy on these operational themes as well as the cultural and institutional context in which the US military approached operational lessons learned and concept writing.

The purpose of this chapter is hence to examine the development of US military doctrine in peace operations in the context of the political dynamics of successive US administrations, the inherent institutional needs of the military services, and the demands of a complex environment. The United States, which is the world's dominant power and, particularly since the end of the Cold War, the only superpower, has at times exhibited exceptionalist tendencies, and with well-established checks and balances in its domestic politics, a coherent peacekeeping policy was hard to come by. Moreover, the US military has traditionally considered that it has an advantage in "fighting the nation's wars" with decisive, conventional warfare. "Nation-building," being the world's global police force, or peacekeeping were not its preferred options, even though it has engaged in these types of operations consistently throughout its history. This chapter will hence demonstrate how the development of peace operations concepts and doctrine, as well as the overarching stability concepts, have become embedded in the inherent tensions that characterize the continuing debate over the appropriate role for the US military in so-called low-intensity conflict.

Having specified the political context of US doctrine formation, this chapter will then posit the following three arguments pertaining to US peace operations doctrine. First, that the development of US peace operations doctrine has historically been influenced by related operational areas, namely, post-conflict occupation and administration, counterinsurgency, and stability, and that eventually all these fields came to be integrated within the full-spectrum approach adopted in the mid-2000s by the US Army, where peace operations became one of the operational themes contained within that spectrum. The US Army's focus on the full-spectrum approach reflected the country's ever-increasing engagement in "small wars" in the 2000s, and this meant in doctrinal terms that US peace operations doctrine could develop and evolve only in the context of the full-spectrum approach. The idea of full-spectrum operations is that all military operations are composed of offence, defense, and stability, and each operational theme is explained as a combination of these elements. As such, since the 2000s, US approaches to peace operations have been linked to developments in the "stability" segment of the doctrine. This made it somewhat inevitable that peace operations concepts and doctrine would be influenced by events outside peace operations, most notably counterinsurgency and stabilization, such as those non-United Nations (UN)-led missions in Iraq or Afghanistan. Revisions in the doctrine under these categories also tend to go hand in hand.

The second argument presented here is that, against the background of increasing importance of civil-military coordination in peace operations since the end of the Cold War, the US historical experience in civil-military operations (CMOs) stands in uneasy relation to the UN concept and practice of civil-military coordination. The US military approach to CMOs contains two separate traditions that are contradictory to one another—i.e., those from the standpoint of enabling the commander's missions, on the one hand, and those as a support role for civilian agencies operating in a peace operations context on the other. Civilian agencies, by comparison, approach civil-military coordination as supporting their mission only in exceptional cases, and in the case of the UN, the idea of integrated missions is making the binary approach to civil-military coordination less central to the purpose of achieving system-wide coherence in peace operations. Such differences in approach and structure potentially place the United States at odds with the UN on the issue. The current US approach is accentuated by the very lack of interagency machinery, that is, the lack of an integrated approach at the strategic and operational level that addresses not only US interagency relations but also relations with the nongovernmental, intergovernmental, and private sectors, except, perhaps to some degree through a US Embassy Country Team.

Lastly, in evaluating the current state of US military doctrine and the tensions and opportunities presented by the UN initiatives launched by President Obama on 15 September 2015, we argue that US military peace operations doctrine is increasingly focusing on specific themes such as the protection of civilians and conflict transformation. The preparation of such doctrines and guidelines are welcome developments, particularly as the United States provides for mentoring, and logistical and other support for regional peacekeeping operations. However, the impact of these initiatives is diminished as long as the United States remains ambivalent about contributing US military units to UN peace operations.

The US military considers doctrine to be much more than guidance. Doctrine enables national security strategy by providing bridges between objectives and actions. It informs the senior political leaders about the strengths, capabilities, and proper employment of military forces as well as their limitations. It provides the concepts and framework to guide the senior military leaders in determining the size and composition of the force, the direction of research and development, the acquisition and subsequent distribution of personnel and materiel, the requirements for education and training, and the deployment, development, and sustaining of that force. Doctrine is hence central to a well-functioning military. Yet, doctrinal development cannot be free from the policies surrounding certain types of operations. Closer political interest and leadership in operations can create an environment where doctrinal development is more resourced and prioritized, with civilian interest and at times oversight. However, where such genuine political interest or political direction is lacking— as has at times been the case historically in the US stance towards UN peacekeeping—doctrine is often institution-driven and developed in isolation, without coordination with other agencies or clear links with policy.

The chapter first examines the political context of the evolution of the doctrine of US military peace operations. This is followed by an explanation of the origin and evolution of that doctrine, and culminates in an examination of the full-spectrum approach adopted in the mid-2000s. Then it will discuss the opportunities and tensions inherent in US thinking about CMOs and broader civil-military coordination, followed by an analysis of emerging issues important for the US peace operations doctrine. The conclusion will discuss the doctrinal and educational implications of the recent Obama initiatives, while identifying major gaps in US doctrinal approach.

US interests and peace operations: The policy context

The policy and stance of the United States towards peacekeeping, as the world's dominant power, inevitably have a great influence on peacekeeping in general. As a permanent member, with huge resources at its disposal, the United States' vote on the UN Security Council concerning whether to authorize peacekeeping missions has mattered greatly.[1] In accounting for the post-Cold War proliferation of UN peacekeeping, US preferences and advocacy were instrumental, albeit with some fluctuations.[2] The United States is also the largest financial contributor to UN peacekeeping operations, with about 28 percent of total contributions by formal assessment of the UN peacekeeping budget as of 2013/15. The US has also enhanced training for peacekeepers globally, through mechanisms it created such as Global Peace Operation Initiative (GPOI), which was established in 2004. The United States has also provided for logistical capabilities and intelligence in support of various UN peacekeeping missions.

The influence that the United States exerts on global peacekeeping trends has, however, not always been matched by a clear-cut policy. Rather, the ambivalence of the American stance towards the United Nations itself has applied to UN peacekeeping as well, especially with regard to having its own military contribute. The United States has to date played only a limited operational role in UN peacekeeping operations, opting rather for a support role, albeit to an extent that is indeed critical, and providing only a small number of uniformed personnel to a limited number of UN missions.[3] In general, successive US administrations found it hard to convince the American public and legislature of the virtues of engaging American forces in peacekeeping, particularly if it involves long-term commitment, or "nation-building" tasks. It has preferred that these jobs be undertaken by others—other UN member states, allies, or the global community at large.[4] Gradually, more formal and explicit links were made between US support for, or participation in, peacekeeping and vital US national security interests.

During the early Cold War years, the United States contributed personnel in support of the 1948 Truce Commission for Palestine and the 1949 UN Truce Supervision Organization (UNTSO). However, the Security Council was largely paralyzed during the Cold War and this made expansion or effective use of UN peacekeeping machinery unrealistic. In addition, the strategic utility of UN peacekeeping was found in its neutrality *vis-à-vis* the Cold War rivalry, hence there was not much strategic logic in having the superpowers providing UN peacekeepers. More substantial engagement by the United States in peacekeeping and equivalent activities during the Cold War was in non-UN missions, namely, the Multinational Force mission in Lebanon (1982–4), and the Multinational Force and Observers (MFO) which came into existence with the Camp David Accords (the US forces deployed 19 March 1982 and are still there today as the largest contingent of over 700). The US military were also deployed in the Dominican Republic in 1965, to protect lives and property during the country's civil war. This preceded the Mission of the Representative of the Secretary-General in the Dominican Republic (DOMREP) that followed. Nonetheless, given the scarcity of political interest in sending American troops to serve under the command of the UN, initial enthusiasm in the US military for UN peacekeeping quickly waned and gave way to the conventional focus of its fighting ethos.

Since the end of the Cold War, the issue of how the United States should support and strengthen the UN, including most notably UN peacekeeping, attracted renewed attention as both presidents George

H.W. Bush and Bill Clinton initially pursued the optimistic goal of promoting the UN role in international security. President Bush declared the emergence of a "new world order" as Cold War confrontation gave way to seeming harmony of the great powers' interest in supporting a stronger role for the UN. For Bush, the Gulf War was an exemplary expression of this order and during his term, new UN peacekeeping missions were established in El Salvador, Angola, Yugoslavia, Cambodia, Iraq-Kuwait, and Somalia.[5] Furthermore, US forces led the multinational force in Somalia to stop starvation, the first peace enforcement action under a humanitarian banner.

President Clinton continued with the enthusiasm of his predecessor, under the banner of "assertive multilateralism," although the UN mission in Somalia replacing the US-led multinational force there was something it inherited, rather than initiated. Bosnia, with ongoing ethnic civil war, presented another challenge. Indeed, between November 1992 and March 1996, the United States had a large number of personnel under UN command (in Somalia, Haiti, and the former Yugoslavia).[6]

However, after the failed mission in Somalia, forcing US forces to withdraw, initial enthusiasm for assertive multilateralism gave way to a policy of realism, or selective engagement. On 3 October 1993, when a team of US Army Rangers sent to capture Mohammed Farah Aideed was ambushed in Mogadishu, resulting in 18 American deaths, the sight of dead US soldiers being dragged through the city's streets hit the evening news.[7] This event, coupled with resistance from within the military about being bogged down in supporting UN peacekeeping missions at a time when resources were being cut, and concerns in Congress about diverting US resources from domestic needs, changed the thrust of US support to UN peace operations.

Presidential Decision Directive (PDD) 25 was the first explicit peacekeeping policy published by the Clinton administration, and this set out to create conditions for US support for UN peacekeeping that focused more narrowly on vital US national interests.[8] The application of this policy had a devastating effect, because the reluctant Security Council failed to adopt an effective policy just at the time a genocidal tide was rising in Rwanda in 1994. The scale of UN peacekeeping as a whole was limited in terms of personnel numbers and budget in the latter half of the 1990s; it was only for East Timor and Kosovo from the late 1990s that larger missions again started to be created.

A critical development in terms of US military doctrine came in the Clinton era, with increased and longer term involvement in the former Yugoslavia. US troops participated in the post-Dayton North Atlantic

Treaty Organization (NATO) peace support mission in Bosnia and also in the Kosovo Force (KFOR). These operations were conducted by NATO, not under UN command but with UN authorization. These peace support missions had a great impact on US military doctrine on a host of peace-operation-related issues. This impact notwithstanding, US troop presence in these missions was quickly drawn back, with more of the burden shifted to its European allies.[9] Direct US troop presence (in 2001, about 6,000 in Bosnia and 5,500 in Kosovo; in 2004, 2,000 and 1,900, respectively) was larger than its participation in UN missions. In 2001, the United States had 44 military and 844 police personnel under UN command.[10]

It was the 9/11 terrorist attack on the United States that inadvertently shifted the US stance on stability operations and quite unexpectedly, on peace operations as well. The George W. Bush (Jr) administration came to office from a position of strong skepticism about US multilateral engagement, in particular military involvement in peacekeeping globally—as expressed in Bush's infamous statement that he would withdraw US troops from the Balkans. Later, however, the administration shifted position, embracing the UN multinational fora for increasing international cooperation to tackle global terrorism, an outgrowth of his declared Global War on Terror.

The administration also embraced UN peacekeeping when it suited US national interests or values. Despite initial reticence, UN peacekeeping expanded dramatically in size and number of missions under Bush. The US supported the expansion of the mission in the Democratic Republic of the Congo in 2002, and supported the establishment of several large-scale peacekeeping missions in Liberia, Cote d'Ivoire, Haiti, and Darfur.[11] It also supported the UN move to support the African Union mission in Somalia. In 2004, the United States also launched the Global Peace Operations Initiative and funded it, in order to train and equip peacekeepers from across the world, with particular focus on 25 African nations.[12] Police training was another focus, with the GPOI assisting training of police trainers from 29 countries at the Center of Excellence for Stability Police Units (CoESPU).[13]

The most immediate impact of 9/11 was the US embrace of stability operations, and it was this and the full-spectrum approach that would have a deep influence on the US approach to peace operations. Stability missions had long been submerged in the notions of low-intensity conflict and MOOTW, in the US strategic and military orientation, and, together with "nation-building," were considered largely redundant in the political and strategic climate after the Vietnam War.

Nonetheless, the fact was that the US military was squarely embroiled in stability and counterinsurgency missions in Iraq and Afghanistan, and the Bush administration had to come to terms with that fact. Notably, in 2006 the Department of Defense issued Directive 3000.05 on "Stability Operations," which declared that such operations were, along with combat, part of the core mission of the US military. In 2013 the secretary of defense conducted an assessment based on the directive that required biannual review, and determined that the military needed to continue to be prepared to address complex environments that were not going away. That assessment led to a series of recommendations to distill the lessons of the last several years and prepare a doctrine, structures, and materiel that would address the emerging situation.

Under the Obama administration, the initial instinct was the reverse of the previous administration, toward multilateral rather than unilateral engagement. Nonetheless, in terms of peacekeeping policy, the administration did not develop a concrete position until September 2015, when a position paper was published for the UN General Assembly. That month President Obama convened a Summit at the UN "to strengthen and reform U.N. peacekeeping because our common security demands it." The president also issued *United States Support to United Nations Peacekeeping Operations*, the first US policy document on peacekeeping since the PDD 25 during the Clinton administration. Obama directed that the United States use the experience, technology, doctrine, and expertise gained over 15 years of engagement in conflict to improve the performance of the UN. The major areas of the policy are building partner capacity to support UN peace operations, contributing US diplomatic support, providing enabling capabilities and personnel, and leading and supporting efforts at the UN for systemic reform.[14]

The United States is set to continue to assist in developing the capacity of the UN to achieve operational and tactical success through the Global Peace Operations Initiative, through which resources and training for member states and to the UN staff and missions are provided. One of the supporting initiatives is the African Peacekeeping Rapid Response Partnership. Over the 2016–20 period the United States plans to invest $110 million in a core group of six African countries that have demonstrated a commitment to protecting civilians from violence. Although the program has been slow to be executed, the US goal is to encourage countries to be proactive in using force to uphold mandates. The United States also plans to share knowledge and technology for global logistical support and information management as well as develop a better common understanding of the operational area. In the Central African Republic, the United States sold its expeditionary modular bases to the UN mission, allowing the latter to establish sector headquarters outside of the capital city of Bangui. With the new Acquisitions and Cross Servicing Agreements that have been negotiated with the UN, the United States will be able to supply support in a more expeditious manner and assist with technical solutions.[15]

Obama offered to double the US contribution of military staff, individual police, and military observers, from the current 40. However, the president has not yet proposed the provision of a formed military unit. The policy incorporates other institutional initiatives that will enhance Department of Defense representation in peacekeeping. It directs the department to "seek to find ways to credit, professionally reward, and more readily track UN mission experience and expertise of U.S. military and civilian personnel within their respective personnel systems," hence pledging to address the long-standing obstacle to mainstreaming UN experience within the US military. The Department of Defense will also develop a "cadre of military personnel able to serve in leadership roles in UN headquarters and field missions."[16] These are welcome developments, with implications for doctrine, education, and training.

These initiatives, if fully implemented, will enhance US support for UN peacekeeping through a renewed focus on the training/capacity-building, support, and educational aspects of UN peacekeeping. Yet the long-held ambivalence towards increasing the operational role of the US military in UN peacekeeping seems to remain in place, and so Obama administration policy towards UN peacekeeping may not be that marked a departure from the past.

The origin and development of US peace operations doctrine: Convergence into "stability"

The often-ambivalent policy towards UN peacekeeping, especially direct participation, has provided the basis for the US military's doctrinal development, which historically had a tendency to focus on conventional, high-intensity warfare.

Although the US military has, in fact, engaged in peace operations and related operations more often than in major inter-state warfare, such operations have been considered less relevant to the core mission of conducting major inter-state, high-intensity warfare. These "lesser" operations have been seen as either not the job of the military or activity inappropriately assigned to it by politicians. They are thought of as jobs the military would easily and quickly complete, handing them back to civilians before getting back to the real job of fighting "big conventional war." Moreover, peace operations were seen as diverting limited resources that should be husbanded for the major crisis. Larry Yates, writing for the US Army Combat Studies Institute, summarizes this attitude:

> Yet, in the past, war-fighting doctrine, supported by military education and training programs and reflecting the Army's institutional biases, has instilled the conviction in most officers that, despite war's diversity, "real" war is primarily a conventional undertaking—one in which the regular armed forces of a given state wage large-scale and sustained combat operations against the regular armed forces of an enemy state.[17]

If America's armed forces have fought fewer than a dozen major conventional wars in over two centuries, they have, during that same period, engaged in several hundred military undertakings that would today be characterized as stability operations. The Army was involved in many of these; as an institution, however, it developed, in the words of analyst James Carafano, "a tradition of forgetting" its own experience. The primary reason for this is simple enough: throughout most of its history, the Army has regarded stability operations as "someone else's job," an unwanted burden, a series of sideshows that soldiers performed either separately from war or in the wake of war.[18]

Given this institutional climate, it is important to understand that peace operations doctrine in the United States developed in stages, and that it has precursors in the related activities of post-conflict occupation and stability/counterinsurgency, as these activities were imposed upon the US military at particular historical and political junctures. The peace support operations like these that proliferated during the 1990s are the direct precursors to US peace operations doctrine. Gradually, driven by after-action reviews inside and outside of the US government, and pressure from political leadership starting in 2005 when the secretary of defense issued Directive 3000.05 making "stability operations" a core task of the US military along with combat, these operations have become the overarching framework unifying these streams of doctrine.[19]

Post-conflict civil administration and support

The multinational occupation of the German Rhineland at the end of World War I (WWI) was the first time that the US military had engaged in the occupation and administration of another nation in

what would later be termed a stabilization operation. As the US Army attempted to impose public order in collaboration with Great Britain, France, and Belgium, it discovered that there were different approaches among the allies on how to accomplish this task. The United States desired to use only its military forces while the other nations had combinations of civilian and military structures to administer the occupied areas. This led to debates and friction as the US commander, Major General Henry T. Allen, refused to surrender any authority to civilian oversight.[20] The responsibilities and relationships between civil and military would be an ongoing theme of doctrinal debates.

The WWI experience led to several studies on occupation in post-conflict situations and what kind of preparations that the US military should make. In 1920 Colonel Irving L. Hunt wrote a report based on his occupation experience calling on the US Army to educate and train for civil administration in post-conflict situations. *Military Aid to Civil Power*, published by the Army in 1925 on the basis of Hunt's report, was to provide the post-conflict framework after WWII.[21]

In the post-WWII era, moreover, in the Philippines, Korea, Lebanon, Central America, and the Dominican Republic, the US military faced the issue of post-conflict support for civil authorities, where the focus was supporting friendly governments in building their capacity to deal with instability. The US government considered such foreign assistance the key to fighting communism. The so-called Draper Committee (the President's Committee to Study the United States Military Assistance program), established in 1958 by the administration of President Dwight Eisenhower to provide for an independent and bipartisan analysis of US military foreign assistance programs, validated the need to develop the capability to assist friendly countries. The findings of the Draper Committee were expanded in the 1960s by President John F. Kennedy's push to assist governments around the globe to deal with communist insurgencies. Post-conflict support for rebuilding a nation was now associated with counterinsurgency as an internal development. From Vietnam onward these doctrinal strands would intertwine.[22]

Small wars and counterinsurgency

As studies on post-conflict administration after WWI were being undertaken in the 1920s, the US Army and the US Marine Corps (USMC) were conducting complex operations in Haiti, Nicaragua, Honduras, Cuba, and the Philippines. Both the Army infantry and the USMC officers who had been engaged in these expeditionary missions believed that similar operations would be most likely in the future. The Army's *Small Wars and Punitive Expeditions* and the USMC's *Small Wars* were published prior to WWII in an effort to provide guidance amid the complexities. They reflected the struggles between conventionally minded leaders and those who had been engaged in occupation environments, as Keith Bickel chronicles in his book *Mars Learning*.[23] Both publications emphasized the need to develop and assist local civil authorities and consider civil measures in addition to military responses in order to ensure lasting peace. They emphasized that police and civil order had to include gaining popular support and providing protection for civil populations. With the coming of WWII both of these works were put aside as all services faced worldwide war.[24]

Germany's counter-guerrilla operations during WWII exerted a profound influence over American post-war doctrine. The US Army translated many of the German doctrinal materials and pamphlets captured, and when the US Army was engaged against communist guerrillas in South Korea this body of knowledge was put into action. FM 31–20, *Operations Against Guerrilla Forces*, was the key document. It recognized that guerrillas were dependent on the support of the population and this became a key tenet in the counter-guerrilla approach.[25]

The FM 31–20 manual recognized the political, economic, and social dimensions of the struggle and advocated a proactive approach to address these issues and focus on the drivers of conflict. It called for a broad political-military plan based on "detailed analysis of a country, the national characteristics and the customs, beliefs, cares, hopes, and desires of the people."[26] This was the lesson that the Germans had not learned in dealing with the Russian resistance. The manual also called for population-control measures, such as taking hostages and conducting reprisals against civilian communities believed to be supportive of guerrilla forces. As Andrew Birtle, historian of this doctrine, writes: "FM 31–20's mixed message with regard to the treatment of a population under conditions of irregular warfare thus reflected the symbiotic relationship that benevolence and repression had long enjoyed in American military thought and practice."[27]

The tenets of Geneva Convention IV as well as lessons from the field were gradually incorporated into the doctrine concerning treatment of civilian populations, but again by 1958 the Army had lost interest and counter-guerrilla doctrine disappeared. Soon the Army would be facing Vietnam.

In the 1960s, President Kennedy compelled the US military to prepare itself to deal with conflicts of national liberation. The military responded by publishing a family of manuals on counterinsurgency. FM 31–15, *Operations against Irregular Forces*, in 1961 was the base document. It was developed by the special operations community and built on the basis of FM 31–20. It addressed the basic civil issues while emphasizing the defeat of insurgents by isolating them from the people. It also recognized the importance of civil assistance, police action, and training and assistance for a host nation's military. This of course depended upon the willingness of the host nation. Follow-up manuals called for stern measures against civilians who were supporting insurgents.

Following the American tradition, the FM 31–15 manual advised commanders to apply a judicious mixture of moderation and fairness on the one hand and "vigorous enforcement and stern punishment" on the other, warning that "half-heartedness or any other sign of laxness will breed contempt and defiance."[28]

In 1962, with the Army's publication of its overarching operational doctrine, FM 100–5, the military approach toward the civilian population shifted. The manual recognized the centrality of civilian populations and the need to not only gain their support but protect them as well. It also recognized that military authority has its limitations and that the host nation was a key actor.[29] These themes would reappear in later peace operations doctrine.

In the wake of Vietnam, the US Army shifted its focus to conventional war. Counterinsurgency and all other "low intensity/less than war" operations were relegated to the backwaters. The Army eliminated most of this type of instruction from its schools and centers. The Army was trying to forget Vietnam, and was rebuilding itself toward defeating the Soviets on the central front in Europe. The 1973 Arab-Israeli War was the catalyst for this change and its tenets dominated doctrine for several years to come. In 1974, the terms "counterinsurgency" and "stability operations" were both eliminated from the doctrine; they were replaced by "internal defense and development." Counterinsurgency would not enter the Army lexicon again until 2006.[30]

Peace operations

As seen in the previous section, from 1948 throughout the Cold War the US military was involved in supporting United Nations missions, but that support remained quite limited. It did not formally address peacekeeping before the 1990s, and doctrine in this area was long neglected. From 1948 to the 1980s the only official doctrine publication that even used the term "peacekeeping" was 1969's FM 7–20, *The Infantry Battalion*. This document provided no discussion of any fundamentals other than the brief mention that peacekeeping was an operation that an infantry battalion might be called upon to perform.

During this time, hence, military thinking on peace operations was limited to writings by individual officers. From 1971–5 students at the Command and General Staff College studied and wrote about peacekeeping. Major Charles Raymond's graduate thesis in 1974 was later to provide one of the basic documents for the development of the US Army peace operations doctrine, but Raymond's groundbreaking work did not find its way into Army doctrine for another 20 years. He considered all of the international work that had been done, especially that by the Australian, British, Canadian, American, and New Zealand Standardization Group (ABCA) in 1970.[31]

That year, the ABCA, an organization chartered in 1947 to maintain and extend the cooperation, interoperability, and standardization achieved during WWII, met to consider the future security challenges for the period 1981–90. It believed that peacekeeping would be a key concern and developed a concept for success which consisted of six elements: timely planning, clear mandates, proper command and control, well-trained combat forces, strategic air lift, and cutting-edge technology.

Raymond's study captured the standard principles of peacekeeping outlined by the United Nations but went on to emphasize the need for "unified or concurrent" peacekeeping and peacemaking. If a peacekeeping mission was to have long-term success, it had to do more than freeze the situation. Concurrent action had to be taken to relieve the causes of conflict. He saw the operation as transforming the environment. Today, conflict transformation is central to the US peacekeeping doctrine. He did not advocate the use of force: "The peacekeeping force does not defend territory nor impose its will by use of force. It provides the opportunity for the belligerents to avoid conflict."[32]

With the fall of the Berlin Wall in 1989, a new era of peace operations opened. President George H.W. Bush (Sr.), as a former US ambassador to the United Nations, embraced this opportunity especially after the Gulf War in 1991. He ensured that key national security documents reflected increased support for the UN. The 1993 *National Security Strategy* described the UN as a "central instrument for the prevention and resolution of conflicts and the preservation of peace," and stated that the United States would pay its full dues and take "an active role in the full spectrum of UN peacekeeping and humanitarian relief planning and support."[33]

The US military responded with the publication in 1990 of FM 100–20, *Army Operations in Low Intensity Conflict*, where peacekeeping was seen as a category of US military operations in low-intensity conflict, but applying the same principles of "political dominance" (akin to what is today termed the primacy of political aims), "legitimacy," "unity of effort," and "perseverance and adaptability" applied to all of these operations. *Peacekeeping* was defined in the manual as "Chapter VI operations" with full consent. Peace enforcement was called *peacemaking* and placed in the chapter named "Peacetime Contingency Operations" alongside "raids." Peacekeeping embraced Raymond's concepts that include use of force only for self-defense. *Peacemaking* emphasized the political nature of the operation, the need for restricted rules of engagement, the need for an appropriate foreign authority, and the rule that force used be appropriate to the environment. The objective of peacemaking was to achieve a concentration of force at the critical time and place to achieve a "military victory." *Peacemaking* was described as a "combat operation" to advance US interests using all means necessary.[34]

General Gordon Sullivan, chief of staff from 1991 to 1995, guided the Army to address the issue of operations in complex environments, including the need for a comprehensive approach. He had been faced with the Kurdish operations in northern Iraq, Rwanda, and Somalia and understood that this was going to be a prevalent contingency for US forces in the foreseeable future. He was concerned that the doctrine was inadequate, given the increasing potential for US involvement in internal crises, as demonstrated by the deployment to Somalia and the problems in the Balkans. He wanted to bring together all of the various strands of doctrine previously advanced and make a coherent peace operations concept.

The June 1993 FM 100–5 Army operational manual included an entire chapter on military operations other than war. For the first time in a capstone manual, the Army acknowledged this environment and established a separate set of principles for it. The doctrine established the term *peace operations* as a category and divided it into two aspects, "peacekeeping" and "peace enforcement" (as "peacemaking" came to be called), based on UN Secretary-General Boutros Boutros-Ghali's "An Agenda for Peace." The principles of war applied to all operations that the US Army was conducting, including peace operations. However, in addition those principles were added that included legitimacy, perseverance, and restricted use of force that should also apply to all of the components of operations other than war. The various strands of doctrine were starting to converge in the US capstone doctrine:

peacekeeping, peace enforcement, counterinsurgency, and nation assistance were now under the same category with the same set of principles.[35]

The doctrine writers at US Training and Doctrine Command reached out to the United Kingdom because of the latter's experience in the UN Protection Force (UNPROFOR, 1992–5) and established a dialogue with the writers of the British military doctrine manual, *Wider Peacekeeping*.[36] These discussions led to the publication in 1994 of the first US peace operations manual. It was divided into three parts, now taking into consideration the thinking in the UN and the United Kingdom: peacekeeping, peace enforcement, support to diplomacy that included peacebuilding, peacemaking, and preventive diplomacy. Although it brought together these various parts, each was considered separately, as done in *Wider Peacekeeping*. A military force was either in a peacekeeping mission, a peace enforcement mission, or conducting support to diplomacy. Success in peace operations depended on the ability of the commander to exercise situational dominance with respect to the variables to avoid "inadvertently slipping from one type of peace operation to another." The events in the Balkans and the lingering fear of being sucked into a Vietnam type of situation with no end in sight influenced this doctrine. Peace enforcement was seen as a separate operation that could make way for a peacekeeping force.

Peace enforcement operations are military intervention operations in support of diplomatic efforts to restore peace or to establish the conditions for a peacekeeping force to work between hostile factions that may not consent to intervention and may be engaged in combat activities. Peace enforcement implies the use or threat of force to coerce hostile groups to cease and desist from violent actions. Units conducting peace enforcement, therefore, cannot maintain objective neutrality in every instance. They must be prepared to apply elements of combative power to restore order, to separate warring factions, and to return the environment to conditions more conducive to civil order and discipline.[37]

As noted, the enthusiasm of President Bush (Sr.) for peace operations was continued by President Clinton, who, during his early days in office pursued a policy of "assertive multilateralism." He authorized US ground forces to deploy to Macedonia under the blue helmet (the UN Preventive Deployment Force, UNPREDEP). However, the eventual failure in Somalia and the adoption of PDD 25 in May 1994 precluded any further development in terms of US military unit participation in UN peacekeeping. PDD 25, which included strict guidelines for US participation in UN peace operations along with a list of required reforms for the UN, influenced the development on the next iteration of US military doctrine.

In 1999, JP 3–07.3, *Joint Tactics, Techniques, and Procedures for Peace Operations* reflected this changed approach. The definition of peace operations was narrowed to include only peacekeeping and peace enforcement. The rewrite was being done in the wake of Implementation Force (IFOR) deployment in Bosnia, during which the fear of "mission creep" significantly narrowed its mandate for the participating US forces. There were two reasons for the narrow definition: The Joint Staff J5 team directed that PDD 25 be used as the authoritative guide for the joint doctrine. Importantly, PDD 25 only recognized peacekeeping and peace enforcement as categories of peace operations. The J5 thus directed that the tactics, techniques, and procedures doctrine should focus only on the military role of peacekeeping and peace enforcement.

Accordingly, the other roles of peacebuilding were seen as civilian, and not military. There was no recognition of the role of the military in support of civilian operations, indicating a weak development in the civil-military coordination aspect of peace operations doctrine. However, the assumption within the military back then was that peace operations were political/civil missions that the military supports; hence it was not the remit of the military to propose principles and fundamentals for the peacebuilding/civilian dimensions or civil-military coordination dimension of peace operations. That was thought to be the responsibility of the UN, NATO, or US interagency policy. The military should only concern itself with the "military" dimension of peace operations, i.e., peacekeeping and peace enforcement. They should also be kept separate as clear and distinct operations with clearly defined objectives. In this way, the military could meet the requirement set down by PDD 25.

A change came in 2000 when the Peacekeeping Institute (PKI) at the US Army War College was tasked to re-write FM 100–23, FM 3–07, and eventually JP 3–07.3. Based on the experience of the Balkans, Haiti, and Somalia, the PKI argued that peace operations should be considered in a continuum that matched the new doctrinal concept of full-spectrum operations and that it should be incorporated into the overarching stability doctrine, FM 3–07. Peace operations now included peacebuilding, peacemaking, and conflict prevention as separate but related categories. Additionally, the PKI posited that peace operations were transformative and that the US military needed to be able to work simultaneously across the spectrum, collaborating with civilian counterparts in addressing the drivers of conflict by building up host nation capabilities and using all necessary force to deal with the demands of an environment where consent and levels of violence could shift.

In 2006, with the publication of the US Army's counterinsurgency manual, followed by the publication of the stability operations manual in 2008, the doctrine recognized that in all of these operations certain tasks needed to be performed across all operations to achieve success.

Stability ultimately aims to create conditions that the local populace regard as legitimate, acceptable, and predictable. These conditions consist of the level of violence; the functioning of governmental, economic, and societal institutions; and the general adherence to local laws, rules, and norms of behavior. *Stabilization* is a process in which personnel identify and mitigate underlying sources of instability to establish the conditions for long-term stability. While long-term development requires stability, stability does not require long-term development. Therefore, stability tasks focus on identifying and targeting the root causes of instability and by building the capacity of local institutions.[38]

Full-spectrum approach

The idea of the full-spectrum approach finally provided an overall structure in which various operational themes could be identified and defined: to successfully engage in a complex environment, the military commander must continuously and simultaneously combine offense, defense, and stability tasks.[39] The 2012 Army doctrine calls this "decisive action." Missions in any environment require Army forces to conduct any combination of these tasks.

The operating concept of unified land operations reflects the fundamental nature of the Army contribution to operations conducted outside the United States and its territories. The concept of unified land operations describes how the Army seizes, retains, and exploits the initiative to gain and maintain a position of relative advantage in sustained land operations through simultaneous offensive, defensive, and stability tasks in order to prevent or deter conflict, prevail in war, and create the conditions for favorable conflict resolution. Army forces employ synchronized action—nonlethal and lethal—proportionate to the mission and informed by a thorough understanding of all relevant aspects of an operational environment. Commanders carefully balance offensive and defensive tasks with stability tasks to create an environment that accomplishes the national objectives.[40]

What this means for peace operations, as experience has demonstrated, is that the boundaries between peacekeeping, peace enforcement, and peacebuilding do not exist in reality, and that these operations can be conducted simultaneously in the same geographic area. The situation on the ground can be fluid and the military force must be prepared to address all of these situations. This is illustrated in Figure 1.1 below from the 2006 JP 3–07.3.

The challenges in Figure 1.1 lie in the areas of intersection. The US doctrine alerts the military commander to be prepared to respond flexibly with a combination of offensive, defense, and stability tasks. The doctrine is clear that the capability of the force must match the environment as modulated by the level of consent and legitimacy. Consent and legitimacy are not static, so the force commander must consistently assess the situation to adjust his force to increase capability if consent decreases or to reduce the force if consent increases.

For example, if, during a peace operation, an insurgency is uncovered then the military commander using the concept for decisive operations

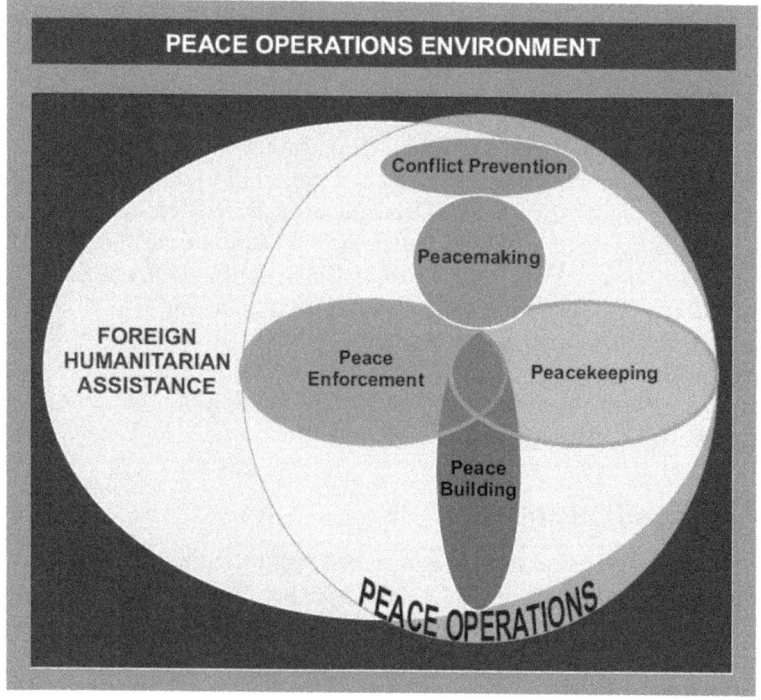

Figure 1.1 The peace operations environment
Source: Joint Staff, JP 3-07.3 *Peace Operations* (draft), 2006, 1–14.

will rearrange the offensive, defensive, and stability tasks to meet the new threat. This may require an adjustment or increase in the forces capability and possibly the rules of engagement. The new threat fits easily within the overarching doctrinal framework.

The implication of the full-spectrum approach is that, given that the majority of US troops have been deployed to non-UN stability operations in the past decade (i.e., Iraq and Afghanistan), the developments or experiences gained in these theaters have naturally impacted peace operations doctrine as well, through the incorporation of these lessons. This reflection of experience remains the core feature of the US approach to peace operations doctrine. It can have various implications for UN missions, as the doctrine is applied in the field by supporting or participating US contingents. For example, the Obama administration pledged, as part of the aforementioned concept paper presented to the UN summit, to provide materiel, monetary, resources, knowledge, technology, and bilateral support to both troop-contributing countries (TCC) and police-contributing countries (PCC) as well as to the UN itself. It is understood that the United States will put to use the doctrine, education, and capabilities that were honed in the conflicts of Afghanistan and Iraq. For example, improvised explosive devices (IEDs) have become a significant threat. The US has a great deal of experience dealing with IEDs and in defeating the network that constructs and emplaces them, so this knowledge will be offered to the UN. In Mali, in support of a UN Department of Peacekeeping Operations (DPKO) request, the United States recently sent an asymmetric warfare team to assess the threat that IEDs create for UN peacekeepers. Such support transported to UN peacekeeping missions from different theaters of operations may seem more technical and neutral. However, in general, knowledge acquired in a quite different operational context (e.g., counterinsurgency) should be applied, bearing in mind differences in political, social, and operational conditions.

Peacekeeping principles and the use of force

US military doctrine reflects a bias towards conventional warfare, and has always emphasized using all force necessary to dominate the situation. Particularly given the tradition of American warfare, where firepower and technology is favored, this interpretation comes into conflict with peacekeeping, the principle of which is the use of minimum necessary force (or in the UN's parlance, no use of force except for self-defense and defense of the mission, the latter involving robust rules of engagement).

Furthermore, with regard to the definition of peacekeeping and peace enforcement, in contrast to the UN stipulation involving the use of force at the strategic level, the United States defines *peace enforcement* as the use of force to implement the mandate. So, if force is necessary to protect civilians, deliver humanitarian aid and assistance, enforce sanctions, separate belligerents, and restore order—it is "peace enforcement." Therefore, all the UN missions today operating under Chapter VII would be considered peace enforcement according to US doctrine and not as "robust peacekeeping," which in UN parlance refers to the use of force at the tactical level with the consent of the main parties to the conflict.[41] *Robust peacekeeping* has no meaning in US doctrine.

The issues of impartiality, restrictive use of force, and protection of civilians have developed over time. Impartiality is still seen as a viable concept when force is used. It is true that people against whom the force is used will perceive that it is anything but impartial. The civil-military team must thus have a public communications strategy to deal with these perceptions. The idea is that the force is impartial in relationship to the mandate; those that oppose the mandate are not enemies but spoilers who must be dealt with like police deal with criminals who break the law.

How should the force be used? In 1966 a major study, "Counter Guerrilla Doctrine," was completed by the US Army's Special Warfare Agency. This document recommended the selective use of force to preclude harming the population. The concept, called *discriminate force*, began to be worked into the doctrine, although military commanders at the time were not willing to allow any limitation on their use of force.[42]

The term that was finally settled upon was *restricted use of force*. Now called *restraint*, the concept appeared for the first time in the 1993 FM 100–5 manual. This was based on General Sullivan's historical assessment of the US Army's response to complex environments throughout history and the preceding struggles in Central America, and global responses to natural disasters, as well as Operation Provide Comfort—the post–Gulf War operation to protect the Kurds in northern Iraq.

The US does not use the UN terms *non-use of force* and *minimum necessary use of force*, as they are understood to lead to confusion. The US assessment of the complex environment is that force may be necessary given the dynamic nature of the situation in order to achieve the goals established for the mission. The level of force used in those situations must be sufficient for the military unit to dominate. The use of force therefore should be necessary, proportional, and sufficient to the situation to achieve the desired outcome.

US civil-military operations and UN civil-military coordination

The nature and complexities of today's multidimensional operations are such that no single organization, department, or agency has all the requisite resources, authority, or expertise to single-handedly provide an effective response. With the changing nature of challenges faced internationally, the role of the military has expanded in peace operations, incorporating not only use of military and police resources to provide, support, or complement the provision of emergency humanitarian relief, but participation in peacebuilding efforts. This has resulted in increasing interaction among the military, civilian, police, and various civilian elements in areas not directly related to security.

This has been a challenge for military and civilian agencies alike, but the key dilemma in this context for the US government and for the military is that there are crucial differences in the US and UN approaches to civil-military relations. In essence, the US concept of civil-military operations retains a historical struggle between the traditional notion of CMO, with its primary military focus, and which is binary in the definition of issues pertaining to civil-military relations, and a newer model that aims at "enabling" civilian agencies to achieve the overall purpose of peacebuilding and state-building. The UN, on the other hand, focuses on enabling civilian agencies to accomplish the overall mandated mission through an integrated approach.

In the US tradition, CMOs were conducted as part of a military operation to advance military objectives. During WWII, these operations were designed to provide the US military maneuvering room to engage with the enemy, while keeping civilians from impeding the maneuvering forces and addressing civil issues as mandated by international law.[43] During the limited period where post-conflict occupation was conducted in Germany and Japan following WWII, civil-military operations supported military governments in both countries.

After the war, support to developing nations, especially if they were facing an insurgency, became a key issue of US civil affairs forces supporting CMO. Civil affairs officers assumed advisory roles in the Philippines and Vietnam, assisting as part of large US military advisory missions in support of a US embassy. They also supported joint military operations in Grenada, the Dominican Republic, Panama, and Haiti as part of military joint task force or military advisor groups, working out of the US embassies.[44]

During the 1960s, however, there emerged two competing views about US CMOs. The traditional school depicted civil affairs as an important, yet distinctly auxiliary weapon whose utility lay in facilitating military operations. The second school, which was a newer approach responding to operations providing a supporting role to host governments in the developing world, adopted a more expansive view, in which soldiers would don the mantle of social engineers to implement the latest nation-building theories. Since both philosophies found expression in Army texts, confusion inevitably arose as to the proper aims and boundaries of Army-civil activities.

When, peace support operations proliferated globally in the post–Cold War era, it was the operations in the Balkans that forced the US military to adapt to this new environment. As the US military operated in the context of peace operations, international civilian agencies now led transitional governments, and nongovernmental organizations and military actors sought to sort out roles in the shared space. There was a deliberate effort on the part of the US military to compartmentalize the military and civilian missions and tasks in Bosnia, as reviewed above, and indeed, that model had profound influence on NATO peace support operations in the Balkans and beyond. By 1997, however, that model was seen as a recipe for failure in coordinating civilian and military tasks for peace support.[45] US military officers were increasingly expected to enable civilian agencies so that the civilian part of the mission could succeed. This concept of using civil affairs officers to conduct CMOs and to facilitate civilian agencies to achieve their objectives was a challenge for the US forces. The concept of enabling civilian agencies, which first emerged as a school of thought in the 1960s, has since been written into relevant joint and service doctrines, namely, the 2011 joint stability doctrine and the joint operations capstone manual.[46] However, implementing this remains difficult.

UN civil-military coordination, on the other hand, has developed in such a way as to be increasingly molded and incorporated in a broader "integrated approach" to ensure all intra-agency, interagency, and system-wide coherence, including relations with the host-nation actors.[47] This has meant that UN peacekeeping is part of an overall architecture, in support of a host of political, peacebuilding, humanitarian, and development goals. In the peacekeeping context, the UN has an established notion of integrated mission, which is designed to "generate and sustain a common strategic objective, as well as a comprehensive operational approach, among the political, security, development, human rights, and where appropriate, humanitarian UN actors at country level."[48] In addition, the UN has an important humanitarian focus in its assistance programs, where UN civil-military coordination (CMCoord) is a prominent concept. CMCoord is broadly supported by the UN and broader humanitarian communities, and is endowed with a set of guidelines to ensure the civilian-led nature of UN assistance, where the military role is strictly subordinated to civilian needs, priorities, and guidance.[49]

The US doctrine, on the other hand, still contains some inconsistencies in the way CMO works within its mission. The 2011 *Army Manual on Civil Affairs Operations* states that the purpose of such operations is "to facilitate military operations and consolidate operational objectives." The document, hence, retains the military-centric logic. JP 3–57, *Civil-Military Operations*, on the other hand, states that the purpose of CMO is "establish, maintain, influence, or exploit relationships between military forces and indigenous populations and institutions, by directly supporting the attainment of objectives relating to the reestablishment or maintenance of stability within a region or host nation." The Joint Stability Manual goes further by stating that success is not defined in military terms but also involves "rebuilding infrastructure, supporting economic development, establishing the rule of law, building accountable governance, establishing essential services, and building a capable host-nation military responsible to civilian authority." In the next paragraph, it states that "the primary military contribution to stabilization is to protect and defend the population, facilitating the personal security of the people and, thus, creating a platform for political, economic, and human security."[50]

An additional US-UN difference is that the civil affairs section in a US Joint Force is staffed by military personnel in support of the military commander while the civil affairs section in the UN mission headquarters is a civilian component in support of the senior leadership team. In the UN integrated approach, the overall integrated effort that covers political, security, development, justice, and reconciliation, is led by a senior leadership team headed by a civilian. The military is part of this overall team, representing the "security" line of the overall effort while "enabling" civilian lines of the work. The UN senior military staff is part of the senior UN integrated leadership team and reports to the special representative of the secretary-general. The civil affairs officer, instead of serving a civil-military function in the UN, is responsible for representing the UN with the local authorities, such as acting as liaison with national government departments, and with provincial and local government entities. In this larger context, UN civil-military cooperation (CIMIC) is a section in the military force that coordinates the support that the military provides to the rest of the mission. Hence, the military force in an integrated mission does not form a binary relationship with the civilian, but rather, forms part of an integrated team.

To add to the challenge presented by the contending US approaches, the United States has no developed concept or doctrine of "integrated approach" at the government level, supported by relevant governmental structures and institutions. The Joint Staff assessment in 2012 that analyzed US engagement in stabilization and peace operations in the past decade identified two of the greatest shortfalls in the US conduct of these operations: lack of an integrated approach among all of the agencies, and the resulting lack of effective planning and execution of the transition back to the host nation. The assessment report noted that in both Iraq and Afghanistan, for example, "interagency unity of effort was a resounding failure." It further asserted that the "DOD partnering with other US departments and agencies during the first half of the decade consistently failed to harness the strengths and resources of the respective organizations," and that the United States failed to apply its resources in a "concerted and coherent way."[51] Rather, the study found that, where it was tried out—such as in Iraq—unity of effort was heavily dependent on personality.

Given the ongoing destabilization and breakdown of the regional order and national order in large swaths of the Middle and Near East, North Africa and the Levant, combined with the return of great power politics, the stability operations the US military conducts today should increasingly be seen as, and should function as part of, a comprehensive strategy that serves the US (and broader international) interests. It is highly desirable that CMO and civil-military coordination are made integral to (a notion of) an "integrated approach" at the government level. Such a concept should be clarified in a government-wide interagency doctrine, and it should be supported by a clear structure in the US government that ensures policy and operational coordination. The reality, however, seems to be going the other direction. For instance, the Office of the Coordinator for Stabilization and Reconstruction (SCRS) within the State Department established a whole-of-government approach with appropriate structures and procedures after 2005, but that approach was lost after SCRS was re-missioned as the Bureau of Conflict and Stabilization Office (CSO). The bureau now assists the department in understanding conflict and bringing appropriate solutions—some of them civ-mil or interagency but with no overall convening function.

Currently, no US agency is endowed with authority for interagency coordination in US engagement in peace and stability missions.

Emerging thematic focus

Aside from the main doctrinal issues discussed above, there are a number of emerging issues in the thinking behind US doctrine about peace operations. This sections discusses two: the protection of civilians and conflict transformation.

Protection of civilians

The military is faced with particular difficulties when operating in the presence of civilian populations. Most of the US capstone doctrines published in recent years consider civilian populations as a hindrance to military operations. They discussed gaining their support or getting them out of the way, so that the military could perform their tasks. Meanwhile, the idea that civilian populations were in fact central to the success or failure of an operation had been addressed in detail in the counterinsurgency strand of doctrine in the post-WWII years.[52] It was only in 2011 that the same idea was addressed in the US joint capstone doctrine.

In addition, in counterinsurgency doctrine, support by local populations is the central goal of operations and also the key to the legitimacy of an operation. This point has not been made in US peace operations doctrine, however, even though legitimacy is a key principle. There was little formal doctrine or guidelines about protection of civilians in a peace operations context from the UN, NATO, or other countries until very recently—although since 1999 the UN Security Council has dealt extensively with the matter through various resolutions. Military forces have dealt with the situation on the ground with little doctrinal guidance.

A protection of civilians doctrine for the US military grew out of an initiative in 2007 by Sarah Sewall of the Carr Center at Harvard University called the Mass Atrocity Response Operations (MARO) Project. Driven in part by the "responsibility to protect" (R2P) principles agreed at the 2005 World Summit of the United Nations and the Genocide Prevention Task Force of 2007 by the US Institute for Peace, the Holocaust Museum, and the American Academy of Diplomacy, it was a collaborative effort of the Harvard Kennedy School and the US Army Peacekeeping and Stability Operations Institute (PKSOI). The goal of the MARO Project was to enable the United States and other militaries to prevent and halt genocide and mass atrocity, when directed, as part of a broader integrated strategy.

The project produced a handbook on mass atrocity response and led to a MARO appendix in the joint doctrine on peace operations, a policy planning guide for mass atrocity prevention and response, and the military handbook *Protection of Civilians*.[53] The situation in Afghanistan involving civilian casualties and concerns of other commands such as the European Command and the Africa Command became the catalyst that moved these handbooks into doctrine. In June 2008, shortly after General David McKiernan assumed command, the International Security Assistance Force (ISAF) was involved in two high-profile incidents resulting in numerous civilian casualties. Information on these events from local nongovernmental organizations, the Taliban, and international organizations differed so dramatically from ISAF's data that it recognized the need for action. Studies were commissioned resulting in the establishment of a Civilian Casualty Mitigation Team (CCMT) in 2011 and a recognized need for new doctrine. The Army responded by designating PKSOI as the lead agency responsible for doctrine development as well as training and education in this area, a move that led to the publication of an initial Army manual on *Civilian Casualty Mitigation* that was subsequently incorporated into the 2015 Army Technical Publication 3.07.6, *Protection of Civilians*.[54]

By 2016 protection of civilians was being mainstreamed into capstone military doctrine manuals and was recognized as being applicable to all operations, not just peace operations. This doctrine takes into consideration the framework outlined in the DPKO and UN Department of Field Support (DFS) guidelines for protection of civilians as well as their operational concept and identifies the need for swift and decisive action.

Conflict transformation

JP 3–07.3, the joint publication on peace operations, states that peace operations are essentially crisis response and as such their core mission should include "international efforts and military missions to contain conflict, redress the peace, and shape the environment to support reconciliation and rebuilding and to facilitate *the transition to legitimate governance.*"[55]

In light of this assertion, conflict transformation *should be* the centerpiece of the US approach to complex environments, with the focus on converting the dynamics of conflict into processes for constructive, positive change. This consideration has been part of stability operations doctrine and is currently being introduced into relevant Joint capstone doctrine manuals.

According to US Army doctrine, as stated in Army Doctrinal Publication 3–07, *Stability*:

Conflict transformation focuses on converting the dynamics of conflict into processes for constructive, positive change. The process of conflict transformation reduces the means and motivations for violent conflict while developing more viable, peaceful alternatives for the competitive pursuit of political and socioeconomic aspirations. It aims to set the host nation on a sustainable, positive trajectory in which transformational processes directly address the dynamics causing instability or violent conflict. Conflict transformation is based on identifying and mitigating the root causes of conflict and instability while simultaneously building the capacity of local institutions to prevent future instability.[56]

Real transformation alters the existing war-hardened power structure—otherwise it is not transformation, but more likely a stalemate or temporary ceasefire. The means to a transformed society is through local leaders and emerging social groups, or the "host nation." Because not only the existing power structure but also at times the emerging new power leaders must be changed toward moderation, this requires a comprehensive framework and an integrating method and structure understood and accepted by all participants. Such frameworks, methods and structures cannot be foisted upon an unsuspecting populace, but must be developed in partnership with local leaders; the pace and sequencing will be determined by local realities.[57] The implication is that the US military is expected to be supportive and engage with peacebuilding efforts.

International peacebuilding, at its heart, is transformational and a national (host-nation) challenge and responsibility, and national factors will shape its pace and sequencing. Even though the international community will be directly engaged in assisting a country, local political processes will be fundamental for success and will include extensive political mediations and compromises. The military will be asked to undertake a wide variety of tasks beyond its basic combat skills because of its ability to plan, organize, respond, and mobilize resources. It is an institution noted for seizing the initiative, taking action, and getting results. Addressing the drivers of conflict, supporting legitimacy, and building institutional capacity are key toward achieving transformation, stabilizing a situation and allowing peacebuilding to proceed.

First, addressing the drivers of violent conflict begins with a thorough assessment. This analyzes the conditions of an operational environment, including how the operation affects the situation on the ground and how locals perceive the conditions. This conflict assessment ensures that planning focuses on the root causes of conflict or strife and prescribes integrated approaches to resolution.

Second, supporting legitimacy is central to building trust and confidence among the people. Legitimacy is a multifaceted principle that impacts every aspect of stability operations from every conceivable perspective. Within the scope of national strategy, legitimacy is a central principle for intervention: both the legitimacy of the host-nation government and the legitimacy of the mission. The legitimacy of the government has many facets. It generally represents that of the supporting institutions and societal systems of the host nation. Legitimacy derives from the legal framework that governs the state and the source of that authority. It reflects not only the supremacy of the law, but also the foundation upon which the law was developed: the collective will of the people through the consent of the governed. It reflects, or is a measure of, the perceptions of several groups: the local populace, individuals serving within the civil institutions of the host nation, neighboring states, the international community, and the American public.

Building institutional capacity in the host nation is the third key component of transformation. The aim of capacity building is to create an environment that fosters development to improve governance, community participation, and human resource development, and that will result in legitimate institutions capable of addressing the drivers of conflict. The US Army *Stability Operations* manual states that building institutional capacity in the host nation is "fundamental to success" in stability operations, and that capacity-building includes efforts to improve governance capacity, political moderation, and good governance, in both norms and governance structure, supported by appropriate policy and legal frameworks.[58] In this way, transformation can be achieved over the long term.

The UN capstone doctrine, *United Nations Peacekeeping Operations: Principles and Guidelines*, does address this issue under multidimensional peacekeeping operations. The document recognizes the need to reform institutions, to assist in the transition to sustainable peace, and to facilitate political processes toward establishing legitimate and effective institutions of governance in the host nation. Under the heading of promotion of national and local ownership the peacekeeping mission is asked to manage the tensions that will occur in the country from the transformational change that the peacekeeping mission will bring. The problem with the US doctrine is that it does not consider what role the military should play in supporting peacebuilding that will bring about the transformation.[59]

The UN and the US doctrines describe the various parts of peace-building. US doctrine delineates the potential roles that its forces should play in support of peacebuilding activities. It looks at each of the peacebuilding sectors of security, humanitarian assistance and social wellbeing, justice and reconciliation, governance and participation, and economic stabilization and infrastructure, and suggests potential military tasks. These activities appear as US stability sectors that would apply to a counterinsurgency or a post-conflict reestablishment of a country like Iraq or Afghanistan but under different principles.[60]

Conclusion

The chapter reviewed the development and core characteristics of US peace operations doctrine. It also discussed current concerns and emerging issues in US doctrinal thinking. We noted the close relationship between the development of US peace operations and the political stance of the US government with regard to low-intensity operations. The US military, with its own institutional preferences and approach, has also created a context in which these policies are implemented. As observed, the development of peace operations concepts and doctrine has been embedded in inherent tensions over the proper role of the US military in low-intensity conflicts.

Doctrine writing on peace operations has accelerated since the end of the Cold War, driven by the practical need of the US military to engage or support such operations. In the case of US doctrine, thinking on peace operations was influenced by developments in related operations, most importantly stability operations, the notion that was elevated to an overarching concept under the full-spectrum approach. Against the background of historical American engagement in post-conflict occupations, civil-military operations, counterinsurgency, and stability operations, contemporary doctrinal thinking about peace operations and related areas has coalesced into the notion of stability operations. Furthermore, in the current doctrine-writing process, specific themes, such as protection of civilians and conflict transformation, are assuming importance.

With the planned updates of the Army and Joint manuals on *Operations, Stability, Counterinsurgency* and *Peace Operations* by the end of 2017, US doctrine will continue to evolve. It is hoped that the themes and approaches discussed in this chapter would be brought together in a coherent framework. These manuals embrace the concept of operating across a conflict continuum. The situation in a region may demand that the military force deal with insurgents as well as concurrently support political processes and build up the local capacity of the host government.

The new *Stability* manual will also address many of the issues that were identified by the 2015 United Nations High-level Independent Panel on Peace Operations (HIPPO).[61] Especially, the four essential shifts called for by the panel should be addressed by the new stability doctrine. First, HIPPO emphasizes the importance of the political process as central, and the need for the military to take the political process into consideration when designing operations. Secondly, HIPPO calls for the United Nations to use a "full-spectrum" approach to respond in a flexible way to the needs on the ground, as does the US *Stability* manual, which states that operations require nesting military operations within a comprehensive framework, bringing many stakeholders together. Third, the HIPPO and the US manuals emphasize partnership and the need for conflict prevention. Fourth, the panel calls for field-focused and people-centered approaches. The addition in the new doctrine of protection of civilians will address this issue.

The Obama administration's recent initiative on US support for UN peacekeeping will also have doctrinal impact. Specifically, the initiative pledged to provide material, money, resources, knowledge, technology, and bilateral support to both troop- and police-contributing countries, as well as the UN itself. In so doing, it will provide doctrine, education, and capabilities that have been developed as the United States engaged in conflicts globally in the past two decades, including in Afghanistan and Iraq. For example, the United States will use its technology to enhance peacekeeping globally, in the area, for example, of tackling the threats from IEDs, as noted above. The US already sent, in support of a DPKO request, an asymmetric warfare team to Mali to assess the threat that IEDs create for UN peacekeepers.

Indeed, the Obama administration (albeit nearing its final months) has tried to reinvigorate interest in UN peacekeeping and related operational doctrine and education. Again, this most recent trend speaks to the close link between policy and doctrines. With the history of US ambivalence about peacekeeping, particularly with regard to military engagement in peace operations on a large scale, both at the political- and military-institutional levels, the recent rise in political interest in US contributions to peace operations, including doctrine and education, is noteworthy.

At the same time, this chapter noted various gaps in peace operations concepts and practice. The first involved the conceptual gap between the United States and the UN with regard to use of force and scope of peacekeeping/peace enforcement. The second gap relates to the differences between the UN concept of civil-military coordination and the US approach to civil-military operations. The third main gap can be found within the US lack of an integrated approach at the government-institutional level. The recognized doctrinal principle of "unity of effort" is not accompanied by strategic- or operational-level interagency machinery, and this gap complicates US-UN coordination on civil-military relations. These gaps suggest future directions where more thinking and political initiatives will have to be explored in order to enhance US support for UN peacekeeping.

Notes

1 Ian Johnstone and Ethan Corbin, "Introduction: The US Role in Contemporary Peace Operations: A Double-Edged Sword?" *International Peacekeeping* 15, no. 1 (2008): 1–17; and Victoria K. Holt and Michael G. Mackinnon, "The Origins and Evolution of US Policy Towards Peace Operations," *International Peacekeeping* 15, no. 1 (2008): 18–34.

2 Adam C. Smith, "The United States of America" in *Providing Peacekeepers: The Politics, Challenges, and Future of United Nations Peacekeeping Contributions*, ed. Alex J. Bellamy and Paul D. Williams (Oxford: Oxford University Press, 2013), 71.

3 Ibid.

4 Ivo H. Daalder, "Knowing When to Say No: The Development of US Policy for Peacekeeping" in *UN Peacekeeping, American Politics and the Uncivil Wars of the 1990s*, ed. William J. Durch (New York: St. Martin's Press, 1996); and Mats R. Berdal, "Fateful Encounter: The United States and UN Peacekeeping" *Survival* 36, no. 1 (1994): 30–50.

5 Quynh-Nhu Vuong, "U.S. Peacekeeping and Nation-Building: The Evolution of Self-Interested Multilateralism" *Berkeley Journal of International Law* 21 (2003): 810.

6 Smith, "The United States of America," 72.

7 J. William Snyder, "'Command' vs 'Operational Control': A Critical Review of PDD 25," 1995, www.ibiblio.org/jwsnyder/wisdom/pdd25.html.

8 Daalder, "Knowing When to Say No"; Berdal, "Fateful Encounter"; and Vuong, "U.S. Peacekeeping and Nation-Building."

9 As of March 2001 the European nations had provided more than 60 percent of the approximately 57,000 military troops and most of the special constabulary forces deployed in NATO-led operations in Bosnia and Kosovo. See US General Accounting Office, "European Security: U.S. and European Contributions to Foster Stability and Security in Europe," Report to the Congressional Committees, doc. no. GAO-02-174, November 2001, 6, www.investigativeproject.org/documents/testimony/214.pdf.

10 Smith, "The United States of America," 72.

11 Ibid., 76.

12 Ibid.

13 Ibid.

14 Paul D. Williams, "Keeping a Piece of Peacekeeping: The United States Doubles Down at the UN," *Foreign Affairs*, 6 October 2015, www.foreignaffairs.com/articles/20151006/keepingpiecepeacekeeping.

15 Ibid.

16 The White House, *The United States Support to United Nations Peace Operations*, 28 September 2015.
17 Lawrence A. Yates, *The US Military's Experience in Stability Operations 1789–2005*, Global War on Terrorism Occasional Paper 15 (Fort Leavenworth, Kans.: Combat Studies Institute Press, 2006), 2–3.
18 Ibid., 2–3; Walter E. Kretchik, *U.S. Army Doctrine From the American Revolution to the War on Terror* (Lawrence: University Press of Kansas, 2012) identifies this lack of sustained institutionalized doctrine until the 1990s.
19 Association of the United States Army (AUSA) and Center for Strategic and International Studies, *Play to Win: Final Report of the Bi-partisan Commission on Post-Conflict Reconstruction*, (Arlington, Va.: AUSA, 2003); James Dobbins, John G. McGinn, Keith Crane, Seth G. Jones, Rollie Lal, Andrew Rathmell, Rachel M. Swanger, and Anga R. Timilsina, *America's Role in Nation-Building: From Germany to Iraq* (Santa Monica, Calif.: RAND Corporation, 2003), www.rand.org/pubs/monograph_rep orts/MR1753.html; Brent Scowcroft, Samuel Berger, and William Nash, *In the Wake of War: Improving US Post Conflict Capabilities* (Washington, DC: Council on Foreign Relations, 2005); Robert Orr, ed., *Winning the Peace* (Washington, DC: Center for Strategic and International Studies, 2004); and Jock Covey, Michael Dziedzic, and Leonard Hawley, *The Quest for Viable Peace* (Washington, DC: United States Institute for Peace, 2005).
20 Jolyon P. Girard, "American Diplomacy and the Ruhr Crisis of 1920," *Military Affairs* 39, no. 2 (1975): 59–61.
21 Janine Davidson, *Lifting the Fog of Peace: How Americans Learned to Fight Modern War* (Ann Arbor: University of Michigan Press, 2011), 53.
22 US President's Committee to Study the United States Military Assistance Program (Draper Committee), Records, 1958–59, Dwight D. Eisenhower Library, Abilene, Kansas, Accession 67–9 Processed by SLJ; Date Completed: February 1977.
23 Keith B. Bickel, *Mars Learning: The Marine Corps' Development of the Small War Doctrine 1915–1940* (Boulder, Col.: The Westview Press, 2001).
24 Ibid.; USMC, *Small War Manual* (Washington, DC: US Government Printing Office, 1940).
25 Andrew J. Birtle, *US Army Counterinsurgency and Contingency Operations Doctrine 1942–1976* (Washington, DC: Center of Military History, 2006), 134.
26 Ibid.
27 Ibid., 173. Birtle reminds the reader that this was one of the factors that led the United States to reject the 1977 Geneva Convention amendment that would forbid reprisals.
28 Ibid., 242.
29 Kretchik, *U.S. Army Doctrine From the American Revolution to the War on Terror*, 185; Department of the Army, *Field Service Regulation Operations*, FM 100–5 (Washington, DC: Department of the Army, 1962), 136, 139.
30 Department of the Army, *Internal Defense and Development U.S. Army Doctrine*, FM 100–20 (Washington, DC: Department of the Army, 1974).
31 Charles W. Raymond, "A Military Perspective of International Peacekeeping: The Nature and Characteristics of Peace Operations and Review and Evaluation of some Peacekeeping Concepts and Doctrine," Master of Military Art and Science thesis, the United States Army Command and

General Staff College (USACGSC), Fort Leavenworth, Kansas, 1975. *Low Intensity Conflict Selected Readings*, FC 100–39, USACGSC, Fort Leavenworth, 1984 presents the background to his study.

32 Raymond, "Military Perspective."

33 The White House, *National Security Strategy of the United States*, January 1993, 7.

34 Department of the Army, *Army Operations in Low Intensity Conflict*, FM 100–20, (Washington, DC: Department of the Army, 1990), 5–7.

35 Ibid., 13–20.

36 UK Ministry of Defence, *Wider Peacekeeping* (London: Her Majesty's Stationery Office, 1996).

37 Ibid., 13–17.

38 Department of the Army, *Stability*, Army Doctrine Publication ADP 3–07 (Washington DC: Department of the Army, 2012), 1.

39 The stability tasks from joint doctrine are: create a safe and secure environment, and ensure the rule of law, stable governance, a stable economy, and social wellbeing.

40 Department of the Army, *Stability*, 7.

41 DPKO/DFS, "United Nations Peacekeeping Operations: Principles and Guidelines" (so-called "Capstone Doctrine"), United Nations, New York, 2008, www.un.org/en/peacekeeping/documents/capstone_eng.pdf.

42 Birtle, *US Army Counterinsurgency and Contingency Operations Doctrine 1942–1976*, 425.

43 Department of the Army and Department of the Navy, *United States Army and Navy Manual of Civil Affairs Military Government*, doc. no. FM 27–5 (Army) and OPNAV P22–1115 (Navy) (Washington, DC: US Government Printing Office, 1947), 5, www.loc.gov/rr/frd/Military_Law/pdf/FM-27-5-1947.pdf. This doctrine states that the purpose of CMO is to assist military operations and do the duty required by international law.

44 Edward Bernard Glick, *Peaceful Conflict: The Non-Military Use of the Military* (Harrisburg, Pa.: Stackpole Books, 1967); and Birtle, *US Army Counterinsurgency and Contingency Operations Doctrine 1942–1976*.

45 Thijs Brocades Zaalberg argues that NATO civil-military cooperation (CIMIC) doctrine adopted the US approach, centering on the military dimensions of such tasks and relying on a group of specialized CIMIC officers, but that this was a wrong foundation upon which to build civil-military operations for the organization in the following decade. See Thijs Brocades Zaalberg, "Countering Insurgent-terrorism: Why NATO Chose the Wrong Historical Foundation for CIMIC," *Small Wars & Insurgencies* 17, no. 4 (2006): 399–420.

46 Joint Chiefs of Staff, *Stability Operations*, Joint Publication (JP) 3–07 (Washington DC: Joint Staff, 2011); and the capstone manual, Joint Chiefs of Staff, *Doctrine for the Army Forces of the United States*, JP 1 (Washington, DC: Joint Staff, 2013), I-5.

47 Cedric de Coning, "The United Nations and the Comprehensive Approach," Report 2008–14, Danish Institute for International Studies, 2008, 4–5.

48 Ibid., 10, citing the United Nations, *Integrated Missions Planning Process (IMPP)*, guidelines endorsed by the secretary-general on 13 June 2006, New York, 2006, 3; and DPKO/DFS, *United Nations Peacekeeping Operations*, 69–74.

49 UN CMCoord is defined as: "The essential dialogue and interaction between civilian and military actors in humanitarian emergencies that is necessary to protect and promote humanitarian principles, avoid competition, minimize inconsistency, and when appropriate, pursue common goals. Basic strategies range from co-existence to cooperation. Coordination is a shared responsibility facilitated by liaison and common training." See UN MDCA Project, "Guidelines On The Use of Military and Civil Defence Assets to Support United Nations Humanitarian Activities in Complex Emergencies," March 2003 (and Rev. 1, January 2006).

50 Department of the Army, *Civil Affairs Operations*, FM 3–57 (Washington, DC: Department of the Army, 2011), 1–1; Joint Chiefs of Staff, *Civil Military Operations*, JP 3–57 (Washington, DC: The Joint Staff, 2013), ix; and Joint Chiefs of Staff, *Stability Operations*, JP 3–07, vii.

51 Joint and Collation Operational Analysis (JCOA), Joint Staff, "Decade of War Vol 1: Enduring Lessons from the Past Decade of Operations." (Suffolk, Virg.: Joint Staff, 2012), 15, 25.

52 See Department of the Army, *Stability Operations*, FM 31–20 (Washington, DC: Department of the Army, 1967), 24.

53 Joint Chiefs of Staff, *Peace Operations*, JP 3–07.3 (Washington, DC: Joint Staff, 2012); Sarah Sewall, Dwight Raymond, and Sally Chin, *Mass Atrocity Response Operations (MARO): A Military Planning Handbook* (Cambridge, Mass.: The President and Fellows of Harvard College, 2010); Dwight Raymond, Cliff Bernath, Don Braum, and Ken Zurcher, *Mass Atrocity Prevention and Response Options (MAPRO): A Policy Planning Handbook* (Carlisle, Pa.: Peacekeeping and Stability Operations Institute, 2012); and Dwight Raymond, Bill Flavin, and Jurgen Prandtner, *Protection of Civilians Military Reference Guide* (Carlisle, Pa.: Peacekeeping and Stability Operations Institute, 2013).

54 Jennifer Keene, *Civilian Harm Tracking Analysis of ISAF Efforts in Afghanistan* (Washington, DC: Center for Civilians in Conflict Copyright, 2014), 3–5; Sarah Sewall, *Joint Civilian Casualty Study* (Norfolk, Va.: Joint Center for Operational Analysis, 2010); Department of the Army, *Civilian Casualties Mitigation*, Army Tactics, Techniques, and Procedures (ATTP) 3–37.31 (Washington, DC: Department of the Army, 2012); and Department of the Army, *Protection of Civilians*, Army Techniques Publication (ATP) 3–07.6 (Washington, DC: Department of the Army, October 2015).

55 Joint Staff, *Peace Operations*, JP 3–07.3, vii. Emphasis added.

56 Department of the Army, *Stability*, Army Doctrine Publication (ADP) 3–07 (Washington, DC: Department of the Army, 2013), 2.

57 Ibid., 1–2.

58 Department of the Army, *Stability Operations*, Field Manual (FM) 3–07 (Washington, DC: Department of the Army, 2008), 1–8.

59 DPKO/DFS, "United Nations Peacekeeping Operations," 22–9.

60 Joint Staff, *Peace Operations*, JP 3–07.3, Chapter IV.

61 José Ramos-Horta, *Uniting Our Strengths for Peace Politics, Partnership and People: Report of the High Level Independent Panel on United Nations Peace Operations* (New York: United Nations, 2015).

2 The United Kingdom and UN peacekeeping

David Curran and Paul D. Williams

- **The Cold War**
- **UNPROFOR and the United Kingdom's doctrinal evolution**
- **Peace support operations**
- **The "War on Terrorism"**
- **Stabilization**
- **A return to peacekeeping?**
- **Conclusion**

In line with this volume's central focus, this chapter concentrates on the United Kingdom's roles in relation to the evolution of United Nations (UN) peacekeeping doctrine—or at least its major principles and guidelines given that the UN has yet to write formal doctrine for its peacekeepers. It does so by analyzing the evolution of the United Kingdom's experiences in UN peacekeeping operations and how these influenced British military doctrine relevant to peacekeeping. On occasion, particularly during the late 1990s, British doctrine also influenced the UN approach to peacekeeping, particularly concerning the concepts of consent, minimum use of force, and impartiality.

We adopt a broadly chronological approach in order to illustrate the sometimes interrelated nature of the debates. This covers the largely ambivalent approach to peacekeeping doctrine through the Cold War, and the transformation of British approaches to peacekeeping doctrine. It also covers alternative forms of engagement in the twenty-first century, where instead of deploying "boots on the ground," the United Kingdom called for specific UN peacekeeping reform through its support for the "Brahimi Report," published in 2000, and its "non-paper" with France in 2009 which fed into the "New Horizon" framework adopted by the UN later that year. From this, we also briefly discuss the British input on relevant thematic issues, including on the protection of civilians and sexual violence in armed conflict. Additionally, the chapter offers a summary of the debates that emerged about the United Kingdom's contribution to UN peacekeeping operations after the withdrawal of its troops from Afghanistan in October 2014. In late 2015 Britain announced it would roughly double the number of uniformed personnel it contributes to UN peacekeeping operations. In 2016, it started deploying up to 70 personnel to the UN Support Office in Somalia (UNSOS) and 250–300 personnel to the UN Mission in the Republic of South Sudan (UNMISS).

As a permanent member of the UN Security Council, Britain has played a leading role in the evolution of UN peacekeeping operations. Its principal contributions to UN peacekeeping have come in the form of financing, deployed personnel, mandate formulation and doctrinal development, as well as various forms of relevant capacity-building initiatives for other troop- and police-contributing countries.

In financial terms, until 2016 the United Kingdom had been the fifth largest contributor to the UN's assessed peacekeeping budget, paying just under 7 percent of the total. In 2016, however, the United Kingdom assessed rate dropped to 5.8 percent, placing it sixth, behind the United States, China, Japan, Germany, and France. It also makes periodic voluntary contributions in-kind and to relevant trust funds. As one of the pen-holding countries on several UN peace operations—in Cyprus, Darfur, and Somalia—as well as relevant thematic issues— notably civilian protection and women, peace, and security—the United Kingdom plays a leading role in mandate formulation and the evolution of guidelines in these areas. More generally, along with France, Britain has been one of the most active P5 members when it comes to proposing Security Council resolutions.[1]

The United Kingdom's contributions of personnel include deployments in the field as well as staff in the UN Secretariat, including some senior positions such as the head of the Department of Political Affairs (from 1993–2005). In field missions, Britain's first UN deployment was to its former colony of Cyprus in the 1960s, where until 2016 it maintained the majority of its "blue helmets." After the Cold War, the United Kingdom's major deployments of UN peacekeepers came in the Balkans, specifically to Bosnia-Herzegovina and later Kosovo. Indeed, for one month during 1995 the United Kingdom's contribution of approximately 10,000 troops to the UN Protection Force (UNPROFOR) made it the UN's top troop contributor. Following the terrorist attacks on the United States in September 2001, Britain's major military campaigns in Afghanistan (2001–14) and Iraq (2003–11) put its armed forces under considerable strain and severely limited its ability to provide any contingents to UN operations.[2]

The exceptions were small deployments maintained in Kosovo and Cyprus (where reservists were used instead of regular army personnel until 2014). As already noted, in 2016 Britain deployed the first of potentially up to 370 troops to the UN missions in Somalia and South Sudan. The United Kingdom's major capacity-building initiatives have been delivered in various formats, notably Military Advisory Training Teams and Peace Support Teams.

The Cold War

Owing to its position as a permanent member of the Security Council, Britain has always had the ability to influence UN peacekeeping. However, British political and military elites have at times had a rather ambivalent attitude towards the UN and its peace operations. The United Kingdom's first significant impact was its unsuccessful attempts to stop the UN's first armed peacekeeping force, the UN Emergency Force I. After British, French, and Israeli troops had occupied the Suez area, the United Kingdom, along with France, resisted all efforts in the Security Council for a withdrawal of its soldiers and the establishment of a peacekeeping force. This forced the United States to act through the General Assembly and the "Uniting for Peace" resolution 997. Passed on 2 November 1956 by 65 votes to 5, the United Kingdom was one of the countries that voted against it.[3] Hence Britain's early engagement with UN peacekeeping was conflictual because it signaled the old imperial order was crumbling and the UN's membership would not always comply with British demands.[4]

The end of empire was also at the heart of Britain's next major engagement with UN peacekeeping, this time as part of the UN Peacekeeping Force in Cyprus (UNFICYP). Following constitutional breakdown and inter-communal violence between Turkish and Greek Cypriot communities, the United Kingdom deployed forces into Cyprus in late 1963, patrolling an agreed "green line" separating the two communities. After trying to deal with the issue through the North Atlantic Treaty Organization (NATO), Britain eventually agreed to the creation of the UN force in March 1964. It would play a leading role in the mission from this point on. Indeed, it remains the United Kingdom's largest contemporary deployment of about 275 UN peacekeepers.

For a considerable period of time, UNFICYP was the venue for arguments between British policymakers and senior military officials over whether or not the force, and peacekeepers in general, should adopt a more robust posture to potentially coerce the parties towards a political settlement. British troops also had a hard time adjusting to a peacekeeping posture. As one contemporary commander put it, his troops had "never before been placed in this 'in-between' position where weapons were the last thing to be used—and none of them liked it."[5]

In spite of these debates, Britain did not develop any specific peacekeeping doctrine until 1988. *Army Field Manual Volume V, Pam I Peacekeeping Operations* was largely composed of "mundane but necessary tasks, associated with operations in Cyprus and the Middle East," and predominantly focused on inter-state conflict situations. It also emphasized that peacekeeping did not involve powers of enforcement, and any unnecessary or illegal force could create the conditions where the peacekeepers become "part of the problem."[6] Both of these assumptions were to be challenged in the early post–Cold War era.[7]

UNPROFOR and the United Kingdom's doctrinal evolution

For the United Kingdom, it was the war in Bosnia-Herzegovina (1992–5) that provided the main crucible in which its ideas about traditional and other forms of peacekeeping were tested. At one stage, Britain deployed over 10,000 blue helmets, briefly making it, in 1995, the UN's top troop-contributing country. It also provided a force commander for UNPROFOR.[8] Unsurprisingly, this major commitment heavily influenced British military thinking about peacekeeping. The mission also became the major (mainly negative) point of reference for how many of the senior British officers who served in UNPROFOR understood UN peace operations.

The first major doctrinal statement came in 1994. It was called *Army Field Manual: Wider Peacekeeping*—in large part to capture the idea that troops were asked to perform a much wider range of tasks than traditional peacekeeping but often had to do so in a context of ongoing violence.[9] The doctrine used feedback from British troops serving with UNPROFOR to illustrate the wide range of characteristics of intra-state conflict and how British soldiers could forge good relationships with the multitude of actors in such conflict zones. Thus issues of liaison, respect for the host country's religion, customs, language, and culture, as well as effective communication skills were covered.

One of the most widely discussed limitations of *Wider Peacekeeping* was what one analysis called its "absolutionist view of consent," which posited a rigid distinction between peacekeeping and peace enforcement depending on whether peacekeepers enjoyed consent from the local parties.[10] If peacekeepers were to use force they would likely lose their impartiality and ultimately jeopardize the mission by tipping it into one of peace enforcement. As the *Army Field Manual* put it, resort to force would likely become a source "of future resentment and hostility which may inhibit control and manifest in outbreaks of further violence and prolongation of the conflict."[11]

In practice, however, UNPROFOR witnessed considerable use of force, albeit sometimes supplied by NATO air power and a parallel Anglo-French Rapid Response Force. Such escalation in force ran counter to the doctrinal guidance. Thus while the doctrine was based on a clear distinction between UN Charter Chapter 6 "peacekeeping" and Chapter 7 "peace enforcement," the peacekeepers on the ground found themselves oscillating between the two. It therefore became necessary to once again review British military doctrine in this area. The subsequent debate centered on two issues: how to conceptualize consent and whether there existed a middle ground between peacekeeping and peace enforcement.

In relation to consent, the starting point was recognition of the multiplicity of actors in contemporary war zones and whether the consent of all such belligerents was a requirement for peacekeeping. The principal author of *Wider Peacekeeping*, Major Charles Dobbie, argued that the proliferation of actors did not alter the foundational role of consent in peacekeeping activities. He noted how, for example, UNPROFOR commanders in Bosnia successfully negotiated their way through checkpoints, and used consent-promoting techniques to good effect. This led Dobbie to conclude that:

> avoidance of escalation, impartiality, negotiation, patience, trust, confidence, the developing of relationships, mediation and restraint do not constitute a disparate collection of useful characteristics and principles. They each serve to develop cooperation by protecting and supporting consent. The requirement for consent is the parent of the principles and techniques described in the foregoing practitioners' reports.[12]

And yet, consent on the ground was often contested, even by the forces of parties whose leaders may have given their formal consent for the presence of a peacekeeping mission. This led to calls for a more pragmatic approach. John Mackinlay, for instance, argued that peacekeepers were being held hostage to the consent of warlord factions and as a consequence, the "uncertainty of consent has become a fatally disabling characteristic of the new generation of missions."[13] This was particularly true when peacekeepers were confronted by "insurgent leaders," who often demonstrated little "concept of statesmanship or the rule of law" and even when they gave assurances, were not always able to "exercise control" over local factions.[14] In sum, it was time to rethink whose consent was required and how peacekeepers should seek to manage consent among a wide range of actors.

As to whether a middle ground was possible between peacekeeping and peace enforcement, the evidence coming out of Somalia during 1993 and Bosnia during 1994 suggested there was not, with UN-authorized forces effectively declaring war on particular local factions within the context of an ongoing peacekeeping operation. In Somalia this led to the collapse of the operation while in Bosnia the mission morphed into a NATO-led enforcement operation after a fragile peace deal was constructed in Dayton in 1995.

In May 1994, Colonel Allan Mallinson, who was responsible for the development of British Army doctrine for "operations other than war," argued that the case for a "middle ground" was unconvincing. Rather, the UN must decide whether it was to be a true third party to the conflict or become one of the combatants: it could not be both. Quoting General Sir Michael Rose's phrase "you don't fight war from white-painted vehicles," Mallinson argued that if peacekeepers were to "dine a la carte from both doctrine menus" they would lose impartiality and be at a huge disadvantage militarily.[15] Mallinson also contended that past experiences suggested that peacekeeping successes were a direct result of the application of the traditional principles of consent, impartiality and minimum use of force, of which *Wider Peacekeeping* was an extension.

Similarly, *Wider Peacekeeping*'s principal author, Major Charles Dobbie, also concluded that the peacekeeping failures in the 1990s stemmed from the inability to "distinguish adequately between peacekeeping and peace enforcement—two activities that require radically different conceptual approaches."[16] Whereas peacekeeping doctrine was an impartial, third-party approach, peace enforcement required a war-fighting doctrine. For Dobbie, they were "mutually incompatible," not poles at either end of the same spectrum. Using a soccer analogy, he likened peacekeepers to referees and peace enforcers to the players. Each had very different jobs to do on the field and they should not be mixed, as one will ultimately prejudice the other. Pushing for "middle ground peacekeeping," however, was precisely asking to blur the distinction between referees and players, which could only result in chaos.

On the other side of the argument, some American policy makers began pushing for a more forceful approach to peacekeeping in Bosnia (notably through the "lift and strike" strategy) and in Somalia. In late

1993, John Gerard Ruggie argued that the solution lay in developing doctrine that mixed elements of peacekeeping and peace enforcement. "Strategically," Ruggie argued,

> the United Nations' new domain resembles a suasion game: because there is no clear-cut aggressor, U.N. forces, by presenting a credible military threat, seek to convince all conflicting parties that violence will not succeed. International force is brought to bear not to defeat but neutralize the local forces. The political objective is to prevent local force from becoming the successful arbiter of disputes and to persuade combatants that they have no viable alternative but to reach a negotiated settlement. The military objective of the strategy is to deter, dissuade and deny.[17]

Ruggie concluded that the UN had to occupy the space between peacekeeping and peace enforcement. The policy challenge was for this type of approach to be integrated effectively within national military doctrines and capabilities, particularly those of the UN's major troop-contributing countries.[18]

Like Ruggie, John Mackinlay also called for a new peacekeeping doctrine for the new post-Cold War environments in which peacekeepers were being deployed. To ignore this "doctrinal void" was to leave UN peacekeepers badly exposed. As Mackinlay put it, "The UN has begun a new chapter of military assignments with no idea how to address them. The UN commander is like the conductor of a scratch orchestra whose musicians are without sheet music; the score has to be written as each concert progresses."[19]

Peace support operations

In the United Kingdom, the result of these debates was the publication of new doctrine anchored on the concept of "peace support operations" (PSO). First outlined in the 1997 "Joint Warfare Publication 3–01," and updated in the 1999 "Joint Warfare Publication 3–50," PSO doctrine effectively outlined the necessity for a robust, combat-capable peacekeeping force to be deployed at the outset into areas of low consent, with the end goal of gaining consent and handing over to a civilian-led peacebuilding operation. The term "peace support operation" was thus used generically to cover all peace-related operations, including conflict prevention, peacemaking, peacebuilding, and humanitarian operations. The doctrine was based on the premise that peacekeeping needed to be updated to cope with conflicts where belligerents showed little respect for international and humanitarian law, and peacekeepers had to be "sufficiently flexible, robust and combat-capable to deal with a wide range of scenarios, including operating in a non-permissive environment."[20]

Thus, according to PSO doctrine, a peace enforcement posture would be deployed from the outset, to ensure that if belligerent parties did not consent to the presence of peacekeepers, the peacekeeping force would be capable of moving towards a robust posture:

> [A] PK [peacekeeping] force that is not capable of combat beyond self-defence, and which relies on the consent of the parties for its freedom of action, will be more constrained in its actions than a combat-capable PE [peace enforcement] force, especially if consent is withdrawn. . . . A lightly armed force, in dispersed and vulnerable locations is not capable of conducting PE and combat operations which may escalate to war.[21]

Now, the British military's assumption was that consent was a variable from the outset, and should not be treated as an absolute. Moreover, a "middle ground" between peacekeeping and peacebuilding was identified, its agent being a combat capable force with the necessary firepower to deter (or perhaps coerce) any "spoilers" to the peace process.

Nevertheless, PSO doctrine still maintained that deployments would rely on consent, impartiality, and "the minimum necessary force."[22] While consent would likely vary at the start of a PSO deployment, over time the situation would stabilize and the PSO could be scaled down to a peacekeeping force. PSO doctrine saw this scaling down of the military contribution as an indicator of success:

> In military terms success may be measured by a reduction of the military profile and the early achievement of an exit strategy. In the context of a complex, multinational PE operation, carried out by a military alliance or coalition of willing states, military success may be created by the creation of conditions for the handover of the operation to a UN PK [peacekeeping] force or CIVPOL [civilian police].[23]

This understanding of consent meant that it was crucial for a force to retain its impartiality. Whereas *Wider Peacekeeping* examined impartiality as a factor in a consent-based peacekeeping mission, JWP 3–50 examined impartiality in the context of a robust peace enforcement operation. The importance of impartiality in peace enforcement under a PSO is explained in the following manner: "Given the impartial manner of PSO, a PE force will therefore need to be prepared to use both coercion and inducement in an even handed manner, against any or all of the parties depending on their demonstrated level of compliance."[24]

It was suggested that the best way to maintain impartiality was to ensure transparency in the force. If the mandate and objectives of the force were outlined clearly to all parties, when the peacekeepers employed coercion to ensure compliance among the parties, they could do so while retaining their impartiality.

Importantly, the PSO doctrine utilized both coercion and persuasion to manage the consent of the conflict parties. In this sense, it drew upon many of the techniques of consent promotion identified in *Wider Peacekeeping*. These were important to build good relations with the local population and maintain the force's credibility and impartiality. In the end, the PSO doctrine spelled out that consent was still crucial, for without it, there could be no exit strategy. As JWP 3–50 stated: "Without the active co-operation and consent of the parties and the indigenous population, there can only be subservience and a dependency culture, not a self-sustaining peace. This requirement, and the long-term demands of peace, will constrain the use of all military techniques and not just the use of force."[25]

The impact of PSO doctrine was felt beyond the United Kingdom. The UN's "Brahimi Report," published in August 2000, for instance, had echoes of it, and was strongly supported by the British government. Indeed, Britain's support was an important part of overcoming some opposition to the panel and its call for a fundamental overhaul of the way UN peacekeeping operations were conducted and managed.[26] Like British PSO doctrine, the panel that created the Brahimi Report recognized that consent could easily be manipulated by belligerent groups but also managed by peacekeepers. In such fluid environments, it might be possible for UN peacekeepers to use force in an impartial manner against "spoilers" to the peace process.[27] Furthermore, in a significant development for peacekeeping operations, Brahimi's panel recommended a more robust force posture for future operations:

> Rules of Engagement should not limit contingents to stroke-for-stroke responses but should allow ripostes sufficient to silence a source of deadly fire that is directed at United Nations troops or at the people they are charged to protect and, in particularly dangerous situations, should not force United Nations contingents to cede the initiative to their attackers.[28]

Impartiality was defined in the Brahimi Report as the adherence to the "principles of the [UN] Charter and to the objectives of a mandate that is rooted in those Charter principles."[29] And in that sense, peacekeepers were once again asked to play the role of referees and sanction those players that broke these rules. Once again, this was in line with the proposals outlined in British PSO doctrine.

In May 2000, the United Kingdom's intervention in Sierra Leone provided an opportunity for the doctrine to be put to use. Here, the British unilaterally deployed troops (at the invitation of the host government) to support the faltering UN Mission in Sierra Leone (UNAMSIL) operation, which was suffering from disagreements amongst the major troop-contributing countries and had some 500 of its peacekeepers kidnapped by rebels. While the immediate task of the British operation was to evacuate its citizens, subsequent engagement resulted in the British forces working in tandem with UNAMSIL, including to conduct more traditional peacekeeping tasks as well as to combat the Revolutionary United Front rebels. British forces also engaged in a major unilateral operation in September 2000 to rescue nearly a dozen British soldiers who had been taken hostage the previous month by rebel fighters.

British forces thus conducted "operations across the complete spectrum of PSO and partial enforcement operations."[30] After the kinetic missions subsided with the end of the civil war, British forces remained engaged in various security sector reform activities. Within a decade, these reforms enabled the Republic of Sierra Leone Armed Forces to contribute troops to both UN peacekeeping operations and the African Union (AU) mission in Somalia.

The "War on Terrorism"

As it turned out, the terrorist attacks on the United States in September 2001 meant that the United Kingdom's Sierra Leone operations became the anomaly rather than the norm as a new era unfolded under the label of the "global war on terror." Since then, the campaigns in Afghanistan (2001–14) and then Iraq (2003–11) meant that Britain deployed very few troops in UN operations (the residue being in Kosovo and Cyprus) or in theaters working alongside them. These campaigns are also highly likely to shape the way senior British military commanders think about similar operations for some time to come.[31]

It was also apparent that the United Kingdom maintained a reliance on more traditional force structures, as opposed to the lighter forces that would fit better the requirements for rapid deployment in PSOs. This was partly due to pressures defined by the war on terror, partly because of the drop in public support for more expeditionary campaigns beyond Afghanistan and Iraq, and partly because the British military was keen to focus its efforts on traditional war-fighting as opposed to PSOs.[32]

This combination of factors created a situation whereby Britain's involvement in UN and PSO-type operations was highly unlikely unless they could be sold domestically as aiding the so-called war on terrorism. Unsurprisingly, therefore, British military doctrinal debates after 2001 focused almost entirely on the lessons derived from the campaigns in Afghanistan and Iraq, and paid relatively little attention to what was happening in the world of UN peace operations. Ironically, since 2010 in particular, a number of new UN peacekeeping missions have come to resemble some aspects of the British campaigns in Afghanistan and Iraq, particularly their focus on the concept of stabilization (see below).

The context of fighting a "war on terrorism" inevitably led some analysts to highlight the links between counter-insurgency and peace operations.[33] Regarding British approaches, links were made between PSO doctrine and counter-insurgency in areas such as information operations and unity of effort.[34] More broadly, some analysts viewed the International Security Assistance Force in Afghanistan as embodying key elements of PSO doctrine.[35] Although similar techniques to those outlined in the PSO doctrine were used in Afghanistan and Iraq, the British doctrine itself defines the relationship between PSO and counterinsurgency (COIN) in the following manner:

> The conduct of PSO may appear very similar to Counter Insurgency (COIN), and PE can perhaps be described as COIN in a UN rather than colonial context. However, the impartial nature of a PSO, and in their reference to and international mandate and International Humanitarian Law (IHL), rather than directly to national interests, makes them distinct. PSOs are neither in support of, nor against a particular party, but they are designed to restore peace and ensure compliance with the mandate in an even-handed manner. The conduct of a PSO force should be analogous to that of a third party referee, even if only one party persistently fails to comply with the mandate and suffers the consequences.[36]

Stabilization

It was in the context of the campaigns in Iraq and Afghanistan that the United Kingdom developed its military doctrine on stabilization.[37]

Indeed, 2009 was a busy year for both the United Kingdom's doctrine writers and the UN Secretariat. Following on the back of the publication of the UN's principles and guidelines document on peacekeeping operations, the British pushed for further reforms in a joint initiative with France. Specifically, in January 2009 they circulated at the UN a "non-paper" that sketched ideas for ensuring better strategic oversight of UN peacekeeping operations. The non-paper defined this in terms of reforming the preparation, planning, monitoring, and evaluation of missions.[38] This initiative fed into the wider UN reform efforts that produced the "New Horizon" framework for peacekeeping operations.[39] Among other things, the partnership agenda led to greater emphasis being placed on consultation with major troop-contributing countries (TCCs) and police-contributing countries (PCCs) before establishing mandates, and the creation of an annual open meeting with UN force commanders to bring field perspective to the Security Council. It also generated considerable interest in the need for "benchmarks" for UN missions.[40] The United Kingdom provided material assistance for the implementation of the "New Horizon" recommendations.[41]

Part of this effort entailed a specific focus on the protection of civilians in armed conflict, on which the United Kingdom had been a leading voice at the Security Council. After the test case of the UNAMSIL operation in Sierra Leone in 1999, most new UN peacekeeping operations were given explicit civilian protection mandates, albeit with various caveats.[42] In 2009, the United Kingdom would go on to chair the newly established informal Security Council Expert Group on the Protection of Civilians and in 2011 it released its "Strategy on the Protection of Civilians in Armed Conflict." A short, strategic-level document, this established four policy areas for joint action principally between the British Ministry of Defence (MOD), Foreign and Commonwealth Office (FCO), and Department for International Development (DFID): political engagement, protection by peace support operations, humanitarian action, and state capacity.[43]

While the New Horizon agenda and the civilian protection initiatives focused on UN peacekeeping reforms, British decision-makers were far more interested in what had become the central focus of their campaigns in Afghanistan and Iraq: stabilization.

The British approach was set out most clearly in "Security and Stabilisation: The Military Contribution" published in November 2009. Based on the experience of British armed forces in Afghanistan and Iraq, this defined *stabilization operations* as long-term, multidimensional, but primarily political affairs that included important role(s) for the military. It is particularly important to note that stabilization operations can deploy into situations where no political settlement or even peace agreement exists. Consequently, *stabilization* was defined as:

> the process that supports states which are entering, enduring or emerging from conflict, in order to prevent or reduce violence; protect the population and key infrastructure; promote political processes and governance structures, which lead to a political settlement that institutionalises non-violent contests for power; and prepares for sustainable social and economic development.[44]

Although this document borrowed heavily from US approaches in several respects, it attempted to strike a more civilian-oriented tone throughout and hence define a more precise role for the military.

For the British government, the military contribution to the stabilization process should be based on nine security principles:

- there should be primacy of political purpose;
- soldiers must understand the context in which they operate—described as a dynamic "conflict ecosystem;"
- they should stay focused on the needs of the population;
- the goal is to foster host state governance, authority and indigenous capacity;
- there should be unity of effort between military and civilian agencies;
- irregular actors should be isolated and neutralised;
- the military should exploit credibility as a lever to gain support;
- soldiers should be prepared for the long-term through perseverance and building sustainability; and
- they must anticipate, learn and adapt to the dynamic operating environment.[45]

In implementing these principles, the military would be expected to transition between combat, peacekeeping and humanitarian assistance operations, sometimes very rapidly. They would also need assistance from local parties, particularly those with indigenous policing and paramilitary expertise. By utilizing these different techniques and supporting forces, the military would aim to facilitate a viable political settlement, which would reverse any spiral towards state collapse and from which the elements of a stable state could emerge. To maintain a degree of stability, the central importance of the triangular relationship between the host government, competing local elites, and the wider population was emphasized. The principal threat to the stabilization process was likely to come from what the doctrine writers termed *irregular activity*, defined as "the use, or threat, of force, by irregular forces, groups or individuals, frequently ideologically or criminally motivated, to effect or prevent change as a challenge to governance and authority."[46] All these areas place major demands on the intelligence community within a stabilization operation.

The overall British joint doctrine summarizes the operational framework for conducting all these activities as: shape, secure, hold, and develop.[47] Also in operational terms, military progress during the stabilization process was largely understood in terms of facilitating a transition to a situation where police forces could assume the lead role in providing security. This would not only require the neutralization of key irregular actors but also considerable progress in building indigenous security force capacity, as well as on reforming the local security and justice sectors.

Turning back to developments in UN peacekeeping for a moment, it is important to note that since this British doctrine was published, three UN peacekeeping operations have been deployed with the term *stabilization* in their title: in the Democratic Republic of the Congo (2010), Mali (2013), and the Central African Republic (2014). Given the United Kingdom's use of stabilization to include situations without political settlements in place, it is interesting to recall the warning issued by the UN secretary-general's report, "The Fall of Srebrenica" (1999), that "[p]eacekeepers must never again be deployed into an environment in which there is no ceasefire or peace agreement" and where the necessary resources are not provided.[48]

A return to peacekeeping?

After the end of British combat operations in Iraq in 2009, and the subsequent withdrawal of all British troops in 2011, attention turned to how the campaign in Afghanistan might end. This was also a period in which the Labour Party lost its hold on power and handed over to a coalition of the Conservatives and Liberal Democrats. The new government ushered in a series of key strategic documents that would set the tone and approach of its national security policies. Although they made few references to the UN or peacekeeping, they framed the political and strategic context in which the United Kingdom's engagement with the UN would occur. The two most important documents were the "Strategic Defence and Security Review" (2010) and the "Building Stability Overseas Strategy" (2011).[49] While the latter represented the first integrated cross-government strategy to address conflict issues, covering early warning, response, and upstream pre-vention, the former set out how the United Kingdom would operate with a 20–30 percent cut in its armed forces' operational ambition and deployable capability. Specifically, as part of "Future Force 2020," British regular forces would be reduced from 102,000 to 90,000 by 2015, and to 82,000 by 2020. The only areas that received an increase in resources were some special forces, cyber capability, and the reservists (to a trained strength of 30,000).[50]

Although the UN did not feature prominently in either document, it was not entirely absent.[51] The Strategic Defence and Security Review defined Britain's priority areas for UN reform as: a more representative Security Council, greater UN budgetary discipline and more equitable allocation of UN costs among member states, a greater role for conflict prevention alongside peacekeeping and peacebuilding efforts, greater integration of UN efforts across the political, security, development and humanitarian sectors, and better UN coordination with NATO and the European Union (EU), including more strategic dialogue and coopera-tion on planning operations.[52] The Building Stability Overseas Strategy called for the United Kingdom to play a leading role to improve the "efficiency and effectiveness" of operations, to ensure such operations support peace processes, and that they "stay no longer than necessary."

At the same time, some segments of the British government and military establishment began to reflect once more on the concept of peacekeeping. In part, this was because of the different political and economic context from the days when the PSO doctrine was written. But it was also partly a product of the idea that Britain might want to increase its contributions to blue helmet operations after the withdrawal of its forces from Afghanistan.

The result was the publication in July 2011 of a Joint Doctrine Note: "Peacekeeping: An Evolving Role for Military Forces" (JDN 5/11). Intended as an interim step in preparation for a more formal and wholesale review of JWP 3–50, JDN 5/11 sought to analyze the chief characteristics of the contemporary context in which such missions were operating, outline the military and planning implications of engaging in such operations, and go some way towards filling the gap in British doctrine related to the protection of civilians.

Unlike stabilization operations, JDN 5/11 emphasized that peace-keeping is "predicated on a peace agreement or ceasefire where a ces-sation of major violence has occurred."[53] Such an agreement may break down for any number of reasons but peacekeeping starts from the assumption that such an agreement exists. Also unlike stabilization operations, peacekeepers "should not have a designated enemy" but may be required to use coercive measures against perpetrators of acts that contravene the mission mandate. JDN 5/11 therefore defined *peacekeeping* as "a technique designed to support the implementation of a ceasefire or peace agreement, however fragmented, where major hostility has halted, and to assist in implementing agreements achieved by the peacemakers."[54]

For the British government, this meant that peacekeeping was best understood as a set of activities guided by seven principles, which distinguishes it from other types of operations: consent ("strategic consent of the main parties to the conflict"); impartiality (explicitly not neutrality); minimum force for self-defense and implementation of the mandate; political primacy; legitimacy (especially with local audiences); causing no harm; and pursuing an integrated approach.[55] JDN 5/11 went on to emphasize that the protection of civilians in peacekeeping missions would likely be undertaken for rather different, moral and legal reasons, than in a COIN environment, where the overarching goal was to reduce local support for insurgents.[56]

In May 2012, the United Kingdom launched the "Prevention of Sexual Violence Initiative."[57] This was an attempt to focus its diplomatic energies on one particular aspect of its civilian protection agenda, an area of crucial importance for UN peacekeeping operations. The British initiative involves attempts to ensure that at both the UN and African Union the "protection of civilians includes action to prevent and respond to sexual and gender-based violence, zero tolerance of sexual exploitation and abuse committed by UN and AU personnel in peacekeeping settings, and women's participation and the promotion of gender equality in all peace and security efforts."

Moreover, with the UN calling for European states to "return" to its peacekeeping operations, the United Kingdom is well positioned to support UN missions in certain areas.[58] This idea has also resonated in some areas of the British military and political establishment. For example, the current chief of the defence staff, General Nick Houghton, has said that the United Kingdom needs "to be far more pro-active in our investment in United Nations Operations" not least because "such operations come pre-funded and with the benefit of an extant legal mandate which confers legitimacy."[59] Similarly, another official directly engaged with the United Kingdom's peacekeeping policies recently called for greater British engagement with UN peacekeeping in order to preserve and maintain "skills within our own forces that have utility across all operations."[60] The United Kingdom's major military exercise, "Agile Warrior," also suggested that the army should recommend itself for such operations. Specifically, "it should not hold back from conducting a cost-benefit analysis of the merits of greater engagement in [peacekeeping operations]."[61]

The year 2015 proved to be even more significant for British engagement with UN peace operations. In January, the MOD signed a Memorandum of Understanding with the Irish Department of Defence to enhance cooperation in supporting "UK Armed Forces engagement in peacekeeping operations, through the provision of peacekeeping training and addressing the potential of joint Ireland/UK contributions to UN mandated and UN led peacekeeping operations."[62] In September that year, at the Peacekeeping Leaders' Summit, Prime Minister Cameron pledged to deploy up to 370 British blue helmets to UN missions. This was followed in November by the 2015 Strategic Defence and Security Review, which formalized this pledge, stating that the United Kingdom would "double the number of military personnel" that it contributes to UN missions, as well as committing to establish a cross-Whitehall/joint-UN Peacekeeping Policy Unit.[63] Britain also committed to host the following Peacekeeping Leaders' summit in London in September 2016. During that year Britain started deploying the first of these new peacekeepers to UNSOS and UNMISS.

Conclusion

As the preceding analysis demonstrates, the United Kingdom has moved from an initially ambivalent attitude towards UN peacekeeping in the 1950s and 1960s to one of its principal supporters. That support has only sporadically translated into the deployment of British blue helmets, but it has been important in some UN peacekeeping theaters with regard to mandate formulation as well as support for wider reforms of the UN peacekeeping architecture. It remains to be seen whether the United Kingdom's doctrine on stabilization plays a significant role in reforming how the UN defines guidelines for its peacekeeping operations.

With the end of its military campaigns in Iraq and Afghanistan and the initial deployments of new contingents of peacekeepers to Somalia and South Sudan, the United Kingdom currently stands at an important domestic crossroads concerning its engagement with UN peacekeeping. In the context of the austerity measures imposed by the ruling coalition government, Britain is undergoing significant reductions in the resources available to its armed forces as well as to their numbers. The country's finances also have significant consequences for what form British contributions might assume.[64]

The end of the Iraq and Afghanistan campaigns did not therefore automatically equate with spare deployable capacity at the levels witnessed during the height of these campaigns. But the case for greater British participation in UN peacekeeping has been made and has gained significant acceptance.[65] During the 2000s, for instance, the British military did not need UN peacekeeping to make a case for relevance or the relevance of particular assets. But when the British military considered its potential post-Afghanistan business, UN peacekeeping operations become a more attractive proposition, especially if they occurred in areas Britain considers strategically important such as the Middle East and Mediterranean or helped address national security threats such as terrorism.

It is also important that the United Kingdom's latest blue helmets are military engineers, given the UN's need for force enablers of this kind. Indeed, Britain's future contributions to UN peace operations should arguably focus on providing specialist capabilities. Relevant options might include logistics, medical and engineering units, including counter-improvised explosive device (IED) elements from the British Army's Counter-IED Task Force. Another option would be intelligence, surveillance, and signal intercept capabilities (or training for other countries in their use). Important here might be the use of Watchkeeper unmanned aerial vehicles (UAVs) with their ability to conduct surveillance at night. In terms of mobility assets, Britain could help with strategic lift issues as well as helicopter capabilities. The United Kingdom also has a sizable inventory of armored vehicles, one legacy of its campaigns in Iraq and Afghanistan.[66] Another option is for Britain to become what Walter Dorn has called a "technology-contributing country" or TechCC.[67] Designed to complement existing notions of troop- and police-contributing countries, a TechCC would provide other contributors, field missions, and UN headquarters with technological concepts, equipment, advice, and support.

Whatever options the British government chooses, its doctrinal journey towards a more "pragmatic approach" has helped set the parameters for peacekeeping operations to be more resilient and more robust. This, in turn, raises some big questions for the UN as it more regularly sends its peacekeepers into areas where there is no peace to keep.

Notes

1 For a discussion see Thierry Tardy and Dominik Zaum, "France and the United Kingdom at the UN Security Council," in *The UN Security Council*, ed. Sebastian von Einsiedel, David Malone, and Bruno Stagno Ugarte (Boulder, Col.: Lynne Rienner, 2015).
2 At its peak, during 2007, the United Kingdom deployed over 15,000 troops to the campaigns in Afghanistan and Iraq.

86 *David Curran and Paul D. Williams*

3 Oliver Ramsbotham and Tom Woodhouse, *Encyclopaedia of International Peacekeeping Operations* (Santa Barbara, Calif.: ABC-CLIO, 1999), 262.
4 Neil Briscoe, *Britain and United Nations Peacekeeping 1948–1967* (Basingstoke: Palgrave-Macmillan, 2003), 54.
5 Michael Harbottle, *The Impartial Soldier* (Oxford: Oxford University Press, 1970), 46.
6 Robert M. Cassidy, *Peacekeeping in the Abyss: British and American Doctrine and Practice after the Cold War* (Westport, Conn.: Praeger, 2004), 137–8.
7 Lieutenant Colonel Philip Wilkinson, "Sharpening the Weapons of Peace: the Development of a Common Doctrine for Peace Support Operations," *British Army Review*, April 1998, 1–2.
8 Gen. Sir Michael Rose, *Fighting for Peace: Lessons from Bosnia* (London: Warner Books, 1998). See also Jane M.O. Sharp, *Honest Broker or Perfidious Albion: British Policy in the Former Yugoslavia* (London: Institute for Public Policy Research, 1997); Richard Caplan, *Post Mortem on UNPROFOR* (London: Brassey's, 1996); and Brendan Simms, *Unfinest Hour: Britain and the Destruction of Bosnia* (London: Penguin, 2001).
9 Ministry of Defence, *Army Field Manual: Wider Peacekeeping* (London: HMSO, 1995).
10 John Mackinlay and Randolph Kent, "Complex Emergencies Doctrine: The British Are Still the Best," *RUSI Journal* 142, no. 2 (1997): 43.
11 Ministry of Defence, *Wider Peacekeeping*, Chapter 4, 2–9.
12 Charles Dobbie, "A Concept for Post-Cold War Peacekeeping," *Survival* 36, no. 3 (1994): 126.
13 John Mackinlay, "Improving Multifunctional Forces," *Survival* 36, no. 3 (1994): 151.
14 Ibid., 150.
15 Colonel Allan Mallinson, "No Middle Ground for UN," *Jane's Defence Weekly* 14 (1994): 19.
16 Dobbie, "A Concept for Post-Cold War Peacekeeping," 121.
17 John Gerard Ruggie, "Wandering in the Void: Charting the U.N.'s New Strategic Role," *Foreign Affairs* 72, no. 5 (1993): 29.
18 Ibid., 31.
19 Mackinlay, "Improving Multifunctional Forces," 152.
20 Philip Wilkinson, "Peace Support Under Fire: Lessons From Sierra Leone," *International Security Information Service*, Briefing Series, 2 June 2000, 1.
21 Permanent Joint Headquarters, Ministry of Defence, "Peace Support Operations," *Joint Warfare Publication* 3–50, 1998, Chapter 3, 2.
22 Philip Wilkinson, "Sharpening the Weapons of Peace," in *Peacekeeping and Conflict Resolution*, ed. Oliver Ramsbotham and Tom Woodhouse (London: Frank Cass, 2000), 77.
23 Permanent Joint Headquarters, "Peace Support Operations," Chapter 3, 3.
24 Ibid., 4.
25 Ibid., Chapter 4, 2.
26 See Mats Berdal, "United Nations Peace Operations: The Brahimi Report in Context," in *Peace Support Operations: Lessons Learned and Future Perspectives*, ed. Kurt Spillmann, Thomas Bernauer, Jurg Gabriel, and Andreas Wenger (Bern: Peter Lang, 2001), 49.

27 The term *spoilers* is also used in Permanent Joint Headquarters, "Peace Support Operations."

28 UN, "The Report of the Panel on United Nations Peace Operations," UN doc. A/55/305-S/2000/809, 2000, 9.

29 Ibid., 9.

30 Wilkinson, "Peace Support Under Fire," 6.

31 As noted in Ministry of Defence, "Peacekeeping: An Evolving Role for Military Forces," Joint Doctrine Note 5/11, July 2011, para. 306.

32 Andrew Dorman, "The United Kingdom," in *Forces for Good: Cosmopolitan Militaries in the Twenty-First Century*, ed. Loraine Elliot and Graeme Cheeseman (Manchester: Manchester University Press, 2004), 246.

33 See, for example, John Mackinlay, "Opposing Insurgents, During and Beyond Peace Operations," in *Peace Operations After 11 September 2001*, ed. Thierry Tardy (London: Frank Cass, 2004); and John Mackinlay and A. Al-Baddawy, *Rethinking Counterinsurgency: RAND Counterinsurgency Study, Vol. 5* (Santa Monica, Calif.: RAND, 2008), 55.

34 Richard P. Cousens, "Amristar to Basra: The Influence of Counter-Insurgency upon the British Perspective of Peacekeeping," in *Major Powers and Peacekeeping*, ed. Rachel Utley (Aldershot: Ashgate, 2006), 53, 59.

35 For example, Alex J. Bellamy and Paul D. Williams, *Understanding Peacekeeping*, 2nd edn. (Cambridge: Polity, 2010), chapter 12; and Thijs Brocades Zaalberg, "Counterinsurgency and Peace Operations," in *The Routledge Handbook of Insurgency and Counterinsurgency*, ed. Paul B. Rich and Isabelle Duyvesteyn (London: Routledge, 2012), 80–98.

36 JWP 3–50, Chapter 3, 1.

37 Ministry of Defence, "Security and Stabilisation: The Military Contribution," Joint Doctrine Publication 3–40, November 2009.

38 The non-paper is available at www.franceonu.org/IMG/pdf_09-0116-FR-UK _Non-Papier_-_Peacekeeping_2_-2.pdf.

39 UN DPKO/DFS, "A New Partnership Agenda: Charting A New Horizon for UN Peacekeeping," July 2009.

40 See, for example, UN doc. S/PRST/2009/24, 5 August 2009.

41 FCO-DFID-MOD, "Conflict Pool Annual Report 2009/2010," 2010, 42, www.gov.uk/government/uploads/system/uploads/attachment_data/file/67639/ conflict-pool-annual-report.pdf.

42 See Victoria Holt and Glyn Taylor with Max Kelly, "Protecting Civilians in the Context of UN Peacekeeping Operations," UN DPKO/OCHA, New York, November 2009.

43 Foreign and Commonwealth Office, "UK Government Strategy on the Protection of Civilians in Armed Conflict," December 2011, www.fco.gov. uk/resources/en/pdf/about-us/our-publications/ukstrategy-protect-cvilians-a rms-conflict.

44 Ministry of Defence, "Security and Stabilisation," 239.

45 Ibid., 59.

46 Ibid., 3.

47 Ibid., 55.

48 UN doc. A/54/549, 15 November 1999, para. 498.

49 British Cabinet Office, "Strategic Defence and Security Review," October 2010, www.gov.uk/government/publications/the-strategic-defence-and-secur ity-review-securing-britain-in-an-age-of-uncertainty; and FCO-DFID-MOD,

"Building Stability Overseas Strategy," 2011, www.gov.uk/government/uploa ds/system/uploads/attachment_data/file/67475/Building-stability-overseas-strate gy.pdf.

50 These targets have remained under constant review, not least because of criticism from the House of Commons Defence Committee.

51 In the United Kingdom, the Foreign and Commonwealth Office leads on UN policy, although strategic guidance on priority issues comes from the Prime Minister's Office or the new National Security Council. Under the Conservative-Liberal coalition government, the Prime Minister's Office has not been particularly interested in UN peacekeeping, which gives the Foreign Office further latitude. Drafting of Security Council resolutions is mainly done in London, and coordinated by the FCO's International Organisations Department. Discussions of changes to the mandates of peacekeeping operations, or about transition from peacekeeping to special political missions or UN country teams will involve significant input from staff in relevant British embassies or DFID country offices. See Tardy and Zaum, "France and the United Kingdom."

52 British Cabinet Office, "Strategic Defence and Security Review," 61–2. The sixth priority referred to ensuring the appropriate governance of cyberspace.

53 Ministry of Defence, "Peacekeeping: An Evolving Role for Military Forces," 1–1.

54 Ibid., 1–5. Defined in this manner, it raised the question of whether the United Kingdom should continue to use its previous doctrinal concept of PSOs. Ibid., 1–8.

55 Ibid., 2–1.

56 Ibid., 4–4.

57 See, for example, British Government (Gov.uk), "Speech: Preventing Sexual Violence Initiative, UK Team of Experts," William Hague, 30 January 2013, https://www.gov.uk/government/speeches/preventing-sexual-vio lence-initiative-uk-team-of-experts.

58 See, for example, Hervé Ladsous, "UN Peacekeeping Operations in Africa: Change in 2013 and Priorities for 2014," speech at Chatham House, London, January 13, 2014.

59 Nick Houghton, Annual Chief of Defence Staff Lecture, the Royal United Services Institute (RUSI), 18 December 2013, https://www.rusi.org/event s/past/ref:E5284A3D06EFFD.

60 Mike Redmond, "UK Defence and UN Peacekeeping: Time to Put our Forces Where Our Money Is," *British Army Review* 159, no. 14 (2013): 91.

61 "Agile Warrior" report, 2014, 19, cited in Adrian Johnson, "Back in Blue? A British Return to United Nations peacekeeping," *RUSI Journal* 60, no. 1 (2015): 14–24.

62 British MOD/DoD Ireland, "Memorandum of Understanding between the UK Ministry of Defence and the Department of Defence Ireland on the Enhancement of Bilateral Engagement on Certain Aspects of Defence and Security Cooperation," London and Dublin, 2015, 5.

63 HM Government, "A Secure and Prosperous United Kingdom: National Security Strategy and Strategic Defence and Security Review 2015," London, 2015, 60.

64 This is partly down to the way in which British contributions to UN peacekeeping are funded. The financial set up in Whitehall means that

deploying a small contingent of British troops to a UN mission would come at the expense of some other conflict management–related programs operating with the joint FCO-MOD-DFID Conflict Pool funds. This is because the United Kingdom's Peacekeeping Budget pays for its legally binding commitments (assessed costs) to UN, Organization for Security and Co-operation in Europe (OSCE), and EU peacekeeping missions, while the Conflict Pool funds discretionary activities that support conflict prevention and stabilization and contribute to peacekeeping overseas. Ironically, this means that it might be easier for Britain to fund a major troop contribution to a UN peacekeeping operation, i.e. of several thousand soldiers, because in that scenario, the Treasury would probably consider such a deployment a major operation and fund it directly from the contingency reserve.

65 For example, David Curran and Paul D. Williams, "The UK and UN Peace Operations: A Case for Greater Engagement," Oxford Research Group, May 2016, www.oxfordresearchgroup.org.uk/publications/briefing_papers_a nd_reports/uk_and_un_peace_operations_case_greater_engagement.

66 See Adrian Johnson, "After Afghanistan: A British Military Return to Peacekeeping?" Paper presented at the NIDS International Symposium on Security, "New Trends in Peacekeeping: In Search for a New Direction," Tokyo, 5 November 2014.

67 A. Walter Dorn, "Smart Peacekeeping: Toward Tech-Enabled UN Operations," IPI project, Providing for Peacekeeping, no. 13, July 2016, https://www.ipinst.org/2016/07/smart-peacekeeping-tech-enabled.

3 France and the evolution of the UN peacekeeping doctrine

Alexandra Novosseloff and Thierry Tardy

- The early stage of post–Cold War peacekeeping: No doctrinal framework and lessons learned
- An uneasy doctrinal adaptation
- The difficulty of existing between peacekeeping and war-fighting
- France shaping the peacekeeping debate at the United Nations
- Conclusion

France's current relatively modest troop and police presence within UN-led operations[1] contrasts with its role at the political level, particularly at the UN Security Council where France actively participates in debates and resolution drafting. Overall, while the UN remains for France at the center of the international security architecture, including in its legitimizing role of peacekeeping operations and other military interventions, it is still perceived as structurally ill-adapted to France's conception of military crisis management. As a result, the UN as an operational framework is not prominent in recent French military doctrine. This reflects a certain mistrust *vis-à-vis* the UN as a possible tool of French security policy, in a context where the North Atlantic Treaty Organization (NATO) operation in Libya, the French intervention in Mali and the one in Central Africa are perceived to have raised the merits of swift coercive action over those of long-term peacekeeping. Overall, France has preferred to operate in other frameworks over the last decade, including those of NATO (Afghanistan, Kosovo), the European Union (Democratic Republic of Congo, or DRC; antipiracy operation in the Gulf of Aden, Chad, and the Central African Republic, or CAR), or the national framework (operation Licorne in Côte d'Ivoire, Serval in Mali, Sangaris in CAR). The French narrative emphasizes that these other missions are UN-mandated and therefore are complementary with UN-led operations.

Moreover, peace operations are not considered by France as a specific category of military operations in which different principles would apply. French doctrinal texts of the last decade are explicit on the need to ensure that wherever the French armed forces are deployed, they are engaged in accordance with some key military principles, among which are the freedom of action and the possibility of resort to coercion.[2] Also, for the French military establishment, a contribution to peace operations must not jeopardize the identity of the soldier as a "warrior." This partly explains the weak French presence in UN operations due to the inherent difficulty of reconciling the constraints of contemporary peace operations (and the implications of the consent-based and noncoercive approach) with the imperative of military action.

This chapter examines France's doctrinal evolution *vis-à-vis* UN peace operations in three parts. It first looks at the immediate post–Cold War era when the French engagement in UN-led operations—in Bosnia and Herzegovina in particular—did not proceed with a sound conceptualization of the meaning of peace operations. The difficulties encountered led to a series of lessons learned that resulted in France moving away from UN-led operations while maintaining a strong presence in crisis management outside of the UN operational framework. The second part goes through France's doctrinal adaptation and attempts to grasp the complexity and multidimensionality of contemporary peace operations. Incrementally, France's doctrinal documents factor in the necessity of a wide-ranging response that goes beyond the military aspects, while reasserting the key principles of military action.

Finally, the chapter sheds light on some ambiguities of the French doctrinal effort regarding peace operations and most specifically the role that force should play in them. By acknowledging that the role of force is not necessarily central in multidimensional operations where the political/economic dimension takes precedence over a too narrowly defined security imperative, France has confronted the difficulty of reconciling the virtues of the use of force with the political and operational constraints of contemporary peace operations. From the Balkans to Lebanon or even Africa, the question is posed as to what can be achieved through the use of force in missions that are not primarily of a military nature; that are inherently constrained at the political level; and that, for the most part, are not deployed to defend the type of strategic interests that would justify a sustained use of force.

The early stage of post–Cold War peacekeeping: No doctrinal framework and lessons learned

France's commitment to UN peacekeeping in Bosnia and Herzegovina

Early in the 1990s, France was an active supporter of the UN revitalization and its impact on peacekeeping.[3] In 1992–5, France became one of the top troop contributors to UN operations with more than 6,000 personnel deployed in 1993–4, mainly in former Yugoslavia, but also in Cambodia and Somalia.[4] France's commitment to the UN derived from the post–Cold War evolution of conflict management practices and the need to multilateralize national policies. If France then significantly participated in UN-led missions, the implied change for the military was not reflected in doctrinal terms. On the contrary, one key characteristic of the French participation in the UN Protection Force (UNPROFOR) in the former Yugoslavia was the mismatch between a political and military commitment to a complex operation and the weakness of concomitant strategic thinking on the implications for the military.

In particular, the conditions of the use of force by "blue helmets" in an operation dominated by a humanitarian protection mandate were not initially thought through. Nor was any typology of multi-dimensional operations agreed upon, be it at the national or multi-lateral level.[5] This absence of doctrinal reflection led to general improvisation. Blue helmets resorted to force—or abstained from doing so—in scenarios based neither on a traditional conception of the use of armed force, nor on a conception specific to peacekeeping. In the end, the mandate was implemented by member states and the UN Secretariat in a way that prevented an open interpretation of the use of force, but rather restricted it. This was tragically illustrated in May 1995 when Bosnian Serbs took blue helmets hostage, followed by the fall of the enclave of Srebrenica despite its status as a safe area placed under UN protection.

In this debate over the virtues of force in peace operations, French leaders often put the blame on the UN and its structural incapacity to operationalize the use of force. This was by and large the spirit of the French Parliamentary Mission on the fall of Srebrenica as well as of most official declarations on the difficulties encountered by the UN in the early 1990s.[6] As with many other countries, France tended to transfer the responsibility of mistakes to the institution rather than to adopt a self-critical approach. In the case of UNPROFOR in Bosnia and Herzegovina, this approach was all the more paradoxical as

France had largely contributed to the design of the operation's mandate within the Security Council and influenced its implementation on the ground. Interestingly enough, while, as of 1994–5, France became adamant that the military needed to be able to shift quickly from one "passive" peacekeeping posture to a more aggressive one (resorting to force as required in force protection or defense of their mandate), the use of force was largely underplayed in UN operations during the early 1990s. In fact, the UN weaknesses in former Yugoslavia should not hide a general passivity from all countries involved that was grounded in a mix of weak conceptual thinking and intentionally renouncing the use of force. In other words, the philosophy on the use of force was the result of both under-conceptualization and *Realpolitik*, according to which no country was ready to take the risks of military escalation.

In May–June 1995, France eventually rejected this ambivalence when the French forces (under the framework of the Rapid Reaction Force[7]) took military action against the Serbs in Sarajevo, but this came only after three years of field presence and strong political commitment. Overall, for the military the Bosnian episode epitomized what military operations should not look like and then profoundly influenced subsequent doctrinal development and practice.

Lessons learned: Moving away from UN peacekeeping

In fact, France's engagement in UN missions in the early 1990s and the difficulties encountered marked an important shift in its conceptualization of peace operations. First, contrary to the French position right after the end of the Cold War, the UN was, in 1994–5, no longer seen as an appropriate vehicle for French policy in peace operations, and therefore had to be replaced by other instruments, be they institutional or state led. This disavowal stemmed from a distrust in the command and control structure of the UN as well as the acknowledgment of a certain incompatibility between the UN's culture and the requirements of military action. For former French defense minister François Léotard, the only way out of the Bosnian quagmire was to "move away from the UN system."[8]

The 1998 and 2013 White Papers on Defence confirmed this trend, by raising doubts about the ability of the UN to live up to the expectations of peace maintenance. The 2013 document observed that "[w]hether the result of a growing aversion to risk-taking, doubts about the effectiveness of recent operations or the impact of financial constraints, Europe and the United States have greater misgivings about committing to large scale, extended foreign intervention," before deploring that "attempts at reform launched in the first decade of the 21st century have not achieved the expected results" and that "UN reform has thus far been a failure."[9] This mistrust led to a reorienta- tion of the French crisis management policy that took the form of renationalization: France wanted to favor frameworks, such as NATO, the European Union (EU), or national operations, that better suited its military requirements.

Second, France—and here most specifically the French Ministry of Defence—concluded that the mandates of UNPROFOR, or the UN Assistance Mission for Rwanda (UNAMIR) in Rwanda, were not to be repeated where the interpretation of the principle of use of force in self-defense prevailed while massive violations of human rights were perpetrated, and where the requirements for force protection were bla- tantly overlooked. What was at stake was the compatibility of the key principles of UN peacekeeping operations (consent of the host state, impartiality, and non-resort to force except in self-defense) with those of military action.[10] The French military peacekeeping operations were in contradiction with the principles of military action as they increased the vulnerability of the military and limited their freedom of action.[11]

Compatibility between the principles of UN peacekeeping opera- tions and those of military action was further undermined by the humanitarian and political dimensions of UN operations that pulled the military away from its core function. In accordance with their colonial past and recurrent reference to Marshal Lyautey, the French military were not *a priori* against a social role towards the civilian populations, and would even put forward a certain French specificity in this respect (which they would contrast with American forces that are seen as less forthcoming with the local populations). However, the French military were eager to preserve their know-how as soldiers, and saw the so-called humanitarian missions of the early 1990s as a dilu- tion of what they should be best at—waging war. With these lay the risk of humiliation—let alone human losses—for soldiers that were denied their core attributes while confronted with regular assault on the ground. With Operation Turquoise in Rwanda and the Rapid Reaction Force in Bosnia and Herzegovina, France established opera- tions that constituted breaks with UN practice in the sense that they abided by the principles of military action and therefore put the mili- tary "back on track." Inevitably, by framing a doctrine that defined the use of force as one of its key parameters, France moved away from the UN and its peacekeeping culture.

These two orientations were not specific to France; they were by and large shared by the United States as well as by most European countries.[12] It followed an emerging division of labor between coalitions of states or Western regional organizations implementing stabilization operations—when necessary with a coercive dimension—and the UN that continues to embody peacekeeping orthodoxy with, at best, a willingness to move towards "robust" mandates.

An uneasy doctrinal adaptation

Doctrinal adaptation in France really started in 1994, in parallel with similar processes in most Western countries. The 1994 White Paper on Defence is one of the first official documents explicitly dealing with peace operations and their integration in the French military posture. What the document called "operations in support of peace"[13] appeared as one of six scenarios of the use of armed forces. The white paper also drew lessons from the recent UN engagements through the definition of criteria for French participation in UN missions, including a clear distinction between the UN authority for the overall implementation of the mandate and the "responsibilities of the military command in the conduct of the military aspects of operations," as well as the necessity of having rules of engagement approved at the political level, both national and multinational.[14]

In the same vein, a French parliamentary inquiry conducted after the Rwandan genocide put forward recommendations in relation to French participation in peacekeeping operations. First, it was suggested that when "[French] forces operate under Chapter VI [of the UN Charter], they be given real self-defence, or even combat, capacity, so that they can face any change in the situation." Furthermore, in case of a "brutal deterioration of the situation or outbreak of a violent crisis, the resort to Chapter VII that allows the use of force must be a condition of [France's] participation in a peace restoration intervention." Most importantly, when considering such a hypothesis, the document added that the intervention mode that had proven its effectiveness was "the establishment of a force under national or international command, at the request of the Security Council," where the "responsibility for running the operation falls on a lead-nation or a defence regional organization,"[15] i.e. not the United Nations.

The documents dealing with peace operations produced in the mid-1990s were written in reaction to the early 1990s experiences and were aimed at reasserting a certain number of principles relating to military action that had been neglected in the UN context. However, while those documents did clarify the conditions of the use of force in peace operations, they tended to focus on the military requirements at the expense of a broader approach taking account of the new political environment and its consequences for the nature of military action.

By contrast, French doctrinal texts adopted in the first decade of the twenty-first century paid more attention to the evolution of conflicts—its actors and dynamics—and, as a result, to the evolving role of the military in tackling them. In particular, the idea came to be formulated that "international interventions show the limits of the military tool,"[16] that the use of military force is only one dimension of the success of multidimensional operations, and that a "destructive capability" no longer "leads directly to the achievement of the strategic objective, but merely contributes to it."[17] Expressions such as "winning the peace" and "comprehensive approach" also started to appear in French MOD doctrinal texts.

As an example, a 2007 document elaborated by the Centre of Doctrine on the Use of Armed Forces (*Centre de Doctrine d'Emploi des Forces*) and titled "Winning the Battle, Building Peace: Land Forces in Present and Future Conflicts" talked about the need to adapt to the new environment, including in the way force is used:

> By changing its purpose, the use of force adapts to the changes in international relations. Since it no longer conquers but works in the service of the rule of law and peace, force acts at the very heart of life: human society. While always necessary each time an army needs to fight, the defeat of the enemy is no longer enough to ensure the success of the engagement, nor does it constitute the main objective of the use of force.[18]

The Afghan context no doubt influenced this approach, and some of the wording recalls that of counterinsurgency.[19] Yet it also applies to more traditional peacekeeping environments, and "Winning the Battle" explicitly referred to operations Artemis in the DRC and Licorne in Côte d'Ivoire, which fall within the broad peace-operations spectrum.

By reflecting the understanding that military operations are part of a broader effort to stabilize countries at risk, the French doctrine moved towards the idea of a comprehensive approach and the need for the military to think about their own role in relation with other actors. This is what the 2010 "Capstone Concept on the Employment of Armed Forces," elaborated by the Joint Centre for Concepts, Doctrine and Experimentation of the Joint Headquarters, said when stating that "the management of current crises shows that resolution is not only military but multifaceted, requiring a comprehensive approach based on adequate use of diplomatic, economic and military resources."[20] This reflects a general evolution in Western thinking on the nature of military operations and the centrality of the use of force in achieving success.

This being said, two related issues characterize French doctrinal evolution. First, the variety of doctrinal documents has been accompanied by various characterizations of French military operations and how "peace operations" fit into them. Different documents have used different terms to talk about such operations. For example, the typologies of operations differ between the 2006 "Doctrine d'Emploi des Forces Terrestres en Stabilisation" that framed the concept of *stabilization operations*, and the 2010 "Capstone Concept on the Employment of Armed Forces" that did not mention stabilization operations, but rather talked about *crisis management*, and also of "missions to establish and maintain peace" that are part of "combat operations."[21] The 2008 white paper adopted a slightly different typology, by making the distinction between *stabilization operations* and *large-scale military operations*.[22] With this, two categories of operations were conceptualized, based on their degree of coercion. The 2013 white paper referred to *coercive operations* as opposed to *crisis-management operations* that encompass "peace-keeping, interposition, securing the maritime or air approaches of failed States, combating trafficking, piracy or terrorism, assistance to a government or counter-insurrection."[23] Similarly, the 2013 "Capstone Concept for Military Operations" distinguished between *crisis-management operations* that include "peace keeping or peace restoration" and *coercive operations* that are about "international engagement in a major conflict" as well as "peace enforcement."[24]

This conceptual evolution has to some extent reflected unease with the concept of peace operations and how it should be defined; peace operations have indeed lost preeminence in the spectrum of military operations. They remain an option, but shall not be a reference point for military planning and organization.

Second, a key feature of doctrinal evolution is the absence of a clear-cut rupture between what falls within "crisis management" and what falls within "coercive operations." Typologies do list these different levels of operations, but also make the point that various types of engagement are not mutually exclusive. As the 2013 "Capstone Concept for Military Operations" stated, "Given the threats' hybrid nature and variety of possible operational situations, one operation can thus, simultaneously or sequentially, include both coercive and crisis management actions."[25]

Within crisis management operations, different stages of intervention are introduced, from intervention to stabilization and normalization.[26]

The intervention phase is the most coercive. It generally "aims at establishing temporary order by the use of force to defeat violence and chaos." The following phase is that of stabilization, where the "aim is to consolidate the transitional order previously imposed through the reduction and the containment of the violence, allowing all to set off on the path towards peace." Stabilization is presented as "the decisive phase of a military operation" as it is here that "armed forces establish the conditions for strategic success." Finally, the normalization phase "focuses on the installation and strengthening of an enduring political, judicial and social system accepted by the protagonists in the conflict."[27] Here again, all stages are presented as being part of a continuum of military operations in which the use of force is never *a priori* excluded. They "all, to varying degrees, contain moments of coercion and of control of violence, i.e. low- and high-intensity moments,"[28] and they therefore do not require specialized forces or training. The 2008 white paper emphasized the absence of a strict distinction between stabilization and war-fighting that explains the choice not to specialize units but rather to opt for the polyvalence of the French forces.[29] In the same vein, the 2013 white paper stressed that "[French] forces could, on an irregular basis, be forced to conduct several types of operation simultaneously," and they must therefore be "capable of deploying both permanent resources allowing actions of coercion and local attrition in centres of population, and resources responding to the need to control vast areas, often in support of local security forces."[30]

The difficulty of existing between peacekeeping and war-fighting

The conceptual basis provided by the French military and largely endorsed at the political level has shaped French military engagement over the last 20 years. Following Operation Turquoise in Rwanda in 1994 and the Rapid Reaction Force in Bosnia in 1995, the following operations have all met French political and operational requirements: the NATO-led operations in Bosnia from December 1995 to December 2004 (the Implementation Force, IFOR, followed by the Stabilization Force, SFOR), and Kosovo as of June 1999 (the Kosovo Force, KFOR); and the EU-led operations in Bosnia beginning December 2004 (EUFOR Althea), in the Democratic Republic of the Congo in 2003 (EUFOR Artemis) and 2006 (EUFOR DRC), in Chad in 2008–9 (EUFOR Chad/CAR), and in the Central African Republic (EUFOR RCA) in 2014.

An example of the kind of crisis-management mission that France wishes to establish on a national level, both in terms of command and control structure and in relation to a simultaneous UN (or African Union) presence is operation Licorne, deployed in Côte d'Ivoire as of February 2003,[31] partly to support the UN Operation in Côte d'Ivoire (UNOCI). Another is operation Sangaris in the Central African Republic as of December 2013, established partly to support the African Union operation the African-led International Support Mission to the Central African Republic (MISCA), and then the UN Multidimensional Integrated Stabilization Mission in the Central African Republic (MINUSCA).

Over the last five years, the evolution towards more robustness was further illustrated by a series of engagements that arguably fall outside the remit of crisis management. Following the French contribution to the International Security Assistance Force (ISAF) in Afghanistan, both the Libya operation in 2011 and operation Serval in Mali in 2013 (and then Barkhane as of August 2014) are illustrations of engagements that belong to the category of "coercive operations."[32] While this clarifies the French position on the role of the military, it also raises questions as to the compatibility between such a posture and the requirements of contemporary peace operations.

First, if military operations of the last decade have by and large met the French conditions for engagement, new doctrinal developments nonetheless raise the question of French compatibility with what UN operations are about. The fact that France has distanced itself from UN missions still leaves the latter with the issue of the level of coercion it can possibly implement, in particular in the absence of significant contributions from Western states. This relates to the notion of "robust peacekeeping" and the ability and will of current troop contributing countries (TCCs), mainly coming from the Global South,[33] to resort to force in defense of the mandate, i.e. beyond force protection. The debate touches upon states' capacities in key areas of complex operations (rapid reaction, logistics, communication, intelligence, etc.) and also upon their own conception of the use of force.

Moreover, by contending that peace operations are not "wholly distinct from war-fighting,"[34] France runs the risk of amalgamating policy responses that vary significantly from one type of operation to the other. In other words, the French policy may prove to be difficult to square with the constraints of multidimensional peace operations. Beyond the acknowledgement of this contradiction, this means that France is unlikely to reengage troops in UN-led operations in the medium-term. As stressed in the 2013 white paper, despite the different reform processes that have been engaged internally,[35] France still sees the UN as ill-equipped to match the criteria that it defines for itself.

Yet the UN can be seen as part of France's exit strategy in a division of labor whereby France—or a coalition to which France would contribute—would lead the entry force before a longer-term UN presence would take over.

This leads to the inherent difficulty to reconcile the nature of contemporary peace operations with the imperative to preserve the core tasks of soldiers. All French doctrinal texts of the last decade have been explicit on the need to ensure that wherever the French armed forces are engaged, it should be in accordance with some key military principles, among which is the possibility of resort to coercion.

However, the complex political context in which peace operations are deployed, the nature of the tasks that militaries perform in those operations, as well as the centrality of nonmilitary tasks in the stabilization phase, make it extremely difficult to guarantee the coherence of a military engagement. Operations in Bosnia and Herzegovina with NATO, in the DRC or Chad with the EU, or in Lebanon with the UN, all attest to the difficulty for the military of sticking to purely military tasks and retaining the initiative in military terms. In each case, the multinational dimension or the nature of the potential spoilers inevitably undermine the military approach that doctrinal texts describe. Another important factor is the nature of the engagement: in support of a peace process where military are often used for police tasks and where reaching out to the civilians is essential.

The idea of a continuum between different types of operation implies that there is compatibility between them; yet reality on the ground may offer a different picture. The resort to force was possible in Afghanistan in a way that it is not in Lebanon, where a military confrontation with Hezbollah is to be avoided. And while KFOR in Kosovo or the UN Interim Force in Lebanon (UNIFIL) may abide by military principles, most French military would not consider them—in comparison with Libya or Serval for example—as "real" operations.

In this environment, there also appears to be an un-theorized qualitative distinction between short-term semi-coercive operations, such as Turquoise in Rwanda, Artemis in the DRC, or EUFOR RCA, and longer-term operations that contain a peacebuilding dimension, and therefore the necessity to think about the role of the military in different terms. France clearly positions itself on the former range of operations rather than on the latter, yet the latter is essential to "winning the peace." The extent to which crisis management operations that have been militarily tested—Licorne in Côte d'Ivoire or Sangaris in the CAR—can simultaneously be part of a broader peacebuilding endeavor is yet to be demonstrated. Here lies the most fundamental problem of the French policy *vis-à-vis* peace operations: It has yet to conceptualize peace operations so as to capture the tension between short-term robust military action on the one hand, and longer term police-type activities on the other. By insisting on one narrow aspect of crisis management, France runs the risk of being simply absent from long-term crisis management operations, as well as from the development of a comprehensive approach.

More broadly, this raises the question of the role of armed forces in tackling issues that fundamentally are not of a military nature. This leads to the distinction, made by British general Rupert Smith, between what the use of force can *do* as opposed to what it can *achieve*.[36] As we have seen, the use of force has been theorized over the last 15 years mainly as a tool to give the French armed forces the required freedom of maneuver and force protection. Less attention has been paid to the ultimate purpose of the use of force, i.e. what is to be achieved through the recourse to force. This is all the more crucial, as the very nature of multidimensional peace operations, in which the military component is one among many, makes the articulation between the use of force and long-term political objectives central to the effectiveness of their actions and the sustainability of peace consolidation. In other words, while operations Turquoise, Artemis, or Licorne may meet the French requirements as defined in the latest doctrinal papers, the extent to which these operations have been effective in supporting a broader political agenda remains an open question.

France shaping the peacekeeping debate at the United Nations

UNIFIL and its consequences

Among all French participations in the twenty-first century peace operations, the 2006 contribution to UNIFIL constitutes an exception. After 15 years of quasi-absence from UN-led operations, deploying forces under UN command was a source of major concern within the military.[37] Following French activism in the negotiating process leading to the adoption of UN Security Council Resolution 1701 (2006), which authorized an expanded UNIFIL, the UN Secretariat requested that France provide a major contribution to the operation and provide its backbone. The French authorities were initially hesitant due to France's links with Lebanon and the implications for regional issues. There was also a concern about the French soldiers being overexposed. As they eventually acceded to the UN request, conditions on their contribution were put forward. These were: robust rules of engagement that "must guarantee the freedom of movement of the Force and its capacity for action;" means for the protection of the force (which led to the deployment of Leclerc Main Battle Tanks and Short Range Air Defense); and a clear (that is, "simple, coherent, and reactive") military chain of command with the establishment of a dedicated cell for UNIFIL at UN Headquarters in New York.[38]

The establishment of this dedicated cell—called Strategic Military Cell (SMC)—was the most notable specific development in the expanded UNIFIL. Initially, the purpose of the SMC was to become UNIFIL's operations headquarters, at the strategic level of command and decision. The second idea was to have a permanent direct link with New York for the force in Naqoura, Lebanon in case of a crisis, allowing the force commander to talk directly to the "operations commander" (the SMC director). The French military establishment therefore conceived a small military structure built on the "J Structure" of military head-quarters, composed of representatives of TCCs (at the time 70 percent of which were Europeans) and representatives of the permanent members of the Security Council. It was commanded by a three-star general with a direct link to the political level in New York (the secretary-general or the head of the Department of Peacekeeping Operations, DPKO). This structure was placed within DPKO (although outside the Military Division), against France's wishes. The nature of this cell (created for only one peacekeeping operation, and furthermore dominated by European countries), and the fact that it was breaking the decentralized way of running peacekeeping operations (PKOs) caused some opposition among traditional TCCs as well as within the Secretariat.

French–British initiative

France drew on the SMC to promote some reforms within DPKO, in particular the transformation in 2007 of the Military Division into an Office of Military Affairs (OMA) with the increase of its personnel (30 plus) and of the ranking of its head (from senior level professional D2 to assistant secretary-general), as well as the strengthening of planning and information capacity within OMA.

As it promoted the strengthening of military expertise within the Secretariat, France also worked on this within the Security Council, in partnership with the United Kingdom. In the fall of 2008, in the con-text of a new crisis in the DRC, the two countries presented a non-paper titled "Improving the Preparation, Planning, Monitoring and Evaluation of Peacekeeping Operations" that suggested reforms in four areas: reinforcement of the council and the Secretariat's work on preparation, planning, and monitoring operations at the strategic level; ensuring that each council member receives coherent and accurate military analysis; reinforcement of the dialogue between the council and the Secretariat on the military dimension of PKOs; and effectiveness of forces, rules of engagement, and mobilization of contributors, as well as best practices.[39] This work was endorsed by a presidential statement on 5 August 2009, by which the Security Council agreed:

> to develop the following practices: (i) regular dialogue with the Secretariat on the general challenges of peacekeeping; (ii) efforts to deepen consultations with troop and police contributing countries, including through the Security Council's Working Group on Peacekeeping Operations; (iii) organisation of political-military meetings on specific operations to improve the shared analysis of operational challenges; (iv) encouraging regular updating of planning documents by the Secretariat to ensure consistency with mandates; (v) improved monitoring and evaluation, through the use of benchmarks, as and where appropriate, that enable progress to be charted against a comprehensive and integrated strategy.[40]

This work subsequently led DPKO to launch a new reform process named "New Horizon."

Since then various changes have been implemented: The Security Council holds regular meetings on peacekeeping operations; the Working Group on Peacekeeping has been revitalized and holds regular meetings on issues ranging from the use of technologies to regional partnerships, triangular cooperation (between the Security Council, the Secretariat, and troop and police contributing countries), safety and security, and the protection of civilians. Although still very general, benchmarks are identified for each PKO mandate and the operational documents for each operation are regularly updated.

In 2010–11, the P3 in the council (the United States, France, and the United Kingdom) also introduced reviews of operations that they run by themselves. These reviews aim at "right-sizing" operations, rationalizing and adapting them to their evolving environment (i.e., looking at ways of reducing their format when the conditions allow, as in Haiti and Côte d'Ivoire), and thus reducing their budget. This allows for the coordination of positions among the P3 and the elaboration of a common position towards DPKO/the Department of Field Support (DFS). These P3 reviews are conducted in parallel with the Secretariat's own "strategic reviews," completed prior to the renewal of operational mandates.

Support of ongoing reform processes

Finally, France has been broadly supportive of efforts towards more robust peacekeeping operations, the use of new technologies in support of operations, and the necessity for all operations to protect the civilian population in a more proactive way. This has been done within the Security Council and the General Assembly's Special Committee on Peacekeeping Operations (C34) as well within the EU. France had also taken the lead (together with Jordan) of the Working Group on Special Forces as part of a larger DPKO-led doctrinal development work.[41] It has also supported the reform process initiated by the High Level Independent Panel Report on Peace Operations, released in June 2015, in four main areas: strengthening consultations with regional players and neighboring countries; dialogue with troop- and staff-contributing countries; the negotiation of compacts with host states; and the improvement of rules governing logistics and medical care.[42] At the September 2015 "Obama summit" on peacekeeping operations, France's pledges were rather modest and centered on providing French language training to 25,000 troops and to train 80,000 African troops.[43]

Overall, this activism has allowed France to remain a driving force among the P5 on reflecting on improving the effectiveness of peacekeeping operations, thus justifying its leadership of DPKO and overcoming possible critiques about its weak troop contribution to operations.

Conclusion

France has been one the most active supporters of the broad notion of crisis management, be it within the Security Council, the European Union, or through its own national policy and operations. In the meantime, the French doctrine towards peace operations has, over the last two decades, reflected the ambivalence of France's position, stretched between a military culture that places the use of force at the center of strategy and multidimensional operations that by nature integrate a larger range of activities. In the end, while France has been significantly involved in peace operations since the end of the Cold War, the military has never felt comfortable with the peacekeeping concept, seen as a dilution of what they should be trained for.

This tension has shaped both doctrinal development and operations. Twenty years after the French engagement in the former Yugoslavia, lessons have been learned, and the military have become aware of the evolution of conflict management and the subsequent necessity to integrate the military dimension into a broader framework. This is the rationale behind the concept of a comprehensive approach that has become a central theme of military thinking.

However, France still finds it difficult to reconcile the nature of contemporary peace operations with the imperative to preserve the core tasks of soldiers. Indeed, the complex political context in which peace operations are deployed, the nature of the tasks that the military performs in those operations, as well as the centrality of nonmilitary tasks in the stabilization phase make it difficult to guarantee the coherence of a military engagement the way the French think of it.

Furthermore, the extent to which a comprehensive approach reconciles the centrality of military principles—among which is the use of force—with the characteristics of multidimensional peace operations, is yet to be demonstrated. And as long as peace operations attempt to combine different types of military functions, the soldier's identity debate is likely to remain.

In this context, France, or at least the French Ministry of Defence, still resists the idea of contributing directly to UN operations as these operations are seen as too conceptually remote from France's vision of military engagements. The French doctrinal apparatus has therefore refrained from conceptualizing what a French participation in UN peacekeeping operations could potentially be and imply. Paradoxically, the field absence contrasts with a high level of political commitment within the Security Council, where France acts as a "pen holder" for quite a few peacekeeping operations, and was behind the establishment of the latest two large missions in Mali and the Central African Republic. In the end, France appears to be quite effective in pushing in various political fora for its own agenda, ensuring that the UN, the EU, or bilateral partners endorse the French vision of peace operations and back up France's own operations.

Notes

1 As of the end of April 2016, France has contributed 875 personnel (830 troops, 9 military experts, and 36 police officers), mainly deployed in UNIFIL in Lebanon (790 troops). Its ranking position is thirty-fourth over 123 troop-contributing countries. See www.un.org/en/peacekeeping/resour ces/statistics/contributors.shtml.
2 See Joint Centre for Concepts, Doctrines and Experimentation (CICDE), French Ministry of Defence, "Capstone Concept on the Employment of Armed Forces," Joint Concept JC-01, Paris, 2010.

3 See Francis Delon, "Le rôle joué par les membres permanents dans l'action du Conseil de sécurité," in Académie de droit international de La Haye, *Le développement du rôle du Conseil de sécurité*, La Haye, Colloque 21–23 juillet 1992 (Dordrecht: Martinus Nijhoff, 1993); and Brigitte Stern, ed., *La vision française des opérations de maintien de la paix* (Paris: Montchrestien, 1997).

4 See Thierry Tardy, "France," in *Providing Peacekeepers: The Politics, Challenges and Future of UN Peacekeeping Contributions*, ed. Alex Bellamy and Paul Williams (Oxford: Oxford University Press, 2013).

5 Within NATO, the first document defining peace operations was issued by the Military Committee in 1993 (NATO Military Planning for Peace Support Operations, MC-327, August 1993), but was only adopted by the North Atlantic Council in 1995. In the United States, the Field Manual on Peace Operations was released in December 1994, a few months after the release of the Presidential Decision Directive 25 (PDD-25), "Clinton Administration's Policy on Reforming Multilateral Peace Operations," US Department of State, Washington, DC, May 1994.

6 See French National Assembly, "Srebrenica: rapport sur un massacre," Volume 1—Report and Annexes, Joint Information Mission, report no. 3413, Paris, 2001.

7 Security Council Resolution 998, UN doc. S/RES/998, 16 June 1995.

8 French National Assembly, Testimony of François Léotard, "Srebrenica: rapport sur un massacre," Volume 2—Hearings, Joint Information Mission, report no. 3413, Paris, 2001, 260.

9 Direction de l'information légale et administrative, Government of France, *French White Paper on Defence and National Security*, Paris, 2013, 31.

10 The "Joint Concept on the Employment of Armed Force" defines five principles of military action: freedom of action, concentration of effort, economy of resources, surprise, and controlled use of force. See CICDE, "Joint Concept on the Employment of Armed Force," January 2010, 28–30.

11 See hearings by Generals Cot, Morillon, and De La Presle before the Parliamentary Mission ("Srebrenica: rapport sur un massacre," Volume 2). See also Centre de Doctrine d'Emploi des Forces, French Ministry of Defence, "Enseignements Tactiques. Les opérations terrestres de l'armée de terre des années 90—Témoignages," *Cahier de la réflexion doctrinale*, Paris, 2005, 37–8.

12 The United Kingdom operated a similar policy shift, which found an illustration with British operation Palliser in 2000 in Sierra Leone. Since then the United Kingdom and the United States have become even smaller contributors to UN peacekeeping, with respectively 302 and 74 personnel as of the end of April 2016. The British have, however, evolved recently (see Chapter 2 by David Curran and Paul D. Williams in this volume).

13 Government of France, *White Paper on Defence*, no. 10/18, Paris, 1994, 115.

14 Ibid., 76.

15 French National Assembly, "Rapport d'information sur les opérations militaires menées par la France, d'autres pays et l'ONU au Rwanda entre 1990 et 1994," no. 1271, Paris, 1998.

16 Alain Juppé and Louis Schweitzer, "La France et l'Europe dans le monde," white paper on France's foreign and European policy, 2008–20, 2008, 20.

17 Centre de Doctrine d'Emploi des Forces, "Winning the Battle, Building Peace: Land Forces in Present and Future Conflicts," FT-01, January 2007, 5.
18 Ibid., 20.
19 See CICDE, "Counter-Insurgency," 5 November 2010.
20 CICDE, "Capstone Concept on the Employment of Armed Forces," 17.
21 Ibid., 32.
22 Odile Jacob, "White Paper on National Defence and Security," Paris, 2008, 129–30.
23 Ibid., 81, 83.
24 CICDE, "Capstone Concept of Military Operations," Paris, 2013, 14.
25 Ibid.
26 CICDE, "Comprehensive Approach to External Crisis Management (Military Contribution)," Paris, 2011, 23.
27 Centre de Doctrine d'Emploi des Forces, "Winning the Battle," 10–13. See also Centre de Doctrine d'Emploi des Forces, "Doctrine d'Emploi des Forces Terrestres en Stabilisation," Paris, 2006, 3–5.
28 Centre de Doctrine d'Emploi des Forces, "Winning the Battle," 10.
29 Jacob, "White Paper on National Defence and Security, 2008, 130.
30 Government of France, *French White Paper on Defence and National Security*, 2013, 82.
31 The French-led (and UN-mandated) operation Licorne was deployed to help stabilize Côte d'Ivoire following the signature of the Linas-Marcoussis Agreement and to protect French citizens within the country. See Alexandra Novosseloff, "UNOCI," in *Oxford Handbook on United Nations Peacekeeping Operations*, ed. Joachim A. Koops, Norrie MacQueen, Thierry Tardy and Paul D. Williams (Oxford: Oxford University Press, 2015), 708–19; and Arthur Boutellis and Alexandra Novosseloff, "Côte d'Ivoire," in *The UN Security Council in the 21st Century*, ed. Sebastian von Einsiedel, David Malone and Bruno Stagno Ugarte (Boulder, Col.: Lynne Rienner, 2015), 681–98.
32 Operation Serval (and its follow-on mission Barkhane) is, however, also deployed in support of the UN Multidimensional Integrated Stabilization Mission in Mali (MINUSMA) as stated in Security Council resolution 2100, UN doc. S/RES/2100, 25 April 2013, para. 18, which authorizes it "to intervene in support of elements of MINUSMA when under imminent and serious threat upon request of the Secretary-General."
33 As of April 2016, the top ten troop and police contributors to UN operations were: Ethiopia, India, Pakistan, Bangladesh, Rwanda, Nepal, Senegal, China, Burkina Faso, and Ghana. See www.un.org/en/peacekeeping/contributors/2016/apr16_2.pdf.
34 See Victoria Holt and Tobias Berkman, *The Impossible Mandate? Military Preparedness, the Responsibility to Protect and Modern Peace Operations* (Washington, DC: Stimson Center, 2006), 123.
35 See DPKO/DFS, "United Nations Peacekeeping Operations: Principles and Guidelines" (so-called "Capstone Doctrine"), New York, 2008; and DPKO/DFS, "A New Partnership Agenda: Charting a New Horizon for UN Peacekeeping" (New York: United Nations, 2009).
36 See Rupert Smith, *The Utility of Force: The Art of War in the Modern World* (New York: Knopf, 2007). Also see on this distinction Mats Berdal, "Lessons Not Learned: The Use of Force in 'Peace Operations' in the

1990s," in *Managing Armed Conflicts in the 21st Century*, ed. Adekeye Adebajo and Chandra Lekha Sriram (London: Routledge, 2001), 55–74. See also Mats Berdal and David H. Ucko "The United Nations and the Use of Force: Between Promise and Peril," *Journal of Strategic Studies* 37, no. 5 (2014): 665–73.

37 The military establishment had planned until the very last moment for a force that would be outside the UN institutional framework. A week after the vote of 1701, the French defense minister, Michèle Alliot-Marie, was still talking about the possible deployment of a French "rapid reaction force" in support of UNIFIL. See Philippe Bolopion, "La France réticente à engager son armée au Liban," *Le Monde*, 17 August 2006.

38 See Alain Pellégrini, *Un été de feu au Liban. 2006, les coulisses d'un conflit annoncé* (Paris: Economica, 2010), 131–4. See also Richard Gowan and Alexandra Novosseloff, "Le renforcement de la Force intérimaire des Nations Unies au Liban: Etude des processus décisionnels au sommet," *Annuaire français de relations internationales*, volume XI (2010), 245–67.

39 See UN Security Council meeting, UN doc. S/PV.6075, 23 January 2009, www.un.org/News/Press/docs/2009/sc9583.doc.htm.

40 Statement by the president of the Security Council, Un doc. S/PRST/2009/24, 5 August 2009.

41 See Alexandra Novosseloff, "La professionnalisation du maintien de la paix ou le travail de Sisyphe," *Global Peace Operations Review*, 30 March 2016, http://peaceoperationsreview.org/thematic-essays/la-professionnalisation-du-maintien-de-la-paix-des-nations-unies-ou-le-travail-de-sisyphe/.

42 Statement by François Delattre, Permanent Representative of France to the United Nations, on Security Council peacekeeping, "The Application of the PKO Depends on the Understanding of the Mandates," 20 November 2015.

43 See UN, Leaders' Summit 2015, www.un.org/en/peacekeeping/operations/leadersummit.html.

4   China's doctrine on UN peacekeeping

He Yin[1]

- **China's active participation in UN peacekeeping**
- **Analytical framework**
- **China's peacekeeping doctrine before the twenty-first century**
- **China's peacekeeping doctrine in the twenty-first century**
- **The PLA's understanding of UN peacekeeping**
- **Conclusion**

The past four decades have witnessed China's increasingly active participation in United Nations Peacekeeping Operations (UN PKOs). The existing literature on China's participation has two features. First, it has largely focused on the country's changing attitude towards UN peacekeeping and the reasons behind these changes.[2] Few researchers have examined in depth the doctrine that guides China's peacekeeping behavior. An analysis of China's peacekeeping doctrine can help understand its participation in UN peacekeeping affairs from a special perspective. Key questions regarding the article may include: Does Beijing have a peacekeeping doctrine, and if it does, what are the contents of the doctrine? Second, in the existing literature most of the writing is limited to policy analysis or review; few researchers have conducted research from a theoretical perspective. This author believes that an analysis of Beijing's peacekeeping doctrine from such a perspective can help understand China's participation in UN peacekeeping.

A member state's doctrine on UN peacekeeping usually consists of two pillars: policy doctrine and operational doctrine. The former serves as policy guidance for the state's participation in UN peacekeeping while the latter serves as operational guidance for the state's peacekeeping activities. However, distinct from some other member states, who tend to regard UN peacekeeping mostly as a military problem, China regards it as a political issue. In other words, it is policy doctrine rather than operational doctrine that guides China's peacekeeping behavior. In fact, according to the information that this author has obtained, the People's Liberation Army (PLA) has not issued an explicit operational doctrine on UN peacekeeping. Therefore, this chapter chooses to analyze China's doctrine mainly from a policy angle. Nevertheless, it also makes efforts to discuss the PLA's understanding of UN peacekeeping.

The first section of the chapter introduces the facts and figures regarding China's current active participation in UN peacekeeping. The second presents an analytical framework, proposing an examination of China's doctrine through describing its international identities in different historical eras since its return to the UN system in 1971. The third section discusses China's peacekeeping doctrine before the twenty-first century. The fourth section analyzes China's peacekeeping doctrine in the twenty-first century. The fifth section discusses the PLA's understanding of peacekeeping. The last section concludes this chapter.

China's active participation in UN peacekeeping

There are many reasons to believe that present-day China is an active peacekeeper. As of 30 April 2016, China had 3,042 peacekeepers, including 2,833 troops, 28 UN military experts on mission (UNMEM) and 171 police officers, in 10 of the 16 ongoing UN PKOs (see Table 4.1). China ranked number eight among the 123 troop- and police-contributing countries (TPCCs) and number one among the five UN Security Council (UNSC) permanent members in terms of the contribution of personnel.[3] So far China has contributed a total of more than 33,000 military and police peacekeepers to UN-commanded PKOs and special political missions.[4]

In December 2013, China for the first time deployed a security company to a UN PKO, the UN Multidimensional Integrated Stabilization Mission in Mali (MINUSMA). More significantly, in 2015 it deployed a 700-person infantry battalion to the UN Mission in South Sudan (UNMISS).[5]

China is now the second largest UN peacekeeping budget contributor among all the 193 UN member states as well as the largest UN peacekeeping budget contributor among the developing countries. Its assessment rate in contribution to UN peacekeeping in 2016 is 10.2855 percent. China has also invested heavily in setting up peacekeeping training facilities. Both the Chinese military and police forces have their own peacekeeping training centers,[6] which serve as venues not only for training of Chinese peacekeeping personnel but also for relevant international cooperation activities.

Table 4.1 China's contribution of peacekeeping personnel to ongoing UN PKOs, as of 30 April 2016

Operations	Host country	Police	Military experts on mission	Troops	Total
MINURSO	Western Sahara		10		10
MINUSMA	Mali			402	402
MON-USCO	DRC		13	221	234
UNAMID	Darfur, Sudan			235	235
UNIFIL	Lebanon		10	408	418
UNFICYP		6			6
UNMIL	Liberia	152	2	512	666
UNMISS	South Sudan	13	3	1,045	1,061
UNOCI	Cote d'Ivoire		6		6
UNTSO	Middle East		4		4
Total		**171**	**48**	**2,823**	**3,042**

Source: UN Department of Peacekeeping Operations and Department of Field Support, "UN Mission's Summary Detailed by Country," 30 April 2016, http://www.un.org/en/pea cekeeping/contributors/2016/apr16_3.pdf.

Today's China is becoming increasingly active in participating in international affairs regarding peace and security. It has nominated special representatives for hotspot regions like Africa and the Middle East. Beijing was believed to have played an important role in per-suading Sudan to accept UN peacekeeping in 2006.[7] Working together with their international colleagues including those from the United States and Europe, the Chinese special representatives and minister of foreign affairs have made significant contributions to the peace process in South Sudan, Darfur in Sudan, the eastern part of the Democratic Republic of the Congo (DRC), Mali, Afghanistan, and the Middle East.[8] Besides, China has given strong support to UNSC Resolution 1816, which calls for international efforts to fight pirate activities in the Gulf of Aden. It has deployed People's Liberation Army Navy (PLAN) ships to conduct escort missions in the region's international waters since 2008. On 4 January 2014, China sent the frigate Yancheng to join the international escort mission for the disposal of Syrian chemical weapons in response to appeals from the UNSC and the Organisation for the Prohibition of Chemical Weapons (OPCW).[9]

Most significantly, on 28 September 2015, in his statement at the General Debate of the 70th Session of the UN General Assembly and remarks at the UN Peacekeeping Summit respectively, Chinese president Xi Jinping announced six important measures to support the improvement and strengthening of UN PKOs:

> First, China will join the new UN peacekeeping Capability Readiness System and set up a permanent peacekeeping police squad and build a peacekeeping standby force of 8,000 troops. Second, China will give favorable consideration to UN requests for more Chinese engineering soldiers and transportation and medical staff to take part in UN PKOs. Third, in the coming five years, China will train 2,000 peacekeepers from other countries, and carry out 10 demining assistance programs which will include training and equipment provision. Fourth, in the coming five years, China will provide free military aid of US$100 million to the African Union to support the building of the African Standby Force and the African Capacity for Immediate Response to Crisis. Fifth, China will send the first peacekeeping helicopter squad to UN PKOs in Africa. Sixth, China will establish a 10-year, US$1 billion China-UN peace and development fund to support the UN's work, advance multilateral cooperation and contribute more to world peace and development. Part of the fund will be used to support UN PKOs.[10]

Analytical framework

A state's peacekeeping doctrine consists of a set of policy guidelines and principles that guide and regulate its peacekeeping behavior, as does China's. Although some researchers have already discussed a few doctrinal elements of China's peacekeeping policy,[11] including the "responsibility to protect" (R2P) issue,[12] so far few have gone in depth to examine China's overall peacekeeping doctrine, which this author believes can present a special angle on China's role in UN peacekeeping.

Furthermore, so far most writings on China's participation in UN peacekeeping are about policy analysis or review. Basing their research on policy analysis, many researchers believe that China's current policy of increasingly active participation in UN peacekeeping is largely driven by a long list of pragmatic needs or interests ranging from "multilateralism and image building to more traditional concerns such as isolating Taiwan and securing its investments."[13] According to these authors, China's peacekeeping doctrine is the result of a reactive response to these pragmatic needs or interests.

One cannot deny that national interests, including immediate ones, can shape a state's doctrine of international behavior. However, one will also find it hard to believe that a realism-oriented policy analysis approach can show the full picture of China as an active peacekeeper, in particular, the dynamics of a rising China's evolving peacekeeping doctrine. In fact, many arguments based on policy analysis are easy to refute. For example, some point to South Sudan and argue that China's participation in UN peacekeeping is driven by its increasing need for natural resources such as oil.[14] However, this kind of argument is questionable because China has also deployed many troops to UN PKOs in places like Darfur, Mali, Lebanon, and Haiti, where there are not many natural resources at all. Some also argue that Beijing's one-China policy is a key factor affecting the country's peacekeeping behavior.[15] However, as is shown in its continuous support to the UN peacekeeping efforts in Haiti, a poverty-stricken Caribbean state that has long adopted a pro-Taiwan policy, Beijing has a peacekeeping strategy beyond the "Taiwan Question." In sum, although traditional approaches highlight some motivations for China's peacekeeping behavior, a policy-analysis approach does not help us understand China's peacekeeping strategy.

This chapter adopts a theoretical approach to analyze China's peacekeeping doctrine. It explores the key variable that affects China's peacekeeping behavior. As mentioned above, China's attitude towards UN peacekeeping has kept changing over the past decades, which means China's peacekeeping doctrine is not static; instead, it has been evolving over time. What is worth noting is that since the People's Republic of China was admitted into the UN and assumed its seat as a veto-wielding permanent member of the UNSC, it has been increasingly integrated into the international community. Also, since its adoption of the reform and opening-up policy at the end of the 1970s, China's power has increased dramatically, and so has its status in the international community. Starting from these assumptions, this author argues that the changes in China's international identity have led to changes in its foreign policy doctrine, including that on peacekeeping.

China's changing international identity provides a new angle for understanding the country's peacekeeping doctrine. In this chapter, the concept of "identity" is based on but not limited to that in the constructivist literature. Distinct from what some constructivists believe is a shared culture—largely unaffected by material factors—identity here is conceptualized as being affected by both ideational and material factors. Although the chapter does not take a purely theoretical stance, it adopts an eclectic analytical framework which draws theoretical support from mainstream IR meta-theoretical approaches, including realism, institutionalism, and constructivism. To be more specific, China's international identity is mainly affected by three factors: the country's national strength, its participation in the international institution regime, and its socialization within the international community.

China's peacekeeping doctrine before the twenty-first century

Significant political, military, and social change tend to generate shifts in a state's national identity.[16] In general, since 1971 China's national identity has undergone three phases of development: from semi-revolutionary in the 1970s, to a normal member of the international community in the 1980s and 1990s, to a rising power in the twenty-first century. This section examines China's international identity and corresponding peacekeeping doctrine in the first two phases. The next section examines China's international identity in the twenty-first century and the corresponding peacekeeping doctrine in depth. Although so far neither the Chinese Government nor the PLA has issued any specific policy paper to explain their doctrine on peacekeeping, one can gain a general understanding of their doctrine on peacekeeping by interpreting their words and deeds, including official documents, public announcements, and peacekeeping behavior.

In the 1970s, China was to some degree a revolutionary state, which kept a skeptical eye on the existing international institutional system.[17] Although returning to the UN in 1971 and gradually improving relations with the Western powers in the wake of Richard Nixon's historic visit in 1972, China's international outlook did not change significantly. It continued to regard itself as a victim of the imperialist behavior of the two superpowers—the United States (as well as the other Western capitalist powers) and the Soviet Union—as it did in the 1960s, and identified itself with the Third World.[18] During this period, revolution and struggle were the banners of China's diplomacy. China wished to fulfill its international moral responsibility towards other Third World countries by strictly adhering to the Westphalian norms of state sovereignty and nonintervention. As a result, it condemned and opposed the creation and continuation of all UN PKOs, refused to share the burden of the peacekeeping budget or contribute personnel to ongoing operations, and abstained from UNSC voting.[19] The PLA was preoccupied with its traditional task of safeguarding China's territorial integrity and had no interest in international operations like peacekeeping.

In the 1980s and 1990s, as China sought to become a normal member of the international community, it began to selectively embrace UN peacekeeping. Beijing's adoption of a policy of reform and opening up at the end of the 1970s shifted its focus of attention from domestic as well as international revolution to development, especially economic development. After China established diplomatic relations with the major Western countries, especially the United States, its international security environment greatly improved,[20] which enabled it to allocate limited resources towards development-oriented reform and an opening-up strategy. This in turn improved China's international status and self-confidence in addressing international affairs. During the 12th National Congress of the Communist Party of China (CPC) held in 1982, an "independent foreign policy of peace" (*duli zizhu de heping waijiao zhengce*) was formulated, which marked the fact that China effectively abandoned its ideological disagreement with the West, and was determined to seek peaceful coexistence.[21] China's adoption of the independent foreign policy of peace showed its pragmatic strategy of integrating into the international community and its willingness to become a normal member. Despite changes in both the international and domestic environment, Beijing largely stuck to this strategy throughout 1980s and 1990s. To become a normal member, China needed to make good use of its limited domestic and international resources. Being a veto-wielding permanent member in the UNSC, China found that its policy on UN peacekeeping, if well designed, could generate precious political capital for its integration into the international community. As a result, Beijing gradually accepted the concept of UN peacekeeping.

First, China adjusted its attitude towards UN peacekeeping by providing financial support for UN PKOs and by participating in UNSC voting. In 1981, China for the first time voted in the council, in favor of Resolution 495, which extended the ongoing UN Peacekeeping Force in Cyprus (UNFICYP). In 1982, China began to pay its dues for peacekeeping. Then, it began to show interest in participating in UN peacekeeping. In November 1988, China joined the UN Special Peacekeeping Committee. Five months later, Ambassador Yu Mengjia, in an unprecedented move, called on the international community to give "powerful support" to UN peacekeeping. Finally, in 1990, China became a peacekeeper by deploying five military observers to the UN Truce Supervision Organization (UNTSO) in the Middle East.

China's peacekeeping doctrine in 1980s and 1990s largely reflected a balance between its traditional normative position and pragmatic concerns for its national interests, in particular, those regarding its strategy of attempting to be accepted as a normal member of the international community. Therefore, Beijing had two major considerations regarding peacekeeping doctrine: on one hand, it needed to uphold its political position on the Westphalian norms of state sovereignty and non-intervention, and on the other it was aware that non-obstructionist behavior could yield much-needed political and diplomatic gains.[22]

During this period, especially in the 1990s, driven by the strategy of integrating into the international community, it had shown a certain degree of flexibility regarding peacekeeping doctrine, in particular on the use of force. Thirty-six UN PKOs were established between 1988 and 1998. China voted in favor of all operations that carried out traditional peacekeeping tasks and all peacebuilding operations as well as the continuation of all ongoing traditional UN PKOs that were established during the Cold War era. At the same time, it did not veto any peace enforcement missions. Most notably, in November 1990 China chose abstention rather than a veto during the voting on UNSC Resolution 678, which authorized member states to use "all necessary means" to restore international peace and security in Kuwait. Moreover, in the early 1990s, China voted in favor of all peace operations in Somalia, including the UN Operation in Somalia II (UNOSOM II), which was adopted with a peace enforcement mandate under Chapter VII of the UN Charter. Of course, it should be noted that occasionally China also blocked UN peacekeeping efforts in countries that openly challenged its core interests in the Taiwan Question, as it did in the cases of Guatemala in 1997 and Macedonia in 1999.[23]

China's peacekeeping doctrine in the twenty-first century

China is a rising power in the twenty-first century. It has a peace-keeping doctrine increasingly aligned with other member states, which fits into its strategy for peaceful rise. China's low-profile strategy of becoming a normal member of the international community in 1980s and 1990s paid off. Continuous adoption of the development-oriented policy, increasing socialization into the international community, and active participation within the international institutional regime have all contributed to growing national strength and confidence, which have encouraged China to find a new identity for itself. As early as 1999, former premier Zhu Rongji declared that China wanted to be a "responsible power."

Entering the twenty-first century, China's further integration into the global economy, marked by its participation in the World Trade Organization, among other factors, secured the prospect of continuous high-speed economic growth. In 2003, Zheng Bijian, then executive vice-president of the Party School of the CPC Central Committee, introduced the concept of "peaceful rise" at the Boao Forum for Asia. In September 2005, while addressing an audience of state leaders from around the world at the UN headquarters in New York, Chinese President Hu Jintao called for a "harmonious world." If the pronouncements of "responsible power" and "peaceful rise" can be interpreted as China's changing perception of its international identity—from a normal member to a rising power—then, Hu's "harmonious world" can be understood as the rising power's confident proposal regarding international order. These pronouncements were met with some degree of acceptance from abroad. A few days after Hu's UN summit speech, then US deputy-secretary of state Robert B. Zoellick proposed the idea of China being a "stakeholder." Zoellick pointed out in a speech to the National Committee on US-China Relations: "It is time to take our policy beyond opening doors to China's membership into the international system: we need to urge China to become a responsible stakeholder in that system."[24]

China's new identity of a rising power defines its interests in and shapes its doctrine on peacekeeping. UN peacekeeping has three core principles—consent, impartiality, and non-use of force—which China believes are "fundamental to winning the confidence and support of Member States for peacekeeping operations and ensuring their smooth conduct."[25] Although today's China still insists that peacekeeping should adhere to these principles, some changes have taken place to its position on them. Moreover, entering the twenty-first century, the post-Westphalian interventionist concept of R2P, promoted mostly by Western countries, has begun to challenge many non-Western states' traditional position on these fundamental principles. An analysis of China's understanding of both the three principles and R2P presents a general picture of the country's doctrine on UN peacekeeping.

Consent

China insists that the consent of a host country is a prerequisite to establishing a UN PKO. This stance is in concord with its traditional position on Westphalian norms of state sovereignty and noninterference. If a host country has consented to host a PKO, Beijing will usually not only show its support for the authorizing UNSC resolution but also contribute peacekeepers.

China is also aware that sometimes consent may not be obtained without effort. However, Beijing is against the threat or use of sanctions and force; it prefers noncoercive means, like persuasion and influence. China is believed to have joined the international community in persuading Sudan, South Sudan, the DRC, and Syria to accept UN peacekeeping or cooperate with the UN in recent years.[26]

Impartiality

China insists that the principle of impartiality should be abided by in peace efforts by the international community: "The international community should adhere to the principle of 'impartiality, objectiveness and neutrality' . . . refrain from interfering in local political disputes or impeding the peace process."[27] As Ambassador Wang Min warns: "Any practice that deviates from or weakens [the guiding principles of peacekeeping] will hamper the operation's impartiality and objectivity and, worse yet, could transform the United Nations into a party to conflict, thereby undermining the conflict resolution efforts of the international community."[28]

Beijing is very wary of a regime change agenda. For example, it abstained when the UNSC voted on Resolution 1973, which decided to establish a "no-fly zone" over Libya to "help protect the civilians."[29] China had serious reservations concerning some contents of the resolution due to concern that it might be abused by some countries to legitimize the use of force in violation of Libya's sovereignty.[30] Later, NATO-led multinational forces distorted Resolution 1973 as a green light to launch air strikes against Libya and brought about regime change. Having learned a lesson from Libya, China became extremely cautious of the West's regime change impulse. When Beijing perceived that some Western states intended to support Syrian opposition forces and force the Assad government to relinquish power, it showed strong opposition without hesitation. In June 2012, during Russian president Vladimir Putin's visit to China, Beijing and Moscow issued a joint statement reiterating that the Syria crisis should be resolved in an impartial and peaceful way: The two countries "strongly oppose[d] any attempt to impose a regime change in the insurgency-ridden country."[31] On 22 May 2014, when the UNSC voted on a French-drafted resolution referring the situation in Syria to the International Criminal Court (ICC), China joined Russia in vetoing the draft resolution. Foreign Ministry spokesman Hong Lei said during a press conference:

> With regard to the Syrian issue, what the international community should do now is to stay committed to the Syrian issue through political means, strive to realize a ceasefire and cessation of

violence, improve the humanitarian situation, and encourage the two parties in Syria to pursue a "middle way" that is consistent with Syria's national conditions and accommodates interests of all parties through Geneva talks in particular.[32]

Being a rising power, China practices the principle of impartiality with flexibility. That is, on one hand, Beijing maintains that the internal affairs of these three states should not be interfered with. On the other hand, it is willing to play an active role in these countries' peace processes through different means, including engaging with opposition parties.

In early June 2011, China confirmed that its ambassador to Qatar, Zhang Zhiliang, had met with the chairman of Libya's National Transitional Council, Mustafa Abdel Jalil.[33] One retired Chinese diplomat noted that China's engagement with the Libyan opposition leader before the fall of Gaddafi's government showed a high degree of flexibility in its principle of nonintervention.[34] Ambassador Zhong Jianhua, the special representative of the Chinese government on African affairs, has had talks with South Sudan's opposition forces since 2012.[35] On 5 February 2013, the Chinese ambassador to Egypt, Song Aiguo, met with Syrian National Coalition for Opposition and Revolutionary Forces chairman Ahmed Moaz Al-khatib in Cairo.[36] Chinese Foreign Ministry spokesperson Hua Chunying noted during a press conference: "What is the core is that we should push both sides in Syria to blaze a 'middle way' by keeping in mind Syria's national conditions and the interests of all parties."[37] When asked to confirm the report about an Afghan Taliban delegation's visit to Beijing in late November 2014, another Chinese foreign spokesperson, Hong Lei, said:

> As a friendly neighbor of Afghanistan, China attaches great importance to developing relations with Afghanistan, hopes to see Afghanistan achieve lasting peace, stability and development at an early date, supports the "Afghan-owned" process towards peace and reconciliation and wishes to play a constructive role to that end.[38]

Non-use of force

China maintains that peaceful settlement of international disputes and non-use of force in international relations is an important principle of the UN Charter and a basic norm of international law. It opposes the threat or use of force in international relations.[39] Nevertheless, Beijing does not rule out the necessity of using force under exceptional circumstances. It insists that use of force should meet two basic requirements: "one is the authorization of the UNSC, the other for the purpose of self-defence or defence of the mandate." Moreover, "it advocates whether to use force or not should be decided by the UNSC in light of the reality of conflicts on a case-by-case basis."[40]

In practice, China's peacekeeping doctrine regarding non-use of force is mainly reflected in its voting behavior in the UNSC as well as in its contribution of peacekeepers to UN PKOs. In the UNSC, as long as there is an invitation or acquiesce from the host country, China will usually vote in favor of the establishment of new UN PKO or the continuation of an existing one, even if mandated under Chapter VII. It has supported the establishment of robust UN PKOs in places including the DRC, Haiti, southern Sudan (later the state of South Sudan), Darfur, Chad, and Mali. At the same time, Beijing does not believe in a "victor's peace," and keeps a cautious eye on peace enforcement attempts by some UN member states, most notably the United States and its Western allies. Along with other key UN member states, such as France, Russia, and Germany, China stood against the American attempt to apply for UNSC authorization of peace enforcement in Iraq in 2003. It also opposed the threat or use of sanctions and force against Sudan, Zimbabwe, and Myanmar. In relation to Myanmar, in 2007 Beijing even resorted to a rarely used veto in the UNSC to block US- and UK-backed draft resolutions[41] that might have given a green light to a Western-led enforcement action on the long-sanctioned state. Beijing insists that sanctions cannot help solve the problems in Myanmar. More importantly, it believes that international intervention may lead to a deterioration of conditions in its poverty-stricken neighbor,[42] and endanger China's geopolitical and economic interests.[43]

The international community has long expected China to contribute "combat troops" to UN PKOs.[44] During the 1990s, China did not contribute any armed peacekeepers. However, this has changed in the twenty-first century. In January 2000, China began to deploy civilian police officers to the UN Transitional Administration in East Timor (UNTAET). As UNTAET was a Chapter VII mission, UN civilian police officers were authorized to carry handguns and could use force when their law enforcement mandate deemed it necessary. In 2004, China deployed a 125-person formed police unit (FPU) to the UN Stabilization Mission in Haiti (MINUSTAH). According to the authorization from the UNSC, the Chinese FPUs carried not only nonlethal weapons—such as batons, shields, pepper sprays, and water canon—but also lethal ones, including short guns, rifles, sniper guns, and light machine guns. During its six-year mission in Haiti, the Chinese FPU performed various public control duties including combat ones. More significantly, China's contribution of a 135-person security company and a 700-person infantry battalion to MINUSMA and UNMISS respectively shows that although in the twenty-first century the rising power still has concerns regarding the use of force, it no longer minds being directly engaged in the use of force in UN-commanded PKOs when there is UNSC authorization.

R2P

China's position on the above-mentioned three fundamental principles is also well reflected in its attitude towards R2P. Although Beijing has in principle endorsed R2P by supporting the 2005 World Summit Outcome, it has never accepted the interventionism embodied in the concept. According to the 2005 World Summit Outcome, R2P has three pillars:

Pillar One: Each individual state has a responsibility to protect its population from mass atrocities.
Pillar Two: The international community has a responsibility to assist the state to protect its population.
Pillar Three: If the state fails to protect its citizens from mass atrocities and peaceful measures have failed, the international community has the responsibility to intervene through coercive measures. But military intervention is the last resort.[45]

China insists that most of the weight of R2P should fall on Pillar One. It is concerned that R2P may serve as a sharp tool for the West, which prefers Pillars Two and Three, to skip the consent of host countries and penetrate the wall of traditional sovereignty.[46] On 24 July 2009, the Chinese ambassador to the UN, Liu Zhenmin, made a statement at the plenary session of the General Assembly on the question of R2P, insisting that:

> [t]he government of a given state bears the primary responsibility for protecting its citizens. The international community can provide assistance, but the protection of the citizens ultimately depends on the government of the state concerned ... there must not be any wavering over the principles of respecting state sovereignty and non-interference of internal affairs ... it is necessary to prevent "R2P" from becoming another version of "humanitarian intervention."[47]

According to one Chinese veteran diplomat, the government regards R2P as a concept or a good wish, which solely has significance as political morality.[48] Nevertheless, China has not adopted a rigid policy on R2P that would rule out international intervention under any circumstances. It does recognize that the concept of R2P can apply to the four international crimes of "genocide, war crime, ethnic cleansing, and crimes against humanity."[49] Moreover, China insists that implementation of R2P should strictly abide by three principles: (1) Intervention is a last resort, (2) the authority of relevant UNSC resolutions should be respected, and (3) the implementing party (when it is not the UN itself) should regularly report to the UNSC.[50] Whenever it involves enforcement actions, there should be more prudence in the consideration of each case.[51]

One major concern of the supporters of R2P is with the concept of the protection of civilians (PoC). As is shown in China's support to the UN guiding principles on the use of force, which makes it clear that force can be used only as a last resort in implementation of a PKO mandate authorized by the UNSC under Chapter VII, China basically agrees to the concept PoC. However, as Sarah Teitt points out, "China prefers political rather than coercive solutions, and accepts the use of force for civilian protection purposes only as a last resort and after the consent of the parties to the conflict has been secured."[52] Moreover, when coercive solutions like sanctions or use of force are necessary, Beijing insists that they should be authorized by the UNSC. In a statement at a UNSC open debate on PoC in armed conflict, Chinese ambassador Wang Min stated:

> [W]hen considering a protection-of-civilians mandate for a peace-keeping operation, it is crucial to respect fundamental principles, such as the consent of host countries ... [peacekeeping operations] should ... respect the sovereignty of the host country, ensure objectivity and impartiality and avoid becoming a party to the conflict.[53]

In recent years, the Chinese academic community has also begun to discuss R2P. In 2012, Ruan Zongze coined the concept of *responsible protection* (RP) *vis-à-vis* R2P.[54] RP has six elements:

Element One: Any intervention should protect innocent civilians in the country concerned as well as regional peace and stability, rather than specific political factions or armed forces.
Element Two: The UN Security Council is the only body with the legitimacy to implement "humanitarian intervention".

Element Three: The necessary precondition for the implementation of force must be that all diplomatic and political means of settlement have been exhausted.
Element Four: The goal of protection should be to prevent or alleviate a humanitarian disaster, rather than the overthrow of a government.
Element Five: National reconstruction after intervention and protection should be given sustained support.
Element Six: The UN should establish a monitoring mechanism, and an effective evaluation and accountability system.[55]

As the six elements of RP are basically in line with China's official discourse regarding R2P, many international academics regard RP as expressing the Chinese protection approach in relation to R2P.[56] The greatest significance of RP is not how it differs from R2P, but that it symbolizes a turn of China's attitude towards international norms, from passive acceptance or rigid rejection in the past to increasingly active participation in debate. Being a rising power in the twenty-first century China "increasingly sees itself as a norm-shaper and norm-maker with the international system."[57]

The PLA's understanding of UN peacekeeping

In 1990, the PLA for the first time participated in UN peacekeeping by deploying five military observers to UNTSO. However, during in 1990s the PLA only contributed UN military observers (UNMOs) except in the case of Cambodia, where from April 1992 to September 1993 it deployed two 400-person engineering units.[58] In 2003, the PLA deployed a 178-person engineering company to the UN Mission in the Democratic Republic of the Congo (MONUC), which marked the beginning of increasingly active participation in UN peacekeeping in the twenty-first century. However, for more than a decade the PLA had not contributed combat troops—only troops in engineering, transportation, demining, and medical roles.

The PLA, which has more than two million soldiers, is the largest national military force in the world. The international community has long expected the PLA to contribute combat troops to UN peace-keeping. Its deployment of security troops to Mali and South Sudan implies that it will play a more and more active role in UN peacekeeping.

So far the PLA has not issued any doctrinal documents on UN peacekeeping. Nevertheless, in 1998, China for the first time issued a defense white paper, *China's National Defence in 1998*, which uses a few paragraphs to explain China's policy on UN peacekeeping and introduce the PLA's participation in UN peacekeeping.[59] Since then China has issued a defense white paper every two years. The PLA's increasingly active participation in noncombat missions in the twenty-first century has encouraged China to redefine the PLA's missions including military operations other than war (MOOTW). In January 2009, the Ministry of National Defence (MND) issued *The Planning on Capacity Building of PLA's Military Operations other than War*, which imposed clear guidelines, principles, objectives, force scale as well as measures and requirements on the PLA's MOOTW capacity building. In December 2011, The Military Operations Other Than War Research Center was founded at the Academy of Military Sciences.

In March 2013, the MND issued a white paper called *The Diversified Employment of China's Armed Forces*, which for the first time systematically explained the PLA's missions in the twenty-first century.[60] It states that the PLA has diversified its missions to include defending national sovereignty, security and territorial integrity, supporting national economic and social development, and safeguarding world peace and regional stability. It explains that the PLA should assume its due international responsibilities, and play an active role in maintaining world peace, security, and stability.[61] Regarding the legal issues of the PLA's MOOTW, the white paper states: "On the basis of the UN Charter and other universally recognized norms of international relations, they [the PLA] consistently operate within the legal framework formed by bilateral or multi-lateral treaties and agreements, so as to ensure the legitimacy of their operations involving foreign countries or militaries."[62]

At the operational level, the PLA's deployment of a security company to Mali and an infantry battalion to South Sudan shows that Chinese military forces are willing to carry on security tasks in UN peacekeeping. When mandated by the UN, the PLA peacekeepers will accept the necessity of using force to fulfill their peacekeeping tasks. On 25 September 2014, MND spokesperson Geng Yansheng said in a press conference:

> The United Nations' Security Council resolution authorizes the United Nations Mission in South Sudan to take the protection of civilians, UN employees and humanitarian workers as one of its main tasks. The Chinese peacekeeping troops will strictly abide by the international law and stick to their mandate. They will provide protection to the local people and other countries' personnel engaged in such peaceful activities as peacekeeping, humanitarian assistance and economic development in the area to the best of

their ability. And their actions will be taken as required by the situation, or upon the instruction from the headquarters of the mission, and they will also follow the rule of engagement.[63]

Nevertheless, the spokesperson also emphasized that it is not accurate to call the Chinese peacekeeping infantry battalion to South Sudan "combat troops": "The peacekeeping infantry battalion, called security troops by the UN, is tasked to implement security and protection, rather than to carry out traditional combat tasks. ... The UN peacekeeping troops will not get directly involved in the armed conflicts of the mission country."[64]

Conclusion

Since China's return to the UN, great changes have taken place to the country's international identity. China's peacekeeping doctrine has been changing accordingly. In the 1970s, China was to some degree a revolutionary state. It had very negative views on UN peacekeeping. In the 1980s and 1990s, China identified itself as a normal member of the international community. Its position in the UN peacekeeping regime was used to foster its integration into the international community. However, constrained by limited strength and influence, China was busy adapting to the changing international environment during these decades, in particular in the early 1990s. As a result, China adopted a peacekeeping doctrine which could balance a traditional stance on Westphalian norms with pragmatic concern for its relations with the international community. Occasionally, China showed flexibility in the three peacekeeping principles when reacting to calls for cooperation from the international community, in particular, from the Western powers. Its peacekeeping doctrine in the 1980s and 1990s could be characterized as "reactive cooperation."

China is a rising power in the twenty-first century. Backed with enhanced national strength, improved international status and accumulated knowledge about the international community, including the UN peacekeeping regime, China is increasingly aware of its rights and responsibilities as a rising power. In other words, China needs a peacekeeping doctrine in concord with its strategy of peaceful rise. The doctrine should serve its strategic interests in being a responsible power and building a peaceful international environment. Therefore, instead of playing a reactive or passive role in UN peacekeeping, as it did in the 1980s and 1990s, today's China is playing an active or sometimes even proactive role in UN peacekeeping. China's peacekeeping doctrine in the twenty-first century can be characterized as "active participation."

Its increasingly active participation, for example, its recent deployment of security troops to Africa in particular, shows that at the operational level, the PLA is willing to accept protection tasks in UN-commanded PKOs. When necessary, PLA peacekeepers will be ready to use force as long as it is authorized by their mandate.

On 1 June 2016, terrorists attacked the barracks of the Chinese peacekeeping security company located in Gao, Mali with a vehicle bomb, leading to the death of one Chinese peacekeeper and four injuries. A few weeks later, on 10 July, another two Chinese peacekeepers were killed and five more injured in a mortar exchange between the government forces and the rebel army in Juba, South Sudan. In both cases the Chinese peacekeepers acted according to the respective rules of engagement of the two PKOs and refrained from overreaction. Most notably, the Mali attack has aroused heated discussion among the Chinese public on counter-terrorism in UN peacekeeping. However, China is unlikely to give a green light to any PKOs with a counter-terrorism mandate because it is aware that the UN lacks both the capabilities and political will to implement it. A counter-terrorism mandate in PKOs will result in more casualties and injuries of peacekeepers.[65]

Beijing has not shown any intention to withdraw troops from Mali or South Sudan after the attacks. On the contrary, it is going to deploy a 140-person PLA air unit with four multifunctional helicopters in the African Union/United Nations Hybrid Operation in Darfur (UNAMID) very soon. Apparently, a rising China is determined to be an active UN peacekeeper in spite of increasing fatalities among and injuries to Chinese peacekeepers.

Given the changing nature of conflicts and disputes in recent years, the concept and practices of peacekeeping operations have displayed new trends and characteristics.[66] UN peacekeeping is at a crossroads where the traditional principles of peacekeeping are faced with challenges of post-Westphalian norms of limited state sovereignty and interventionism. As an active peacekeeper as well as a rising power, China has its own distinct peacekeeping doctrine. In the twenty-first century this will not only affect the development of UN peacekeeping doctrine but also influence world politics.

Notes

1 He Yin, PhD, is associate professor at the China Peacekeeping Police Training Center (CPPTC) of the Chinese People's Armed Police Forces

Academy. The views expressed here are the author's personal opinions. They do not represent the views of the CPPTC or the Chinese Ministry of Public Security. This research was supported by the China National Social Sciences Fund (15BFX187).

2 He Yin, "China's Changing Policy on UN Peacekeeping Operations," Asia Paper, Institute for Security & Development Policy, Stockholm, July 2007; Stefan Stahle, "China's Shifting Attitude towards United Nations Peace-keeping Operations," *The China Quarterly*, no. 195 (2008): 631–55; Bates Gill and Huang Chin-Hao, "China's Expanding Role in Peacekeeping: Prospects and Policy Implications," SIPRI Policy Paper 25, Stockholm International Peace Research Institute, 2009; International Crisis Group, "China's Growing Role in UN Peacekeeping," *Asia Report* no. 166, Beijing, 2009; and Mac Lanteigne, "China's Peacekeeping Policies in Mali: New Security Thinking or Balancing Europe?" MFC Working Paper no. 11, MFG Research Group, Berlin, 2014.

3 United Nations, "Ranking of Military and Police Contributions to UN Operations," 30 April 2016, www.un.org/en/peacekeeping/contributors/2016/apr16_2.pdf.

4 It should be noted that uniformed personnel, including military observers and police officers, on political missions commanded by the UN Department of Political Affairs are UN peacekeepers too.

5 *Xinhua*, "China to Send 700 Peacekeepers to South Sudan for UN Mission: Defence Ministry," 25 September 2014, http://news.xinhuanet.com/english/china/2014-09/25/c_133672485.htm.

6 In August 2000, the China Peacekeeping CIVPOL Training Center was established in Langfang, Heibei Province and later renamed as the China Peacekeeping Police Training Center (CPPTC). The MND Peacekeeping Center was established in June 2009 in Huairou district, Beijing.

7 International Crisis Group, "China's Growing Role in UN Peacekeeping," 19–22.

8 Interview with an official from the Chinese Ministry of Foreign Affairs, Beijing, 18 June 2014.

9 *Xinhua*, "Chinese Frigate Starts Escort Mission for Chemical Weapons: FM," 8 January 2014, http://news.xinhuanet.com/english/china/2014-01/08/c_133026228.htm.

10 Xi Jinping, "Working Together to Forge a New Partnership of Win-win Cooperation and Create a Community of Shared Future for Mankind," Statement by H.E. Xi Jinping, President of the People's Republic of China at the General Debate of the 70th Session of the UN General Assembly, New York, 28 September 2015, www.fmprc.gov.cn/mfa_eng/zxxx_662805/t1305051.shtml; Xi Jinping, "China is Here for Peace," Remarks by H.E. Xi Jinping of the People's Republic of China at the United Nations Peacekeeping Summit, New York, 28 September 2015, www.fmprc.gov.cn/mfa_eng/topics_665678/xjpdmgjxgsfwbcxlhgcl70znxlfh/t1302562.shtml.

11 He Yin, "China's Changing Policy on UN Peacekeeping Operations"; He Yin, "China-EU Cooperation on UN Peacekeeping: Opportunities and Challenges," in *Europe and China in 21st Century Global Politics: Partnership, Competition, or Co-Evolution?* eds. Frauke Austermann, Wang Xiaoguang and Anastas Vangeli (London: Cambridge Scholars Publishing, 2014), 43–61; International Crisis Group, "China's Growing Role in UN

Peacekeeping"; Bates Gill and Huang Chin-Hao, "China's Expanding Role in Peacekeeping: Prospects and Policy Implications"; and Mac Lanteigne, "China's Peacekeeping Policies in Mali: New Security Thinking or Balancing Europe?"

12 Sarah Teitt, "The Responsibility to Protect and China's Peacekeeping Policy," in *China's Evolving Approach to Peacekeeping*, eds. Marc Lanteigne and Miwa Hirono (New York and London: Routledge, 2011), 56–70; Tiewa Liu, "Responsibility to Protect and Chinese Perspective: China's Attitude towards Libyan Issue as a Case" (baohu de zeren yu zhongguo de shijiao—yi zhongguo dui libiliya de taidu weili), 26 September 2012, www.unachina.org/upload/Attach/default/274269.pdf;   Andrew   Garwood-Gowers, "China's 'Responsible Protection' Concept: Re-interpreting the Responsibility to Protect (R2P) and Military Intervention for Humanitarian Purposes," *Asian Journal of International Law* 6, no. 1 (2016): 89–118.

13 Bates Gill and Huang Chin-Hao, "China's Expanding Role in Peacekeeping: Prospects and Policy Implications," 11.

14 Colum Lynch, "U.N. Peacekeepers to Protect China's Oil Interests in South Sudan," *The Cable*, 16 June 2014, http://foreignpolicy.com/posts/2014/06/16/u-n-peacekeepers-to-protect-chinas-oil-interests-in-south-sudan.

15 International Crisis Group, "China's Growing Role in UN Peacekeeping," 17.

16 Qin Yaqing, "National Identity, Strategic Culture and Security Interests: On Three Hypotheses of the Relations between China and International Society" (guojia shenfen, zhanlue wenhua he anquan liyi: guanyu zhongguo yu guoji shehui guanxi de sange jiashe), in *Power, Institutions, and Culture: Essays on International Relations Theory and Methodology* (qianli zhilu wenhua: guoji guanxi liyu yu fangfa yanjiu wenji), ed. Qin Yaqing (Beijing: Peking University Press, 2005), 351.

17 Compared with the 1960s, China's revolutionist color has already faded a lot due to its engagement with the United States.

18 Yeshi Choedon, "China's Stand on UN Peacekeeping Operations: Changing Priorities of Foreign Policy," *China Report* 41, no. 1 (2015): 39.

19 He Yin, "China-EU Cooperation on UN Peacekeeping: Opportunities and Challenges," 16–17.

20 Kim J. Ilpong, ed., *The Strategic Triangle: China, the United States & the Soviet Union* (Saint Paul, Minn.: Paragon House Publisher, 1987).

21 He Yin, "China-EU Cooperation on UN Peacekeeping: Opportunities and Challenges," 22.

22 Yeshi Choedon, "China's Stand on UN Peacekeeping Operations: Changing Priorities of Foreign Policy."

23 Guatemala has diplomatic relations with Taiwan. It had been active in pushing for Taiwan's membership in the UN. In 1997, China vetoed a UNSC draft resolution to deploy military observers to verify the implementation of ceasefire agreements in Guatemala. Beijing was enraged when Macedonia shifted its recognition from Beijing to Taipei 17 days before the UNSC intended to deliberate upon the extension of the UN Preventive Deployment Force (UNPREDEP) because Taipei promised to provide aid. China vetoed the UNSC draft resolution to extend UNPREDEP.

24 Robert B. Zoellick, "Whither China: From Membership to Responsibility?" 21 September 2005, http://2001-2009.state.gov/s/d/former/zoellick/rem/53682.htm.

25 Chinese Ministry of Foreign Affairs, "Foreign Ministry Spokesperson Hong Lei's Remarks on the UN Security Council's Vote on the Draft Resolution to Refer the Situation in Syria to the International Criminal Court," 23 May 2014, www.fmprc.gov.cn/mfa_eng/xwfw_665399/s2510_665401/t1158923.shtml.

26 Interview with a senior Chinese diplomat, Beijing, 18 June 2014.

27 Chinese Ministry of Foreign Affairs, "Position Paper of the People's Republic of China at the 68th Session of the United Nations General Assembly," 9 September 2013, www.china-embassy.org/eng/zgyw/t1074585.htm.

28 Permanent Mission of the People's Republic of China to the UN, "Statement by Ambassador Wang Min at the Security Council Open Debate on United Nations Peacekeeping Operations," 11 June 2014, www.china-un.org/eng/hyyfy/t1168830.htm.

29 Security Council Resolution 1973, UN doc. S/Res/1973, 17 March 2011.

30 Chinese Ministry of Foreign Affairs, "Foreign Spokeswoman Jiang Yu's Remark on the UNSC Resolution 1973 over Libyan Issue," 18 March 2011, www.fmprc.gov.cn/ce/cekor/chn/fyrth/t807595.htm.

31 *Xinhua*, "China, Russia Urge Impartial, Peaceful Syria Solution," 7 June 2012, http://news.xinhuanet.com/english/china/2012-06/06/c_123245703.htm.

32 Chinese Ministry of Foreign Affairs, "Foreign Ministry Spokesperson Hong Lei's Remarks on the UN Security Council's Vote on the Draft Resolution to Refer the Situation in Syria to the International Criminal Court."

33 *Xinhua*, "China Ready to Receive Libya Opposition NTC Envoys: Diplomat," 9 June 2011, http://news.xinhuanet.com/english2010/china/2011-06/09/c_13919420.htm.

34 Interview with a Chinese ex-diplomat, Langfang, China, 25 May 2016.

35 Interview with Ambassador Zhong Jianhua, Beijing, 12 June 2014.

36 *Xinhua*, "Chinese Ambassador Meets Syrian Opposition Leader in Cairo," 6 February 2013, http://news.xinhuanet.com/english/china/2013-02/06/c_132153328.htm.

37 *Xinhua*, "China Backs UN Syria Mediation," 23 June 2014, http://news.xinhuanet.com/english/china/2014-06/23/c_133431146.htm.

38 Chinese Ministry of Foreign Affairs, "Foreign Ministry Spokesperson Hong Lei's Regular Press Conference on 14 January 2015," January 14, 2015, www.chinaembassy.cz/cze/fyrth/t1228255.htm.

39 Chinese Ministry of Foreign Affairs, "Position Paper of the People's Republic of China on the United Nations Reform," 7 June 2005, www.china-un.org/eng/xw/t199101.htm.

40 Chinese Ministry of Foreign Affairs, "Position Paper of the People's Republic of China on the United Nations Reform."

41 UN News Center, "China and Russia Veto US/UK Backed Security Council Draft Resolution on Myanmar," 12 January 2007, www.un.org/apps/news/story.asp?NewsID=21228&Cr1#.VLEvddKjKlY.

42 Christopher Len and Johan Alvin, "Burma/Myanmar's Ailments: Searching for the Right Remedy," *Silk Road Paper*, Uppsala and Washington, Central Asia-Caucasus Institute (CACI) Silk Road Studies Program (SRSP), March 2007, www.ibiblio.org/obl/docs4/BurmaMyanmar-Len&Alvin.pdf.

43 He Yin, "China's Changing Policy on UN Peacekeeping Operations."

44 International Crisis Group, "China's Growing Role in UN Peacekeeping"; and Bates Gill and Huang Chin-Hao, "China's Expanding Role in Peacekeeping: Prospects and Policy Implications."

45 UN General Assembly, "2005 World Summit Outcome," UN doc. A/60/L.1, 20 September 2005, 31.

46 He Yin, "China-EU Cooperation on UN Peacekeeping: Opportunities and Challenges," 52.

47 Permanent Mission of the People's Republic of China to the UN, "Statement by Ambassador Liu Zhenmin at the Plenary Session of the General Assembly on the Question of Responsibility to Protect," 24 July 2009, www.china-un.org/eng/hyyfy/t575682.htm.

48 Interview with a Chinese veteran diplomat, Langfang, China, 13 December 2012.

49 Permanent Mission of the People's Republic of China to the UN, "Statement by Ambassador Liu Zhenmin at the Plenary Session of the General Assembly on the Question of Responsibility to Protect."

50 Interview with a Chinese veteran diplomat, Langfang, China, 13 December 2012.

51 Chinese Ministry of Foreign Affairs, "Position Paper of the People's Republic of China on the United Nations Reform."

52 Sarah Teitt, "China and the Responsibility to Protect," Asia-Pacific Center for the Responsibility to Protect, 2008, http://responsibilitytoprotect.org/files/China_and_R2P%5B1%5D.pdf.

53 Permanent Mission of the People's Republic of China to the UN, "Statement by Ambassador Wang Min at the Security Council Open Debate on Protection of Civilians in Armed Conflict," 12 February 2013, www.china-un.org/eng/gdxw/t1013938.htm.

54 Ruan Zongze, "Responsible Protection: Building a Safer World," China Institute of International Studies, 15 June 2012, www.ciis.org.cn/english/2012-06/15/content_5090912.htm.

55 Ruan Zongze, "Responsible Protection," *China Daily*, 13 March 2012, http://usa.chinadaily.com.cn/opinion/2012-03/15/content_14838556.htm.

56 Gareth Evans, "From the Responsibility to Protect to Responsible Civilian Protection," *Daily Star*, 28 October 2013; and Ramesh Thakur, "A Chinese Version of 'Responsible Protection'," *Japan Times*, 1 November 2013.

57 Andrew Garwood-Gowers, "China's 'Responsible Protection' Concept: Reinterpreting the Responsibility to Protect (R2P) and Military Intervention for Humanitarian Purposes"; and He Yin, "Norm Competition and Complementation: Peacebuilding as Case Study" (Guifan Jingzheng Yu Hubu: Yi Jianshe Heping Weili), *The World Economics and Politics*, no. 4 (2014): 105–21.

58 Information Office of the State Council, *China's National Defence in 1998*, July 1998, http://eng.mod.gov.cn/Database/WhitePapers/1998.htm.

59 Ibid., 9.

60 Information Office of the State Council, *The Diversified Employment of China's Armed Forces*, 2 April 2013, www.china.org.cn/government/whitepaper/node_7181425.htm.

61 Ibid., 5.

62 Ibid., 7.

63 Ministry of National Defence, "Defence Ministry's Regular Press Conference on September 25, 2014," 25 September 2014, http://eng.mod.gov.cn/Press/2014-09/25/content_4539896.htm.

64 Ibid.

65 He Yin, "100 Peacekeepers Died: What Happened to This State?" (100 Yu Lianheguo Renyuan Gezhong Yuanyin Siwang, Zhege Guojia Zenmela?). 4 June 2016, http://mil.huanqiu.com/observation/2016-06/9008911_2.html.

66 Chinese Ministry of Foreign Affairs, "Foreign Ministry Spokesperson Hong Lei's Remarks on the UN Security Council's Vote on the Draft Resolution to Refer the Situation in Syria to the International Criminal Court," 23 May 2014, www.fmprc.gov.cn/mfa_eng/xwfw_665399/s2510_665401/2535_665405/t1158923.shtml.

5 The Russian perspective on UN peacekeeping

Today and tomorrow

Maxim Bratersky and Alexander Lukin

- Russia and the idea of peacekeeping
- Russian participation in UN peacekeeping
- Russian peacekeeping as policy
- The problem of unrecognized mandates
- Conclusion: Russia's world outlook and recent peacekeeping trends

This chapter discusses the approach of the Russian Federation to United Nations (UN) peacekeeping based on various regional organizations as they functioned at the beginning of the 1990s. Russia, being essentially a status-quo power, supported the traditional UN approach to peacekeeping as well as the procedures on peacekeeping established by the UN Security Council and the Secretariat.

Starting at the end of the decade, international peacekeeping came under the influence of two important trends. First, it became increasingly common for regional organizations or powerful nations acting in coalitions to begin their engagement in peacekeeping operations prior to receiving a mandate from the UN. Either the actors retroactively sought a UN mandate, after an operation had already begun, or they interpreted the mandate in such a way as to allow them to take sides in a conflict, eliminating the need for a mandate all together. The second trend came as the UN reacted to the increase in internal ethnic, religious, and ideological conflicts by modifying mandates to depart from the traditional, nonpartisan nature of its decisions. These developments were seen in Russia as a threat to the existing world order and a challenge to the traditional role of peacekeeping within it, though in some instances the changes were seen as an opportunity to forward Russian security interests.

As these trends are inseparable from discussions of the UN's overall role in world politics, an analysis of how Russia views the evolving role of peacekeeping must begin with a look at how Russia currently views the world and the role of the UN. In this chapter, the discussion is in three sections: the traditional Russian approach to peacekeeping and Russian participation in UN peacekeeping missions; Russian peacekeeping efforts within the framework of non-UN organizations, including the problem of unrecognized mandates; and the adjustment of Russian foreign policy to the realities of peacekeeping in the twenty-first century.

This chapter argues that from the Russian perspective, international peacekeeping is increasingly moving beyond its traditional role as a tool for impartial resolution of conflicts, that it is being used as a foreign policy tool of the great powers, and that it is in this context that we should view Russia's position that UN member-states must strengthen their commitment to finding compromise as a necessary condition for successful international peacekeeping. Similarly, the official Russian demands for the "de-ideologization" of world politics find their concrete expression in Russia's rejection of the use of peacekeeping mandates to topple objectionable regimes and forward the national interests of the United States and its Western allies.

Russia and the idea of peacekeeping

As Russian diplomats have declared on multiple occasions, Russia considers peacekeeping to be one of the main functions of the UN. According to Russian minister of foreign affairs Sergei Lavrov:

> Russia consistently places huge importance on peacekeeping as an important instrument in lessening the level of conflict in international relations and managing the crises which in our turbulent times continue to present a threat to international law and security. … Russia plays and will continue to play an active part in the development of preventative anti-crisis potential of the UN, which includes assigning UN peacekeepers for operations to keep the peace, support peacekeeping operations, and preparing for peacekeeping contingencies.[1]

Russian support for UN peacekeeping activities should be viewed in the context of Russia's broader policy towards the UN. In its vision of the world and the changing world order, Russia attributes enormous importance to the United Nations and the latter's central place in the global political architecture. There are two good reasons for this. First, Russia is by no means a revisionist power. On the contrary, Russia is and has been a status-quo power (some experts would also argue that Russia is a "descending power") and insists on preserving the Yalta–Potsdam international system in its original incarnation.[2]

This is natural, since under conditions of relative weakness in comparison with the United States and its allies, which increasingly see Moscow as a competitor and even opponent, the system of international law established after World War II (WWII) grants Russia the right to preserve its own position. Even the more assertive actions of Russia to defend its own interests, for example in relation to Georgia in 2008 and Ukraine in 2014, should be considered not as revisionist initiatives, but as a reaction to the actions of the West, which, from Moscow's perspective, has gone too far in its efforts to change the status-quo, attempting to bring more and more territory into its sphere of influence. The United Nations has always served as the central pillar of the post-WWII international system, and the Soviet Union (Russia) was guaranteed a central role in the system by its permanent membership on the Security Council, augmented by its veto power.

Another reason for Russia being supportive of the UN's central role in the world system, including its peacekeeping responsibilities, lies in the fact that the current leadership of the Russian Federation in its world outlook stands on the position of realism and sees the world as a competitive arena where nations promote their national interests. Such a vision is in contrast with the liberal world outlook inviting the idea of a world hegemon responsible for preserving stability in the world order. The realist perspective of Russia therefore implies several key assumptions. Most important of these are: the acceptance of the fact that every nation has its national interests, and that nations should seek compromise between their interests; that Russia believes that the United Nations is the key mechanism for seeking compromises among nations and that it is the only institution which could, despite all its problems, make the world political system stable and predictable; and that alternative concepts of the world order are unacceptable. In sum, Russia sees the world without a central role for the UN as dangerous, unpredictable, prone to conflicts, and unfair.

This stance on the UN's world role has always been central to Russian foreign policy, and has been confirmed by all Russian administrations and in all foreign policy documents. The current "Concept of the Foreign Policy of the Russian Federation" of 2013 reads:

> The United Nations should remain the center of international relations and coordination in world politics in the 21st century, as it has proven to have no alternative and also possesses unique

legitimacy. Russia supports the efforts aimed at strengthening the UN's central and coordinating role.[3]

Russia rejects any attempts to reform the UN that risk undermining its central role in the world system. Commenting on the various ideas raised in discussions of UN reform, Russian president Vladimir Putin insisted that:

> we should move toward reform on two main conditions. First— this should be a result of a broad consensus. ... The second compulsory condition is to maintain the fundamental principles of UN efficiency; in particular, the prerogatives and rights of its Security Council.[4]

The Russian vision of the UN's role in international peacekeeping is grounded firmly in its view of the organization's role in world politics more generally. First and foremost, Russia holds that international peacekeeping missions, as a rule, must be sanctioned by the Security Council. To some extent, Russia also accepts the possibility of peacekeeping on the basis of intergovernmental agreements and recognizes the special role that regional organizations often play in initializing peacekeeping missions, but Russia's acknowledgment of this role is based on such organizations acting strictly within the geographic frameworks on which they are based. In other words, according to Russia, a peacekeeping mission should ideally be authorized by the UN. Regional organizations and individual nations also may engage in peacekeeping, but only on the basis of an intergovernmental agreement or on the territory of the members of the organization. Peacekeeping missions outside these legal premises are viewed as in violation of international law.

Russia shares the view that UN peacekeeping operations have not been sufficiently effective and that there is a pressing need for reform in this area. However, Russia also traces the basic reasons behind this crisis in UN peacekeeping not only to organizational failures but, first and foremost, to the attempts of the United States and its Western allies to undermine the leadership role of the UN, and the Security Council in particular, in this and other spheres.

Russia's stance on the West's approach was not always thus. Immediately after the fall of the Union of Soviet Socialist Republics (USSR), Russia began to actively participate in international peacekeeping, fully sharing the goals of the West. The first serious crisis became the peacekeeping operations in the former Yugoslavia, during the course of which, in Moscow's opinion, the United States and the North Atlantic Treaty Organization (NATO) used the Security Council mandate not to end conflict, but to achieve their own political goals: the punishment of the disagreeable Milosevic regime and the breakup first of Yugoslavia, then Serbia. In Russia, this policy led to serious disappointment with the West.

In May of 1999, while NATO bombs were falling on Belgrade, then special representative to the president of Russia for Yugoslavia, former prime minister Viktor Chernomyrdin, wrote:

> During the years of reform, a majority of Russians formed a view of the United States as a genuine democracy, truly concerned about human rights, offering a universal standard worthy of emulation. But just as Soviet tanks trampling on the Prague Spring of 1968 finally shattered the myth of the socialist regime's merits, so the United States lost its moral right to be regarded as a leader of the free democratic world when its bombs shattered the ideals of liberty and democracy in Yugoslavia.[5]

Another serious reason for Russia's disappointment was NATO's abuse of Security Council Resolution 1973 on Libya. Passed in March 2011, it established a no-fly zone and permitted measures for the defense of the peaceful population. However, the forces of the Western powers used the resolution for the complete destruction of the armed forces of one of the sides to the conflict. In essence, the sentiment in Russia was that revisionist governments, first and foremost the United States, themselves were not fulfilling the regulations of the UN Charter, making the peacekeeping operation ineffective.

Criticizing these and similar actions by the United States and its allies, one Russian expert came to the conclusion that:

> towards the middle of the 1990s, the signs of a crisis in the UN's peacekeeping operations became obvious, and the international community began to search for a way out of the crisis. The crisis in UN peacekeeping is deeper than it seems at first glance, its roots can be found not only in the shortcomings of the crisis-reaction system itself, but also in weaknesses in the international legal system as a whole.[6]

These and other situations formed the Russian position on reforming the UN peacekeeping system. This is based on the belief that the formation of active mechanisms for preventing crises, the continuous improvement of peacekeeping practices, and the strengthening of the foundations for both, must take place under conditions of tight coordination with regional organizations, but always with the Security Council playing a central role.

Formulating this position, the assistant director of the Department of International Organizations of the Russian Ministry of Foreign Affairs, Vladimir Zaemskii, wrote:

> A new level of regulations put forth by the world community on the issue of peacekeeping activities, substantially broadened the range of goals and means for their attainment. On one hand, the established methods of peacekeeping have undergone a substantial evolution, on the other, the number of tasks that must be addressed in the course of peacekeeping operations have multiplied exponentially. The variety of forms of modern peacekeeping methods, including with the participation of regional organizations or coalitions, is a natural and necessary development, but what must remain immutable is the lead role of the UN as the only universal organization of its kind, to whose charter all members of the international community are bound to adhere.[7]

From Moscow's perspective, reform must consist of two main components: the perfection of the crisis-reaction mechanism itself (its peacekeeping potential) and the development of clear legal guidelines for the use of force in international relations. In the first instance, Russia calls for realizing a host of new measures, chiefly for heightening the quality of planning and preparation for peacekeeping operations, as well as for greater operational efficiency. The realization of this goal would require, among other things, the creation of well-trained multinational teams of 5,000 people each, which could be deployed to any hotspot in the world within a month. Politically, emphasis should be placed on strict adherence to the operational mandates issued by the Security Council, which for their part must be drafted according to the utmost standards of clarity, must be achievable, and must be backed up by the necessary resources.

Secondly, in Russia's opinion, serious research must be dedicated to improving sanctions regimes. Russia's aim is to have proposed sanctions remain under the consideration of the Security Council not indefinitely, but according to strictly agreed upon periods of time. This would involve a mandatory analysis of the possible humanitarian consequences, with measures generating suffering among the civilian population and negative effects of sanctions on third countries being unacceptable.

Thirdly, Russia continues to press ahead at the UN with its proposal for activating a "Military Staff Committee," which will be possible only through the participation of all permanent members of the Security Council. Finally, Russia supports the expansion of partnership between the UN and regional organizations within the framework of Chapter VIII of the UN Charter. As far as Moscow is concerned, Russia is making progress in this regard, developing coordination between the UN and the Commonwealth of Independent States (CIS) in the area of peacekeeping. Nonetheless, Russia is opposed to the replacement of the UN by regional structures.[8]

As far as the legal aspects of peacekeeping are concerned, Russia underlines the special importance of adhering to the fundamentals of international law as they pertain to peacekeeping, and, first and foremost, in the UN Charter. Russia, for example, has introduced a proposal at the UN on collectively clarifying the legal aspects of the use of force in international relations in the context of a globalizing world. Russia's position is that these legal provisions must not violate the basic principles of sovereignty and the territorial integrity of states. This position is challenged by the constant violation of the Charter by the United States, which defends its actions with theories such as "limited sovereignty," "humanitarian intervention," and the "responsibility to protect," which contradict the principles of territorial integrity and the inviolability of national borders.[9]

Russia, advocating for the necessity of adhering to norms of international law in international relations, calls for giving priority in the use of preventative diplomacy to early warning systems and preventative measures. Speaking at the 54th session of the General Assembly in 1999, Russian minister of foreign affairs Ivan Ivanov warned:

> The founding fathers of the UN envisioned the capability of responding, on a legal basis, to the violation of peace and security. The international community can resort to coercive measures, but this must be done in accordance with the UN Charter and by a decision of the Security Council. Non-legal means can only compromise legal ends. This is precisely the view that informs our understanding of doctrines such as the concept of "humanitarian intervention." We must be exceptionally careful in our approach to any coercive measures, and even more so in not allowing them to become a tool of repression to be used against states or peoples that one or another state finds objectionable.[10]

Russian participation in UN peacekeeping

As the legal successor to the Soviet Union, the Russian Federation inherited the Soviet Union's political assets and responsibilities regarding peacekeeping, including its central role on the Security Council. Russia plays an active role in all council discussions concerning peacekeeping and has taken part in several UN peacekeeping missions.

Since Russia has played a substantial role in the development of UN peacekeeping procedures, there is little disagreement with the key principles developed by the UN concerning such missions: a clear mandate; the consent of the parties to the conflict to a UN intervention and deployment; the impartiality of the missions; and the non-use of force by peacekeepers, except in self-defense and in defense of the mission's mandate. Another principle that Russia does not hold as official, but as a tradition, is nonparticipation of the military contingents of great powers in peacekeeping missions. This tradition originated from the 1974 protocol of the agreement between Israel and Syria and though it has not become official policy, Russia has generally preferred that peacekeeping missions be mostly staffed with military personnel from third countries.

At present, Russia has 80 personnel assigned to UN peacekeeping missions: 13 police officers, 63 military observers, and four troops.[11] This number is lower than average for Russia, which as recently as 2010 had 371 personnel (55 police, 77 military observers, and 239 troops) actively assigned to UN peacekeeping missions. Russian personnel have served with the following missions: the UN Mission for the Referendum in Western Sahara (MINURSO), the UN Mission in the Central African Republic and Chad (MINURCAT), the UN Stabilization Mission in Haiti (MINUSTAH), the UN Operation in Côte d'Ivoire (UNOCI), the UN Mission in the Democratic Republic of the Congo (MONUC), the UN Interim Administration Mission in Kosovo (UNMIK), UN Mission in Liberia (UNMIL), UN Mission in the Sudan (UNMIS), and UN Integrated Mission in East Timor (UNMIT). Russian (at the time Soviet) participation in UN peacekeeping missions dates back to the UN Emergency Forces (UNEF II) mission in 1973, when, after three days of fighting, the first group of Soviet officers arrived in the Middle East and on October 26 received the status of UN military observers.

The largest military contingent ever dispatched by Russia for a UN mission served in the former Yugoslavia. On 6 March 1992, the Supreme Soviet of the Russian Federation passed a resolution sending

900 Russian peacekeepers to Bosnia and Herzegovina, 400 of which were transferred to Kosovo in 1999. In June that year an additional 3,600 Russian troops were sent to Kosovo, where they stayed until July 2003. The most technically equipped mission in which Russia took part was in Sudan in 2006. The Russian contingent there consisted of 120 men and four helicopters.

Russia's contribution to the UN peacekeeping budget is only about 2 percent. According to leading Russian expert Alexander Nikitin, this "reflects the fact that while Russia pays its assessed contributions for UN peacekeeping it does not make significant additional voluntary contributions."[12] At the same time, Russia is the second largest supplier of contractor services: "In 2011, Russian companies held contracts from the UN worth $382 million, which composed 14 percent of UN peacekeeping services; [a]lmost all of this is comprised of aviation transportation services provided by Russian aviation and cargo companies."[13]

Before the mid-1990s, Russian participants in UN peacekeeping operations were trained at the Vystrel Training Center of the Russian Armed Forces Academy in the town of Solnechnogorsk, near Moscow. After that, and until the late 2000s, all military peacekeepers (including those designated for non-UN-mandated regional operations) were trained in the Fifteenth Motorized Infantry Division based near the city of Samara. According to Nikitin, in the late 2000s the training system was reformed again:

> Under these reforms, soldiers eligible for deployment as peacekeepers would be nominated by their division and those designated for joining UN contingents would undergo training in a Ministry of Defence Training Center in Narofominsk, near Moscow. Since June 2005 military cadres from CSTO [the Collective Security Treaty Organization] states became entitled to train and be certified in Russian defence academies and institutions at no cost to their governments. Joint programmes for the training of peacekeepers, anti-terror and anti-drug specialists from all CSTO countries were organized by Russian military academies.[14]

Russian police peacekeepers are trained at the All-Russian Institute for Continuous Education of the Ministry of Interior in the town of Domodedovo, which also provides training for foreign policemen. Thus it trained about 200 police peacekeepers from Africa and 300 policemen from Afghanistan according to an agreement with the UN.[15] The annual budget for peacekeeping operations training accounted for 800 million rubles in 2009, equivalent to US$30–35 million at the time.[16]

Nikitin points out: "Leaving aside the relatively wide geographic presence, one can't fail to point out that the scale of Russian participation in UN peacekeeping is noticeably smaller than what might be expected of a great power with pretensions of playing a global role."[17] By size of contingent participating in UN peacekeeping operations, Russia has historically ranked somewhere between twentieth and fortieth among states, depending on the year in question—significantly lower than the United Kingdom, France, and China, among others. In Nikitin's opinion, the "main factors which limit Russian participation in UN peacekeeping are its domestic situation in the immediate post-Soviet era, its focus on conflict resolution in the post-Soviet space, and tendency to pursue these activities outside the auspices of the UN."[18]

Russian peacekeeping as policy

Russia regularly underlines the special role of regional organizations, which from its perspective must be the core implementers of UN decisions in their respective regions. The major supraregional powers, such as Russia, must act in accordance with these general efforts, not controlling such operations, but assisting and making an important contribution to them. The following two principles give concrete expression to this position.

First, such an approach limits the interference of the United States and its allies (which Russia considers opposed to its interests) in regional conflicts, and likewise does not find the growth in their global influence acceptable. Second, as will be shown below, Russia would like the main actors in post-Soviet space—the region of Russia's traditional influence—to be organizations where Russia plays a leading role, such as the CIS and CSTO.

This position has been stated in multiple statements by leading Russian diplomats. In his closing remarks after meeting with Benjamin Barnaba, the minister of foreign affairs and international partnership of the Republic of South Sudan, in May of 2014, Sergei Lavrov stated that:

> Russia is convinced that the key and leading role in managing various conflicts on the continent must be played by Africans themselves. The African Union and sub-regional organizations on the continent have proven that they are ready to take the initiative and act as peacekeepers, and they deserve all necessary support

from the UN and the Security Council. . . . As far as future con-
flict management is concerned, in Somalia, the Central African
Republic, Mali, the DRC, and the Great Lake Region as a whole,
Russia as a permanent member of the Security Council will con-
tinue to play an important part in peacekeeping on the African
Continent.[19]

The scope of Russia's commitment to deterring and preventing military
conflicts is laid out in Article 19 of the Military Doctrine of the Russian Federation, which calls for Russia "to participate in international
peacekeeping activities, including under the auspices of the United
Nations and within the framework of interaction with international
(regional) organizations."[20] This document serves as an official basis
for Russia's participation in peacekeeping operations undertaken not
only by the UN but by other international (regional) organizations as
well. In addition to its UN commitments, Russia also participates in
peacekeeping efforts on the basis of intergovernmental agreements with
other countries. Russia's first non-UN mandated peacekeeping operations were carried out on the basis of such agreements. The following two
examples of such operations can be considered characteristic of the
Russian approach, and provide a clear picture of the Russian
understanding of the acceptable role and tasks of such activities.

Transdniestria

The first peacekeeping operation carried out by the Russian Federation
took place in Moldavia. Starting in 1989, tensions began to rise
between the nationalist leadership of the Moldavian Soviet Socialist
Republic (and after 1991, the government of the independent Republic
of Moldova) and the Russian-speaking population concentrated in the
Transdniester region, which sought the creation of a separate, Trans-
dniestrian Moldavian Soviet Socialist Republic. In June of 1992, military clashes took place, resulting in casualties among the civilian
population. On July 23, Russia was able to secure the "Agreement on
the Peaceful Resolution of Armed Conflict in Transdniestria," according to which a peacekeeping force was created consisting of units from
the two conflicting sides and Russia. The peacekeeping forces included
12 battalions, six of which were Russian and were responsible for a
secure zone of 220 by 10–20 kilometers.

Responsibility for the coordination of the peacekeeping forces was
given to the so-called "Integrated Control Commission for the Resolution of Armed Conflict in the Transdniester Region," consisting of

six representatives from each of the conflicting parties and six from Russia. The activities of the Russian peacekeepers included the minimal set of measures necessary for the delineation: separating the conflicting parties in the event of tensions, securing weapons stockpiles, and organizing checkpoints and security cordons. Starting in 1992, several attempts were made to find a political resolution to the problem. Towards the end of the year, negotiations were restarted, with Russian mediation, on the question of a special status for Transdniester Region, and the following year the Organization for Security and Cooperation in Europe (OSCE) took over the role of mediator from Russia, to be replaced in 1995 by Ukraine.

In 2003, a proposal was made by Russia to resolve the situation in the form of the so-called "Kozak Memorandum," which called for the integration of Moldova and the Pridnestrovian Moldavian Republic (PMR) on the basis of a new federal Moldovan government. However, the memorandum was never implemented due to fierce contestation from the European Union (EU) and United States. The frozen conflict continues to the present day, creating a serious obstacle to Moldova in its plans for an association agreement with the EU and potential entry into NATO.

South Ossetia

Already in early 1991, the final year of the USSR's existence, the leadership of the Georgian Soviet Socialist Republic attempted to rid the region of South Ossetia of its special status within Georgia. Armed Georgian police units, joined by volunteers, were sent to Tskhinvali, the capital of the autonomous region of South Ossetia, where they were met with armed resistance from the local population. Towards the spring of 1991, it had become obvious that active military engagements between the Ossetian and Georgian formations had ceased, and both sides continued to hold the territory under their control. The fundamental problem in the region became the criminalization of the conflict zone.

With the twin goals of stabilizing the situation and preventing a second flare-up of violence, President Boris Yeltsin of Russia and President Eduard Shevarnadze of Georgia signed the Dagomys Agreements, which provided for the creation of a tripartite peacekeeping force responsible for maintaining law and order and for the settlement of outstanding administrative, agricultural, and economic questions: the Joint Control Commission (JCC). The peacekeeping forces were designed to include three battalions, one each from the armed forces of

Georgia, Russia, and a third drawn from forces under the command of the Russian Autonomous Republic of North Ossetia, which were trusted by the authorities in South Ossetia. The agreement also called for jointly staffed checkpoints along roads, and the general disarmament of the population.

However, the peacekeeping scheme did not go according to plan. Both the Georgian and Ossetian battalions proved to be undisciplined and criminality was widespread, including incidents of gangsterism, looting, and drug trafficking. Under such circumstances, the bulk of the work of maintaining law and order in the region fell to the Russian peacekeeping battalion. Under a somewhat vague mandate to maintain the peace and uphold law and order in the region, Russian peacekeepers essentially served as the primary organ of law-enforcement in South Ossetia where matters of security were concerned.

In 1994, an agreement was reached between the presidents of the member countries of the CIS on the creation of the Collective Peace-Keeping Forces of the CIS (CPKF CIS). On the basis of this agreement, not only Russia but Kyrgyzstan, Kazakhstan, and Tajikistan also pledged to send peacekeeping units to South Ossetia and Abkhazia (another breakaway region of Georgia). Ultimately, these pledges to send peacekeepers to the region were not fulfilled, and Russia remained the only CIS member country with peacekeeping forces in the zone of the Georgian-Ossetian conflict, albeit from then on they were operating in a different official capacity, as forces under the aegis of the CIS. Simultaneously, from December 1992, the OSCE maintained a mission in Georgia. The mission's objective was formulated as "[a]id to the government of Georgia in the sphere of conflict resolution, democratization, human rights, and maintaining the rule of law," as well as to "promote negotiations between the conflicting parties in Georgia which are aimed at reaching a peaceful political settlement."[21] The observers sent by the OSCE were based mainly in the region of the South Ossetian conflict, while representatives of the United Nations worked in the second conflict zone of Abkhazia.

The situation in the South Ossetian conflict zone deteriorated sharply in the summer of 2008, when the Georgian government decided to take military measures to restore the country's territorial integrity. Georgian armed forces attacked Tskhinvali, the South Ossetian capital, which resulted in large numbers of casualties among both the civilian population and the Russian peacekeepers stationed there. The attack resulted in the five-day Russian-Georgian War, during the course of which Russian regular military forces, coming to the aid of the peacekeepers, repelled Georgian forces from South Ossetia.

Characteristically, in defending the operation, Russia first referred to the principle of "enforcing the peace," though it does not authorize Russian actions, since in accordance with Article 53 of the UN Charter, all operations involving armed peace enforcement must be carried out on the basis of a resolution from the Security Council. The stronger rationale used by Russia to justify its actions in the five-day conflict is found in Article 51 of the UN Charter: the right to self-defense.

Tajikistan

The third operation which is considered as peacekeeping by the Russian leadership was conducted to stop the civil war in Tajikistan. However, in this case the Russian forces participated in a CIS regional operation. The operation, which also had no UN mandate, involved troops of three other CIS countries: Kazakhstan, Kyrgyzstan, and Uzbekistan. Russia contributed most troops, about 7,000. The mission, however, regularly reported to the UN and therefore the CIS interpreted it as a case of regional peacekeeping under Chapter VIII of the UN Charter. About 130 UN military observers from 13 countries were also sent to in Tajikistan as part of the UN Mission of Observers in Tajikistan (UNMOT). According to Nikitin, the:

> deployment of two missions and absence of the UN mandate for the CIS operation was caused by the UN Security Council's lack of preparedness to interfere in a civil war in which there was no peace to keep and which contained the presence of many dispersed unauthorized armed groupings inside Tajikistan. The UN tended towards a more cautious and classical interpretation of peacekeeping and was not ready to propose solutions for conflicts in what in 1992 was widely interpreted as "Russia's backyard."[22]

The problem of unrecognized mandates

The increase in the number of regional peacekeeping operations is a serious concern for Russia. In the opinion of some Russian experts, at present, instead of a single peacekeeping system led by the UN with a mandate from the Security Council, in which all states participate equally, there are now two rival models of international conflict intervention that are splitting further and further away from one another.

The first model is the continuation of classic UN peacekeeping according to the mandate (political decisions) of the Security Council or General Assembly. Here, for better or worse, belong the failures (Rwanda, Somalia) as well as the cases generally considered successes (for example, East Timor, now a UN member state). The second model is intervention in conflicts by regional organizations and coalitions of countries, sometimes with mandates from regional organizations, but, most importantly for Russia, without a UN mandate. There have been at least 10 such cases over the past decade, and the countries participating in such non-UN mandated operations have included not only the United States and its allies in NATO, but also the CIS and Russia itself.[23] According to Alexander Nikitin: "As a result of Cold War inertia, military intervention in a series of conflicts by the US, NATO and Western countries on one hand, and interventions by Russia and the CIS on the other, are occurring in greater and greater isolation from each other, with neither side recognizing the activities of the other as *real peacekeeping*."[24]

The United States and its allies do not recognize the legitimacy— especially after the entry of Russian soldiers into Georgia in August 2008—of peacekeeping operations carried out under the mandate of the CIS, in Tajikistan and Abkhazia. Neither does the United States recognize the actions of Russia in signing bilateral agreements in Moldova and South Ossetia. Russia, for its part, never recognized the legality of the West's, and especially NATO's, actions in the Federal Republic of Yugoslavia in 1999, the actions of the United States, Great Britain, and their allies against Iraq without a UN mandate in 2003 (before receiving a Security Council mandate), nor in Syria (attempts to overthrow the lawful government through support for anti-government insurgents without any kind of UN mandate whatsoever).

Nikitin calls for Russia and the West to find common ground to overcome the problem of mutually unrecognized peacekeeping operations: "It is necessary to be able to see disputes through the eyes of the *other side*, to find joint formulas for mutually acceptable use of military force in conflicts."[25] In the majority of cases, it is possible to find agreement among the members of the Security Council to legitimize international intervention with a UN mandate. However, in the current international environment, where areas of confrontation between Russia and the West are increasing, it is unlikely that either side will be willing to take the steps necessary to find common ground. Still, recent developments have shown signs of the potential for a shift in a more positive direction. For example, on the necessity to resolve the ongoing conflict in Ukraine, all sides recognize the positive role being played by the OSCE, which has become significantly more active after decades of relative passivity, at least in the international security sphere. Perhaps at some point these efforts could lead to an agreement which could ultimately be legitimized at the Security Council level. Ultimately however, the increasingly confrontational situation remains a serious obstacle towards international peacekeeping and makes the world substantially more dangerous and unpredictable, and this sooner or later must be addressed by all sides.

Conclusion: Russia's world outlook and recent peacekeeping trends

Russian peacekeeping missions in post-Soviet space are often criticized by the United States and its allies for being little more than an attempt to consolidate Russian influence in neighboring countries, for not allowing the participation of representatives from states outside the region, and for obstructing the freedom of Russia's weaker neighbors to choose their own paths of development. Perhaps unsurprisingly, these criticisms are nearly identical to the ones lodged by Russia against the United States and other NATO member countries. Obviously, such positions demonstrate the importance given to peacekeeping operations within the larger context of Russian foreign policy, but the fact remains that the majority of Russia's operations have been effective insofar as, following the cessation of hostilities, they did not cause further instability—in marked contrast to the operations led by NATO member countries, for example, in Iraq and Libya.

Peacekeeping operations—at least in the "near abroad," a region of direct strategic interest to Russia—are considered by Russia not only as an instrument for keeping the peace and resolving humanitarian problems but also as an important instrument of foreign policy and the pursuit of national interests. Undoubtedly, the most important such interest is the maintenance of peace on the country's borders, but for Russia, peacekeeping operations can serve additional political purposes. It is worth mentioning that in this respect Russian peacekeeping operations differ little from the approaches of other major powers, all of whom take the decision to initiate or participate in such operations on the basis of their own national interests. Russia shares this approach. The combination of a pragmatic foreign policy and a fundamentally realist outlook forms the basis on which Russia determines its approach to the full range of issues related to peacekeeping. All other factors being equal, Russia tends to support peacekeeping efforts aimed at preserving the status quo, in the fullest sense of the term. Russia views peacekeeping first and foremost as a component of its foreign policy, and thus various approaches to resolving a particular situation are assessed by the extent to which they serve Russia's national interests. Such a foundation in many ways determines Russia's position with respect to the new peacekeeping structures and objectives that the international community has witnessed in recent years.

The last decade has been marked by a sharp increase in the scope and mode of UN peacekeeping operations. There have been cases both where UN forces were dispatched to protect a government against militants—Mali—and cases such as South Sudan, where the UN sent peacekeepers to protect civilians in the absence a peace agreement. Both cases represented new UN approaches that differ drastically from the traditional UN principles of peacekeeping.

What was the Russian reaction toward such changes? Russia accepted the necessity to expand the UN mandate to cover these new situations, supporting both Security Council Resolution 2100 on Mali and Resolution 1590 on Sudan. And while Russia voted against the US-sponsored resolution on Syria in 2012, it supported the US resolution on the Islamic State of Iraq and the Levant (ISIL) proposed in 2014. These votes lead one to conclude that Russia accepts a broader reading of UN peacekeeping missions when the situation demands it, and in general is less concerned with the scope or scale of the mission than with its objectives and political consequences.

Thus, modern Russian policy with regards to the form and objectives of peacekeeping operations must be viewed within the framework of Russia's strategic outlook on the world and Russia's understanding of the emerging international order. The key elements characterizing the Russian world outlook can be summarized as follows: upholding the principles of international law (with special emphasis on the principle of sovereignty), maintaining stability (no changes to the existing configuration of the international system), and preserving the Yalta–Potsdam institutions of global governance as the central mechanisms for resolving international disputes.

Russia is loathe to accept the US-centric international order and its unilateralism, and insists on the need for coordination between the great powers of the modern world through compromise and a balance of interests. This view is consistently stated in Russia's key foreign policy documents, including its most recent Foreign Policy Concept, which states clearly that "[i]nternational relations are in the process of transition, the essence of which is the creation of a polycentric system of international relations."[26] The logic of Russia's world vision is as follows: (1) in normal international practice, doubts shall be interpreted in favor of state versus non-state actors; (2) attempts at regime change, including those undertaken by means of peacekeeping operations, are illegitimate; (3) mandates for a peacekeeping operation or any other kind of international intervention can be granted only by the Security Council or be implemented on the basis of an inter-governmental agreement (or agreement by a regional association) involving the state on whose territory such an operation is taking place; (4) all attempts at peacekeeping without such mandates (e.g., "coalitions of the willing") are illegitimate; (5) peacekeeping operations shall not result in geopolitical or economic gains by initiating countries; and (6) neighboring countries have a stronger vested interest—and right—to formulate the objectives and terms of an operation than international actors from outside the region.

Russia shares the general humanitarian concerns of other members of the international community. Moscow remains opposed to violence used in internal conflicts, and sees such conflicts—and peacemaking efforts—that occur in the regions where Russia's national interests are at stake as being a heightened cause for concern. It is also worth noting that Russia uses precedent as a key principle of international law. While Russia protested against granting independence to Kosovo, in 2008 it referred to the principle of precedent when granting recognition to South Ossetia and Abkhazia, and did so again when accepting the results of the Crimean referendum of 2014. Russia rejects the monopoly of a chosen group of countries to interpret, and violate, international law, and does not initiate such moves as a first actor.

Russia's greatest concern in regard to peacekeeping today is formulated in the Foreign Policy Concept of the Russian Federation:

> Another risk to world peace and stability is presented by attempts to manage crises through unilateral sanctions and other coercive measures, including armed aggression, outside the framework of the UN Security Council. . . . Some concepts that are being implemented are aimed at overthrowing legitimate authorities in sovereign states under the pretext of protecting their civilian populations. The use of coercive measures and military force bypassing the UN Charter and the UN Security Council is unable to eliminate profound socioeconomic, ethnic and other antagonisms that cause conflicts.[27]

This quotation allows one to conclude that Russia sees two potentially problematic aspects of changes occurring to the philosophy of UN peacekeeping operations: that these operations may be used unilaterally for geopolitical and economic gains; and that such operations, conceived and carried out for geopolitical objectives, may end up causing even more chaos and instability.

150 *Maxim Bratersky and Alexander Lukin*

Notes

1 Sergei Lavrov, "Rossiia prodolzhit aktivno uchastvovat' v mirotvorcheskoi deiatel'nosti OON" (Russia continues to actively participate in peacekeeping operations), 14 November 2013, http://itar-tass.com/politika/750107.
2 J. Wilson, 2004 [in complete], quoted in David Scott, *China Stands Up: The PRC and the International System* (London: Routledge, 2007), 99.
3 Ministry of Foreign Affairs of the Russian Federation, "Concept of the Foreign Policy of the Russian Federation," approved by President Putin 12 February 2013, www.mid.ru/brp_4.nsf/0/76389FEC168189ED44257B2E0039B16D.
4 Seliger 2014 National Youth Forum, 29 August 2014, http://eng.kremlin.ru/news/22864.
5 Viktor Chernomyrdin, "Comment: Bombs Rule Out Talk of Peace," *The Washington Post*, 27 May 1999.
6 O.V. Kuz'mina, "Reforma Organizatsii Ob'edinennyh Natsii i politika SShAv period administratsii Baraka Obamy (2008–2012)" Reform of the United Nations and Policy of the United States during the Administration of Barack Obama (2008–2012), *Oykumena*, no. 2, 2013, 74.
7 Vladimir F. Zaemskii, "Sovremennye problemy mirotvorcheskoi deiatel'nosti OON. Politicheskie issledovaniia" (Contemporary Challenges of UN Peacekeeping Activities), *Politicheskie issledovaniia* (Polis), no. 2, 2009, 138.
8 L.E. Grishaeva, "Kosovo: Krizis Mirotvorchestva OON" (Kosovo: Crisis of UN Peacekeeping), *Novyi istoricheskii vestnik* 17 (2008): 143.
9 "Vystuplenie Ministra Inostrannyh del Rossiiskoi Federatsii I. S. Ivanova na 54-y sessii General'noi Assamblei OON" (Speech of Minister of Foreign Affairs of the Russian Federation I.S. Ivanov at the 54th Session of the General Assembly of the UN), www.rg.ru/oficial/from_min/mid_99/285.htm.
10 Ibid.
11 United Nations Peacekeeping, Troop and Police Contributors, www.un.org/en/peacekeeping/resources/statistics/contributors.shtml.
12 Alexander Nikitin, "The Russian Federation," in *Providing Peacekeepers: The Politics, Challenges, and Future of United Nations Peacekeeping Contributions*, ed. Alex Bellamy and Paul Williams (Oxford: Oxford University Press, 2013), 163.
13 Ibid.
14 Ibid., 172.
15 Ibid.
16 Vitaliy Denisov, "Missiya mira Rossii" (Russia's Peace Mission), *Kranaya zvezda*, 24 July 2008, http://old.redstar.ru/2008/07/24_07/1_01.html.
17 A.I. Nikitin, *Uchastie Rossii v mezhdunarodnom mirotvorchestve i perspektivy ego reformirovaniia* (Participation of Russia in International Peacekeeping and Perspectives for its Reform), *Indeks Bezopasnosti*, no. 2, 1997, 108.
18 Nikitin, "The Russian Federation," 158.
19 Ministry of Foreign Affairs of the Russian Federation, Department of Information and Press, "Vystuplenie I otvety na voprosy SMI Ministra inostrannyh del Rossii S.V. Lavrova v hode sovmestnoi press-konferentsii po itogam peregovorov s Ministrom inostrannyh del mezhdunarodnyh sotrudnichestva Respubliki Yuzhnyi Sudan B. Barnaboi" (Speech and

Q&A with the media with Russian Minister of Foreign Affairs Sergei Lavrov during the course of a joint press conference on the results of talks with the Minister of Foreign Affairs and International Cooperation of the Republic of South Sudan, Benjamin Barnaba), *Information Bulletin* 23–6 May 2014, Moscow, 26 May 2014, 14 (author's translation).

20 Text of newly-approved Russian military doctrine, 2010, http://carne gieendowment.org/files/2010russia_military_doctrine.pdf.
21 OSCE Mission to Georgia, Mandate, https://archive.is/UjcPP.
22 Nikitin, "The Russian Federation," 164.
23 Nikitin, "Uchastie Rossii v mezhdunarodnom mirotvorchestve i perspektivy ego reformirovaniya," 106.
24 Ibid.
25 Ibid., 109.
26 Ministry of Foreign Affairs of the Russian Federation, "Concept of the Foreign Policy of the Russian Federation."
27 Ibid.

6 The large contributors and UN peacekeeping doctrine

Seun Abiola, Cedric de Coning,
Eduarda Hamann, and Chander Prakash

- Asia: Bangladesh, India, Nepal, and Pakistan
- Key doctrinal considerations among the large TPCCs
- Conclusion

The division of labor in United Nations (UN) peacekeeping stresses the boundaries between North and South, following political power, money and risk taking. As UN secretary-general Ban Ki-Moon stated: "[Among] [t]hose who mandate missions, those who contribute uniformed personnel and those who are major funders are separate groups … tensions and divisions are inevitable, with potentially negative impacts on our operations."[1] This mostly North–South divide is by far the most complex (hard) political issue in the current UN structure of international peace and security. It is complex and difficult because it is linked to deep historical, economic, and political power structures in the global order, and within the UN, and while it needs to be confronted by any serious attempt to reform UN peace operations, the underlying structural causes behind this divide will take many years to evolve. The more immediate question is perhaps what can be done at the policy level to address this divide and to mitigate against its negative consequences. In this chapter we aim to highlight the policy positions, and the factors that motivate them, of the large troop- and police-contributing countries (TPCCs) to UN peace operations, as well as their views on what should be done to address the North–South divide in UN peacekeeping.

The UN Security Council (UNSC), and especially the five permanent members (P5), have the most influence on where UN peacekeeping operations are deployed and what mandates and tasks they are authorized to carry out. Among the P5, France, the United Kingdom, and the United States (collectively known as the P3) are the most active members when it comes to drafting UNSC resolutions. Apart from their political power as permanent members with veto power, they also have a considerable stake in the cost of UN peacekeeping operations, which in 2015 amounted to approximately $9 billion. In 2014–5, the P5 contributed 52 percent of the total cost of UN peacekeeping operations. The P3 contributed 42 percent of the total cost of UN peacekeeping operations. The top 10 financial contributors in 2015, apart from the P5, included Japan, Germany, Italy, Canada, and Spain.[2]

In the early period of the UNSC's operation, and throughout the Cold War, countries like Canada, Finland, India, Norway, and Sweden were prominent peacekeepers, but since the 1990s, the majority of peacekeepers have been provided by the Global South.[3] As of 31 March 2016, African and Asian countries were contributing approximately 75 percent of the 105,381 military and police UN peacekeepers serving at that time. The top 10 total contributors at that time were Ethiopia, India, Pakistan, Bangladesh, Rwanda, Nepal, Senegal, China, Burkina Faso, and Ghana. China is the largest contributor among the P5 and the eighth largest contributor overall; France is the second-largest contributor. Latin America's participation increased tenfold between 2000 and 2010, from 753 to 7,523. Despite this impressive growth, the overall numbers from Latin America are low compared to the Asian and African contributions. Latin American countries contribute with only 6.4 percent of all uniformed personnel.[4]

There is a range of motivations for countries to contribute troops or police officers to UN peacekeeping operations, including political, security, economic, moral, and professional. Although the majority of the TPCCs analyzed in this chapter do deploy their nationals to robust missions, or to missions that somehow challenge the core principles of UN peacekeeping, the level of satisfaction with the current system is rather low. For example, Asian and African countries are expected to take the highest risks when deploying troops to missions with mandates to protect civilians. At the same time, however, they have limited or no access to the elaboration of the mandates they would have to implement. This widens the gap between North and South, something that is felt in New York, in national capitals, and in the field, affecting not only the effectiveness but also the legitimacy of the mission. As a result, some TPCCs are still willing to provide continued support to more robust missions, but when it comes to actually committing to military operations in the field, the results are mixed. And some countries have chosen a non-anticipated and dangerous solution to this challenge, highlighted in a recent study by the UN's Office of Internal Oversight Services (OIOS).[5] These troop-contributing countries (TCCs) deploy their nationals to more robust missions, but with caveats or orders from the capital that prevent their troops from actually taking part in more robust military operations in the field. The current dilemmas facing the largest TPCCs reinforce the main argument of this book, namely that the gap that exists between North and South is further exacerbated by the tensions between peacekeeping doctrine and current praxis.

In the following sections we discuss the effective engagement of selected countries from Asia, Africa, and Latin America that regularly deploy uniformed personnel to UN peacekeeping operations.

Asia: Bangladesh, India, Nepal, and Pakistan

Bangladesh, China, India, Pakistan, and Nepal together currently account for almost 30 percent of the uniformed peacekeepers contributed by 123 countries to UN peacekeeping operations. Bangladesh, Pakistan, and India have consistently occupied one of the top four places in the troop contributor lists for over a decade. Countries participate in UN peacekeeping of their own will and therefore have some good reasons for their contributions. Most contributors claim that their engagement is for the maintenance of international peace and security. However, in real terms it is for prestige and economic gains—and experience, training, and exposure for their national uniformed forces. Possibly it is also for better relations with host countries, while some may also contribute to showcase their military.[6] It would not be incorrect to state that a country's degree of commitment to UN peacekeeping is directly related to the intent to pursue its national interests.

Bangladesh, a small country with a high density of population and gross domestic product (GDP) per capita of US$3,600 (2015 estimate), despite political instability and the relatively small size of its armed forces, ranks fourth in the number of peacekeepers deployed in UN peacekeeping operations.[7] It has 7,145 uniformed personnel deployed in various peacekeeping operations across the globe. Its first set of deployments came in 1988, when it participated in the UN Iran-Iraq Military Observers Group (UNIIMOG) in Iraq, and the UN Transitional Assistance Group (UNTAG) in Namibia. Since then, Bangladeshi troops have participated in 52 UN missions in 40 countries, with 120,587 uniformed personnel from three services of the defense forces and police.[8]

Bangladesh pursues a policy of active participation in global and regional peace processes. It is a country that has recognized the UN Charter in its national constitution. By participating in UN peacekeeping missions, Bangladesh benefits politically, diplomatically, financially, and militarily. Being a low-income country, the financial package it receives from the UN is an attractive incentive. From 2001 to 2010, Bangladesh received $1.28 billion from the UN, and 67 percent of this is on account of troop costs and the balance is equipment reimbursement. Thus, UN peace operations help subsidize Bangladesh's armed forces.[9]

Notwithstanding the benefits that accrue to Bangladesh from participating in peacekeeping operations, it has some challenges in highly multidimensional contemporary peacekeeping. Generally speaking, Bangladesh responds pragmatically to requests to commit troops to the UN or other nonaggressive partners. Sometimes it even volunteers to offer peacekeepers, especially due to humanitarian considerations. However, Bangladesh does not send troops into conflict situations or into circumstances where they might look like aggressors. Nor does Bangladesh compromise its national interests or values.[10]

India, with 7,700 military and police deployed across the globe on peacekeeping duties, is the second-largest contributor to UN operations. It has suffered the highest number of fatalities in UN peacekeeping, 162 against a total of 3,471. India began contributing to UN missions for two overarching reasons: to provide training for its soldiers (no longer a relevant consideration), and to improve its clout and standing within the international community with an eye to securing a permanent seat on the Security Council. India aspires to be recognized as a great power that can influence the world stage. This ambition is also one of the reasons for its efforts in international affairs, including UN peacekeeping. Today, the traditional benefits that troop contributors derive from UN peacekeeping operations are not necessarily relevant in India's case, especially the access to better training, and the opportunity to subsidize defense costs.[11]

India's first participation in a UN operation was in Korea in 1950 with a medical unit. After the conflict ended India also provided a Custodian Force for the Neutral Nations Repatriation Commission, which arranged for an exchange of prisoners of war. It also contributed significantly to the Indo-China Supervisory Commission deployed in Cambodia, Laos, and Vietnam from 1954 to 1970. The use of armed military contingents was first authorized by the Security Council for deployment with the UN Emergency Force (UNEF I) in the Gaza Strip and Sinai after the Arab-Israeli war in 1956. From 15 November 1956 to 19 May 1967, 11 infantry battalions from India successively served with this force.[12]

India readily agreed to participate in the UN Operation in the Congo (ONUC), whose purpose was to end secession and reunify the country. The rules of engagement were modified to cater for use of force in defense of the mandate, in carrying out humanitarian tasks, and in countering mercenaries. India's contribution to the operation was not only substantial but also robust and most vital. Between 14 July 1960 and 30 June 1964, two successive Indian brigades participated in these operations. Some 36 Indian personnel lost their lives and 124 were wounded.[13] Thus, India had clearly demonstrated its willingness to use force and commitment to the objectives of the UN Charter.

In the post–Cold War era, India has continued to provide contingents, military and police officers, and also enablers and force multipliers in the form of attack and utility helicopters, until it had to withdraw them from the Democratic Republic of the Congo (DRC) and Sudan in 2011 due to domestic pressure. Indian contingents understand the complexities of modern day peacekeeping. This has been more than amply demonstrated by their performance in Cambodia, Somalia, Mozambique, Angola, Rwanda, and Sierra Leone. It also continues to be demonstrated by those deployed in the DRC, South Sudan, and in Lebanon.

India is of the view that the international community must grasp the rapid changes that are underway in the nature and role of contemporary and multidimensional peacekeeping operations involving intra-state conflicts. Mandates of UN peacekeeping operations need to be rooted in ground realities and correlated with the resources provided. It has been voicing concerns that troop and police contributing countries are not being sufficiently involved in mandate formulation and in all aspects of mission planning. There need to be greater financial and human resources for peacebuilding in post-conflict societies where UN peacekeeping operations have been mandated. India has also expressed caution regarding what it has labeled *interventionist mandates*, as have some other countries, particularly from Asia, because it views such mandates as unrealistic and unachievable.[14]

Nepal's major engagement in UN peacekeeping operations came during its second democratic period, 1990–2005. Nepal started sending troops under the provisions of Chapter VII of the UN Charter when its troops participated in the mission in Somalia, in 1993.

It is one of the very few member states whose constitution provides that the UN Charter principles are guidelines in the conduct of its foreign relations. It is worth mentioning that Nepal has provided troops to UN missions in the most complex conflict zones even during its decade-old People's War (1996–2006).

Nepal has substantially increased its troop and police contribution to UN peacekeeping in the past decade and has become a major contributor, with 5,298 peacekeepers deployed worldwide. Since 1958 Nepal has participated in 29 peacekeeping missions and has suffered 70 fatalities. The country is currently participating in all 16 current peacekeeping missions, including a political mission in Afghanistan led by the UN Department of Peacekeeping Operations (DPKO). Nepal has a standby arrangement with the UN for 2,000 troops for peacekeeping purposes. Peacekeeping allows Nepal to be seen as a relevant player at the international level *vis-à-vis* its larger neighbors, while pursuing an independent and even autonomous foreign policy.[15] Nepali troops as well as police have remained in high demand for peacekeeping missions around the world, particularly ones that require working under hazardous conditions.

Pakistan's journey with UN peacekeeping began in July 1960, when it deployed its first contingent to the Congo (ONUC). Since then, Pakistan has participated in 42 UN missions in 24 countries across the globe. Pakistan has contributed more than 154,000 troops for peacekeeping operations and suffered 138 fatalities. Its major contributions have been in Somalia, Sierra Leone, Bosnia, Congo, and Liberia. Some 7,394 Pakistani men and women are currently serving with complex and challenging peacekeeping missions, including those in Darfur, Haiti, and the DRC, making it the second-largest contributor of troops.

For Pakistan, working with the UN is a way to identify itself as a responsible member of the international community.[16] It has an ambition to become a "good international citizen" with "international responsibilities," which include preserving international peace and security through a proactive involvement in UN peacekeeping. Political image is very important to Pakistan, as it does not want to be regarded as a weak or "failed" state. Pakistan's image as a stable nation has been blemished by internal conflicts and military coups, and it struggles to project an image of a country that values peace. It also aims to establish bilateral relations with major powers such as the United States.[17] Peacekeeping also provides economic benefits and international exposure to Pakistan's armed forces.

Pakistan, like India, is also of the view that precise and achievable mandates, backed by adequate resources, are critical. Early inclusion/ engagement of TPCCs in the mandate formation phase would create a buy-in and help devise achievable mandates. It is of the view that UN peacekeeping is fundamentally different from peace enforcement and this distinction must be maintained. Pakistan has emphasized that venturing into grey zones would confuse the mission, erode the neutrality of peacekeeping, and undermine its reputation and success, besides endangering the safety and security of peacekeepers. It has reiterated that the Force Intervention Brigade (FIB) in the DRC—which forms part of the UN Stabilization Mission in the Democratic Republic of the Congo (MONUSCO)—is a measure agreed to on an exceptional basis and should remain an exception. It has expressed concerns over the safety and security of peacekeepers due to the nature of conflict, proliferation of armed groups, and other elements in the field, including criminality, transnational organized crime, and terrorist threats. Pakistan has also mentioned publicly that peacekeepers are often faced with overwhelming situations beyond their capabilities and resources.[18]

Africa: Ethiopia, Nigeria, Rwanda, and South Africa

Currently, African countries account for 51 percent of contributions of uniformed personnel to UN peacekeeping operations.[19] Of the top 20 contributors, 14 are African countries; five of which are in the top 10 (Ethiopia, Rwanda, Senegal, Burkina Faso, and Ghana). Ethiopia is the number-one contributor with 8,321 uniformed personnel deployed, and Rwanda takes fifth place with a deployment of 6,141. Senegal has seventh place, and has consistently been the largest police-contributing country (PCC), with 1,395 police currently deployed out of a total deployment of 3,727 uniformed personnel. Burkina Faso takes ninth place with a deployment of 2,901, and has been ranked as one of the top 20 since 2013. Ghana has tenth place with a deployment of 2,886, and along with Nigeria, Rwanda, Senegal, Ethiopia, and Egypt, has been consistently ranked as part of the top 10 contributors over the last decade. South Africa has also been consistently in the top 20 over the same period.

African countries have a long history of contributions to UN peacekeeping operations, even before the 1990s shift towards greater contributions from the Global South than the North. Ethiopia and South Africa's participation in such operations dates back to the 1950s, as part of the UN Command (UNC) multinational force in the Korean War. Ethiopia also participated in the 1960s operation in the Congo (ONUC), and subsequently in UN missions in Rwanda, Burundi, Chad and the Central African Republic (CAR), Liberia, Côte d'Ivoire, and the Sudans (Darfur, South Sudan, and the contested area of Abyei on the Sudan-South Sudan border). Nigeria, currently ranked as the thirteenth largest contributor (2,796 uniformed personnel), also participated in ONUC in 1960 shortly after the Congo's independence, and has contributed to UN missions in different parts of the world, including Bosnia and Herzegovina, Iraq, Kuwait, Western Sahara, Rwanda, Somalia, Mozambique, Cambodia, Lebanon, Angola, Beirut, and India and Pakistan.

Since 2004, Rwanda has emerged as one of the top contributors for both UN and African Union (AU) missions, emerging in 2008 as one of the top ten contributors to UN peacekeeping operations. South Africa, currently the eighteenth largest contributor to UN peace-keeping (1,589 uniformed personnel), participated in the UN Mission in the Democratic Republic of the Congo (MONUC) in 1999, but made its first major contribution in 2004 when its troops, as part of the African Mission in Burundi (AMIB), were re-hatted for the UN Operation in Burundi (ONUB).[20]

These countries mainly deploy uniformed personnel to UN peace-keeping missions in Africa, where the majority of missions are located. Security issues in one's own neighborhood have been a motivating factor for increased contributions to address the continent's own crises, acknowledging that regional security is intricately linked to national security interests. Noticeably, major contributions originate from countries located in the problematic Horn of Africa, Great Lakes, and West Africa/Sahel regions, where most of the demand is for international support to manage conflict, in Somalia, the DRC, Mali, the Sudans, Liberia, and CAR.

For example, in 2013, Ethiopia set a new precedent in the history of UN peacekeeping operations by supplying almost the entire military component (nearly 4,000) of the UN Interim Security Force for Abyei (UNISFA), and in December 2014 became the largest contributor to peace operations in the world, when combining both UN and AU missions. Ethiopia, Nigeria, Rwanda, and South Africa have all contributed troops to AU and sub-regional peace operations, including the AU missions in Burundi, Sudan, and Somalia, as well as the African-led International Support Mission to Mali (AFISMA, 2013) and the African-led International Support Mission to the CAR (MISCA, 2014), and the AU/UN Hybrid Operation in Darfur (UNAMID).

Concerns for national and regional security have not only motivated African contributions to UN, AU, and sub-regional interventions, but also support from African TPCCs for more peace enforcement and robust mandates. For example, Rwanda supported the deployment of the FIB to the MONUSCO operation in eastern DRC with the belief that such a tool would assist with the security challenges affecting the region.[21] South Africa has become a prominent supporter of robust peacekeeping, and has contributed troops, attack helicopters, and special forces to the FIB. Alongside South Africa, Malawi and Tanzania provide three infantry battalions, one artillery, and one "special force and reconnaissance" company to the FIB. African support for the FIB has to be understood in the context of regional politics, and South Africa, together with other countries in the region, has been careful to contextualize the use of force by the FIB within a larger political process embedded in the International Conference on the Great Lakes Region (ICGLR), the Southern African Development Community (SADC), and the African Union.

Another example of support and contribution to robust missions in response to regional insecurity is that of Nigeria to the UN Multidimensional Integrated Stabilization Mission in Mali (MINUSMA). Nigeria has recognized the use of force as a necessary strategy to address the immediate terrorist threat and instability in Mali and the West Africa sub-region as a whole, but has also noted that this is not an effective long-term solution.[22] The fight against terrorism is a high priority for Nigeria, and security concerns relating to the Islamist terrorist group Boko Haram in the Lake Chad region have united Nigeria, Benin, Cameroon, Chad, and Niger to contribute 8,700 troops to a Multinational Joint Taskforce (MNJTF). However, these security issues have also limited Nigeria's engagement in operations abroad, especially since 2013, when it withdrew its troops from both MINUSMA and UNAMID to address its own domestic response to Boko Haram. As a result, Nigeria's contributions to the UN have declined to the extent that it is no longer ranked amongst the top 10 contributors to peacekeeping operations.

African countries' contributions continue to be motivated by their own experiences. Ethiopia and Rwanda as major contributors have themselves been beneficiaries of UN peacekeeping operations: UN Mission in Ethiopia and Eritrea (UNMEE) and the UN Assistance Mission for Rwanda (UNAMIR). In particular, Rwanda has been motivated in its contributions by moral reasons. Its contributions to peace operations is part of its post-genocide national identity, and casualties in both UN and AU/UN missions are perceived as sacrifices and made transparent to the extent of public recognition of injuries and fatalities. This is different from other countries who have to persuade the public that such costs to human life are worth taking. Indeed, Rwanda's past experience of delayed international intervention during the 1994 genocide of an estimated 800,000 to one million civilians has fuelled its advocacy of more robust responses to crises. It has called for the operational capacities of the UN to be developed for better crisis-response, including the development of the UN's capacity to deploy quickly instead of mobilizing only after a crisis had erupted; enhanced cooperation with regional and sub-regional organizations as "first responders" to crises with the necessary geographic proximity and political leverage to respond; as well as capacity-building with local and regional actors, who have greater incentive to respond to crises in their back yard.[23]

The contributions by Ethiopia, Nigeria, and South Africa coincide with their role as sub-regional powers. As part of the Economic Community of West African States (ECOWAS), Nigeria plays a dominant regional role, and along with Senegal and Ghana has also contributed uniformed personnel to ECOWAS's multilateral armed force, the Economic Community of West African States Monitoring Group (ECOMOG), which was first established in 1990 to intervene in the civil war in Liberia, and has since deployed to Sierra Leone (1997), Guinea-Bissau (1999), Liberia (2003), and most recently Mali.[24]

One of South Africa's most prominent international activities has been its contributions to several peace processes in Africa, including in Burundi, the Comoros, Côte d'Ivoire, the DRC, Zimbabwe, Sudan, and Madagascar. Peace diplomacy, understood as the country's involvement in peacemaking, peacekeeping, and peacebuilding, thus plays a critical, if not dominant, role in South Africa's foreign policy towards Africa. South Africa's contributions to UN and African peacekeeping operations have been closely linked to its own involvement in peacemaking initiatives, including to Burundi and the DRC and perhaps to a lesser extend to Darfur.[25] Ethiopia is also a regional power in its sub-region, contributing to regional peace and development for the sustainability of its own national development priorities.[26] It hosts the AU, is the chair of the Intergovernmental Authority on Development (IGAD), is the largest contributor to UN peace operations, and actively contributes to peace processes in Somalia, the contested region of Abyei, and civil conflict in South Sudan.

There are also economic incentives for contributing to UN peacekeeping. Globally, armed forces are experiencing budget cuts, and contributions to UN operations provide opportunities for the military to utilize their training, equipment, and capabilities. However, it has been highlighted that many African TCCs provide poor quality contingent-owned equipment (COE) and lack sophisticated capabilities, amidst the growing complexity of UN peacekeeping mandates. Some African TCCs gain in international exposure and military support from donor countries, including training, with the potential to develop strong modern armed forces.

The economic gain of reimbursements has been mentioned as a key motivating factor for some African countries' engagement in UN peacekeeping. This may be the case for some countries, but most large African TCCs seem to be motivated more by global and regional power and security dynamics than by the potential economic gain. South Africa and Nigeria stand out as African countries with middle-income economies. South Africa is the only African member of both the BRICS (Brazil, Russia, India, China, and South Africa) and IBSA (India, Brazil, and South Africa) groups of countries, identified with the biggest and fastest growing economies. In recent times, oil-rich Nigeria's accelerated economic growth has led it to overtake South Africa as the continent's biggest economy, and it is a part of MINT (Mexico, Indonesia, Nigeria, Turkey) as an alternative to BRICS. In 2010, reimbursements from the UN for peacekeeping contributions accounted for around 70 percent of Rwanda's defense budget.[27] Ethiopia withdrew five tactical helicopters from UNAMID apparently for financial reasons, namely the negotiations process for reimbursement, which culminated in inadequate compensation according to Ethiopian officials.

Whilst international prestige may be attributed to all African TPCCs as a major motivating factor, Security Council aspirations have been a significant motivating factor for both Nigeria and South Africa. Nigeria has been the long-time chair of the General Assembly's Special Committee on Peacekeeping Operations (C34), and the most elected African non-permanent member of the Security Council.[28] Since the end of apartheid, South Africa has undergone a radical transformation from international pariah to a prominent, albeit somewhat controversial international actor. South Africa also played a leading role in the transition from the Organization of African Unity (OAU) to the new AU, and along with Algeria, Nigeria, and Senegal, in the creation of the New Partnership for Africa's Development (NEPAD). It has been a regular member of the AU's Peace and Security Council, and has to date served twice in the UN Security Council.

Latin America: Uruguay and Brazil

Latin America has only two countries who participate with more than 1,000 troops in robust peacekeeping and peace enforcement missions: Uruguay and Brazil. Uruguay has provided a significant number of troops to UN peacekeeping since the end of the Cold War, particularly since 2002. This is part of a broader strategy that includes a search for regional and especially international prestige, together with a pragmatic vision to keep its armed forces up to date in terms of doctrine, training, and equipment. The reimbursements by the UN correspond to a large proportion of its national military spending.[29] And the country is proud to have experience in the implementation of the most complex mandates and in the toughest settings.[30]

Throughout the 1990s, a type of expeditionary battalion was first deployed to increasingly instable situations: the UN Transitional Authority in Cambodia (UNTAC) in 1992–3, followed by the UN Operation in Mozambique (ONUMOZ) in 1993–5, and the UN Angola Verification Mission (UNAVEM) in 1995–7. In 2002 Uruguay started deploying more than 1,000 troops, apparently targeting Chapter VII missions. The main destination has been the Democratic Republic of Congo, where Uruguay has kept a regular deployment of an expanded battalion (approximately 1,300 troops) since 2002. In Latin America and the Caribbean, Uruguay contributed to the UN Stabilization Mission in Haiti (MINUSTAH), another Chapter VII mission, with approximately 1,100 troops at its peak in 2006, remaining stable until a partial withdrawal started in 2012. In 2010, for example, 25 percent of the country's operational defense forces were committed to UN peacekeeping, keeping it among the top 10 TCCs for several years in a row.[31] Today, after reducing its troops in MINUSTAH, Uruguay is still the twenty-first largest TCC, with almost 1,500 troops in UN missions. Meanwhile it is the second smallest nation in South America, with a population of only 3.5 million: It is the largest TCC per capita in the world.

Brazil in turn is the largest country in Latin America and, as one of the founders of the UN, has been a regular TCC since the 1940s. When it comes to Chapter VII missions, however, Brazil is not comfortable with the UN taking up deep and robust responsibilities, and has avoided the deployment of its own troops to missions under Chapter VII, or those containing Chapter VII provisions. It has consistently defended the delegation of such missions to multinational forces or, depending on the case, to regional and sub-regional organizations.[32] In fact, when Brazil has been a nonpermanent UNSC member, its statements have usually challenged the engagement of the UN in Chapter VII missions, even in cases of major violations of human rights, such as in Kosovo, Darfur, and Libya, with the notable exception of Rwanda.[33] There is also a deep concern to avoid UN mandates receiving a similar scope and scale to mandates by the North Atlantic Treaty Organization (NATO), to prevent the risk that the agendas of the P5, especially the P3, could prevail over broader UN interests.[34]

Brazil has only deployed large contingents, such as a battalion or more, three times: Suez (UNEF), Angola (UNAVEM III), and Haiti (MINUSTAH). And it was in 2000 that the country first participated in a Chapter VII mission, in Timor-Leste (East Timor)—first the International Force for East Timor (INTERFET), which is not a peacekeeping mission, although authorized by the UNSC, and then the UN Transitional Administration in East Timor (UNTAET) and the UN Mission of Support to East Timor (UNMISET). While in Timor-Leste, Brazil had an agreement which did not allow its troops to engage with combat operations, and its military performed typical policing tasks.[35]

MINUSTAH represented the country's most relevant challenge, both politically and militarily. Brazil supported the mission while serving on the UNSC, having actively participated in the definition of the mandate so that it would also include development issues, and not only security tasks. It has also negotiated with other key South American TCCs in order to build consensus in the region for a Chapter VII mission.[36] Brazil deployed one battalion between 2004 and 2009 and, in the immediate aftermath of the earthquake on 12 January 2010, it mobilized and deployed a second battalion (between 2010 and 2013). Since then, Brazil has maintained one full battalion in Haiti. It is also relevant to add that the mission has been under the military command of a Brazilian general, nominated by the government, from the very beginning, with no rotation between nationalities, which has broken a pattern for UN standards. Moreover, when Brazil was actually using force in Haiti (2005–7), both military and diplomats were able to capitalize on it. Instead of criticism, the country's feat was mostly praised by the UN and among international public opinion.

It is also worth mentioning that a Brazilian general was the force commander of MONUSCO between April 2013 and December 2015. He commanded the only intervention brigade in the UN history, with a warlike mandate to "neutralize and disarm." General Santos Cruz was never appointed by the Brazilian government and his achievements while MINUSTAH's force commander were solely responsible for bringing him to the DRC. However, due to foreign policy calculations, the Brazilian government has been forced to officially acknowledge that there are two Brazilian force commanders in the field, generating an awkward situation since Brazil is opposed to MONUSCO's overall goals and especially the means. Brazil supported General Santos Cruz's mandate with a handful of staff officers for about two years. As soon as his mission was over, in late 2015, Brazil withdrew completely from MONUSCO.

Was MINUSTAH an exception or a precedent? The conditions which would allow for another Brazilian contribution to a Chapter VII mission are still being debated by the government. Despite UN interest at the highest levels, clearly expressed on several occasions, there is no guarantee that Brazil will deploy troops to another robust mission. This does not seem to be included in Brazil's calculations for strengthening its credentials in an attempt to become a permanent member of the UNSC. In fact, diplomats believe that the country's role as a major cooperating partner, and not necessarily a large TCC, will strengthen its negotiating position.[37]

Finally, it is interesting to add that, unlike for Uruguay and other large TCCs, financial reasons do not represent a real motivation for Brazil. For example, between 2004 and 2013 the Brazilian government invested approximately US$700 million (R$2.1 billion) in preparing, deploying, and maintaining its peacekeepers in MINUSTAH. According to the Ministry of Defense, only 35 percent of this amount was actually reimbursed by the UN.[38]

Key doctrinal considerations among the large TPCCs

The focus of this section is on the perspectives of TPCCs with regards to the major doctrinal issues on the UN peacekeeping agenda. It sheds light on key discussions among TPCCs related to: (i) robust mandates; (ii) new trends in peacekeeping, such as the use of new technologies, inter-mission cooperation, and regional partnerships; and (iii) issues relating to mandate setting and resourcing, transparency, and equitable representation in decision-making.

Robust mandates: A trend in peacekeeping

The trend whereby the Security Council has been authorizing more robust mandates, such as in the deployment of the FIB in eastern DRC, the use of intelligence in Mali, and an executive police mandate in CAR, has generated wider debates on the changing nature of violent conflict and its implications for UN peacekeeping. In those cases where more robust mandates we approved, provisions were inserted in the UNSC resolutions to preserve the traditional boundaries of peace-keeping. For example, the emphasis on the exceptional nature of Resolution 2098 (FIB); and the reaffirmation of the agreed principles of peacekeeping, "including consent of the parties, impartiality and non-use of force, except in self-defence and defence of the mandate" in Resolution 2100 (Mali).

Discussions on robust mandates are important given the complexities of such peacekeeping operations. For TPCCs, discussions on the trend of Security Council authorization of robust mandates have included issues such as the implications of robust mandates for the fundamental principles and practice of UN peacekeeping, operational challenges due to the complexity of mandates and environments, and the safety and security of personnel. These three issues are discussed in turn below.

Implications of robust mandates for the fundamental principles and practice of UN peacekeeping

There have been discussions amongst TPCCs on the issue of the use of force, in relation to the authorization of robust mandates to stabilize situations where security is minimal. Such discussions are important because of the recent trend of Security Council authorization of robust mandates; the complexities of robust peacekeeping operations, including the blurred lines between robust peacekeeping and peace enforcement; and the perceived compromise with the impartiality of UN peacekeeping operations.

Discussion on robust mandates has included the impact on the traditional boundaries of peacekeeping, in particular concerns about a potential shift away from traditional peacekeeping principles, such as consent of the local parties, impartiality, and the use of force only in self-defense. For example, UN peacekeepers may no longer be perceived as impartial but as a party to an armed conflict, with implications under international humanitarian law as combatants and legitimate targets, and consequences for the legal protection for peacekeepers. The perception of the robust mandates in Security Council Resolution 2098 (FIB in DRC) and Resolution 2100 (Mali) as peace enforcement has led to discussions on whether or not UN peacekeepers should engage in such activities, as well as on the legal, logistical, and political ramifications for UN operations.

Indeed, the creation of the FIB with an explicit mandate to "neutralize" rebel groups[39] has resulted in a debate on the opacity in current practice of the conceptual difference between robust peacekeeping and peace enforcement, made explicit only in 2008 with the Capstone Doctrine. Latin American and Asian TCCs, for example, have questioned whether current robust mandates authorizing the use of force are an expansion of the fundamental principles. Such norms related to peacekeeping, although not mentioned in the UN Charter, have been defined and codified as a result of lessons learned by trial and error.

Latin American countries also raise concerns with regards to the higher risks to personnel, and so tend to refrain from engaging their troops in robust peacekeeping (except for Uruguay). Of note, the safety and security of peacekeeping personnel has become an important issue for member states, most especially for TCCs. With mandates such as in the case of MONUSCO and MINUSMA interpreted as "peace enforcement,"[40] it has been argued that labeling them as "peacekeeping missions" masks the political constraints and risks that peace enforcement or even robust peacekeeping usually offer to TPCCs.[41]

TPCCs on the Security Council in 2013 did not oppose robust mandates for MONUSCO and MINUSMA, but, along with other member states, they perceived these developments to be both urgent and inevitable. In the case of the DRC, the FIB was established as a result of a lack in alternatives and as part of the wider process of the Peace, Security and Cooperation Framework for the DRC and the Great Lakes Region. In the case of Mali, the UN was not prepared to provide a logistics support package funded through UN-assessed contributions in order to sustain AFISMA alongside a UN special political mission. The UNSC has generally acknowledged that the "static" approach to civilian protection has proven insufficient, as evidenced in the DRC, and hence the need for robustness of the FIB.[42] Rwanda has strongly criticized the failures of the UN missions MONUC and MONUSCO to stabilize the region,[43] and supported and facilitated the deployment of the FIB with the belief that such a tool would assist with the security challenges in the DRC which affect the region.[44]

African member states, both individually and as part of regional coalitions, have played an important role in calling for more robust mandates. The DRC, the International Conference on the Great Lakes region and the Southern African Development Community lobbied for the deployment of the FIB, and the AU Peace and Security Council asked that MINUSMA be given a mandate to "actively sustain efforts aimed at dismantling the terrorist and criminal networks operating in the north of the country."[45]

Most member states in Africa support robust mandates authorizing the use of force for the protection of civilians under the imminent threat of physical harm and other humanitarian concerns. This alludes to proactive strategies, such as deterrent posture, as well as the "deadly" use of force as a means of last resort. Noting that robust mandates have been authorized for missions in Africa, the overall reaction of African countries has been largely positive, especially among countries to which the robust mandates have been applied, as well as their neighbors. For example, Mali acknowledges the need for MINUSMA to respond to the threat of "jihadist aggression."[46] The Central African Republic has also called for a robust Chapter VII mandate, which would enable the mission to address the difficult pre-genocide conditions.[47] Rwanda's past experience has meant the advocacy of more robust responses, including in non-African crises such as in Syria.[48] Since the tragedy, Rwanda acknowledges the improvement in the UN's capacity to prevent genocide and mass atrocities, although it notes the perceived challenges faced by the UN "struggling to match its normative principles with realities on the ground" in CAR, Syria, and South Sudan.[49]

Some Asian TPCCs are still not in agreement with the concept of robust peacekeeping and prefer the traditional approach, with clarity on the minimal use of force, the consent of parties to the peacekeepers' presence, protection of civilians, and upholding human rights.[50] The same is true for most Latin American countries. Some of these countries argue that the actual implementation of the robust mandate for MONUSCO reflects the challenging reality of the FIB alongside the existing military contingents. Namely that there are several military units operating under one single command, implementing a single mandate but with different levels of force and with no differentiation in physical appearance. They have argued that the UNSC decision for the FIB was taken without a holistic consideration of the full potential of extant capacities and chain of command in the mission, and also without consulting the TCCs of already deployed personnel.

Operational challenges due to the complexity of mandates and environments

There have been discussions amongst TPCCs on the issue of operational challenges due to the complexity of both mandates and environments. Such discussions are important because, as well as the trend in complex robust and multidimensional mandates, a number of the missions are currently operating in challenging environments, where there is no peace to keep. The views of TPCCs on this issue have been important, given the risks faced by peacekeepers to fulfill their mandates effectively.

Discussions have been geared towards resolving the political, security, and logistical challenges as a consequence of developments with new forms of mandates. These solutions have included the need for: the provision of a more comprehensive doctrine, including clarity in the concept of operations, command and control structures, and the rules of engagement; provision of training and equipment necessary to implement such mandates; and the application of lessons learned. In particular, providing clearer priorities and greater clarity to tasks within mandates, particularly regarding protection of civilians and the associated need for robust peacekeeping, has been identified as critical for achieving the desired result. For example, a 2014 report by the Office of Internal Oversight Services on the evaluation of the implementation of protection of civilians mandates in UN peacekeeping operations noted that there is "a persistent pattern of peacekeeping operations not intervening with force when civilians are under attack."[51]

Discussion in relation to complex environments reflect recent developments in the UN Disengagement Observer Force (UNDOF) due to the escalating spillover of the Syrian civil war into the mission's area of operations; the challenges of uncertain security environments of fragile states such as CAR, Somalia, and the Sudan; and the deployment of UN peacekeepers in challenging security environments where there is no peace to keep, with asymmetric threats posed by terrorist and transnational organized crime groups, as is the case in Mali.

Complex environments also include situations where host government consent has proven tenuous. This includes Chad's request for the withdrawal of the UN Mission in the Central African Republic and Chad (MINURCAT), whose mandate ended in 2010; the DRC not expressly consenting to the extension of MONUSCO's mandate in 2012; and recent examples related to consent for UNAMID and the UN Mission in South Sudan (UNMISS). Discussions in relation to this issue include managing consent in peacekeeping operations, including the idea of qualified consent; the implications of more legal contract with host governments; and the need to establish national consent at the beginning of a mission for the expected period anticipated for achieving the goal of the mission, rather than consent for the initial mandate period only.

Safety and security of personnel

There have been discussions amongst TPCCs on the issue of the safety and security of personnel. Several current missions in complex operational environments have experienced direct attacks on peacekeepers, such as kidnappings and malicious acts, which have resulted in injury and death to peacekeepers, placing TPCCs under great strain. Also, the impact of robust mandates on the safety and security of peacekeepers remains unclear.

Peacekeepers have lost their lives as a result of direct targeting in missions such as the UN Operation in Côte d'Ivoire (UNOCI),

MINUSTAH, MINUSMA, and the three missions in the Sudans. The deliberate targeting of MINUSMA by terrorist groups has involved the killing of and injury to peacekeepers mostly as a result of improvised explosive devices and other explosive ordnance, which reflects the change in the nature of the threats faced in the field. The increased risk to peacekeepers has led to a crisis of confidence amongst TPCCs, and is not limited to missions with more robust mandates. In UNDOF, a traditional observer mission, the decisions by Croatia, Japan, and in 2014 the Philippines to withdraw their troops were a result of the violence in Syria, and the attendant deteriorating security situation and direct attacks on peacekeepers.

Discussions have included the role of host countries in ensuring the safety and security of peacekeepers and the operational gaps and challenges in managing and mitigating risks, given limited resources. TPCCs are directly affected, and particularly interested in discussions on the link with the authorization of more aggressive mandates. In the negotiations for both Resolution 2098 (FIB) and Resolution 2100 (Mali), council members, including TPCCs such as Pakistan, expressed concern about the implications for the safety and security of peace-keepers.[52] These more aggressive mandates have led to a significant rise in peacekeeping casualties, especially in Mali, and this risk may influence contributions by TPCCs in the future. Debates have been necessary in recent times on a shared understanding about the new boundaries of peacekeeping to highlight the broader legal, political, and operational implications. The increased risk has the potential to widen the divide between those states that mainly contribute troops and those that mainly contribute funds to UN peacekeeping. TCCs are influenced in their decision-making by their perception of the risks in peacekeeping, most especially the perceived linkage between casualties and more robust peacekeeping. Particularly amongst TPCCs, there are serious concerns about the effectiveness and viability of peacekeeping in a rapidly changing and volatile environment.[53] Even countries like Japan, which do not contribute with uniformed personnel, are very sensitive to the casualties and fatalities suffered during UN peace operations.[54]

Latin American countries are definitely not willing to bear such risks. Apart from the logistic and financial constraints inherent to their location on the other side of the Atlantic, there seems to be a perception that missions in Africa tend to represent higher safety risks to personnel in the field. Moreover, there is a perception that only a few TPCCs can provide the necessary assets for robust operations.[55] In fact, only Guatemala and Uruguay have deployed troops to UN robust missions such as the one in the DRC, and their lessons could inform new perceptions and policies.[56] Evidence of this risk-averse politics among Latin American countries is seen in the fact that their contributions to robust missions are mainly restricted to deploying police offices (in individual missions, not through formed police units), or to deploying no more than one platoon.[57] This is evident in the numbers for the entire last decade in UN missions in Mali, the DRC, Darfur, South Sudan, and Sudan (Abyei)—all of them in Africa.

New trends in peacekeeping

New trends include the increase of robust mandates, multidimensional mandates, the use of new technology, inter-mission cooperation, regional partnerships, transnational crime, and climate change. Discussions on new trends in peacekeeping are important in order to reflect on key peace and security issues at the strategic level. In particular, there is a need to identify the growing challenges to peace and security, and proffer solutions to improve the on-the-ground response of peacekeeping operations. For TPCCs the focus of discussions on new trends has included the following three issues discussed below: new technology, inter-mission cooperation, and regional partnerships.

New technology

As discussed further in Chapter 11 by John Karlsrud, there have been discussions on the issue of new technology, since some argue that improvements in the use of technology could enhance the effectiveness and cost-efficiency of UN peacekeeping missions. They argue that the effective use of technology promotes the safety of peacekeepers, increases the responsiveness of peacekeeping operations, and, in general, helps them to carry out their mandates more effectively. These improvements are in line with the UN's "capability-driven approach" to peacekeeping, outlined in the 2009 New Horizon document, which emphasized the need to move from a quantitative focus on numbers to a qualitative focus on the generation of capabilities.

For example, a new peacekeeping tool is the use of unarmed unmanned aerial vehicles (UAVs) in the DRC to enhance situational awareness, in order to identify armed movements, and monitor camps for internally displaced persons, as well as provide timely reconnaissance and rapid reaction forces over vast and sensitive areas. Other types of technology include infrared systems on aircraft and helicopters and GPS technology in vehicles, which add night-sight capacity for weapons and man-portable surveillance radar. Other use of new technology includes the investigation by MINUSMA of the possibility of generating water from humidity in the Kidal area of Mali in order to avoid sapping the local supply of water.[58]

Overall, there is widespread interest in how a broad range of technologies can be used to enhance the effectiveness and cost-efficiency of peacekeeping.[59] In particular, it has been widely accepted that peacekeeping must adapt its toolbox to meet the demands of "increasingly hostile environments, battling asymmetric unconventional threats where there was no peace to keep and no viable political process upon which to build."[60] The changing nature and mandate of UN peacekeeping operations calls for personnel to be properly equipped to effectively respond to the challenges they face on the ground. The use of modern technology is perceived as a necessary investment in order to adapt to the new demands of deployments in hostile environments.

However, some large TPCCs have concerns about the use of UAVs. Issues raised regarding their deployment include access to the information gathered by these systems (operated by commercial contractors), and concerns about sovereignty whenever they fly over border zones. For example, South Sudan did not accept their deployment in UNMISS. Rwanda discussed the need to assess the performance and utility of UAVs in MONUSCO in light of their potential use in other missions, including MINUSMA and UNOCI.[61]

Discussions on technology have also included gaps in its use in specific peacekeeping operations; the type of training needed for TPCCs in new technologies; and the financial implications of new technologies on the peacekeeping budget, including the issue of whether Security Council approval is needed before new technologies are used.

Inter-mission cooperation

There have been discussions amongst TPCCs on the issue of cooperation between missions. Inter-mission cooperation can provide key assets through pooling or temporary redeployment of equipment and personnel at times of crisis or at mission start-up. Cooperation could also be expanded to include a wider range of "enablers," including special forces, hospitals, or reserve battalions. For example, inter-mission cooperation was used for UNMISS in order to respond to the crisis at the end of 2013, although there was limited success with the inter-mission cooperation arrangements to provide the mission with additional troops; the slow pace in the reinforcement was due to legal, political, and logistical challenges in shifting of assets requiring the approval of TPCCs.

Inter-mission cooperation has been identified as a short-term response to critical capability gaps rather than a long-term solution. Discussions have highlighted the limitations of such cooperation as a manner of effectively responding to unforeseen events in peacekeeping operations, and in particular the constraints related to securing timely TPCC consent. Morocco convened a meeting on inter-mission cooperation, which led to the proposal for the standardization of inter-mission cooperation provisions in the memoranda of understanding with TPCCs, as well as the standardization of language on inter-mission cooperation in council mandates.[62] The issue of standardization has also been raised with regards to functions to be carried out by contingents, since the standardization of some functions in peacekeeping would include compatibility of military hardware and software to enable more effective cooperation amongst contingents.

Discussions have emphasized the need for TPCCs to be consulted with regards to inter-mission cooperation, and concerns have been raised with regards to its financial implications, as well as command and control issues.[63] There is a wider need for regular and substantive discussions on key peacekeeping issues, as well as mission-specific consultations with TPCCs.

Regional partnerships

There have also been discussions amongst TPCCs on the role of regional and sub-regional organizations in UN peacekeeping. Such discussions are important because the UN has had to rely on regional organizations to support its peacekeeping efforts, especially in Africa. On the whole, such organizations are well positioned to understand and respond to armed conflicts in their own regions, owing to their knowledge of the root causes of the conflict, their regional proximity, and their political legitimacy. Regional and sub-regional players include the Association of Southeast Asian Nations (ASEAN), NATO, the Organization of American States (OAS), the AU, ECOWAS, the Economic Community of Central African States (ECCAS), IGAD, the Union of South American Nations (USAN), the League of Arab States, and the Organisation of Islamic Cooperation (OIC).

Amongst these organizations, the AU has been the most noticeable for its increased contribution to the maintenance of regional peace and security, including in Sudan (Darfur), Mali, CAR, and Somalia. Examples of regional partnerships with the UN include UNAMID, the provision of a logistics support package funded by UN assessed contributions for the African Union Mission in Somalia (AMISOM), and the authorization of two African-led missions by the council that were subsequently re-hatted into UN peacekeeping missions: AFISMA and MISCA.

Discussions have focused on the need to ensure that such partnerships are effective at the strategic, operational, and tactical levels; and in particular on the need for logistical and financial support to ensure that regional partners possess the required operational capabilities when the UN authorizes them to deploy on their behalf. The need for UN support to regional peace operations has been an important topic given the financial limitations of AU operations. These limitations are due to inadequate equipment and transportation capabilities and other operational weaknesses, and have implications for their re-hatting as UN peacekeeping operations. For example, the difficulties in ensuring that the re-hatted contingents in the Central African Republic or Mali meet UN standards for contingent-owned equipment. Discussions have included financing AU peace operations, planning for and managing mission transitions, enhancing the prospects for rapid deployment, and improving institutional collaboration between the UN Security Council and the AU Peace and Security Council (PSC).

New mandates and resources

The principles and practices of UN peacekeeping have developed over time and are codified in the 1992 "Agenda for Peace," the 2000 "Report of the Panel on UN Peace Operations" (commonly known as the Brahimi Report), and the 2008 "UN Peacekeeping Operations: Principles and Guidelines" (otherwise known as the Capstone Doctrine). Such milestones in developing the framework of UN peacekeeping have contributed to improvements to peacekeeping as a tool. In 2014, the secretary-general announced the launch of a review of UN peacekeeping almost 15 years after the Brahimi report, which would focus on "mandates, political leverage, logistical support, training, accountability, rules of engagement, technological innovation, and clarity on caveats of TCC and PCCs." The successful pursuit of Resolution 2086 (2013) by Pakistan, noted as the most authoritative of council decisions on peacekeeping, follows consensus within the council that peacekeeping missions are one of the most significant tools at its disposal.[64]

Opportunities to discuss the wider issues of peacekeeping are important in order to assess its effectiveness as one of the tools for peace and security, most especially granted the significant changes in the global peace and security environment. Amongst the TPCCs, such discussions, discussed in turn below, have included a focus on: mandate design and implementation; resources and cost efficiency; inclusiveness and transparency; and an issue shaping the normative discussions on peacekeeping—"responsibility while protecting."

Mandate design and implementation

There have been discussions amongst TPCCs on the issue of mandate design and implementation. Such discussions are important given that one of the main shortcomings of UN peace operations is the lack of full implementation of mandates. In particular, the trend in the council in designing detailed mandates hinders the ability of missions to prioritize demands as needs change in the field. Establishing or renewing council mandates is a process that requires huge investment of time and resources from all council members.

Discussions have included ensuring that mandates are realistic and achievable; set clear tasks for the missions and their leadership; and leave room for flexibility and responsiveness. There have also been discussions related to resource constraints, alignment of mandates, and budgets. In particular is the issue of the increasing adoption of complex multidimensional mandates *vis-à-vis* limited operational and financial resources. Malawi, Egypt, Senegal, and Tanzania, for example, are among the states who have stated that mandates must be realistic, which includes ensuring that they are commensurate with the resources allocated for the successful fulfillment of assigned tasks, as well as political support.[65] There is a steady stream of complaints from troops on the ground about unrealistic and confusing mandates and rules of engagement (ROE), as well as the provision of inadequate resources for implementation of the mandate.

Discussions have also focused on peacekeeping's role as part of holistic long-term efforts, including peacebuilding activities, and the implications for mission transitions, namely thinking strategically beyond the 12-month mandate cycle. The 2010 debate on transition and exit strategies acknowledged that successful transitions are ensured by developing clear, credible mandates matched by appropriate resources, and highlighted the importance of "coherence between peacemaking, peacekeeping and peacebuilding to achieve effective transition strategies."

There is agreement that the peacekeeping–peacebuilding nexus is an important consideration for transition. For example, Mexico and Brazil would like to see a natural and effective intersection between peace-keeping and peacebuilding at some point in the life of a mission.[66] However, most members question whether the council is able to address such issues. Brazil believes that sustainable peace should be the end goal of a peacekeeping mission and that exit strategy language is unhelpful to a more holistic approach.[67] Nigeria prefers to talk about achieving objectives and meeting benchmarks rather than talking about an exit.[68]

An important issue is ensuring adequate funds for peacekeeping to effectively conduct peacebuilding tasks. The high cost of UN peace-keeping is of particular concern to some council members given the global financial environment. Certain members that are also key TPCCs have concerns about the implications for peacekeeping resour-ces if peacebuilding tasks are increasingly taken on by peacekeepers, and in particular are concerned about the role of the military compo-nent being made redundant and thus leading to a reduction in the numbers of peacekeepers, should there be an increase in UN personnel involved in peacebuilding tasks.

Resources and cost efficiency

There have been discussions TPCCs on the issue of resources and cost efficiency. Such discussions are important because of the key role peacekeeping mission capabilities play in effectively delivering the mandates of the Security Council. However, expanding demand has led to the serious problem of capacity and resources. There is an over-stretch in peacekeeping, with the increased financial and technical capacity needs of missions as a result of the increasing complexity of mandates, as well as additional resources needed for new missions. As mentioned above, the high cost of UN peacekeeping is of particular concern to some member given the global financial crisis.

There is a persistent division between financial contributors and TPCCs. The disproportionate division of amongst member states pro-viding the financial and human capital has also been a point of con-tention. At a time when the cost of UN peacekeeping is at an all-time high, many countries who are large contributors to the assessed con-tributions for peacekeeping operations, including the P5, are reluctant to take on greater financial commitments, and instead prefer to keep the cost of peacekeeping down. On the converse, significant TPCCs remain concerned about improving the framework for peacekeeping rather than trimming it.

The developing countries that are now the major TPCCs of UN peacekeeping typically face challenges such as lack of equipment and training which often leads to underutilization of their resources in the field. The goal is to achieve better use of resources in the field and better outcomes, improved efficiency, and hopefully reduced costs. Discussions have included the link between the status of contingent-owned equipment and troop reimbursements, as well as developing performance-related financial incentives for TPCCs.

On 10 May 2013, the General Assembly, acting on the recommendation of its Fifth Committee, decided to adjust, for the first time in more than a decade, reimbursement rates to TPCCs. Included in the decision was a provision for the reduction of personnel reimbursement rates when the unit is lacking major equipment, and the payment of premiums for the contribution of key enablers in short supply.[69]

Discussions have included better agreement between council members and TPCCs on the establishment and renewal of mandates within the framework of a capability-driven approach, which requires the right number of military, police, and non-uniformed peacekeepers, as well as adequate force enablers (specialized units such as helicopters and crews, transport companies or medical personnel) to fulfill the council's mandates. Discussions have also included the importance of improving the current coordination mechanisms between TPCCs, the council and the UN Secretariat in order to lessen the possibility of a security vacuum between the deployment or the re-hatting of a mission and its full operational capability; the difficulties encountered by TPCCs in providing critical assets or utilizing them in an optimal way due to external factors or internal capacity issues; and bridging these gaps, including through inter-mission cooperation and commercial options. In particular for TPCCs is the importance of validation of pre-deployment training in peacekeeping, for the contingents' operational readiness. Although TPCCs are responsible for pre-deployment training, early in-mission assessment of pre-deployment training and the TCCs' capability to self-sustain would help to identify and bridge rather common capability gaps in the ability to conduct essential mission tasks or in the maintenance of the contingent's equipment.

Inclusiveness and transparency

There have been discussions amongst TPCCs and other stakeholders on the planning phase of peacekeeping operation, in order to design mandates that reflect better the balance between resources and tasks. It is common for the implementation of mandates to be hindered by insufficient planning or operationally unrealistic recommendations.

Ensuring that the council is presented with sound information and realistic options for the mandates requires careful consideration of operational challenges, and linking achievable mandates with adequate force generation arrangements.

The Brahimi Report addressed the link between commitment gaps in the provision of troops and police for the peacekeeping operations, and the need for better coordination and consultation among TCCs, the council and the Secretariat. Article 44 of the UN Charter states that when calling on states not represented on the council to provide armed forces it should "invite that Member, if the Member so desires, to participate in the decisions of the Security Council concerning the employment of contingents of that Member's armed forces." Better information-sharing on military operational challenges and more meaningful engagement with TPCCs is important for improving the quality of the substantive interaction in the design of mission mandates. TPCCs directly take part in peacekeeping operations, which gives them a technical advantage in terms of analyzing issues. Discussions have included the need for more effective formats for two-way exchanges of information, to improve the creativity and effectiveness needed in the planning, and for the implementation of peacekeeping operations to address challenges in the field.

Overall, discussions have been linked to the wider debate of how to close the gap between those who are deciding on the mandate, and the countries contributing troops and police. TPCCs have limited opportunities for input on management issues and strategic decisions directly affecting their national contingents, including into the early planning stages of a new mission or changes to a mandate, and updating the concept of operations, rules of engagement, and directives on the use of force. Some council members perceive that much of the interest for TPCCs in peacekeeping lies in economic gain, which limits their interest in substantive issues and affects their decisions on issues such as mission downsizing.[70] However, TPCCs state that they are concerned about the lack of understanding of the problems they face. While the problem of inadequate consultations with TPCCs has always existed, there is a need to address the dissatisfaction of TPCCs at a time of peacekeeping overstretch and global financial crisis. It is also apparent that in the background lie additional serious political issues. There is a need to distinguish between the political issues and technical issues in mission planning. Both the Military Staff Committee and the Working Group on Peacekeeping offer various options for addressing and depoliticizing these issues.

"Responsibility while protecting"

Numerous countries from the Global South, many of which are large TPCCs, have reacted negatively to the concept of the "responsibility to protect" since it was agreed to at the UN in 2005. Although the original expression received the in-principle endorsement of virtually all UN member states, when it comes to actually applying the concept, the discussions have been closely followed by the South.

Latin American representation in the UNSC in the last five years is a strong indication of how most Southern countries tend to react. The results are mixed. The region has recently been represented by Brazil (2010–1), Guatemala (2012–3), Argentina (2013–4) and Chile (2014–5), who were at the council when robust peacekeeping and peace enforcement operations were regularly discussed and actually authorized. Their positions shed light on at least three underlying aspects of the mandates authorizing the use of force: concern about sovereignty as a rule, but not in absolute terms; the use of protection language; and attaining an adequate balance between means and ends, during negotiations and especially during implementation.

Brazil, for example, was vocally against providing the UN or regional organizations with a blank check when mandating robust operations or peace enforcement operations. The country abstained from voting on Resolution 1973, which approved a mission in Libya in 2011, even though one of the purposes of the mandate was to protect civilians. Later that year, Brazil launched the concept of "responsibility *while* protecting" to emphasize that the use of force, when necessary, must follow a specific set of principles, rules and procedures, such as proportionality and accountability, to avoid harming those very civilians who are to be protected.[71]

Argentina was in favor of MONUSCO's FIB in 2013, arguing that it would protect civilians in an increasingly complex situation, and explicitly acknowledging there had been a formal request by the local government. It expressed concern, however, about the speed of negotiations that led to the resolution.[72]

In Asia, most TPCCs have not been comfortable with an expanding role for peacekeeping, especially when employed for humanitarian concerns under the "responsibility to protect" mandate.[73] India, for example, also abstained from supporting Resolution 1973 during the Libyan crisis. In fact, without very clear provisions and safeguards, it became clear that such provisions could become a basis for regime change and consequently a violation of state sovereignty.[74]

Conclusion

In this chapter the focus has been on the views and perceptions of the large-troop- and police-contributing countries. The division of labor that has emerged in UN peacekeeping since the end of the Cold War—where the North is engaged in peacekeeping mostly at the strategic level and through its financial contributions, whilst the South mostly contributes the civilian, police, and military personnel—has placed renewed strain on the relationship between the North and South. This is one of the most challenging political issues in the structure of UN peacekeeping, and although there seems to be an interest by some European countries to increase their contributions,[75] it is hard to see how the gap between those providing the bulk of the financing and those providing the bulk of the uniformed personnel is going to change in the medium- to long-term.

The chapter has looked at the doctrinal positions of the countries that contribute the most troops or police officers to UN peacekeeping operations, including political, security, economic, moral, and professional considerations. One of the observations is that the level of satisfaction with the current system is rather low. Asian and African countries are expected to take the highest risks when deploying troops to missions with mandates to protect civilians. However, they have limited or no access to the elaboration of the mandates they would have to implement. As a result, some TPCCs are still willing to contribute troops, but, when it comes to actually committing to military operations in the field, they employ caveats or orders from the capital that prevent their troops from actually taking part in more robust military operations.

The issue that is causing the most serious tension among TPCCs, between the North and South and between the UN Secretariat and contributors, is differences in opinion and interpretation when it comes to the trend towards the more robust use of force in UN peacekeeping. Given their significant contributions and the risks their personnel face in the field, the views of the large TPCCs from the Global South are an important factor in this debate.

Another observation is that there is a wider need for regular and substantive discussions on key peacekeeping issues, as well as mission-specific consultations with TPCCs. The large TCCs and PCCs feel marginalized in the decision-making processes at the UN, and this results in some of them then using caveats to get their way at the tactical level, regardless of where the high-debate may be taking UN peacekeeping at the strategic level. These dilemmas facing UN peacekeeping and especially the large TPCCs reinforce the main argument of this book, namely that the tensions between peacekeeping doctrine and current praxis is undermining the overall effectiveness of UN peacekeeping, and that these need to be resolved. Leaving the doctrinal issues unresolved in order to avoid diplomatic tensions only exacerbates the problem in the medium- to long-term.

Notes

1 UN secretary-general's remarks at the Security Council debate on peacekeeping, New York, 26 August 2011.
2 Department of Peacekeeping Operations, "Financing Peacekeeping," 2014, www.un.org/en/peacekeeping/operations/financing.shtml.
3 Chris Perry and Adam C. Smith, "Trends in Uniformed Contributions to UN Peacekeeping: A New Dataset, 1991–2012," International Peace Institute, New York, 2013, 2–5.
4 All deployment and related contributor statistics in this chapter are based on the UN Fact Sheet as of 31 March 2016, www.un.org/en/peacekeeping/resources/statistics/factsheet.shtml, unless otherwise referenced. As actual deployment figures differ from month to month, we have used rounded up numbers to give a more approximate sense of trends and developments.
5 Office of Internal Oversight Services, "Evaluation of the Implementation of Protection of Civilians Mandates in United Nations Peacekeeping Operations," UN doc. A/68/787, New York, 7 March 2014.
6 Priscilla Cabuyao, "UN Peacekeeping: Bangladesh, India and Pakistan's Troop Contributions," 18 June 2014, www.e-ir.info/2014/06/18/un-peacekeeping-bangladesh-india-and-pakistans-top-troop-contributions.
7 CIA "The World Factbook: Bangladesh," www.cia.gov/library/publications/the-world-factbook/geos/bg.html.
8 Providing for Peacekeeping, "Peacekeeping Contributor Profile: Bangladesh," October 2015, www.providingforpeacekeeping.org/2014/04/03/contributor-profile-bangladesh.
9 Rasheed Uz Zaman and Niloy Ranjan Biswas, "Bangladesh's Participation in UN Peacekeeping Operations and Challenges for Civil-Military: A Case for Concordance Theory," International Peacekeeping 21, no. 3 (2014).
10 Mohammad Humayun, "Global Benefits, National Motives," 18 December 2013, www.dandc.eu/en/article/why-bangladesh-sends-troops-un-missions-and-how-world-benefits-such-engagement.
11 Varun Vira, "India and UN Peacekeeping: Declining Interest with Grave Implications," Small Wars Journal, 13 July 2012, http://smallwarsjournal.com/jrnl/art/india-and-un-peacekeeping-declining-interest-with-grave-implications.
12 Lt. Gen. Satish Nambiar (Retd.), "India and UN Peacekeeping Operations," Media Center, Ministry of External Affairs, Government of India, 26 January, 2014, http://mea.gov.in/articles-in-indian-media.htm?dtl/22776/India+and+United+Nations+Peacekeeping+Operations.
13 Ibid.
14 Compiled from various statements to the Security Council by the Permanent Representative of India to the UN.

15 Alex J. Bellamy and Paul D William, eds, *Providing Peacekeepers: The Politics, Challenges and Future of United Nations Peacekeeping Contributions* (Oxford: Oxford University Press, 2013), 292–3.
16 Kabilan Krishnasamy, "Recognition for Third World Peacekeepers: India and Pakistan," *International Peacekeeping* 8 no. 4 (2001): 56–76.
17 Ibid.
18 Statement by Ambassador Masood Khan, Permanent Representative of Pakistan, at the UNSC Open Debate on "Peace Operations: the UN-AU Partnership and its Evolution," New York, 16 December 2014.
19 Deployment and related contributor statistics are based on the UN Fact Sheets: www.un.org/en/peacekeeping/resources/statistics/factsheet.shtml.
20 International Peace Institute, "Contributor Profile: South Africa," as of 11 September 2013, www.providingforpeacekeeping.org/wp-content/uploads/2013/09/South-Africa-Lotze-deConing-Neethling-11-Sept-2013.pdf.
21 Statement of Ms. Louise Mushikiwabo, Permanent Representative of Rwanda to the United Nations, at the Security Council 7011th meeting, on "The situation in the Great Lakes region," New York, 25 July 2013.
22 Statement of Ambassador Usman Sarki, Deputy Permanent Representative of the Federal Republic of Nigeria to the United Nations, at Security Council 6905th meeting, on "The situation in Mali," New York, 22 January 2013.
23 Ibid.
24 Muhammad Juma Kuna, "The Role of Nigeria in Peace Building, Conflict Resolution, and Peacekeeping since 1960," paper presented at the Workshop on Nigeria and the Reform of the United Nations, organized by the Centre for Democratic Development, Research and Training, Hanwa, Ahmadu Bello University, Zaria, Nigeria, 11 June 2005, www.academia.edu/255514/The_Role_of_Nigeria_in_Peace_Building_Conflict_Resolution_and_Peacekeeping_in_Africa_since_1960.
25 Cedric de Coning and Walter Lotze, "South Africa," in *Providing Peacekeepers: The Politics, Challenges, and Future of United Nations Peacekeeping Contributions*, ed. Alex J. Bellamy and Paul D. Williams (Oxford: Oxford University Press, 2013), 376–95.
26 H.E. Dr Tedros Adhanom, Minister of Foreign Affairs of the Federal Democratic Republic of Ethiopia on "Ethiopia's Foreign Policy: Regional Integration and International Priorities," transcript from a meeting organized by the Africa Programme at Chatham House, 23 October 2015, www.chathamhouse.org/sites/files/chathamhouse/events/special/15.10.26.%20Ethiopia%20FM%20Transcript_0.pdf.
27 Nina Wilén, "A Hybrid Peace through Locally Owned and Externally Financed SSR-DDR in Rwanda?" *Third World Quarterly* 33, no. 7 (2012): 1,323–36.
28 Juma Kuna"The Role of Nigeria in Peace Building, Conflict Resolution, and Peacekeeping since 1960."
29 Arthur Boutellis, "Peacekeeping Needs More Uruguayans, Not Fewer," *Global Observatory*, 20 September 2011, http://theglobalobservatory.org/analysis/111-peacekeeping-needs-more-uruguays-not-fewer.html.
30 Permanent Mission of Uruguay to the United Nations, "Candidature of Uruguay to the Security Council: Term 2016–2017," www.un.int/uruguay/submenu-onu/discursos/2013-01-01%20CandidaturaConsejoSeguridad.pdf.

31 UN General Assembly, UN doc. A/67/224/Add.1, 27 December 2012, www.un.org/en/ga/search/view_doc.asp?symbol=A/67/224/Add.1.
32 Paulo Roberto C. Tarrisse da Fontoura, "O Brasil e as operações de manutenção da paz das Nações Unidas," Fundação Alexandre de Gusmão (FUNAG), Brasília, 2005, http://funag.gov.br/loja/download/23-Brasil_e_a s_Operacoes_de_Manutencao_da_Paz_das_Nacoes_Unidas_O.pdf.
33 Eduarda Passarelli Hamann, "Brazil and R2P: A Rising Global Player Struggles to Harmonise Discourse and Practice," in *The Responsibility to Protect: From Evasive to Reluctant Action? The Role of Global Middle Powers*, ed. Malte Brosig (Johannesburg: Hanns Seidel Foundation, 2012), 71–90.
34 Da Fontoura, "O Brasil e as operações de manutenção da paz das Nações Unidas."
35 Ibid.
36 Eduardo Uziel, "O Conselho de Segurança, as Operações de Manutenção da Paz e a Inserção do Brasil no Mecanismo de Segurança Coletiva das Nações Unidas," FUNAG, Brasília, 2010, http://funag.gov.br/loja/downloa d/678-Conselho_de_Seguranca_e_a_insercao_do_brasil.pdf.
37 Ibid.
38 Luís Kawaguti, "Operação militar no Haiti custa R$ 1.3 bilhão em 10 anos," BBC Brasil, 1 June 2014, www.bbc.co.uk/portuguese/noticias/2014/ 06/140601_dez_anos_missao_brasil_haiti_lk_an.shtml.
39 See UN Security Council Resolution 2098, UN doc. S/RES/2098, 28 March 2013.
40 Among the 16 UN peacekeeping missions in May 2015, five were considered to have a peace enforcement mandate, or at least certain aspects of one: MONUSCO (the Democratic Republic of the Congo), UNAMID (Darfur), UNMISS (South Sudan), MINUSMA (Mali) and MINUSCA (the Central African Republic).
41 Stian Kjeksrud, "Matching Robust Ambitions with Robust Action in UN Peace Operations: Towards a Conceptual Overstretch?" Norwegian Defence Research Agency (FFI), Oslo, 2009.
42 Security Council, 7137th meeting, New York, 14 March 2014.
43 Ibid.
44 Statement of Ms. Louise Mushikiwabo, Permanent Representative of Rwanda to the United Nations, Security Council's 7011th meeting, on "The Situation in the Great Lakes Region," New York, 25 July 2013.
45 UN Security Council, "Letter Dated 15 March 2013 from the Secretary-General Addressed to the President of the Security Council," UN doc. S/ 2013/163, 15 March 2013, www.securitycouncilreport.org.
46 Statement of the President of Mali at the Sixty-eighth General Assembly Plenary, New York, September 2013.
47 Statement of Mesmin Dembassa Worogagoi, Representative of the Central African Republic, at the Security Council's 7069th meeting, New York, 25 November 2013.
48 International Peace Institute, 2014, www.ipinst.org.
49 Statement of Eugene-Richard Gasana of Rwanda, at the Security Council's 7155th meeting, New York, 16 April 2014.
50 Ibid.

51 Office of Internal Oversight Services, "Evaluation of the Implementation of Protection of Civilians Mandates in United Nations Peacekeeping Operations," UN doc. A/68/787, 7 March 2014.
52 *What's in Blue*, "Peacekeeping Working Group Meeting on Safety and Security of Peacekeepers," 31 March 2013, www.whatsinblue.org/2013/05/m eeting-of-the-working-group-on-peacekeeping.php.
53 Ibid., 4.
54 Chiyuki Aoi, "Japanese Participation in Peace Operations: The Civilian Contribution?" in *The Asia-Pacific in International Peace Support and Stability Operations*, ed. Chiyuki Aoi and Yee-Kuang Heng (New York: Palgrave Macmillan, 2014), 60–1.
55 Richard Gowan and Benjamin Tortolani, "Robust Peacekeeping and its Limitations," in "Robust Peacekeeping: the Politics of Force," Center on International Cooperation, New York: New York University, 2008, 52.
56 International Peace Institute, "Beyond Haiti: Enhancing Latin American Military and Police Contributions to UN Peacekeeping," 2014, www.ipinst. org/media/pdf/publications/ipi_e_pub_beyond_haiti.pdf.
57 With the sole exception of Uruguay, who has been able to maintain a battalion in the DRC since 2002.
58 Security Council, report of the meeting on "The Situation in Mali," UN doc. S/PV.6985, 25 June 2013, www.un.org/en/ga/search/view_doc.asp?sym bol=S/PV.6985.
59 What's in Blue (2013).
60 Security Council, report on the meeting "Delegates Argue Merits of Unmanned Arial Vehicles, Other Technologies as Security Council Considers New Trends in Peacekeeping," 11 June 2014, www.un.org/press/en/ 2014/sc11434.doc.htm.
61 *What's in Blue*, "Peacekeeping Working Group Meeting on Safety and Security of Peacekeepers."
62 Security Council, report of the meeting on "United Nations Peacekeeping Operations," UN doc. S/PV.6886, 12 December 2012, www.un.org/en/ga/ search/view_doc.asp?symbol=S/PV.6886.
63 Security Council, report of the "Briefings by Chairmen of Subsidiary Bodies of the Security Council," UN doc. S/PV.6881, 7 December 2012, www.un.org/en/ga/search/view_doc.asp?symbol=S/PV.6881.
64 *What's in Blue*, "Peacekeeping Open Debate," 2013, www.whatsinblue.org/ 2013/01/peacekeeping-open-debate.php.
65 Statement of Wilbert Ibuge (Tanzania), Abdou Salam Diallo (Senegal), Osama Abdelkhalek (Egypt), and Charles Peter Msosa (Malawi), at the Security Council Meeting of 11 June 2014.
66 Security Council, report of the meeting on "No Exit without Strategy," of 15 November 2000, available at: www.securitycouncilreport.org.
67 Report of the UN Security Council meeting on "United Nations Peacekeeping Operations," of 5 August 2009, www.securitycouncilreport.org.
68 Ibid.
69 General Assembly Resolution A/RES/67/261, 6 June 2013.
70 Security Council, report of the meeting on "Peace and Security in Africa," 16 April 2008, www.securitycouncilreport.org.
71 For details, see "Responsibility while Protecting: Elements for the Development and Promotion of a Concept," 9 November 2011, www.un.int/brazil/

speech/Concept-Paper-%20RwP.pdf. Also see Passarelli Hamann, "Brazil and R2P."

72 For details, see UN, "Intervention Brigade Authorized as Security Council Grants Mandate Renewal for UN Mission in Democratic Republic of the Congo," press release, 28 March 2013, www.un.org/News/Press/docs/2013/sc10964.doc.htm.

73 Dipankar Banerjee, "Contributor Profile: India," in "Providing for Peacekeeping," International Peace Institute, 2013, 4, www.ipinst.org/images/pdfs/india_banerjee130201.pdf.

74 Ibid.

75 John Karlsrud and Adam Smith, "Europe's Return to UN Peacekeeping in Africa? Lessons from Mali," in "Providing for Peacekeeping" no. 10, International Peace Institute, New York, 2015.

Part II
UN Peacekeeping Practice

7 UN support in the formation of new states

South Sudan, Kosovo, and Timor-Leste

Diana Felix da Costa and Mateja Peter

- Kosovo: The asterisk state
- Timor-Leste: How to build a state from scratch
- South Sudan: From euphoria to estrangement
- Conclusion

Statebuilding refers to activities undertaken to help a society recovering from conflict to create new government institutions and strengthen existing ones. Statebuilding as a form of peacebuilding is a relatively novel concept in international approaches to conflicts. It was not until the mid-1990s that international organizations and Western governments adopted statebuilding as a remedy for "fragile states." The 1992 United Nations (UN) *Agenda for Peace* refers to peacebuilding as "action to identify and support structures which will tend to strengthen and solidify peace in order to avoid a relapse into conflict."[1] The document is ambiguous on whether these structures are state institutions. In contrast, its *Supplement*, prepared three years later, clearly emphasizes the intrinsic connection between peacebuilding and statebuilding: "[I]nternational intervention must extend beyond military and humanitarian tasks and must include the promotion of national reconciliation and the re-establishment of effective government."[2] By the turn of the century the idea of building peace through building institutions found its ideational underpinnings also in scholarly writings. For example, Francis Fukuyama's influential book on statebuilding criticized the international community for failing to make "headway in creating self-sustaining states in any of the countries it has set out to rebuild,"[3] and Roland Paris' core argument in his is that peacebuilders up to that point had not made sufficient efforts in building basic institutional structures.[4]

In the majority of international statebuilding attempts, including those by the UN, assistance is intended to help states with fragile institutions establish functionality and legitimacy after a conflict. In exceptional situations, a conflict results in the emergence of a new state. A statebuilding exercise in these cases raises an additional set of issues as states and their institutions do not have the same kind of legacy. These new states were previously governed by another center, from which they sought independence. Core issues about the nature of the emergent state—administrative divisions, type of a political system, electoral rules, and a broader legal framework—all have to be settled in a relatively short timeframe. The region that now forms a new state has as a rule been disenfranchised in the previous territorial arrangement. In consequence, there is often also a lack of individuals with sufficient expertise and experience to assume vital positions in a new state.

Since the end of the Cold War, the international community has been more willing to assist in the growing pains of new states. On three such occasions—Kosovo, Timor-Leste (East Timor), and South Sudan—such tasks were assigned to a UN peacekeeping operation, albeit with different levels of engagement. Questions about the appropriate role of international actors under such circumstances have been widely debated over the last two decades, with many prominent scholars finding neo-imperial tendencies of Western powers and international organizations in their patterns of supporting new states.[5] As demonstrated in this chapter, UN support for new states also raises important dilemmas for UN peacekeeping principles, in particular regarding consent, impartiality, and the use of force in a new sovereign state. When the magnitude of decisions to be made are about the make-up of a sovereign state, international preferences and support for any option inevitably stretch the doctrinal underpinnings of UN peacekeeping.

The three cases where UN peacekeepers have engaged in support of a new state are very different. In Kosovo, the mission was asked to support a "state" whose sovereignty remains contested, not just by a party to the conflict but also by two permanent members of the UN Security Council. In Timor-Leste, peacekeepers were tasked with building a state virtually from scratch, with no recognized "government." In South Sudan, the UN mission was supporting the establishment of a state through a vast geographical area with almost no physical infrastructure. At the same time, South Sudan reverted into a civil war in which the government became a party to the conflict. Moreover, UN missions in Kosovo and Timor-Leste were established before the so-called Brahimi Report clearly confirmed the peacekeeping principles; their experience fed greatly into the findings of the Brahimi panel. On the other hand, the South Sudan mission could build on more than a decade-long experience of the UN as a state-builder. And lastly, the support for the three new states varies. In two of the earlier cases the Security Council decided to establish transitional international administrations, thus assigning a range of sovereign powers to a UN peacekeeping mission. In South Sudan, peacekeepers were initially tasked to assist the state and simultaneously hold it accountable to international norms and standards, but did not hold legislative, executive, or judicial powers. Following the political and security crisis in South Sudan, the UN mission shifted its focus to protecting civilians.

The three cases all raise questions about UN peacekeeping operations' abilities to live up to their doctrinal principles. However, they point at a diverse range of challenges. In this chapter we thus first treat them separately, allowing for an examination of the specificities of these challenges. The three sections that follow examine each case study along three dimensions: first, an overview of the state of affairs that the UN peacekeeping operation entered, both the international constellation and on the ground; second, the mandate of the UN mission, what is new and what challenges the mandate raises for the peacekeeping doctrine; and third, the implementation of the mandate—how the evolving situation on the ground and the missions' approaches to their mandates challenge the doctrine. The concluding section reflects on the common challenges to peacekeeping principles highlighted by the UN's support in the formation of new states.

Kosovo: The asterisk state

The Kosovo conflict was the last of a series of conflicts that led to the disintegration of the former Yugoslavia in the 1990s.[6] It was and still remains legally and politically the most controversial one. While all other entities that emerged as new states held the status of a republic in the former Yugoslavia, Kosovo was, for historical reasons, a province within the Republic of Serbia. However, Kosovo's population is, unlike Serbia's, largely Albanian (around 90 percent at the time of the conflict). Throughout the two decades preceding the 1998–9 war, Serbia's leadership escalated its marginalization and "Serbianization" of the province, including by curtailing the official use of the Albanian language.

Following a period of nonviolent resistance by the Kosovar Albanians, the conflict escalated after the adoption of the Dayton Accords. In order to secure Belgrade's support for the peace agreement on Bosnia and Herzegovina, international sanctions against the Federal

Republic of Yugoslavia were lifted without addressing the Kosovo problem. The international community initially criticized the armed uprising of the Albanian population, partly due to fears that the Kosovo conflict could spill over into neighboring Macedonia. However, after an increasingly violent response by the Yugoslav army, which resulted in hundreds of thousands of refugees from the contested province, Western governments started to change their attitude. The humanitarian crisis and what was beginning to look like another ethnic cleansing attempt by the Serbian leadership required a response.

The Security Council passed a number of resolutions to address the Kosovar crisis as it was unfolding, but could not agree on a use of force mandate due to Russian and Chinese opposition. The two countries saw the intervention as interference in the internal matters of a sovereign state and a potential threat to its territorial integrity. Bypassing the Security Council, the North Atlantic Treaty Organization (NATO) launched a campaign of air strikes justified as a humanitarian intervention.[7] This action was decisive, and led to the withdrawal of Serb troops from Kosovo. To address the immediate power and security vacuum (in particular, the revenge violence by Albanians against the minority Serb population of Kosovo), it was decided that a UN peacekeeping operation was to administer the territory, with the NATO-led Kosovo Force (KFOR) providing security. This division of labor meant that use of force dilemmas did not pertain directly to a UN peacekeeping operation itself, as the military component was outside its control.

An initial doctrinal dilemma for UN peacekeeping arising out of the Kosovo case concerns how the UN mission came into being and under what conditions the parties had consented to the operation. A UN peacekeeping operation covering Kosovo had been discussed before the escalation of the crisis, with Yugoslav authorities rejecting the possibility. However, after losing control over the territory, Belgrade feared "NATO attempts to deploy its troops in Kosovo and Metohija by way of insisting on some political elements without a decision and a mandate from the Security Council."[8] NATO's air intervention changed the situation on the ground, putting into question how the consent to the international presence was obtained. While Yugoslav authorities openly welcomed the establishment of the UN civil administration, this was militarily supported by NATO-led forces. These same forces were seen by Belgrade as having sided with Albanians during the conflict, making their impartiality suspect by one party from the beginning.

The powers of the UN Interim Administration in Kosovo (UNMIK) established in Security Council Resolution 1244 were unprecedented and virtually suspended Yugoslavia's sovereignty over the territory.[9] UNMIK's authorization provided that "all legislative and executive authority with respect to Kosovo, including the administration of the judiciary, is vested in UNMIK and is exercised by the SRSG [special representative of the secretary-general]."[10] While this was not the first time that the UN assumed some administrative functions inside a state,[11] Kosovo was fully entrusted to the administration of a UN peacekeeping operation. Timor-Leste, discussed below, followed a couple of months later. At the same time, the resolution that established UNMIK is riddled with ambiguities and contradictions. In order to secure the agreement of both conflicting parties and to obtain the support of Russia and China for the resolution, its text affirms the "territorial integrity of the Federal Republic of Yugoslavia," and at the same time repeatedly calls for "the establishment of democratic self-governing institutions" and "substantial autonomy" for the province.[12] Because the UN placed Kosovo under international administration without a clear road map for its final status, the two parties to the conflict understood UNMIK's mandate differently, leading to complications about its perceived impartiality from the beginning.

The Kosovo operation was the first time that UN peacekeepers had had to deal with the dilemmas of establishing a state. UNMIK was asked to provide solutions for administrative questions, which, while interpreted as technical decisions, are highly political and continually drew criticism about the mission's impartiality. For example, while it is important for the functioning of any state to have a clear legal framework, the question of whether and to what extent law as enforced before the conflict is applicable, is laden with political struggles. In the Kosovo case, the decision to apply the Yugoslav legal system led to accusations of partiality of UNMIK and a boycott of the judiciary by Kosovo Albanians. Similarly, the establishment of customs in Kosovo led to protests by Belgrade as they saw this as a sovereign right of a state.[13] As Alexandros Yannis, a political advisor to the first SRSG in Kosovo, summed the situation up: "Any policy or decision by the international administration has been interpreted by Kosovo Albanians and Serbs as promoting either independence or the return to Serb rule, and contested or undermined by one side or the other."[14] Maintaining impartiality when both sides see the conflict as a zero-sum game is virtually impossible.

At the same time, the interim administration and KFOR had immense problems assuming control over the northern municipalities, where the now minority Serb population was concentrated. Regardless of UNMIK's lack of a position on the question of Kosovo's status, the

Serbian minority saw the mission as supporting Kosovar state-like institutions in the provincial capital, Pristina, and thus undermining their aspiration to integrate Kosovo within Serbia. Financed by Serbia, these municipalities maintained "parallel institutions" to Kosovar ones, including law enforcement and judiciary.[15] Through everyday protest the minority population clearly demonstrated the lack of popular consent for UNMIK's authority. The fact that they received support from Belgrade indicates that while the Former Republic of Yugoslavia was *de jure* supporting UNMIK, *de facto* it was not. This situation was exacerbated after Kosovo declared independence in 2008. In one instance, disregarding the fact that its territory was under the jurisdiction of UNMIK, in May 2008 northern municipalities elected their own authorities (parliament) in the municipal elections called by Serbia.[16] These parallel structures have been largely dismantled and integrated into Kosovo's institutions following a European Union (EU) facilitated 2013 agreement on the normalization of relations between Kosovo and Serbia.[17]

What further complicated the impartiality of the UN mission was the magnitude of the Kosovo statebuilding exercise. Given the scale of the task of administering a state and building new institutions, the UN was not able to take on these tasks by itself. UNMIK was thus composed of four pillars, with police and justice (Pillar I) and civil administration (Pillar II) initially UN-led, and democratization and institution building (Pillar III) led by the Organization for Security and Co-operation in Europe (OSCE), and reconstruction and economic development (Pillar IV) led by the EU. Over time, as the UN transferred many of its functions to the institutions of provisional self-government in Kosovo and the EU increased its footprint, the role of the UN in the UNMIK framework decreased. This created problems for the impartiality principle of a UN mission, as EU institutions had been seen by Serbia and Russia as supporting Kosovo's statehood. Such objections were raised despite the fact that several EU member states to this day do not recognize Kosovo as an independent state and that the EU in its own documents refers to Kosovo with an asterisk, denoting that all its actions are without prejudice to positions on status.

The situation reached its height around Kosovo's declaration of independence. In December 2007, a couple of months before Kosovo proclaimed independence, EU leaders decided to send a mission to Kosovo. The mission was to be responsible for rule of law issues, focusing on policing and judiciary problems. This would mean that the EU would lead on the issue of Kosovo's future and effectively take over the remaining functions of the UN. However, Serbia strongly objected, seeing the proposed mission as an EU attempt to recognize Kosovo.[18] Initially, Russia blocked the transfer of functions from the UN to the EU. However, after an agreement was signed between Serbia and the UN, the Security Council approved the addition of the EU Rule of Law Mission (EULEX Kosovo) as an assistance mission subjected to UNMIK, rather than outright replacing it. EULEX is explicitly not allowed to address the Kosovo status question. However, in practice, the mission is tasked to strengthen the state-like structures of Kosovo. *De jure* UNMIK remains in control over political decisions, *de facto* its role is marginal. While EULEX has around 2,000 personnel, only about 100 international civilian personnel remain under the direct control of the SRSG. The UN mission therefore does not have the capacity to guarantee that other institutions subject to its control in practice respect the UN peacekeeping principles. Its own impartiality thus only remains on paper.

Timor-Leste: How to build a state from scratch

Timor-Leste, or East Timor, is a former Portuguese colony that shares the island of Timor with a former Dutch colony.[19] While the Dutch had transferred the western half of the island to an independent Indonesia in 1949, Portuguese control over the eastern part continued for another quarter of a century. In 1975, Portugal hastily withdrew from the island and East Timor declared itself independent, a move that was not internationally recognized. Nine days later, East Timor was overrun and annexed by Indonesia, turning the eastern part of the island into Indonesia's twenty-seventh province. The majority of East Timorese resisted the annexation.

However, the international community was reluctant to support calls for independence, fearing to alienate Indonesia and Australia, both with a vested interest in the oil reserves in the Timor Sea.[20] An independence struggle was brutally suppressed by 1983. Around 200,000 people, out of a population of fewer than one million, died of violence, starvation, and disease.[21] The region was isolated from the rest of the world, with the Indonesian government holding a tight grip over any key political and societal decisions and posts. Nevertheless, the independence movement remained strong in and outside of the country. Following the collapse of the three-decades-long presidency of Suharto, the new president, B.J. Habibie, was more amenable to calls for greater autonomy for Timor-Leste. In early 1999, he agreed to let the East Timorese hold a referendum on autonomy or independence.

In the run up to the popular vote, as pro-independence forces were gaining salience, anti-independence militias supported by Jakarta havocked the region. With violence escalating, UN secretary-general Kofi Annan requested that Indonesia permit UN forces to provide security during the popular ballot.[22] The UN did not want to deploy a peacekeeping mission without the consent of the state. Indonesia denied the request. Instead, Indonesian police oversaw the ballot, with unarmed UN civilian police officers acting as their advisers.[23] The UN Mission in East Timor (UNAMET) administered the vote,[24] which had to be postponed twice due to violence. After voters overwhelmingly rejected a continuing relationship with Indonesia, the anti-independence militias struck in full intensity, looting and burning houses and public buildings, forcing almost the entire population to flee to the mountains or across the border to West Timor.

Outraged by the violence and on request of the traditional leadership of Timor-Leste, Australia and Portugal pushed for a Security Council response. Indonesia initially rejected a military mission, denying the scale of violence. Its consent to an international presence was in the end obtained through threats that its loan requests from the World Bank and the International Monetary Fund (IMF) would be denied. In September 1999, the Security Council authorized the Australian-led International Force for East Timor (INTERFET) to restore peace and security and oversee humanitarian assistance.[25] A month later it authorized a UN peacekeeping operation—the UN Transitional Administration in East Timor (UNTAET)—to provide an interim civil administration over the territory.[26]

UNTAET's mandate on paper in many ways resembled that of the operation in Kosovo: the Security Council gave the operation complete control over the territory.[27] However, there are at least four differences that substantially impacted how UNTAET was able to adhere to UN peacekeeping principles. First, unlike UNMIK in Kosovo, UNTAET operated with the clear parameter that it was preparing Timor-Leste for independence. This, on one hand, eased the strategic orientation of the mission, but at the same time gave it a short time scale for completion of its tasks.

Second, unlike in Kosovo, where northern provinces objected to UNMIK's control, Timor Leste has a fairly homogenous population, which overall supported the presence of UNTAET and its goals. Most anti-independence forces left Timor-Leste after the arrival of the international presence. Third, in stark contrast to UNMIK, the entire operation in Timor Leste was run by the UN, with heads of the various pillars not representatives of other international organizations, but, rather, UN personnel. The UN mission in Timor-Leste was also in charge of the military component. This created a more conducive situation for the whole mission to be able to adhere to UN peace-keeping principles. Fourth, unlike Kosovo, which has a relatively highly educated population and whose post-conflict institutions had a legacy in the former Yugoslavia, Timor-Leste had no functioning institutions and very few trained personnel. The top ranks of the previous admin-istration were almost entirely drawn from the Indonesian civil service, and they had returned to Indonesia after the referendum.[28] UNTAET was thus building a state from scratch.

The mission was initially organized into three pillars.[29] The first and largest was the military pillar in charge of security. The UN blue hel-mets took over from INTERFET in February 2000, with some 70 percent of troops re-hatting into UNTAET. UN peacekeepers inherited a territory where security was largely restored. After re-hatting, Aus-tralia remained the largest troop contributor. Australia's willingness to use force under INTERFET meant that the continued presence of its peacekeepers was enough of a deterrent to prevent major outbreaks of violence. In addition, by the time UNTAET took over, relations between Timor-Leste and Indonesia had improved exponentially due to changes in the Indonesian government. James Sloan argues that these factors explain why security breaches in Timor-Leste were mini-mal and why despite having a robust mandate, UNTAET did not have to resort to the use of force.[30] The second pillar was in charge of humanitarian assistance and emergency rehabilitation. The work of these two pillars resembles traditional peacekeeping tasks.

The third, and the most novel part of the peacekeeping operation, was known as Governance and Public Administration (GPA). This pillar was responsible for "re-establishing governance at the central and district levels, for regenerating public and social utilities, for establish-ing the rule of law, and for encouraging and regulating investment in the private sector."[31] This was an enormous task for an operation headed by the Department for Peacekeeping Operations (DPKO), which possessed little governance expertise or local knowledge. Ques-tions over which personnel to train, which legal provisions to adopt, when to schedule elections, and how to engage the private sector are all highly political questions, making it difficult for a mission to remain impartial. The GPA approach was seen as Dili-centric. Because of low levels of education and development, UNTAET often assumed it was entering *terra nullius*.

Many analyses point in particular to the problems that UNTAET experienced with "inventing" justice and rule-of-law components.[32]

Due to the short-term time line and technocratic practices, the mission relied on Western models for rule of law, "failed to appreciate the resilience of local structures, and therefore did not reconcile the two contrasting systems of justice."[33] It was not seeking consultation or consent from the Timorese, which in the end resulted in two parallel legal systems on the island and little sustainability of the Western model in practice.[34]

One of the biggest challenges for peacekeeping principles stemmed from the concern of the mission to be perceived as impartial. Its ambition to uphold this peacekeeping principle led it to problematically sideline another: the question of consent. The Timorese had no formal standing in the planning process of the UNTAET mission, and very little in its implementation. Astri Suhrke writes that some earlier plans prepared by the UN Department of Political Affairs (DPA) envisaged a dual-structure, where "the Timorese would have political power while the UN would assume legal authority and serve in an advisory role."[35] However, in the final proposal forwarded to the Security Council both the dual structure and the timetable for elections disappeared. In fact, while the resolution establishing UNTAET mentions the importance of consulting and cooperating with the East Timorese people, this was not only completely left to UNTAET's discretion, but was also addressed after the importance of UNTAET's cooperation with Indonesia and Portugal.[36] In practice, the question of Timorese participation in governance was further complicated by the question of whether to recognize the National Congress for Timorese Reconstruction (CNRT)—the faction that led Timor-Leste to its independence—as the Timorese government. Suhrke writes that at the time it was argued that "[e]arly recognition would amount to political favouritism and could encourage corruption."[37] The quest for neutrality and impartiality meant that little Timorese participation and consent to UNTAET's policies was actively encouraged in the first phase. With the first parliamentary elections organized only in August 2001, the peacekeeping mission was operating without a recognized local counterpart for almost two years.

South Sudan: From euphoria to estrangement

South Sudan achieved independence from Sudan on 9 July 2011, the outcome of a process that started with the signing of the Comprehensive Peace Agreement (CPA) in 2005 between the Sudan People's Liberation Movement/Army (SPLM/A) and the Government of Sudan. The CPA was sponsored by the Intergovernmental Authority on

Development (IGAD) composed of East African countries, and a consortium of donor countries, particularly the United States, the United Kingdom, and Norway. It provided for a referendum on southern self-determination, which was held in January 2011 with the support of the UN Mission in Sudan (UNMIS). On the first day of the new nation, UNMIS was succeeded by the UN Mission in South Sudan (UNMISS), shifting from a Chapter VI to Chapter VII mandate and concentrating entirely on internal issues, simultaneously tasked with supporting the host government and holding it accountable.

The independence of South Sudan gave way to a wave of euphoria, hope and optimism, both internally and internationally, but this was to be short-lived. Overcoming the longest civil war in Africa—which had lasted from 1956, when the British left Sudan, until 2005, with a short break between 1972 and 1983—would be no easy feat. The long conflict had claimed at least two million lives, caused the displacement of more than four million people, and destroyed what little infrastructure existed.[38] The provision of essential services such as education, health, and water remain very limited and most service delivery was and continues to be carried out by nongovernmental organizations (NGOs).[39] Most of the country remains isolated with few or no roads, particularly during the long rainy season, and many areas are only accessible by air.

The civil war had been fought between the North and the South, but it had also led to serious internal clashes between different factions in the SPLM/A. Critically, after the 1991 SPLM/A split, more Southerners died at the hands of other Southerners than from clashes with the North.[40] The first two and a half years of independence were tarnished with numerous localized conflicts exploiting ethnic divides for political objectives. By December 2013 the new nation fell into a war between the government's Sudan People's Liberation Army (SPLA), led by President Salva Kiir, an ethnic Dinka, and the SPLA in Opposition (SPLA-IO), led by former vice-president Riek Machar, an ethnic Nuer, yet again tangling political tensions and ambitions with tribal identities and grievances.[41] The conflict quickly spread from the capital Juba to several other states.

Within weeks, thousands of people had been killed or wounded in the violence, and hundreds of thousands displaced from their homes. Under serious pressure from the international community, an IGAD-sponsored peace deal was signed by the two parties in August 2015. As a result, South Sudan formed a Transitional Government of National Unity in late April 2016, led by President Kiir and Riek Machar as first vice-president, with ministers split between SPLM, SPLM-IO, SPLM Leaders (Former Detainees) or G10 group, and other political parties.[42] At the time of writing, 1.69 million people were internally displaced, nearly 180,000 of these seeking protection inside over-stretched UNMISS camps,[43] over 706,000 people had fled to neighbouring countries, and some 2.8 million people were at serious risk of food insecurity.[44]

UNMISS was initially mandated to support the Government of the Republic of South Sudan (GoRSS) to establish the institutions necessary to govern a new country in a complex and fragile regional and internal environment, and to protect civilians at risk of becoming victims of violence. It also had a mandate to promote socioeconomic development, peacebuilding, and recovery efforts.[45] The UNMISS mandate was innovative in the emphasis it placed on the protection of civilians and on its support to peacebuilding, as well as in its attempt to decentralize and operate widely across South Sudan's rural areas through County Support Bases.[46] But reconciling UNMISS' support to the host government with protection of civilians and peacebuilding, in the context of the highly divided socio-political space of South Sudan, proved extremely difficult. Tensions soon emerged between the various aspects of the mandate, leading to questions about the traditional notions of consent and impartiality.

Since UNMISS' start, protecting civilians from violence has been a central part of its mandate, and has had a twofold purpose: to provide advice and assist the GoRSS to fulfill its responsibility towards its own population, but also to "act independently and impartially to protect civilians when the GoRSS is not providing security."[47] A few months into its mandate, it became apparent that these two aspects were not compatible and UNMISS struggled to strike a balance between supporting the host government, and protecting civilians by holding the government accountable. The close relationship between UNMISS and the GoRSS effectively meant that government failures were also perceived as UNMISS failures, tainting the mission's legitimacy and credibility, both in the eyes of South Sudanese and of other international organizations operating in the country.

UNMISS faced intense pressure over the internal political struggles within the GoRSS and the SPLM. The UN mission's approach to asserting its impartiality was oftentimes perceived as a refusal to act. The most serious incidents followed President Kiir's decision on 23 July 2013 to dismiss his entire cabinet, including Vice-President Machar. International actors, including UNMISS, underestimated the significance of these developments.

The tension between the mandate of UNMISS to support the GoRSS to establish the institutions necessary to run a state, and its mandate to hold the GoRSS accountable to international norms and standards became evident. This was notably the case in the context of the alleged abuses of human rights by the SPLA during the forcible disarmament of civilians and during the violence that began in December 2013. Referring to UNMISS's support to the SPLA during the disarmament campaign in Jonglei in 2012, Amnesty International pointed out that "UNMISS continues to provide support to the government's sensitization campaign including by providing transport to government officials to areas where forced disarmament has been carried out."[48] Although UNMISS contends that it only provided logistical support to the GoRSS sensitization campaign on civilian disarmament in March 2012, it is indicative of the wider perception held by the population and many NGOs operating in the country.

Since the 15 December 2013 crisis, UNMISS' mandate, and success, became even more closely connected with protecting civilians from violence, particularly those who fled in large numbers to UNMISS compounds when the fighting started. With over 100,000 people seeking refuge at UN compounds across the country, in May 2014 Security Council Resolution 2155 made protecting civilians the priority in UNMISS' mandate.[49] While the loss of life averted through safe havens has been significant, the interpretation of the protection of civilians mandate was reactive not proactive. In this respect, there were calls for UNMISS to patrol "areas surrounding bases" and "other areas where civilians are present and may be under threat" as well as plan "for extending protection to civilians taking shelter to areas beyond UNMISS bases, such as churches and other community focal points."[50]

Although there have been a large number of humanitarian organizations operating from within UN bases and working side by side with UN peacekeepers, it was hoped that the protection of civilian (PoC) sites would be temporary and hence with very limited humanitarian services. According to Damian Lilly, a former senior advisor on protection of civilians at UNMISS, "there was concern that the PoC sites could act as a magnet for some of the 800,000 IDPs [internally displaced persons] in other parts of the country."[51] Lilly suggests that the term *PoC site* should theoretically "only provide refuge for civilians 'under threat of physical violence,' rather than the broader definition of IDPs who are forced from their homes due to conflict. In reality, though, there was little difference between the status of IDPs sheltered at UNMISS bases and those in other settlements elsewhere."[52]

Paradoxically, the December 2013 crisis represented both the biggest challenge UNMISS faced and an opportunity to change its public image and to revise the way it managed its relationship with the GoRSS. For the first time, UNMISS privileged protecting civilians at risk of violence—whether targeted by the SPLA or the SPLA-IO—over its relationship with the host government. This led to accusations from both sides that UNMISS was supporting "the other side." However, given the challenges UNMISS faced in providing adequate physical security to civilians and the fact that humanitarian conditions in the PoC sites remained extremely poor, the population did not feel UNMISS was doing enough. Crucially, it also led to questions of consent from the GoRSS, which started questioning the need for UNMISS in the country. While formally the government continued to give its consent to UNMISS' presence, in reality the mission faced increased restrictions in movement and access, including open hostility to its civilian staff, making operations extremely difficult.

Estrangement between the South Sudanese, both population and the government, and UNMISS continued to intensify. In March 2014 an UNMISS convoy mistakenly carrying weapons from Juba destined for Ghanaian peacekeepers in Unity State (a rebel disputed area) was seized in Rumbek.[53] UNMISS reacted immediately explaining that "[s]everal containers were wrongly labelled and inadvertently contained weapons and ammunition; [t]his is regrettable."[54] However, the damage had been done and reinforced perceptions of UNMISS' support to the opposition and its lack of legitimacy in the eyes of the population. Having originally arrived at a time of peace and mandated to support the new state, UNMISS found itself estranged from the host government, in the midst of active fighting and limited consent. In turn, the opposition saw UNMISS as remaining too close to the government. In August 2014, a second UN helicopter was shot down in Unity State by the SPLA-IO.[55] The SPLA-IO commander in Unity State had previously accused UNMISS that its aircrafts were being used to transport SPLA troops and had threatened to shoot down the mission's aircraft.[56] Although UNMISS has had a Chapter VII mandate since its inception, allowing it to take "all necessary actions" to protect civilians, its own personnel, and humanitarian workers, including with the use of force, it was for the most part reluctant to do so.[57] In cases where civilians were under direct threat of violence, such as in Pibor county, UNMISS was not willing to use military force to protect people.[58]

Since the December 2013 national conflict, UNMISS became more proactive in resorting to force to protect civilians and its own staff. One instance where it did use force was in April 2014, when Dinka armed youths stormed into and attacked the PoC site inside the UNMISS base in Bor that was hosting over 5000 mostly Nuer civilians.[59] UN peacekeepers responded with a Quick Reaction Force (QRF) that reached the PoC site approximately 30 minutes into the shooting.

According to the UNMISS Human Rights Division: "Once inside the PoC site, the QRF [Quick Reaction Force] opened fire on the attackers, with rifles, machine guns, and rounds from an armoured personnel carrier (APC)" and that "10 to 15 minutes after the QRF's arrival, the attack subsided."[60] The attack in the PoC site left 53 people dead and over 100 wounded.[61]

In light of the ongoing conflict between the SPLA and SPLA-IO, characterized by serious human rights abuses committed by both parties, UNMISS is between a rock and a hard place, reluctantly hosting thousands of IDPs in its bases under appalling conditions while facing threatening language and actions by the host state, as well as the opposition warring party. Yet, one thing that has become evident is that protecting civilians at risk of extreme violence is not a secondary feature in peacekeeping operations, and that at times the use of force may have to be employed for these purposes. Importantly, it has also become very clear that it may not always be compatible for a peacekeeping mission to support a host government in institution-building and extension of state authority, while simultaneously being tasked to hold it accountable in cases of human rights abuses and violence against its citizens.

IGAD-led monitoring and verification teams (MVTs) began their monitoring operations over violations of the Cessation of Hostilities Agreement signed by the SPLA and SPLA-IO in early 2014. Comprised of representatives of the parties to the conflict, IGAD member states, and the African Union, and reporting to the IGAD special envoys leading the South Sudan mediation process, the MVTs were logistically supported by UNMISS. The teams were essentially monitoring a ceasefire that did not exist, and by August they had produced a report listing violations by both parties,[62] leading to further accusations of support by both sides. Any attempt to hold one party accountable has been seen as supporting the other conflict party, again demonstrating UNMISS' continuous challenges to being perceived as impartial.

Conclusion

The three case studies of UN peacekeeping interventions in new states demonstrate a number of commonalities in how they have challenged existing peacekeeping doctrinal principles, particularly those of consent and impartiality, but also of non-use of force and legitimacy, credibility, and ownership.

One major doctrinal dilemma for UN peacekeeping arising out of the country cases concerns how a UN mission comes into being, the conditions under which it is accepted and how the parties consent to its continued operation. Supporting a new state is an inherently political task. It is thus not surprising that in all three cases, as the conditions and the political environment changed and the mandates shifted, questions about the host governments' consent to the peacekeeping mission emerged. *De jure* states consent to the UN missions, partly due to international pressure. However, *de facto* host states often deliberately establish challenging, near-impossible working environments through administrative and operational restrictions by, for example, impeding movement and access. This has been most clearly seen in the northern provinces of Kosovo and in South Sudan.

Under these circumstances, consent came to be understood by new states as conditional to the peacekeeping missions' support and allegiance to the political goals of either the host government or other key parties. In the inevitably fragile and divisive context of state formation where there are a number of actors and factions, and where there may be other contradictory aspects to the peacekeeping mandate (such as protecting civilians from violence, including from the state, or ensuring the territorial integrity of the administered territory), this is not straightforward and affects the ongoing consent to the mission. In order for their presence not to be challenged, peacekeeping missions would not only have to be impartial, but also neutral, something that is virtually impossible in the circumstances under which they are operating and with the mandates that they are pursuing.

In fact, in light of the vast and often contradictory mandates given to UN missions in new states, it becomes problematic to even claim impartiality while simultaneously offering direct support to a host government. In Kosovo, the two parties to the conflict understood UNMIK's mandate differently, with each side interpreting the transitional administration's actions as promoting the others' perspective. Experience in South Sudan demonstrates that protecting civilians from actions of the host government which the mission was expected to support has not been feasible for UNMISS's work. In both contexts, any attempt to hold one party accountable was seen as promoting the opposition's interests. Having said that, going in the opposite direction does not resolve doctrinal dilemmas for UN peacekeepers either. In Timor-Leste, UNTAET assumed full sovereign powers with very little real Timorese participation to avoid any accusations of favoritism and partiality. The mission thus ran into a problem of designing a state with little buy-in from local actors. To achieve impartiality, consent cannot be compromised either. These issues of impartiality are compounded by the fact that due to the extent of the mandates, in all three cases the UN was working side by side with other international actors, particularly regional bodies, which had their own views and biases.

UN missions have traditionally been extremely hesitant to use force, even when they have the mandate to do so.[63] All three cases discussed had a Chapter VII mandate. In the case of Kosovo and Timor-Leste, security was largely restored by the time UNMIK and UNTAET arrived. In South Sudan, despite early optimism around independence, violence reemerged, leading to repeated calls for a more proactive stance from UNMISS in protecting civilians, including by using force. After the attack in the PoC site at UNMISS in Bor, Toby Lanzer, then UNMISS's deputy special representative of the secretary-general, stated that UNMISS would "do everything necessary to protect the lives of people in our protection, including the use of lethal force."[64] The disposition of UN peacekeepers to use force as per their mandates, is contingent on having troops that are appropriately equipped and supported. As mandates become more driven towards protecting civilians, troops also have to become more willing to use force.

To add to the doctrinal dilemmas, all three peacekeeping missions discussed above were instructed to engage in supporting the host government with administrative and governance issues as if these were technical exercises. Such an approach overlooks the highly political nature of the statebuilding process, which requires negotiations and compromise among a wide array of actors. The emphasis on technocratic statebuilding detached the UN missions from the everyday experiences of the citizens of these newly formed countries. It limited UN engagement to a focus only on formal government at the expense of informal structures of authority. This severely affected the UN's legitimacy and credibility in the eyes of the population. Furthermore, in particular Timor-Leste and South Sudan were assumed to be blank slates, with no political histories or local contexts to draw on, either because of presumed low human resources or simply lack of knowledge of these areas. The lack of attention to nation-building and reconciliation partly explains the relapse into conflict in Timor-Leste in 2006 and the ongoing crisis in South Sudan.

Finally, UNMISS' recent reprioritization of its mandate with protection of civilians taking precedence above all else, including its support to the host government, has shown that successfully negotiating relations with a myriad of actors in the context of a new state is extremely challenging and may be too much to ask. Impartiality may in the end mean taking the side of civilians, whatever side they may be from. This certainly carries consequences as to how host government consent has traditionally been understood. Some of the existing doctrinal principles are not compatible with the expanding mandates of UN peacekeeping operations and how they are implemented on the ground. By putting forward all-encompassing peacekeeping mandates and asking these missions to uphold peacekeeping principles, the Security Council may be charging UN missions with the impossible task of trying to fulfill their mandate by continuously compromising on that same mandate.

Notes

1 United Nations, "An Agenda for Peace: Preventive Diplomacy, Peace-making and Peace-keeping," Report of the Secretary-General Pursuant to the Statement Adopted by the Summit Meeting of the Security Council on 31 January 1992, UN doc. A/47/277–S/24111, 17 June 1992, para. 21, www.un.org/Docs/SG/agpeace.html.
2 United Nations, "Supplement to an Agenda for Peace," Position Paper of the Secretary-General on the Occasion of the Fiftieth Anniversary of the United Nations, UN doc. A/50/60–S/1995/1, 3 January 1995, para. 13, www.un.org/Docs/SG/agsupp.html.
3 Francis Fukuyama, *State-building: Governance and World Order in the 21st Century* (Ithaca, NY: Cornell University Press, 2004), 103.
4 Roland Paris, *At War's End: Building Peace after Civil Conflict* (Cambridge: Cambridge University Press, 2004). For similar arguments see also James D. Fearon and David D. Laitin, "Neotrusteeship and the Problem of Weak States," *International Security* 28, no. 4 (2004); and Simon Chesterman, *You, the People: The United Nations, Transitional Administration, and State-building* (Oxford: Oxford University Press, 2005).
5 For a broader discussion see Richard D. Caplan, *International Governance of War-torn Territories: Rule and Reconstruction* (Oxford: Oxford University Press, 2005); and Dominik Zaum, *The Sovereignty Paradox: The Norms and Politics of International Statebuilding* (Oxford: Oxford University Press, 2007). For critical views see David Chandler, *Empire in Denial: The Politics of State-building* (London: Pluto, 2006); Omar G. Encarnacion, "The Follies of Democratic Imperialism," *World Policy Journal* 22, no. 1 (2005): 47–60; and Mateja Peter, "Whither Sovereignty? The Limits of Building States through International Administrations," in *From Mediation to Nation-building: Third Parties and the Management of Communal Conflict*, ed. Joseph R. Rudolph and William J. Lahneman (Boulder, Col.: Rowman and Littlefield, Lexington Books, 2013).
6 For background readings on Yugoslavian disintegration and the Kosovo conflict see Misha Glenny, *The Fall of Yugoslavia: The Third Balkan War* (London: Penguin Books, 1996); Susan L. Woodward, *Balkan Tragedy: Chaos and Dissolution after the Cold War* (Washington, DC: Brookings

Institution Press, 1995); William G. O'Neill, *Kosovo: An Unfinished Peace* (London: Lynne Rienner, 2002); and Marc Weller, *Contested Statehood: Kosovo's Struggle for Independence* (Oxford: Oxford University Press, 2009).

7 Javier Solana, secretary-general of NATO, Press Release no. 1999(040), 23 March 1999. For more on humanitarian intervention see Martha Finnemore, "Constructing Norms of Humanitarian Intervention," in *The Culture of National Security: Norms and Identity in World Politics*, ed. Peter J. Katzenstein (Columbia University Press, 1996), 153–85; Jeff L. Holzgrefe and Robert Owen Keohane, *Humanitarian Intervention: Ethical, Legal and Political Dilemmas* (Cambridge: Cambridge University Press, 2003); Oliver Ramsbotham and Tom Woodhouse, *Humanitarian Intervention in Contemporary Conflict: A Reconceptualization* (Cambridge: Polity Press, 1996); Jennifer M. Welsh, ed. *Humanitarian Intervention and International Relations* (Oxford: Oxford University Press, 2006); and Nicholas J. Wheeler, *Saving Strangers: Humanitarian Intervention in International Society* (Oxford: Oxford University Press, 2000).

8 Statement by the Federal Republic of Yugoslavia, UN Security Council debate, UN doc. S/PV.4011, 10 June 1999.

9 UN Security Council Resolution 1244, UN doc. S/RES/1244, 10 June 1999.

10 UNMIK Regulation No. 1999/1, 25 July 1999.

11 There were a number of cases throughout the Cold War, where the UN exercised some transitional administrative functions. In the post-Cold War era the UN was partly administering Namibia, Cambodia, El Salvador, and Eastern Slavonia in Croatia. For more on the history of UN administrations see Ralph Wilde, *International Territorial Administration: How Trusteeship and the Civilizing Mission Never Went Away* (Oxford: Oxford University Press, 2008).

12 UN Security Council Resolution 1244.

13 For more examples see Alexandros Yannis, "Kosovo under International Administration," *Survival* 43, no. 2 (2001): 31–48.

14 Ibid., 34.

15 For more on parallel institutions see Elena A. Baylis, "Parallel Courts in Post-Conflict Kosovo," *Yale Journal of International Law* 32 (2007): 1–59; International Crisis Group, "North Kosovo: Dual Sovereignty in Practice," Europe report no. 211, 14 March 2011, www.crisisgroup.org/en/regions/europe/balkans/kosovo/211-north-kosovo-dual-sovereignty-in-practice.aspx; Sven Gunnar Simonsen, "Nationbuilding as Peacebuilding: Racing to define the Kosovar," *International Peacekeeping* 11, no. 2 (2004): 289–311.

16 Igor Jovanovic and Blerta Foniqi-Kabashi, "Kosovo Serbs Convene Parliament; Pristina, International Authorities Object," *Southeast European Times*, 30 June 2008.

17 EU External Action Service (EEAS), "Serbia and Kosovo Reach Landmark Deal," 19 April 2013, http://eeas.europa.eu/top_stories/2013/190413__eu-facilitated_dialogue_en.htm.

18 Elitsa Vucheva, "EU Kosovo Mission 'Unacceptable' for Serbia," *EU Observer*, 17 December 2007.

19 For more on the history of Timor-Leste see Andrea Katalin Molnar, *Timor Leste: Politics, History, and Culture* (London: Routledge, 2010).

20 George Junus Aditjondro, *Is Oil Thicker than Blood? A Study of Oil Companies' Interests and Western Complicity in Indonesia's Annexation of East Timor* (Hauppauge, NY: Nova Science Publishers, 1999).

21 James Traub, "Inventing East Timor," *Foreign Affairs* 79, no. 4 (2000): 74–89.

22 For more on the Timor-Leste self-determination process and the UN's role in it see the account of the head of UNAMET Ian Martin, "Self-determination in East Timor: The United Nations, the Ballot, and International Intervention," occasional paper series, International Peace Academy, New York, 2001.

23 Security Council Resolution 1236, UN doc. S/RES/1236, 7 May 1999.

24 Security Council Resolution 1246, UN doc. S/RES/1246, 11 June 1999.

25 Security Council Resolution 1264, UN doc. S/RES/1264, 15 September 1999.

26 Security Council Resolution 1272, UN doc. S/RES/1272, 25 October 1999.

27 There is a dearth of literature on UNTAET's role in Timor-Leste. See for example Jarat Chopra, "The UN's Kingdom of East Timor," *Survival* 42, no. 3 (2000): 27–39; Paulo Gorjao, "The Legacy and Lessons of the United Nations Transitional Administration in East Timor," *Contemporary Southeast Asia* 24, no. 2 (2002): 313–36; Michael Geoffrey Smith and Moreen Dee, "Peacekeeping in East Timor: The Path to Independence," occasional paper series, International Peace Academy, New York, 2003; and Astri Suhrke, "Peacekeepers as Nation-builders: Dilemmas of the UN in East Timor," *International Peacekeeping* 8, no. 4 (2001): 1–20.

28 International Institute for Strategic Studies, "East Timor's Transition to Independence: Starting from Scratch," *Strategic Comments* 7, no. 8 (2001).

29 Security Council Resolution 1272.

30 James Sloan, *The Militarisation of Peacekeeping in the Twenty-First Century* (Oxford: Hart Publishing, 2011).

31 Smith and Dee, "Peacekeeping in East Timor," 63.

32 See for instance Tanja Hohe, "The Clash of Paradigms: International Administration and Local Political Legitimacy in East Timor," *Contemporary Southeast Asia* 24, no. 3 (2002); Tanja Hohe, "Justice without Judiciary in East Timor," *Conflict, Security & Development* 3, no. 3 (2003); Traub, "Inventing East Timor"; and Joanne Wallis, "A Liberal-local Hybrid Peace Project in Action? The Increasing Engagement between the Local and Liberal in Timor-Leste," *Review of International Studies* 38, no. 4 (2012): 735–61.

33 Hohe, "Justice without Judiciary in East Timor," 335.

34 For more on Timor-Leste post-independence see Damien Kingsbury and Michael Leach, *East Timor: Beyond Independence* (Melbourne: Monash University Press, 2007).

35 Suhrke, "Peacekeepers as Nation-builders," 9.

36 Security Council Resolution 1272, paras. 7 and 8.

37 Suhrke, "Peacekeepers as Nation-builders," 11.

38 For a history of the conflict in South Sudan see Douglas H. Johnson, *The Root Causes of Sudan's Civil Wars: Peace or Truce*, 2nd edn (Woodbridge: James Currey, 2011).

39 Jonathan Counsel Agensky, "Dr Livingstone, I Presume? Evangelicals, Africa and Faith-Based Humanitarianism," *Global Society* 27, no. 4 (2013): 454–74.

40 Sharon E. Hutchinson, "A Curse from God? Religious and Political Dimensions of the Post-1991 Rise of Ethnic Violence in South Sudan," *Journal of Modern African Studies* 39, no. 2 (2001): 307–31.

41 International Crisis Group, "South Sudan: A Civil War by Any Other Name," Africa Report, April 10, 2014, www.crisisgroup.org/en/regions/a frica/horn-of-africa/south-sudan/217-south-sudan-a-civil-war-by-any-other-name.aspx; Douglas H. Johnson, "The Political Crisis in South Sudan," *African Studies Review* 57, no. 3 (2014): 167–74; and Øystein H. Rolandsen, "Another Civil War in South Sudan: The Failure of Guerrilla Government?" *Journal of Eastern African Studies* 9, no. 1 (2015): 163–74.

42 BBC News, "South Sudan President Reappoints Rival as Part of Peace Deal," 12 February 2016, www.bbc.com/news/world-africa-35556799.

43 United Nations Mission in South Sudan, "UNMISS 'Protection of Civilians' (PoC) Sites, update 22 April 2016, Juba, http://reliefweb.int/sites/reliefweb.int/files/resources/160422%20Update%20No.%20123.pdf.

44 UN Office for the Coordination of Humanitarian Assistance (OCHA), "South Sudan Humanitarian Bulletin," no. 5, 16 April 2016, http://relief web.int/sites/reliefweb.int/files/resources/160416_OCHA_SouthSudan_humanit arian_bulletin.pdf.

45 UN secretary-general, "Special Report of the Secretary-General on the Sudan," UN doc. S/2011/314, 17 May 2011. For a more extensive analysis of UNMISS see also Diana Felix da Costa and Cedric de Coning, "United Nations Mission in the Republic of South Sudan (UNMISS)," in *The Oxford Handbook of United Nations Peacekeeping Operations*, ed. Joachim Koops, Norrie Macqueen, Thierry Tardy, and Paul Williams (Oxford: Oxford University Press, 2015), 830–41.

46 Diana Felix da Costa and Cedric de Coning, "UNMISS County Support Bases: Peace-keeping–Peacebuilding Nexus at Work?" *NUPI Policy Brief* 4, Norwegian Institute of International Affairs, Oslo, 2013.

47 UNMISS, *UNMISS Protection of Civilians Strategy*, final draft approved by SRSG, 4 June 2012, 1.

48 Amnesty International, "South Sudan: Lethal Disarmament—Abuses Related to Civilian Disarmament in Pibor County, Jonglei State," London, 2012, 17.

49 UN Security Council Resolution 2155, UN doc. S/RES/2155, 27 May 2014.

50 See for example Louise Arbour, "Open Letter to the UN Secretary-General: International Crisis Group," 24 December 2013, www.crisisgroup.org/en/p ublication-type/media-releases/2013/africa/south-sudan-open-letter-to-the-u n-secretary-general.aspx.

51 Damian Lilly, "Protection of Civilians sites: a new type of displacement settlement?" *Humanitarian Exchange* no. 62, Humanitarian Practice Network, September 2014, www.odihpn.org/humanitarian-exchange-magazine/ issue-62/protection-of-civilians-sites-a-new-type-of-displacement-settlement.

52 Ibid.

53 Sudan Tribune, "UNMISS Cargo of Arms Destined for Dr. Riek Rebels Seized by Security Forces in Rumbek," 7 March 2014, http://southsudantribune.org/sta tes-news/128-unmiss-cargo-of-arms-destined-for-dr-riek-rebels-seized-by-securit y-forces-in-rumbek.

54 UNMISS, "The UN Will Investigate Error in Transport of Weapons for New Contingent," 6 March 2014, http://reliefweb.int/report/south-sudan/un-will-investigate-error-transport-weapons-new-contingent.

55 A UN helicopter was first shot down in Jonglei by the SPLA in December 2012. See BBC, "South Sudan Army 'Shoots Down UN Helicopter,'" 21 December 2012, www.bbc.co.uk/news/world-africa-20819468.

56 UN News Centre, "South Sudan: Preliminary UN Probe Shows Helicopter was Shot Down," 9 September 2014, www.un.org/apps/news/story.asp?NewsID=48674#.VLjsx8bA7R0.

57 Jort Hemmer, "'We Are Laying the Groundwork for Our Own Failure'— The UN Mission in South Sudan and Its Civilian Protection Strategy: An Early Assessment," *Policy Brief*, Clingendael Institute Clingendael Conflict Research Unit (CRU) and Norwegian Peacebuilding Resource Centre (NOREF), January 2013, 4.

58 Human Rights Watch, "'They Are Killing Us': Abuses Against Civilians in South Sudan's Pibor County," September 2013.

59 Human Rights Division, UNMISS, "Attacks on Civilians in Bentiu & Bor April 2014," 9 January 2015.

60 Ibid., 21–2.

61 UNMISS, "Attacks on Civilians in Bentiu & Bor April 2014."

62 Office of the IGAD Special Envoys for South Sudan, "Summary of Reports of Cessation of Hostilities (COHs) Violations (as at 21 August 2014)," 21 August 2014, http://igad.int/index.php?option=com_content&view=article&id=944:igad-mvm-reports-on-violations-of-the-coh-agreement-as-of-21-august&catid=1:latest-news&Itemid=150.

63 Simon Chesterman, "The Use of Force in UN Peace Operations," external study, UN Department of Peacekeeping Operations, New York University School of Law, New York, August 2004.

64 Al Jazeera, "Attack on S Sudan UN Base may be 'War Crime,'" 19 April 2014, www.aljazeera.com/news/africa/2014/04/attack-s-sudan-un-base-may-be-war-crime-20144195198569537.html.

8 Protection of civilians in the absence of peace agreements

Darfur, Chad/CAR, and Côte d'Ivoire

John Karlsrud and Ingvild Magnæs Gjelsvik

- **On a treadmill to nowhere? Peacekeeping operations where there is no peace to keep**
- **Mission impossible? PoC mandates in countries with limited consent and no peace to keep**
- **Conclusion and recommendations**

That operations should only be deployed where there is a peace to keep has been a core tenet of peacekeeping, and was reaffirmed by the Brahimi doctrine in 2000 and the report of the High-level Independent Panel on Peace Operations (HIPPO) in 2015. However, we have witnessed a number of peacekeeping operations being deployed during the last decade to theatres where there either has been a situation of no peace, no war—or where a conflict has been raging. These missions have been furnished with a protection of civilians (PoC) mandate, but with little prospect for changing the long-term political realities in which civilians conduct their lives. The results have been mixed—in some countries a modicum of stability has been achieved, while in others the United Nations (UN) has been a very large Band-Aid for the international community, not able to impact the situation in the long-term.

Unfortunately, it does not seem that the UN is willing or able to learn many lessons from these missions. The deployment of a multidimensional mission with a large military component to Darfur has arguably had little impact on the situation on the ground, and with the absence of a peace agreement an exit is nowhere in sight. The deployment of the UN mission to Chad and the Central African Republic (CAR) from 2008 to 2010 was short-lived with no political mandate to deal with the internal situation in Chad, and a Band-Aid deployment of 300 troops to the northwestern corner of CAR. In Côte d'Ivoire, the UN's mandate to guarantee the outcome of presidential elections gave events an unforeseen twist, as the UN mission stood by Alassane Ouattara as the winner and removed President Laurent Gbagbo by force, an unprecedented move motivated by the combined effect of the mandate to protect civilians and verify the outcome of the elections.

In the first section of the chapter we dig deeper into the specificities of each country case study and highlight some of the short- and long-term considerations that were made at key junctures—the situation on the ground and mandates given by the UN (and African Union [AU] in the case of Darfur), and whether these in fact were aligned. We will highlight discrepancies and dilemmas and detail what strategies the missions have made to deal with these. In the second section we provide a backdrop for the increasing willingness by the UN Security Council to furnish UN missions with PoC mandates, flesh out some of the dilemmas that emerge from the case studies, and see what lessons could be learned from these. Finally, we draw some conclusions and also assess the possibility for higher level learning from these experiences.

On a treadmill to nowhere? Peacekeeping operations where there is no peace to keep

This chapter deals with some of the most difficult cases where UN missions have been deployed: where there has been no peace to keep, and, for the cases of Chad and Darfur, little or no ability to influence the political situation on the ground. Although these cases could be considered outliers in UN peacekeeping, there are some important lessons that could be learned from them.

Darfur: State sovereignty before protection of civilians

Darfur is one of the largest humanitarian crises on the African continent, if not globally. The conflict between the army and its proxies and rebel groups started in 2003 and the primary victims are civilians. Large numbers have been killed and millions forced to flee, many dying as a result of disease and malnutrition.

Darfur is seen as the first "test case" of the "responsibility to protect" (R2P), since the endorsement of the concept at the 2005 United Nation World Summit.[1] R2P was at the time widely discussed and the shift from the term "humanitarian intervention" to R2P was to an attempt to move the focus from the protective interveners to the civilians that needed protection.[2] The three pillars behind the R2P doctrine as defined in the World Summit were:

1   the state carries the primary responsibility for protecting populations from genocide, war crimes, crimes against humanity and ethnic cleansing, and their incitement;

2   the international community has a responsibility to encourage and assist States in fulfilling this responsibility; and

3   the international community has a responsibility to use appropriate diplomatic, humanitarian and other means to protect populations from these crimes; if a member state is manifestly failing to protect its populations, the international community must be prepared to take collective action to protect populations.[3]

Despite the fact that Darfur represents a clear example of how the government of Sudan failed to protect its civilians, the international community showed reluctance to intervene. The first statement of the Security Council on Darfur came in 2004 with Resolution 1556 describing the conflict as a threat to international peace and security. However, the demands of the council were not coherent, and not followed by any enforcement mechanisms.[4] This was largely due to strong opposition to any international intervention by the Sudanese government and the consequent UN reluctance to conduct interventions where there is little or no consent from the host state.[5] The first international military response came from the AU in 2004, which deployed 80 monitors, protected by a small force of 300 troops, to oversee the Humanitarian Ceasefire Agreement. Despite growing in numbers—in 2006 the AU Mission in Sudan (AMIS) had about 12,000 troops deployed—the mission was too small and lacked the resources and personnel needed to fulfill its mandate. In addition to monitoring the ceasefire and provide a secure environment for humanitarian relief, AMIS was also tasked with a PoC mandate. This mandate was ambiguous and AMIS had conflicting opinions on how to interpret it, and whether protection of civilians should the sole responsibility of the Sudanese government.[6]

The Darfur Peace Agreement was signed in 2006 but did not lead to sustainable peace. The crisis lingered on and a more substantial UN peace operation was called for with a more robust civilian protection mandate. The Sudanese government objected to such a mission, which led to a compromise operation. This was the AU/UN Hybrid Operation in Darfur (UNAMID), a joint peace operation with forces of predominantly African character but largely financed and structured according to UN command and control.[7] When deployed with the adoption of Security Council Resolution 1769 in 2007, UNAMID consisted of close to 20,000 military personnel, almost 6,500 police personnel, and a civilian component.[8]

UNAMID has the protection of civilians as its core mandate: "The aim is to do everything in [UNAMID's] power to protect civilians in Darfur, facilitate the humanitarian aid operation to all areas, regardless of who controls them, and to help provide an environment in which peace can take root."[9] However, a robust strategy was not in place to prepare the mission's leadership and troops for their role in protecting civilians.[10] Planning and deploying a hybrid mission such as UNAMID comes with large logistical and administrative challenges and little time and resources were devoted to analyze the security challenges in Darfur and divide the responsibility between the key actors.[11] UNAMID was deployed while conflict was still raging in Darfur and its force commander stated that even if the mission was fully deployed in numbers, the peacekeepers would not stand between rival armies and militates engaged in full-scale combat. This was also a concern for the UN Secretariat as the UN is not deployed to wage war and the peacekeepers in Darfur had no peace to keep.[12]

The Darfur crisis emerged just as R2P became accepted as a new principle, which led to increased international attention around the crisis. It was seen as the first test of R2P, a test that it is generally considered to have failed.[13] Both AMIS and UNAMID had minimal success in the protection of civilians, and the security of civilians in Darfur remains poor. There are several reasons for this. Alex de Waal argues that the conceptualization of R2P was inadequate and the expectations that physical protection by international troops within the limits of the military strength was not realistic,[14] which was also highlighted in the Brahimi Report: "Promising to extend such protection establishes a very high threshold of expectation; [t]he potentially large mismatch between desired objective and resources available to meet it raises the prospect of continuing disappointment with United Nations follow through in this area."[15]

Civilians in Darfur got their hopes up when UNAMID was deployed, but the mission did not deliver as expected. Christina Badescu and Linnea Bergholm highlight that military intervention should not have been seen as the central way to operationalize R2P in Darfur, and R2P advocacy turned protection into a question of intervention rather than support for a political process.[16] Another strong argument explaining the failure to protect civilians in Darfur is international actors' reluctance to intervene. Badescu and Bergholm also argue that UN member states viewed protection for Darfur as secondary to their respect for Sudan's sovereignty.[17]

Reluctance to intervene in Darfur can also be seen in the light of geopolitical interests. Darfur was for some international actors not a priority area, while others saw that the intervention could jeopardize interests they had in the region. To conclude, the failure to implement the PoC mandate in Darfur clearly shows that armed intervention in response to humanitarian crisis is highly unlikely unless a state, group of states, or a regional organization become sufficiently motivated and show the political will to incur significant political and material risks to protect civilians and secure international legitimacy in support of their actions.[18]

Chad/CAR: Attempting a protection-oriented peacekeeping mission

While Darfur received widespread attention, the opposite was the case just across the border in Chad. Refugees sought refuge from Darfur in eastern Chad in increasing numbers from 2004, and concurrently the area was plagued with recurrent attacks by the Janjaweed militias operating from Sudan. Adding to this, there were frequent clashes between Chadian rebel groups and government forces. As a result, there were about 180,000 internally displaced in eastern Chad. The refugees, internally displaced, local population, and humanitarian agencies were plagued by widespread banditry, proliferation of small arms and a breakdown of traditional as well as formal conflict resolution mechanisms.

Together this resulted in a precarious situation for the civilian population, leading the UN High Commissioner for Refugees (UNHCR) in 2006 to call for a "stronger international presence in Chad in 2006."[19] The UN Office for the Coordination of Humanitarian Assistance (OCHA) also briefed the Security Council.[20] Towards 2007, humanitarian and human rights organizations added their voices to the call for a stronger international response to the attacks on civilians in eastern Chad.[21] By that year, an estimated 242,600 refugees from Sudan and 46,200 from the Central African Republic were residing in eastern Chad.[22] In addition, an estimated 178,900 locals were internally displaced.[23]

The continued attention led to Security Council Resolution 1706, which called for "a multidimensional presence ... to monitor transborder activities of armed groups along the Sudanese borders with Chad and the Central African Republic."[24] During the lead up to Resolution 1706, the government of Chad presented the crisis as solely a consequence of the conflict in Darfur, and argued that "mercenaries acting on behalf of the Government of the Sudan have been waging a broad offensive" including an attack on the Chadian capital, N'Djamena.[25]

Chad was reluctant to accept a regular UN peacekeeping operation, envisaged in the resolution, and wanted solely a civilian and police operation to secure refugee camps.[26] This was resisted by the UN Secretariat, which warned against deploying a mission without a clear exit strategy and stated that the conditions for deployment "do not, therefore, seem to be in place."[27] However, under French pressure the Security Council mandated a UN civilian and police operation in Chad and the northeastern corner of the CAR. This was the UN Mission in the Central African Republic and Chad (MINURCAT), secured by a small European Union Force (EUFOR).[28] The latter was replaced by UN troops after one year, in March 2009. EUFOR, and later MINURCAT, troops were envisaged to provide security to vulnerable populations in eastern Chad by patrolling main roads and cities and protecting civilians threatened by Janjaweed, rebel groups, and other militia attacks. However, Janjaweed attacks had already subsided prior to the deployment of MINURCAT and EUFOR, and it quickly became clear that the main threat to civilian populations was banditry, which the troops were not configured to prevent. Concurrently the rebel groups based in Darfur made several pushes across the border and attacked government forces as far into the country as N'Djamena during the early deployment of the mission in 2008. However, as long as they did not threaten civilian populations MINURCAT and EUFOR did not intervene. This increased the tension with the host government, which had envisaged the missions acting as a buffer between themselves and the rebel forces.

An innovative component of the mission was an 850-strong Chadian police/gendarme force: the *Détachment Intégré de Securité* (DIS). Trained and mentored by MINURCAT, the DIS increasingly took on difficult policing tasks pursuing hijackers and other bandits, often at great sacrifice. This was the first time in modern UN peacekeeping that a national security force became integrated into and accountable to a UN operation.[29] MINURCAT was supposed to train and equip the DIS and build police stations in six major towns and police posts in 12 refugee camps, but, due to bureaucratic contract hurdles, construction was slow, and so the DIS officers were deployed to camps with only rudimentary equipment, often living in tents. The slow deployment of UN troops after the transfer of authority from EUFOR to MINUR-CAT added to the tension between MINURCAT and the government, as the DIS increasingly took on more robust tasks than originally planned and was perceived to be doing the job that MINURCAT troops were mandated to do,[30] thus removing the rationale for the mission in the eyes of the government. After asking the mission to leave in 2010,[31] the government provided the Security Council with a new concept of operations for the DIS where it would, together with other Chadian security actors, play an expanded and core role across all of eastern Chad.[32]

MINURCAT was the UN's first "pure" civilian protection operation.[33] Although it included a military force during MINURCAT II, the entire mission's mandate was focused on the protection of vulnerable populations, without a mandate to negotiate a political solution to the ongoing conflict between rebel groups and the government. This was a weakness that staff at the UN Secretariat pointed out from the beginning, and the mission never enjoyed the support it needed from either its masters in New York or the host government.[34] Giulia Piccolino and John Karlsrud have argued that Chad is a case of "withering consent," where host governments reluctantly accept peacekeeping operations and try to take advantage of their support to strengthen security as well as make material gains, while shielding their rule from the liberal agenda that these missions advance, including good governance, gender, and strengthening the rule of law.[35]

MINURCAT enjoyed the support of key members of the Security Council because it represented an indirect way of dealing with the Darfur crisis. This meant that member states were willing to deploy a mission without a political mandate, and without acknowledging the ongoing political struggle between the rebels and government. The government only accepted the international presence reluctantly, on the assumption that it would be able to provide some security and material dividends, and it was quick to ask for the departure of the mission when the political will of the Security Council to deal with the Darfur crisis subsided. The Central African Republic was never prioritized by the council, with only 300 mandated troops to patrol the vast northeastern corner of the country.

During the lifespan of the mission, it was clear that it was not configured in a manner that enabled it to efficiently deal with the threats on the ground. EUFOR and subsequently MINURCAT were set up to deal with threats from rebel groups and the Janjaweed, while hijacking, rape, and violence against civilians were the real threats during its deployment. As a result, the mission attempted to deal with these through increased frequency of patrols, but was hampered by the slow deployment of troops, particularly in the most severely affected Ouaddai region. The DIS contributed by filling the security vacuum, often at high cost. This points to a gap in the UN peacekeeping toolbox: The UN does not have an effective tool to protect civilians against low-level threats. Its troops are mostly a deterrent and can be used offensively against armed groups, while the police do not have an executive mandate. The formed police units (FPUs) could have this capability, but their mandate is limited to population control. The fact that the DIS proved to be a fairly effective means of fighting low-level threats in eastern Chad, but had to be financed with voluntary contributions by member states, shows that there is a need for more innovative thinking and more flexible financing options to have a wider toolbox for peacekeeping, peacebuilding, and security sector reform (SSR) operations.

Côte d'Ivoire: The unforeseen consequences of mixing PoC with elections

The UN Operation in Côte d'Ivoire (UNOCI) was in 2004 mandated by the Security Council to monitor the ceasefire between the government and the rebels and assist with national reconciliation in the implementation of the Linas-Marcoussis peace agreement.[36] To maintain national ownership, the mission was mandated to "assist" the government, and President Gbagbo sought to limit the impact of the international presence.[37] Gbagbo had expected that the French *Licorne* force based in Côte d'Ivoire would help him stop the rebels in line with a 1961 agreement between France and Côte d'Ivoire, and was deeply disappointed that *Licorne* instead stopped the civil war in 2002.[38] *Licorne* continued to be deployed alongside ONUCI after 2004, mandated to support the mission as a quick reaction force if needed, thus providing ONUCI with an extra set of sharp teeth. Gbagbo saw UNOCI as an extension of the international and French interference in the country, and sought to limit the influence of the mission. The special representatives of the secretary-general (SRSGs) heading UNOCI— Albert Tévoédjré (2004–5), Pierre Schori (2005–7), and Young-jin Choi (2007–11)—were all accused of partiality by Gbagbo or his supporters. Consent was thus only reluctantly given from the beginning.

However, in contrast to the weak mandate UNOCI had to support the national reconciliation processes, the mission was given a very strong mandate to support and indeed *certify* elections. Already with the Pretoria Agreement of 6 April 2005, the parties to the conflict agreed that the UN would play a central role in the elections and should be part of the Independent Electoral Commission. Subsequently, Security Council Resolution 1603, in June that year, designated:

a High Representative for the elections in Côte d'Ivoire (the High Representative), autonomous from the United Nations Operation in Côte d'Ivoire (UNOCI), to assist in particular in the work of the

Independent Electoral Commission and of the Constitutional Council, without prejudice to the responsibilities of the Special Representative of the Secretary-General and with the following mandate:

> To verify, on behalf of the international community, that all stages of the electoral process, including the establishment of a register of voters and the issuance of voters' cards, provide all the necessary guarantees for the holding of open, free, fair and transparent presidential and legislative elections within the time limits laid down in the Constitution of the Republic of Côte d'Ivoire.[39]

This responsibility was transferred to the Head of ONUCI through Resolution 1765:

> *Decides* to terminate the mandate of the High Representative for the Elections, *decides* therefore that the Special Representative of the Secretary-General in Côte d'Ivoire shall certify that all stages of the electoral process provide all the necessary guarantees for the holding of open, free, fair and transparent presidential and legislative elections in accordance with international standards, and *requests* the Secretary-General to take all the necessary steps so that the Special Representative has at his disposal a support cell providing him all the appropriate assistance to fulfil this task.[40]

Presidential elections were first scheduled for 2005 but were repeatedly postponed until October 2010. President Gbagbo had expected to win, but to his own and perhaps the international community's surprise, the elections were a close race.

Perhaps in response to the weak mandate to support national dialogue and democratization, SRSG Choi had made clear that he was willing to go very far to ensure that his role as a certifier of the elections was implemented. In a frequently asked questions (FAQ) memo which the Certification Cell of ONUCI had posted on its website and circulated prior to the elections, the mission had underscored that the UN had a mandate to *guarantee and uphold* the outcome of the elections:

> The Certifier has received a mandate from the Security Council to *certify that all stages of the electoral process provide all the necessary guarantees for the holding of open, free, fair and transparent presidential and legislative elections in accordance with international standards.* The Certifier therefore has to ensure that all the necessary guarantees are met for the holding of successful elections in

Côte d'Ivoire. This means safeguarding both the process and the results of the elections.[41]

The first round of elections took place on 31 October 2010 and the second round, in which Gbagbo lost to opposition leader Ouattara, on 28 November. After the second round, both candidates claimed to have won, but the UN supported Ouattara's claim, and Gbagbo asked the UN mission to leave the country.[42] With both candidates claiming to have won the elections, clashes continued between their supporters, leaving hundreds of people dead. Both sides were accused of atrocities, and the International Criminal Court decided to investigate the post-election violence.[43]

During the violence, ONUCI and the SRSG were criticized for not taking action, but after the Duékoué massacre on 28–9 March and increasing fighting over the capital Abidjan, the UN started to move.[44] With a full-scale civil war imminent, the Security Council gave the mission a robust mandate, bordering on peace enforcement. Resolution 1975 mandated it to use all necessary means to protect civilians, in particular to "prevent the use of heavy weapons against the civilian population."[45]

In an unprecedented move, on 4 April and 10 April 2011, UNOCI carried out joint helicopter attacks on Gbagbo's residence, together with the French *Licorne* force. According to a senior UN official, as the UN did not have night-flight capability, MI-24 helicopter gunships with the UN force attacked the positions of Gbagbo's forces until nightfall.[46] The *Licorne* force continued to bomb the positions during the night. The UN helicopters had an impact and also helped the Republican Forces of Côte d'Ivoire (FRCI), the country's armed forces, achieve their objective of conquering Gbagbo's forces: "Indirectly, our actions also helped the FRCI to carry out their operations."[47]

As reported by the BBC, SRSG Choi was sharply criticized by the Russian minister of foreign affairs, Sergei Lavrov: "We are now looking into the legal side of the issue because peacekeepers had a mandate which requires them to be neutral and impartial." A few days later, Russian President Medvedev stated: "The United Nations cannot take sides, but that is *de facto* what happened." The critique from Russia would seem to be well founded, keeping in mind that the UN had outlined the principle of "robust peacekeeping" only one year prior:

> *Robust peacekeeping is not peace enforcement.* Robust peace-keeping is distinct from peace enforcement where use of force is at the strategic level and pursued often without the consent of the host nation and/or main parties to the conflict. The threat and use

of force in robust peacekeeping is at the tactical level, limited in time and space, and aimed at countering or containing specific spoiler and residual or looming threat in a conflict or post-conflict environment. Large scale violence or one where the major parties are engaged in violent conflict is no longer a robust peacekeeping context. Robust missions are not configured or intended to address any systemic breakdown in a political process.[48]

However, this concept note was criticized by various countries, including Morocco and South Africa, for being too assertive.[49] Nevertheless, one year later South Africa, after a short visit by President Zuma to Paris, supported Resolution 1975, thus completely changing its position on the issue.

What emerges from Côte d'Ivoire is a case where the norms of PoC and of robust peacekeeping were redefined through actions on the ground. This has a significant impact on the balance between PoC and the other norms of peacekeeping—impartiality, consent of the parties, and minimal use of force. To protect civilians and prevent or stop mass atrocities and crimes against humanity, the UN may at times be willing to use force at the strategic level against one of the main parties to the conflict, turning the operation into a peace enforcement mission and enforcing the responsibility to protect that the government has failed to respect and uphold.

The decision to use force on a strategic level was very controversial also inside the mission, and there was fear that the mission would be seen as partial to the Ouattara camp, which it was by many of Gbagbo's supporters. However, facing a full-scale civil war, the Security Council and the decision to intervene was also by many seen as stopping atrocities and so saving further human suffering.

Mission impossible? PoC mandates in countries with limited consent and no peace to keep

PoC has been a staple ingredient in mandates for UN peacekeeping operations since the UN Mission in Sierra Leone (UNAMSIL) was given a mandate that included "to afford protection to civilians under imminent threat of physical violence."[50] Missions deployed to countries where there is no peace to keep, furnished with a PoC mandate, will quickly find themselves between a rock and a hard place. These missions are, for better or worse, deployed so that the Security Council is perceived to be "doing something." The result can be surprising—in both positive and negative terms. The presence of missions can put particular situations on the international agenda and lead to intensified efforts to solve these with all available means, as recently seen in the Central African Republic, but there is a significant danger that the attention only will be temporarily, until a new crisis takes center stage, leaving the mission to struggle indefinitely with a weak mandate and insufficient resources to implement it.

MINURCAT was such a mission, deployed against the will of the host state, neighboring states, and the Secretariat, so that the Security Council could be seen to be doing something in relation to the Darfur crisis and spillover effects in the region. However, indirectly it contributed to "solving" the Darfur crisis, by drawing more attention to the need for stability between Chad and Sudan on a regional level, and the need for these states to end their proxy war through rebel groups. The leader of the Justice and Equality Movement (JEM), Khalil Ibrahim, was declared *persona non grata* by President Idriss Déby of Chad in 2010, and following this the countries managed to return to a more stable relationship, which also impacted the security situation on the ground in eastern Chad and in Darfur.

Conclusion and recommendations

Darfur, Chad/CAR, and Côte d'Ivoire all show the difficulties of deploying UN peacekeeping operations where there is no peace to keep. UNAMID lingers on in involuntary limbo between a stalled peace process it has little leverage over, and debates between the UN and the AU on the eventual drawdown of the mission. Chad is today quite stable, due to the military prowess of President Déby's army and his ability to fund troops with oil money, but the future is uncertain. CAR, already one of the least governed territories in Africa, has for long been on a downward path where insecurity is turning into religious factionalism and violence, and where the international community is likely to maintain a presence under French and UN flags in 2017 and beyond.

Some of these missions can be considered Band-Aids for the international community, being deployed to show the political will of the Security Council to deal with the situation. However, and as the Brahimi Report and HIPPO report have stated, the mandates of these missions must be realistic, matched with the requisite means and resources, and backed by real political will in the long term. Without these requirements in place, these missions are quite likely to fail to achieve their mandate, and undermine support for UN peacekeeping.

Deployed without a peace agreement and a peace to keep, the missions are likely to face continuous obstacles and can also easily become a party to the conflict, willing or not. In Côte d'Ivoire, the combined effect of the mandate and the role as a guarantor of the election converted the mission into a peace enforcement mission for a short duration. This probably foreclosed such a combination in future missions, something that may be unfortunate. The mission successfully protected civilians at a key juncture of the crisis, and most probably prevented further mass atrocities from occurring. If this had not happened in the shadow of the North Atlantic Treaty Organization (NATO) intervention in Libya, it could have been the successful precedence of employing R2P in a Security Council mandate that the principle sorely needed. History wanted it otherwise, and few now cite the situation as a successful implementation of the principle.

As Darfur was the first test case of responsibility to protect there are many lessons to be learned. Firstly, it shows that protection of civilians mandates need to be clearly stated and defined and that troops need thorough and contextualized training in how to carry out PoC in practice. This includes divisions of labor, especially when it comes to the role of the state and the role of the mission. Secondly, for a PoC mandate to be functional it must be followed by human and economic resources, which was not the case in Darfur. Thirdly, interventions in Darfur showed that PoC mandates in military interventions come with large limitations—even more so when missions are deployed in areas where conflicts are still ongoing. Therefore, PoC mandates in peace operations must be realistic and followed by effective strategies to manage the expectations of the population.

Finally, and this is an enduring and challenging point, UN peacekeeping missions may detract attention from the need to deal with fundamental underlying issues, including political, focusing instead on harder security issues and leading to a securitization of the situation. It should never be forgotten that many of the conflicts stem from particular parts of the population suffering under persistent poverty, inequality, insecurity, and endemic corruption at local and elite levels. Without addressing these, more long-term and systemic issues in tandem with structural and long-term governance and development efforts by national and international actors, UN peacekeeping operations will continue to fight an uphill battle.

Notes

1 Alex. J. Bellamy, "The Responsibility to Protect: Five Years On," *Ethics & International Affairs* 24, no. 2 (2010): 143–69.

2 Christina G. Badescu and Linnea Bergholm, "The Responsibility to Protect and the Conflict in Darfur: The Big Let-Down," *Security Dialogue* 40 (2009): 287.
3 UN General Assembly, "2005 World Summit Outcome," UN doc. A/RES/ 60/1, 24 October 2005, paras. 138–9, http://daccess-dds-ny.un.org/doc/ UNDOC/GEN/N05/487/60/PDF/N0548760.pdf?OpenElement
4 Badescu and Bergholm, "The Responsibility to Protect and the Conflict in Darfur": 287.
5 Ibid.
6 Paul D. Williams, "Military Responses to Mass Killing: The African Union Mission in Sudan," *International Peacekeeping* 13, no. 2 (2006): 168–83.
7 David Mickler, "UNAMID: A Hybrid Solution to a Human Security Problem in Darfur?" *Conflict Security & Development* 13, no. 5 (2013): 487–511.
8 UNAMID, UNAMID Facts and Figures: Current Authorization until 30 June 2017, www.un.org/en/peacekeeping/missions/unamid/facts.shtml.
9 UNAMID, UNAMID Background, www.un.org/en/peacekeeping/missions/ unamid/background.shtml.
10 Badescu and Bergholm, "The Responsibility to Protect and the Conflict in Darfur": 287.
11 Alex de Waal, "Darfur and the Failure of Responsibility to Protect," *International Affairs* 83, no. 6 (2007): 1,039–54.
12 Ibid.
13 See Paul D. Williams and Alex J. Bellamy, "The Responsibility to Protect and the Crisis in Darfur," *Security Dialogue* 38 (2005): 27–47; Badescu and Bergholm, "The Responsibility to Protect and the Conflict in Darfur": 287; Mickler, "UNAMID": 487–511; and De Waal, "Darfur and the Failure of Responsibility to Protect."
14 De Waal, "Darfur and the Failure of Responsibility to Protect."
15 UN secretary-general, "Report of the Panel on United Nations Peace Operations" (known as the Brahimi Report), UN doc. A/55/305–S/2000/ 809, 21 August 2000, para. 63, www.un.org/en/ga/search/view_doc.asp?sym bol=A/55/305.
16 Badescu and Bergholm, "The Responsibility to Protect and the Conflict in Darfur": 287.
17 Ibid.
18 Ibid., 42.
19 UNHCR, "UNHCR Chief Calls for Stronger International Presence in Chad," 21 December 2006, http://reliefweb.int/node/222078.
20 Oxfam, "Oxfam: Eastern Chad Must not Become Another Darfur," 2007; Human Rights Watch, "'They Came Here to Kill Us:' Militia Attacks and Ethnic Targeting of Civilians in Eastern Chad," 2007, www.hrw.org/sites/ default/files/reports/chad0107webwcover.pdf; and Amnesty International, "Chad: Escalating Violence Means UN Must Deploy, But Be Adequately Resourced," 2007, www.amnesty.org/en/library/asset/AFR20/012/2007/en/ 3e8803c2-a2af-11dc-8d74-6f45f39984e5/afr200122007en.pdf.
21 Ibid.
22 Ibid.
23 Ibid.

24 Security Council Resolution 1706, UN doc. S/RES/1706, 31 August 2006, 4.

25 UN, "Letter Dated 13 April 2006 from the Deputy Minister for Foreign Affairs and African Integration of the Republic of Chad Addressed to the Secretary-General," UN doc. S/2006/256, 21 April 2006.

26 Richard Gowan, Alexandra Novosseloff, "Security Council Working Methods and UN Peace Operations: The Case of Chad and the Central African Republic, 2006–2010," NYU Center on International Cooperation, April 2012, 10; UN, "Report of the Secretary-General on Chad and the Central African Republic," UN doc. S/2007/488, 10 August 2007. The latter report stated that "President Déby and his Government expressed concerns relating to the military component of the proposed United Nations mission," 1.

27 UN, "Report of the Secretary-General on Chad and the Central African Republic Pursuant to Paragraphs 9 (d) and 13 of Security Council Resolution 1706 (2006)," UN doc. S/2006/10, 22 December 2006, 17.

28 Security Council Resolution 1778, UN doc. S/RES/1778, 25 September 2007. Hylke Dijkstra argues that France also took on a significant economic burden in addition to shouldering most of the EUFOR military component, amounting to about €500 million. See Hylke Dijkstra, "The Military Operation of the EU in Chad and the Central African Republic: Good Policy, Bad Politics," *International Peacekeeping* 17, no. 3 (2010): 399. See also Roland Marchal, "An Assessment of EUFOR Chad/CAR," in *EUFOR Tchad/RCA Revisited: A Synopsis*, ed. Walter Feichtinger and Gerald Hainzl (Vienna: Institut für Friedenssicherung und Konfliktmanagement, 2011), 19–33.

29 There was a similar arrangement under the UN Temporary Executive Authority (UNTEA) in West New Guinea in 1962–3 when the local Papuan Police remained responsible for routine policing under the UN administration.

30 UN, "Report of the Secretary-General on the United Nations Mission in the Central African Republic and Chad," UN doc. S/2010/611, 1 December 2010.

31 MINURCAT, MINURCAT: "United Nations Mission in the Central African Republic and Chad: Background."

32 UN, "Letter Dated 7 September 2010 from the Permanent Representative of Chad to the United Nations Addressed to the President of the Security Council," UN doc. S/2010/470, 15 September 2010.

33 John Karlsrud, "United Nations Mission in Central African Republic and Chad (MINURCAT)," in *The Oxford Handbook on United Nations Peacekeeping Operations*, ed. Joachim A. Koops, Norrie Macqueen, Thierry Tardy, and Paul D. Williams (Oxford: Oxford University Press, 2015).

34 John Karlsrud and Diana Felix da Costa, "The Elusive Concept of Protection of Civilians: MINURCAT," in *The Protection of Civilians in UN Peacekeeping*, ed. Benjamin de Carvalho and Ole Jacob Sending (Baden-Baden: Nomos Verlagsgesellschaft, 2012), 163–80.

35 Giulia Piccolino and John Karlsrud, "Withering Consent, But Mutual Dependency: UN Peace Operations and New African Assertiveness," *Conflict, Security and Development* 11, no. 4 (2011): 447–71.

36 Security Council Resolution 1528, UN doc. S/RES/1528, 27 February 2004.

37 Ibid.
38 Piccolino and Karlsrud, "Withering Consent, But Mutual Dependency," 454.
39 Security Council Resolution 1603, UN doc. S/RES/1603, 3 June 3 2005, 3.
40 Security Council Resolution 1765, UN doc. S/RES/1765, 16 July 2007, 2. Emphasis in original.
41 ONUCI, FAQ: The Certification of Elections in Côte d'Ivoire, 2010, www.onuci.org/spip.php?rubrique117. Emphasis in original.
42 BBC News Africa, "Gbagbo Orders Peacekeepers to Leave Ivory Coast," 18 December 2010, www.bbc.co.uk/news/world-africa-12028263.
43 BBC News Africa, "ICC to Investigate Ivory Coast Post-election Violence," 3 October 2011, www.bbc.co.uk/news/world-africa-15148801.
44 BBC News Africa, "Ivory Coast: UN Presses Ouattara over Duekoue Massacre," 3 April 2011, www.bbc.co.uk/news/world-africa-12951990.
45 Security Council Resolution 1975, UN doc. S/RES/1975, 30 March 2011, 3.
46 Senior UN official, Oslo, 15 November 2012.
47 Ibid.
48 UN Department of Peacekeeping Operations and Department of Field Support, "Draft DPKO/DFS Concept Note on Robust Peacekeeping," New York, 2010, 3. Emphasis in original.
49 World Federalist Movement and Institute for Global Policy, "IGP Matrix of Issues: General Debate of the Special Committee on Peacekeeping Operations (C34) 2010 Substantive Session," a WFM-IGP project on the UN Peacebuilding Commission, 2010, www.betterpeace.org/files/C34_Matrix_General_Debate_22_23Feb10Final_0.pdf; Permanent Mission of South Africa to the United Nations, "Statement by Ambassadro Baso Sangqu, Permanent Representative of the Republic of South Africa to the United Nations at the Meeting of the Special Committee on Peacekeeping Operations 2010 Substantive Session," New York, 22 February 2010, www.betterpeace.org/files/c34_south_africa_22feb10.pdf.
50 Security Council Resolution 1270, UN doc. S/RES/1270, 22 October 1999, 3.

9 Protecting governments from insurgencies

The Democratic Republic of the Congo and Mali

Stian Kjeksrud and Lotte Vermeij

- MONUSCO's Force Intervention Brigade
- UN Multidimensional Integrated Stabilization Mission in Mali (MINUSMA)
- Changing principles of UN peacekeeping operations
- Conclusion and key considerations for future doctrine development

United Nations (UN) peacekeeping doctrine guiding operational practices must be revised. The UN missions in Mali and the Democratic Republic of the Congo (DRC) utilize military force in ways that fundamentally challenge the bedrock peacekeeping principles of consent, impartiality, and the non-use of force except in self-defense and defense of the mandate. The combination of more assertive mandate language and coercive military action finds few precedents from former UN operations. What will be the consequences for future peace operations if more forceful military operations are conducted without proper doctrinal guidance? To answer this question in the chapter we draw on experiences from Mali and the DRC. We argue that the time has come to revise the UN's bedrock principles to better guide blue helmets in contemporary robust peace operations, as they emerge as an alternative for protecting weak governments and civilians targeted by insurgents and predatory armed groups.

We begin by describing the development of more forceful UN peace operations based on those in Mali and the DRC. We then illustrate why these operations challenge the UN's current peacekeeping doctrine. Finally, we propose a revision of current doctrine that is more in line with recent developments on the ground. We recommend that UN peace operations doctrine must better describe the role blue helmets may fill when coercive military force is meant to protect governments and civilians from insurgent groups and predatory armed actors. In this process, UN peacekeeping could benefit from including doctrinal guidance from existing work on "stabilization operations." Any reform process must tread carefully, though, and take care to develop a unique approach that is still aligned with the UN Charter and (revised) principles of peacekeeping to retain the organization's comparative advantages.

MONUSCO's Force Intervention Brigade

The Force Intervention Brigade (FIB) has moved UN peacekeeping into new territory. The FIB, as part of the UN Stabilization Mission in the DRC (MONUSCO), has been tasked to "prevent the expansion of all armed groups, neutralize these groups, and to disarm them."[1] Late in 2013, the FIB was instrumental in joint efforts with the National Armed Forces of the DRC (FARDC) to defeat the *Mouvement du 23 Mars* (M23), a militarily potent insurgent group in eastern DRC. Joint operations aiming to neutralize remaining armed groups continued for a while, albeit with much more limited effect. In early 2015, planned joint operations against the Democratic Forces for the Liberation of Rwanda (FDLR), a Rwandan Hutu rebel group and now the strongest armed group in eastern DRC, came to a complete halt due to strong disagreement between the Congolese government in Kinshasa and MONUSCO concerning the participation of particular Congolese officers. After a period of unilateral FARDC operations against the FDLR, MONUSCO and FARDC have relaunched joint operations in 2016.

Similar types of robust military operations have usually been performed by regional organizations or by single states with more significant military resources. The European Union's Operation Artemis in the DRC (May–September 2003), the African Union Mission in Somalia (AMISOM, from 2007) and the French operations in Mali (from 2012) and in the Central African Republic (from 2013) are among the most prominent examples.

Two interlinked aspects make the FIB stand out from former UN peacekeeping operations: the explicit use of assertive language in the mandate, and the decisive employment of military force by a brigade-sized unit designed for offensive military operations in support of host-nation security forces. UN Security Council Resolution 2098 displays a clear intention to use military force *proactively* to "neutralize" armed groups through "targeted offensive operations" to "make space for stabilization activities."[2] The Security Council has never been more specific in its intentions to utilize force coercively. It is too early to categorize the assertiveness as an emerging trend. It could be a one-off incident due to context-specific matters related to the situation in the DRC and the wider Great Lakes region at the time. Several observations point towards the "FIB-language" as an outlier.

First, the humiliating fall of Goma in November 2012 created a strong incentive for the Security Council to take action against the M23.[3] The group, supported by Rwanda and Uganda, overran the MONUSCO-supported FARDC units defending Goma with ease.[4] Although it was the last line of defense, MONUSCO troops displayed neither the willingness nor the ability to militarily resist the M23.[5] Second, a robust military response was made possible due to a regional initiative from the International Conference on the Great Lakes Region (ICGLR), supported by the African Union (AU) and the South African Development Community (SADC), to counter M23 activities.[6] Accordingly, South Africa, Tanzania, and Malawi made troops available to the UN, forming a regionally based intervention brigade under UN auspices.[7] They were willing to confront the M23, had the relevant military capabilities, and needed a strong mandate.[8] This is a unique starting point for a UN intervention, more commonly manned by contributors that seldom use force for protection purposes.[9] Third, the FARDC's conduct of operations, morale, and discipline have improved since the defeat against M23 in 2012. This is quite a unique development. The improvement has partly been attributed to a change of leadership and a talented new commander of North Kivu's 8th Military Region, Major General Bahuma Ambamba.[10] For once, MONUSCO had a credible and effective military partner, which significantly increased prospects for success. Finally, and maybe most importantly, in 2012 and 2013, Rwanda and Uganda were put under international diplomatic and economic pressure to end their support of the M23.[11] This encouraged the Security Council to put more military pressure on the armed groups. In October, just before the M23 was defeated, the United States delayed military aid to Rwanda under the pretext of concern over possible recruitment of child soldiers.[12] Consequently, when Rwanda ceased supporting the M23, the armed group was no match for the joint FARDC and FIB operations.

These specific circumstances help explain the unique language which made its way into the FIB-mandate. Subsequently, it is not likely that this approach will be repeated in future UN mandates, although there have already been calls for a similar approach in Mali.[13] The mandate for the UN Multidimensional Integrated Stabilization Mission in the Central African Republic (MINUSCA), just a few months after the defeat of M23, did not display similar language. The security situation, however, was extremely grave and UN forces were expected to use force to stabilize the situation.[14] Also, despite the consensus reached on the robustness of the FIB, there is growing concern among some Security Council members "about the growing shift towards the military aspects of peacekeeping."[15] Undoubtedly, the FIB-mandate has nudged peacekeeping towards stabilization operations or even peace enforcement. On the one hand, matching language and action is a step towards closing the gap between strategic guidance and the operational practice of modern peacekeeping. On the other, using force to "neutralize armed groups" may have far-reaching consequences for the principles of UN peacekeeping.[16] Some of these concerns will be treated later in the chapter.

The second aspect which makes the FIB stand out from other peacekeeping operations is the *decisive employment of military force by a brigade-sized unit* designed for robust military operations. UN peacekeepers have performed robust operations in the past with mixed results. In 2003–5, the UN Mission in the DRC (MONUC), MONUSCO's predecessor, carried out more than 35 military operations to coerce armed groups to enter disarmament processes, to protect civilians, and deter violence between belligerents.[17] These included both successes—defending Bunia from attacks by the *Union des patriotes congolais* (UPC) in 2003—and failures—inability to stop Laurent Nkunda's large-scale attack on Bukavu in 2004.[18] In 2006–7, the UN Stabilization Mission in Haiti (MINUSTAH) used "intelligence-driven" operations to clear urban slums of armed criminal elements.[19] In 2010–1, the UN Operation in Côte d'Ivoire (UNOCI) joined French forces in the destruction of the heavy weapons of Laurent Gbagbo, who held on to power through violent means after having lost the national elections.[20] In late 2012, MONUSCO gunships "delivered 117 sorties, … 500 rockets, and four missiles" in a futile attempt at confronting the M23 in the days leading up to the fall of Goma in 2012.[21]

The joint FIB/FARDC operations in 2013, however, combined "initiative, surprise, unity of effort, leadership, and discipline" to neutralize the M23.[22] The lead-up to the decisive operations in October came with MONUSCO's establishment of a security zone around Goma at the end of July, after heavy fighting between the FARDC and M23 had led to civilian casualties in Goma and surrounding areas.[23] Within a month, the M23 was retreating from frontline positions around Goma as a result of joint FIB and FARDC operations. These operations utilized artillery, attack helicopters, special forces (including snipers), and infantry units.[24] In late October, the M23 was dealt a decisive blow. Attacked on three fronts, the armed group was split.[25] Without military back-up from Rwanda and Uganda, and with FIB units blocking possible escape routes, the M23 was forced into a rushed retreat towards the Ugandan and Rwandan borders.[26] At the beginning of November, DRC officials pronounced the M23's defeat.[27]

The UN has been criticized for suffering from a "deep and abiding confusion between deploying military forces and employing military force."[28] This time, though, the intention of the Security Council was translated into effective military operations on the ground, as a result of quite rare circumstances. After almost 15 years of increasingly challenging, expensive, and seemingly ineffective peacekeeping in the DRC, the decision to deploy the FIB gave the UN a most welcome boost. According to the UN secretary-general: "Resolution 2098 on the Democratic Republic of the Congo was a milestone. It signalled the resolve of the Security Council to address the changing nature of conflict and the operating environment of UN peacekeeping. And it matched that resolve with credible capabilities. ... The results are tangible improvements of the lives of people living in eastern DRC."[29]

UN operations in the Democratic Republic of the Congo (from 1999) have long been at the forefront of developing innovative as well as controversial practices to UN peacekeeping operations.[30] As such, the establishment of the FIB could be regarded as yet another step towards transforming peacekeeping in the DRC to better manage new challenges. A grim fact, however, is that many of the new practices often come about as a result of severe setbacks.[31] This is also true for the establishment and operations of the FIB. These new practices have also put the principles of UN peacekeeping under considerable strain, which is discussed later in the chapter.

UN Multidimensional Integrated Stabilization Mission in Mali (MINUSMA)

MINUSMA has been involved in military operations against insurgent and extremist groups alongside the French military operations Serval and Barkhane, and the Malian army.[32] This has led to direct reprisal attacks against the UN mission. According to UN Under-Secretary-General for Peacekeeping Operations Hervé Ladsous, MINUSMA has turned into the costliest UN mission in terms of blood, where "peacekeepers face assaults on a virtually daily basis, in the form of rocket attacks on bases and targeted attacks with improvised explosive devices."[33] As of December 2014 the mission has taken 44 fatalities and over 100 blue helmets have been wounded in reprisal attacks, while peace negotiations so far have failed to find a comprehensive solution.[34]

MINUSMA was established in April 2013. The UN mission was originally built by re-hatting the African-led International Support Mission to Mali (AFISMA) as UN forces. The aim was to support political processes in Mali, carry out a number of security-related tasks and a broad range of other responsibilities.[35] These tasks included support to the transitional authorities, implementation of the Malian Transitional Roadmap, protection of civilians, monitoring of human rights, creating conditions to facilitate humanitarian assistance and the return of displaced persons, extending State authority, and the preparation of national elections.

After a rocky first year, the Security Council amended the mandate in June 2014 in an attempt to better face the challenges on the ground. A broader emphasis was now placed on security, stabilization and protection of civilians, national political dialogue and reconciliation, the reestablishment of State authority, the rebuilding of the security sector, and human rights issues in Mali.[36] Notably, in this mandate, the Security Council requested MINUSMA to expand its presence in northern Mali beyond key population centers such as Gao and Timbuktu. The aim was to improve the physical protection of civilians. As a result, over 80 percent of all MINUSMA staff and 90 percent of uniformed personnel are now based in the northern regions.[37] Additionally, MINUSMA's efforts at the political level remain a key priority, in particular to facilitate inclusive peace talks.[38]

MINUSMA has from its inception been faced with severe challenges. Many of those challenges are linked to the security threats from insurgents and the lack of a political settlement to end the conflict.[39] During the second half of 2014 alone the UN mission lost 29 peacekeepers to terrorist attacks, with many more injured. Rocket fire targeting MINUSMA bases, improvised explosive devices (IEDs), suicide bombers, and landmines are posing extremely high security threats to peacekeepers, indicating an urgent need to give MINUSMA more military muscle and doctrinal guidance.[40] In light of these challenges, Hervé Ladsous called for the establishment of an intelligence unit in MINUSMA, the All Sources Information Fusion Unit (ASIFU). ASIFU is the most significant intelligence capability the UN has had on the ground so far and consists of tactical intelligence officers and analysts from The Netherlands, Sweden, and Norway.[41] The unit has been tasked to collect, analyze, and produce timely, actionable, and relevant intelligence.[42] Collaborating with the French Operations Serval and Barkhane and other foreign agencies, ASIFU is meant to establish an intelligence hub which could have a lot of potential for MINUSMA.

However, despite some innovative efforts by MINUSMA to stabilize the conflict, the security situation has deteriorated in northern Mali since early 2014. Insurgent groups affiliated to al-Qaeda have increased terrorist activities. Many armed groups now show signs of fragmentation, making it more challenging to assess threats, and in addition, IED-attacks, abductions, and intercommunal violence are increasing. Although the current mandate addresses some of the complex issues UN forces face on the ground, peacekeeping doctrine does not provide much guidance in this situation. Guided by an ambitious mandate and limited military capabilities, MINUSMA has little room to maneuver in an environment which poses serious security risks to its personnel. To sum up: "[W]ith a decrease in security and no progress in negotiations, let alone in dialogue or reconciliation, MINUSMA is moving further rather than closer to the implementation of its mandate."[43] Overcoming these challenges will require revised doctrinal guidance and new practices that put the peacekeeping principles under considerable strain. This is elaborated upon in the following section.

Changing principles of UN peacekeeping operations

FIB operations in 2013 matched the Security Council's ambitions with decisive military action. Paradoxically, this also impacted existing principles for UN peacekeeping operations. Originally, the principles of consent, impartiality, and non-use of force were meant to clarify the UN's limited military role in the aftermath of international conflict *between* states. This made sense during tense Cold War years.[44] Most armed conflicts now unfold *within* states, however. Increasingly complex UN interventions where "there is no peace to keep" combined with a more forceful approach, stretch the principles beyond recognition.[45] The following discussion analyzes how MONUSCO/FIB and MINUSMA are challenging the bedrock principles of peacekeeping operations.

Contemporary UN operations are often deployed to intra-state conflicts recognized by ongoing violent competition for power despite ceasefires or peace agreements. By default, UN operations tend to have closer links to the authorities of the day who must give their *formal* consent to their presence. Also, the UN is inherently biased towards governments and the strengthening of state institutions, rather than exploring which governance system might work best in a given country. Insurgent or predatory armed groups in opposition might or might not consent to a UN presence, depending on their position in negotiations or in the armed conflict. Thereby, UN operations often become *de facto partial* to the host-nation government in violent power struggles. In practice, however, actual consent from both governing parties as well as spoilers tends to fluctuate throughout cycles of intra-state conflict. Moreover, what is new in the case of the FIB is that the mandate goes a long way in making the UN mission a formal part of the conflict already from its inception. The mandate leaves little room for doubt that the Security Council strongly condemns the M23 along with "the FDLR, the ADF, the APCLS, the LRA, the National Force of Liberation (FNL), the various MayiMayi groups and all other armed groups" and that these will be dealt with militarily in joint operations with the FARDC.[46] Impartiality, as elaborated in the Capstone Doctrine from 2008, is now merely an illusion for FIB/MONUSCO.

Although often seen as an undesirable position for UN forces to find themselves in, partiality definitely increased operational effectiveness of joint FIB/FARDC operations against the M23. The areas of eastern DRC formerly dominated by the insurgent group saw immediate posi-tive impact on the security situation. In Mali, however, similar devel-opments have taken a different turn. When Tuareg rebels launched an attack to take over the city of Kidal in May 2014, the Malian govern-ment called for increased international support in order to "prevent northern Mali from slipping into a spiral of violence that risks drawing Mali back to the state of crisis that . . . could destabilize the entire sub-region."[47] The attacks had led to several casualties, hostage taking, and the occupation of government buildings. MINUSMA is expected to support the Malian government and offer protection against the insurgencies that have undermined the state's presence in northern Mali. For insurgent groups, MINUSMA is not perceived as an impartial actor, despite the UN's insisting that it relates to the bedrock principles of peacekeeping. In Mali, the *de facto* partiality of MINUSMA has resulted in a range of retaliatory attacks by various insurgent groups directly targeted at the UN mission. These developments indicate that being partial, *de facto* or formally, may come with a range of poten-tially negative consequences that influence the security of UN personnel.

Consequently, although current challenges may demand more robust approaches by UN peacekeepers, the protection they have enjoyed being impartial can no longer be taken for granted. This is quite dra-matic. Peacekeepers that utilize force to neutralize opponents of the host-state authorities may become legitimate targets by armed groups in opposition and may formally be a belligerent according to the laws of armed conflict.[48] This could increase the human cost of being a peacekeeper. Although a recent study indicates that so-called "robust peacekeeping" has *not* made it more dangerous to be a UN peacekeeper, both MINUSMA and the FIB have been targeted as a result of military operations against insurgent groups.[49] In Mali UN peacekeepers have been killed by targeted retaliatory attacks by groups such as al-Qaeda in the Islamic Maghreb (AQIM), Ansar Dine, and the Movement for Oneness and Jihad (MUJAO). Between May and October 2014, "at least 28 attacks have targeted MINUSMA personnel, resulting in the death of at least 17 peacekeepers and more than 55 injured; [a]lthough mission facilities are subject to rocket attacks, most of the casualties are the result of improvised explosive devices (IEDs), which are sometimes activated in suicide vehicle attacks."[50] So far, this has led to 86 fatalities among MINUSMA's military, police, and civilian personnel.[51] In the aftermath of UN/FARDC-operations in early 2014, where the FARDC took heavy losses, MONUSCO was also directly targeted by both the Allied Democratic Forces (ADF) and the Alliance of Patriots for a Free and Sovereign Congo (APCLS) elements.[52] That fall, UN staff and buildings were also attacked by armed civilians dissatisfied with MONUSCO's efforts to protect them from the ADF in and around Beni in North Kivu.[53]

Increased risk induced by partiality may also scare away some of the major troop contributors.[54] Recent findings from Mali also indicate that troop-contributing countries (TCCs) are less willing to deploy their troops to high-risk areas, as many lack the support, training background, and capabilities for forceful action against insurgent groups. Although 12,640 uniformed personnel have been pledged to the mission, only 9,494 had been deployed by 31 December 2014.[55] One of the reasons is tension between mission leadership and the capitals of TCCs. A senior MINUSMA staff member commented that "most of the TCCs … are not willing to expose their troops to the security threats in Northern Mali and run the risk of getting them back in body bags; [t]here are a number of caveats coming from the capitals, limiting the possibilities for deployments in Mali."[56] By establishing the FIB in the DRC, some of the major troop contributors have been concerned about being associated with a more forceful UN approach.[57] This may indicate that robust mandates imply greater interest by capitals and consequently more interference and micromanagement of troop contributions.

The robust mandates and partial conduct of UN operations in Mali and DRC also impact "softer" parts of the missions, including humanitarian actors outside the UN multidimensional and integrated structure. In the DRC, humanitarians have long been concerned about

MONUSCO's military support to the FARDC. The deployment of the FIB may have deepened these concerns.[58] Now that the FIB has become more forceful, it is even more important for humanitarians to avoid being associated with the military efforts. The main reason is still that the national Congolese army is historically one of the main human rights violators in the DRC.[59] The FARDC units involved in operations against the M23, however, seem to have been quite disciplined and less prone to committing violations than what earlier has been the case in joint operations.[60] Still, a partial and forceful MONUSCO could, at worst, jeopardize humanitarian access, and also reverse gains made in integrating civilian, police, and military UN components in integrated multidimensional missions.

The growing use of IEDs by insurgents in Mali has also led to increased risks for the humanitarian community and casualties among nongovernmental organization (NGO) staff.[61] Being a multidimensional mission with a large humanitarian component, this has complicated the dynamics within MINUSMA. Parts of the humanitarian community are very hesitant when it comes to collaborating with MINUSMA. A representative of the UN Office for the Coordination of Humanitarian Affairs (OCHA) observed:

> The humanitarian community in Mali generally finds it problematic to work with MINUSMA due to different views on the use of armed escorts. As a general rule these organizations only approve the use of armed escorts as a last resort and they have a strict no weapon policy. This makes the cooperation with the military component of MINUSMA quite difficult as they advocate a different view. In addition to that many of the humanitarian organizations are not comfortable associating with MINUSMA as the armed groups increasingly target the mission. Besides their principle of remaining neutral and impartial actors, the humanitarian community does not want their own staff to be exposed to the risks of working alongside MINUSMA.[62]

Another paradoxical aspect of partiality is that cooperation with national actors may actually prove difficult. In the DRC, the UN mission has long struggled to establish fruitful working relations with Congolese authorities. In Mali, differing views on the way forward have led to a tense relationship between the Malian government and the MINUSMA leadership. As a senior MINUSMA official has said, "Limited commitment by the government to establish dialogue and reach a political solution with the parties in Northern Mali hampered progress towards a peace agreement and further complicated the working environment for MINUSMA."[63]

Another key concern is how to avoid the UN mission becoming a tool for the Malian government to clear away armed groups, with no ensuing political dialogue with populations in the north. In return, Mali's minister of foreign affairs, Abdoulaye Diop, asked the Security Council to consider the establishment of "a rapid intervention force capable of effectively combating terrorists."[64] At the same meeting in the council, Hervé Ladsous stated that:

> the lack of Malian security forces in the northern part of the country has created a situation where, in effect, MINUSMA is the main international presence on the ground. That makes us a target for all those spoilers—extremists, jihadists, and traffickers—who would like to have the ground exclusively to themselves so as to be able to continue their nefarious activities.[65]

Furthermore, by supporting one of the parties to the conflicts, both MINUSMA and MONUSCO are caught in a *counterinsurgency logic* where it is no longer just a question of protecting the population from violence but also of winning their support and trust alongside and in support of the Malian government.[66] MINUSMA is aiming to support the process of the Malian state's return to the north of the country. So far, the mission has not made progress in this respect. In fact, the population of northern Mali expressed serious concerns regarding their safety and security in relation to MINUSMA's presence on the ground, resulting in violent demonstrations against the mission. Several inhabitants of Gao moved away from areas close to MINUSMA's base out of fear of being attacked by armed groups.[67]

MINUSMA's ineffectiveness has been utilized by insurgent groups, as they use violence to make the population turn against the mission. In January 2015, for example, MINUSMA attack helicopters struck National Movement for the Liberation of Azawad (MNLA) rebels in Tabankort, as the armed group posed an imminent threat to civilians and MINUSMA peacekeepers. Dutch MINUSMA troops targeted an MNLA vehicle and disabled it, resulting in the death of five rebels and injury to several others. Although in line with the MINUSMA mandate, violent demonstrations occurred in Kidal and Ber, protesting MINUSMA's action.[68] Being close to MINUSMA was perceived as increasing the risk of being attacked. Many residents expressed the wish to see the mission leave.[69] The lack of protection further deteriorated the relationship between the government, population, and

MINUSMA, leading to stalled peace talks and a lack of political dialogue.

In addition to these challenges, the principle of *consent* no longer guides blue helmets. This has mostly to do with the ways in which contemporary conflict unfolds. In the DRC, conservative estimates of active armed groups in 2013 are close to 25.[70] Not many of these have consented to a UN presence, but all are part of the wider conflict. This is also the case in Mali, where the constant fragmentation of insurgent groups poses further challenges to MINUSMA's presence. Few contemporary UN operations are able to perform their tasks without negative, and often violent, interference. Formal consent is supposed to provide the UN with a minimum of political will and support for the operation. Now, however, "some UN peacekeeping operations are being authorized in the absence of clearly identifiable parties to the conflict or a viable political process."[71] The case of M23 in the DRC also amply demonstrates that consent fluctuates. The armed group's name stems from its dissatisfaction with the implementation of the 23 March 2009 *agreement* between the DRC government and the *Congrès National pour la Défense du Peuple* (CNDP), the (former) armed group from which the M23 originates.[72] Many CNDP-elements honored the agreement and integrated into the FARDC. Some, however, mutinied and created the M23. As armed groups emerge from those that are dissolved it is challenging to distinguish between those that should be part of negotiations and thereby provide their consent for UN efforts, and those that should be disarmed by force. The FIB mandate, as shown, had already made that decision before deployment.

Finally, the FIB and MINUSMA operations have definitely impacted the principle of *non-use of force*. They depart considerably from this principle in both language and practice.[73] According to the Capstone Doctrine, UN peacekeepers are expected to be able to "use force at the tactical level . . . to defend themselves and their mandate, particularly in situations where the State is unable to provide security and maintain public order," i.e. mainly for force protection purposes and to protect civilians.[74] The FIB consists of over 3,000 personnel. It has been mandated at the strategic level to neutralize armed groups by proactive use of force through targeted operations. The brigade has been well resourced to do so, including with attack helicopters and special forces.[75] Although a far cry from the tactical level use of force envisioned by the Capstone Doctrine, operations by the FIB and MINUSMA are equally far from being peace enforcement at the strategic international level. As such, the FIB and MINUSMA do not have a "home" in the Capstone Doctrine's spectrum of operations and represent something new.[76]

Conclusion and key considerations for future doctrine development

The FIB and MINUSMA operations against insurgent and predatory armed groups in eastern DRC and Mali deeply impact the principles of peacekeeping operations. Nevertheless, these principles are no longer able to guide blue helmets in contemporary operations as they were developed to suit former eras of peacekeeping. Although at odds with current doctrine, it is not necessarily implied that the FIB and MINUSMA are bad ideas to be shunned in future peacekeeping operations. What it does imply is that there is an urgent need to provide better guidance to UN peacekeepers dealing with similar situations.

The first insight for future revisions of UN peacekeeping doctrine is that partiality may increase operational effectiveness on the ground, but at the same time make peacekeeping a more risky endeavor for everyone involved. The FIB has closely supported the FARDC in the operations against the M23. Human security is much improved in those areas formerly held by the M23. At the same time, there have been fewer human rights violations by the FARDC, which this time around has lessened the UN's burden of being partial. However, a serious consequence of losing impartiality is that UN troops can be seen as legitimate targets by non-consenting parties. MINUSMA troop contributors are currently suffering heavy losses as they are perceived to be supporting the counterinsurgent efforts of the Malian state, and sometimes even performing these tasks in their place. Also, their capabilities do not seem to match the intentions of the Security Council. Undeniably, higher risks are now involved, and a prerequisite for taking sides is to have sufficient capabilities to operate in a more hostile environment.

The second insight is that future doctrine must clarify the role of blue helmets when consent fluctuates. Although formal consent must always be obtained from the outset of any UN mission, *de facto* consent must be continuously managed. As few contemporary UN operations are able to perform their tasks without violent interference, future doctrine must be able to provide answers on what to do when consent is no longer present. Since UN peacekeepers are expected to continue to operate even when the main parties contest their presence, this principle must be reviewed and transformed.

The third insight is that future doctrine must explore and explain what constitutes utility of force for UN peacekeeping operations instead of focusing on the non-use of force. The defeat of M23 undoubtedly protected many civilians from imminent physical threats, a task which is at the top of MONUSCO's list of priorities. A recent investigation into human rights violations committed by the M23 in North Kivu in the period April 2012 to November 2013 noted that it was responsible for the killing of 116 persons, 161 instances of rape, and hundreds of violations of the right to liberty and security.[77] The actual number of violations is probably much higher. The FIB was able to apply relevant use of force both on its own and jointly with the FARDC against one of the main spoilers and perpetrators of violence against civilians. But has the FIB found *utility* of military force? To have utility, military force must be able to create space for other means to work towards long-term peace and stability in the eastern DRC. As long as insurgents and predatory armed groups continue to operate in this area the space for other means to engage in longer-term stabilization efforts will not significantly improve. It signals quite strongly that tactical victories do not infer with strategic success. This dilemma is still at the core of the UN's approach to the use of force and must be addressed in future revisions of UN peacekeeping doctrine.

Finally, the new terminology introduced in this volume aptly describes the actual situation some contemporary UN operations find themselves in. MONUSCO and MINUSMA do indeed protect weak governments (and civilians) from imminent insurgent threats. What the new terminology does not fully capture is the overarching *purpose* of the UN's employment of military force to protect in these more robust operations. In the end, the objective is to establish some level of stability that may facilitate a more lasting political solution, not to continue to protect a fledgling government. In this regard, the UN may also consider reviewing its future doctrinal guidelines in light of existing guidance on stabilization operations.

Stabilization terminology is not unfamiliar to the UN. In fact, existing *stabilization* definitions do not stray far from core UN activities.[78] Several UN operations, including MONUSCO and MINUSMA, already have *stabilization* as part of their name. However, a shift toward UN stabilization operations would undoubtedly be much more ambitious than using force to protect at the tactical level. A UN stabilization doctrine would demand a clarification of the principles of peacekeeping, and in particular UN peacekeepers' impartial status under international humanitarian law. Although a shift towards UN stabilization doctrine may solve some of the conceptual gaps exposed in current guidance, one should tread carefully when amending these gaps. The crux is to balance the need for improved guidance without losing sight of the UN's comparative strengths.

Notes

1 UN Security Council Resolution 2098, UN doc. S/RES/2098, 28 March 2013, 7.
2 Ibid.
3 Arthur Boutellis, "Will MONUSCO Fall With Goma?" *Global Observatory*, 3 December 2012, http://theglobalobservatory.org/analysis/394-will-m onusco-fall-with-goma.html.
4 UN, "Group of Experts on the Democratic Republic of the Congo: Final Report 2013," 12 December 2013; and Naomi Kok, "From the International Conference on the Great Lakes Region-Led Negotiation to the Intervention Brigade: Dealing with the Latest Crisis in the Democratic Republic of Congo," *African Security Review* 22, no. 3 (2013): 175–80.
5 BBC News, "UN under Fire over Fall of Goma in DR Congo," 21 November 2012, www.bbc.com/news/world-africa-20422340.
6 Congo News Agency, "DR Congo, Rwanda Sign Pact to Fight Rebels in Eastern Congo," 15 July 2012, www.congoplanet.com/news/1985/dr-congo-jo seph-kabila-rwanda-paul-kagame-sign-pact-to-fight-rebels-in-eastern-congo.jsp; and Patrick Counsel Cammaert and Fiona Blyth, "The UN Intervention Brigade in the Democratic Republic of the Congo," IPI Issue Brief, International Peace Institute, July 2013.
7 John Karlsrud, "The UN at War: Examining the Consequences of Peace-Enforcement Mandates for the UN Peacekeeping Operations in the CAR, the DRC and Mali," *Third World Quarterly* 36, no. 1 (2015): 40–54.
8 Challenges Forum, "Force Intervention Brigade: A Sea of Change for UN Peace Operations?" *Policy Brief 2014*, no. 1 (2014): 1–4.
9 UN General Assembly, "Evaluation of the Implementation and Results of Protection of Civilians Mandates in United Nations Peacekeeping Operations," UN doc. A/67/787, 7 March 2014.
10 *African Defence Review*, "How M23 Was Rolled Back," 30 October 2013, www.africandefence.net/analysis-how-m23-was-rolled-back.
11 Ida Sawyer, "Dispatches: After the M23—Congo's Next Challenges," *Human Rights Watch*, 5 November 2013, www.hrw.org/news/2013/11/05/dispatches-a fter-m23-congo-s-next-challenges; and Federico Borello, "The Death of M23: Ending Rwanda's Proxy War in the Congo," *Fletcher Security Review* 1, no. 1 (2013), www.fletchersecurity.org/#!call-for-papers-spring-2014/cimm.
12 David Smith, "US Blocks Military Aid to Rwanda over Alleged Backing of M23 Child Soldiers," *The Guardian*, 4 October 2013, www.theguardian.com/ global-development/2013/oct/04/us-military-aid-rwanda-m23-child-soldiers.
13 Security Council, 7274th meeting (on the report of the secretary-general on the situation in Mali), UN doc. S/PV.7274, 8 October 2014, 5.
14 Security Council Resolution 2149, UN doc. S/RES/2149, 10 April 2014.
15 *What's In Blue*, "Open Debate on New Trends in UN Peacekeeping," 10 June 2014, www.whatsinblue.org/2014/06/open-debate-on-new-trends-in-un-p eacekeeping.php.

16 Mona Khalil, "Humanitarian Law & Policy in 2014: Peacekeeping Missions as Parties to Conflicts," *Professionals in Humanitarian Assistance and Protection*, 13 February 2014, http://phap.org/thematic-notes/2014/februa ry/humanitarian-law-policy-2014-peacekeeping-missions-parties-conflicts.

17 Jan Gunnar Isberg and Lotta Victor Tillberg, *Med Alla Nödvendiga Medel: Brigadgeneral Jan-Gunnar Isbergs Erfarenheter Från Tjänstgjöring I Kongo 2003–2005* (Försvarshögskolan, 2011) (in Swedish).

18 Ibid.

19 Walther Dorn, "Intelligence-Led Peacekeeping: The United Nations Stabilization Mission in Haiti (MINUSTAH), 2006–07," *Intelligence and National Security* 24, no. 6 (2009): 805–35; Michael Dziedzic and Robert M. Perito, "Haiti: Confronting the Gangs of Port-Au-Prince, United States Institute of Peace (USIP), Washington DC, 2008; and Marc Lacey, "U.N. Troops Fight Haiti Gangs One Street at a Time," *The New York Times*, 10 February 2007, www.nytimes.com/2007/02/10/world/americas/10haiti.html?_r=1.

20 Rebecca Friedrichs, "Côte d'Ivoire: UN Peacekeeping, Impartiality and Protection of Civilians," The Stimson Centre, 20 April 2011, www.stimson.org/sp otlight/cote-divoire-un-peacekeeping-impartiality-and-protection-of-civilians.

21 *Chicago Tribune*, "U.N. Defends Failed Attempt to Halt Capture of Congo's Goma," 21 November 2012, http://articles.chicagotribune.com/ 2012-11-21/news/sns-rt-us-congo-democratic-unbre8ak1ac-20121121_1_con go-soldiers-congolese-forces-monusco.

22 US Army Peacekeeping and Stability Operations Institute (PKSOI), "UN Force Intervention Brigade against the M23," Stability Operations Lessons Learned & Information Management System (SOLLIMS), 2013.

23 UN News Centre, "UN Mission Sets up Security Zone in Eastern DR Congo, Gives Rebels 48 Hour Ultimatum," 30 July 2013, www.un.org/app s/news/story.asp?NewsID=45535#.U5ggnyi5T5M.

24 Guy Martin, "DRC Sniper Revelation Compromising SANDF Troops," DefenceWeb, 5 September 2013, www.defenceweb.co.za/index.php?option= com_content&view=article&id=31797:drc-sniper-revelation-comprom ising-sandf-troops-expert&catid=111:sa-defence&Itemid=242; and Stephan Hofstatter, "South Africa at War in the DRC: The Inside Story," *The Times Live*, 22 August 2014, www.timeslive.co.za/local/2014/08/22/south-a frica-at-war-in-the-drc–the-inside-story.

25 *African Defence Review*, "How M23 Was Rolled Back"; and PKSOI, "UN Force Intervention Brigade against the M23."

26 UN News Centre, "DR Congo: UN Peacekeeping on Offensive after Defeat of M23, Says Senior UN Official," 11 December 2013, www.un. org/apps/news/story.asp?NewsID=46721#.Uz1yMVe5T5M.

27 BBC News, "DR Congo Claims Defeat of M23 Rebels," 5 November 2013, www.bbc.com/news/world-africa-24815241.

28 Rupert Smith, *The Utility of Force: The Art of War in the Modern World* (London: Penguin Books, 2006), 6.

29 Secretary-General Ban Ki-moon, "Remarks at Security Council Open Debate on Trends in United Nations Peacekeeping," UN News Centre, 11 June 2014, www.un.org/apps/news/infocus/sgspeeches/statments_full.asp?sta tID=2251#.U52H-Ci5T5M.

30 IPI, "Panel Discussions—Ladsous: Congo Is UN 'Laboratory' for Drones and New Technology," 7 April 2014, www.ipinst.org/events/panel-discussions/

details/531-ladsous-congo-is-un-laboratory-for-drones-and-new-technology.htm
l; Stian Kjeksrud and Jacob Aasland Ravndal, "Emerging Lessons from the
United Nations Mission in the Democratic Republic of Congo: Military Contributions to the Protection of Civilians," *African Security Review* 20, no. 2
(2011): 3–16; Thierry Vircoulon, "After MONUC, Should MONUSCO Continue to Support Congolese Military Campaigns?" International Crisis Group,
19 July 2010, www.crisisgroup.org/en/regions/africa/central-africa/dr-congo/vir
coulon-after-MONUC-should-MONUSCO-continue-to-support-congolese-mi
litary-campaigns.aspx; MONUC, "MONUC Joint Protection Teams Making a
Difference in the Field," 2009, http://monuc.unmissions.org/Default.aspx?ta
bid=1042&ctl=Details&mid=1096&Itemid=4778; and Henri Boshoff, "Overview of MONUC's Military Strategy and Concept of Operation," in *Challenges
of Peace Implementation: The UN Mission in the Democratic Republic of the
Congo*, Institute for Security Studies (ISS). Johannesburg and Pretoria, South
Africa, 2004, 135–45.

31 Boutellis, "Will MONUSCO Fall With Goma?"
32 Security Council Report, "October 2014 Monthly Forecast: Mali," 30
September 2014, www.securitycouncilreport.org/monthly-forecast/2014-10/ma
li_14.php.
33 UN News Centre, "Peace Process in Mali at 'crucial Stage' UN Peacekeeping Chief Tells Security Council," 6 January 2015, www.un.org/apps/
news/story.asp?NewsID=49740#.VMkQ8C4X4x-.
34 UN News Centre, "With Mali Peace Talks Set to Resume, Security Council
Urges 'Spirit of Compromise,'" 17 October 2014, www.un.org/apps/news/
story.asp?NewsID=49110#.VEUVpMm5T5M; and UN News Centre,
"Mali: Ban Voices 'Outrage' as UN Peacekeeper Killed in Second Deadly
Attack This Month," 8 October 2014, www.un.org/apps/news/story.asp?
NewsID=49028#.VE46S8m5T5M.
35 Security Council Resolution 2100, UN doc. S/RES/2100, 25 April 2013.
36 Security Council Resolution 2164, UN doc. S/RES/2164, 25 June 2014.
37 Security Council, "Report of the Secretary-General on the Situation in
Mali," UN doc. S/2014/692, 22 September 2014.
38 Security Council Resolution 2164.
39 Lotte Vermeij, "MINUSMA: Challenges on the Ground," Norwegian
Institute of International Affairs (NUPI) Policy Brief, 2015.
40 Dulcie Leimbach, "The UN's Mission in Mali: A Deadly Fight Against
Terrorists," *Pass Blue*, 18 January 2015, http://passblue.com/2015/01/18/
the-uns-mission-in-mali-a-deadly-fight-against-terrorists.
41 Karlsrud, "The UN at War."
42 UN, "Statement of Unit Requirement for All Source Information Fusion
Unit," 2013.
43 Emmanuel Bombande and Peter van Tuijl, "Can MINUSMA's Mandate
Include the People of Mali?" *Global Observatory*, 24 June 2014, http://the
globalobservatory.org/2014/06/minusma-mandate-include-people-mali.
44 Oliver P. Richmond, "Peace During and After the Age of Intervention,"
International Peacekeeping 21, no. 4 (2014): 509–19.
45 Ki-moon, "Remarks at Security Council Open Debate on Trends in United
Nations Peacekeeping."
46 Security Council Resolution 2098, para.7.

47 Adama Diarra and John Irish, "Mali Wants International Inquiry into Northern Attack," *Reuters*, 20 May 2014, www.reuters.com/article/2014/05/21/us-mali-france-violence-idUSBREA4K00G20140521.

48 Khalil, "Humanitarian Law & Policy in 2014"; Cammaert and Blyth, "The UN Intervention Brigade in the Democratic Republic of the Congo"; and Scott Sheeran and Stephanie Case, "The Intervention Brigade: Legal Issues for the UN in the Democratic Republic of the Congo," IPI, November 2014.

49 Alex J. Bellamy, "Are New Robust Mandates Putting UN Peacekeepers More at Risk?" *Global Observatory*, 29 May 2014, http://theglobalobservatory.org/comp onent/myblog/are-new-robust-mandates-putting-un-peacekeepers-more-at-risk-/blogger/Alex%20J.%20Bellamy.

50 Security Council Report, "October 2014 Monthly Forecast: Mali."

51 MINUSMA, MINUSMA Facts and Figures, www.un.org/en/peacekeep ing/missions/minusma/facts.shtml.

52 Security Council, "Report of the Secretary-General on the United Nations Stabilization Mission in the Democratic Republic of the Congo," UN doc. S/2014/450, 30 June 2014; and *What's In Blue*, "Public Briefing by UN Force Commanders," 8 October 2014, www.whatsinblue.org/2014/10/p ublic-briefing-by-un-force-commanders.php.

53 UN News Centre, "DR Congo: UN Mission Comes under Attack, Steps up Security," 22 October 2014, www.un.org/apps/news/story.asp?NewsID=49145#.VEkJssm5T5M; and Jason Stearns, "String of Massacres Report-edly Kills over 80 around Beni," *Congo Siasa*, 21 October 2014, http://con gosiasa.blogspot.com/2014/10/string-of-massacres-reportedly-kills.html.

54 Richard Gowan, "Diplomatic Fallout: Frustrations Mount for India at the U.N.," *World Politics Review*, 15 April 2013, www.worldpoliticsreview.com/articles/12870/diplomatic-fallout-frustrations-mount-for-india-at-the-u-n.

55 MINUSMA, MINUSMA Facts and Figures.

56 Interview with senior UN staff member at MINUSMA headquarters, Bamako, May 2014.

57 Gowan, "Diplomatic Fallout: Frustrations Mount for India at the U.N."

58 Aurelie Ponthieu, Christoph Vogel, and Katharine Derderian, "Without Precedent or Prejudice? UNSC Resolution 2098 and Its Potential Implica-tions for Humanitarian Space in Eastern Congo and Beyond," *The Journal of Humanitarian Assistance*, 21 January 2014, http://sites.tufts.edu/jha/a rchives/2032.

59 UNHCR, "Report of the Mapping Exercise Documenting the Most Ser-ious Violations of Human Rights and International Humanitarian Law Committed within the Territory of the Democratic Republic of the Congo between March 1993 and June 2003," August 2010.

60 *African Defence Review*, "How M23 Was Rolled Back"; Ponthieu, Vogel, and Derderian, "Without Precedent or Prejudice?"

61 Jan Egeland, "Northern Mali Risks Becoming Forgotten Protection Crisis," Norwegian Refugee Council, 19 June 2014.

62 Interview with OCHA representative, Bamako, May 2014.

63 Interview with senior MINUSMA official, Mali, 2014.

64 Security Council, 7274th meeting.

65 Ibid.

66 Vermeij, "MINUSMA: Challenges on the Ground."

67 Interviews with residents of Gao, 2014.
68 David Lewis and Emma Farge, "Dutch UN Attack Helicopters Strike Mali Rebels in North," *Reuters*, 20 January 2015, www.reuters.com/article/2015/ 01/20/us-mali-fighting-un-idUSKBN0KT29520150120; and UN News Centre, "Mali: UN Mission Wards off Rebel Attack; Urges Armed Groups to Respect Ceasefire," 21 January 2015, www.un.org/apps/news/story.asp? NewsID=49866#.VMkoNC4X4x9.
69 Findings from interviews the author conducted with residents of Northern Mali, 2014.
70 Jason Stearns, Judith Verweijen, and Maria Eriksson Baaz, "The National Army and Armed Groups in the Eastern DRC: Untangling the Gordian Knot of Insecurity," Rift Valley Institute, Nairobi, 2013, www.riftvalley.net/ download/file/fid/3072.
71 Ki-moon, "Remarks at Security Council Open Debate on Trends in United Nations Peacekeeping."
72 Jason Stearns, "From CNDP to M23: The Evolution of an Armed Movement in Eastern Congo," Rift Valley Institute, Nairobi, 2012, 41.
73 Security Council Resolution 2098.
74 DPKO/DFS, "United Nations Peacekeeping Operations: Principles and Guidelines" (so-called "Capstone Doctrine"), United Nations, New York, 2008, 19, www.un.org/en/peacekeeping/documents/capstone_eng.pdf.
75 Darren Olivier, "The FIB Goes To War," *African Defence Review*, 29 August 2013, www.africandefence.net/the-fib-goes-to-war.
76 DPKO/DFS, "Capstone Doctrine," 17.
77 UN Joint Human Rights Office (UNJHRO), "Report of the United Nations Joint Human Rights Office on Human Rights Violations Committed by the M23 in North Kivu Province between April 2012 and November 2013," October 2014.
78 UK Ministry of Defence, "Security and Stabilisation: The Military Contribution," Development, Concepts and Doctrine Centre, Joint Doctrine Publication 3–40, November 2009, 409.

Part III
Emerging Issues

10 Exploiting the water

Naval involvement in UN
peacekeeping—prospects and difficulties

Ian Bowers

- **The record of naval peacekeeping**
- **Trends**
- **Difficulties**
- **Organizational learning and the future**
- **Conclusion**

Given that over 80 percent of the world's population lives within 100 miles of the water, it is perhaps surprising that the United Nations (UN) has traditionally eschewed the use of maritime power in its peacekeeping operations. There has been an understandable institutional bias towards developing ground-based operational procedures and capabilities. In recent years this has begun to change. Historically, UN peacekeeping operations (PKOs) used the sea for the transport of troops, equipment, and supplies. They are now using maritime capabilities to support the implementation and fulfilment of their mandates.[1]

Maritime forces, be they blue-water, littoral, or riverine, are inherently versatile and are capable of undertaking a wide variety of missions.[2] This multi-functionality combined with an underlying mobility allows maritime units to switch missions quickly and effectively, transitioning from peace to combat operations without the need for extensive re-equipping or retraining. These characteristics are of increasing utility as UN mandates and PKOs become more robust and complex and the forces required more specialized.[3]

The UN faces substantial difficulties in utilizing maritime forces for PKOs, including the lack of available vessels and ensuring efficient and effective operations. The evidence also suggests that the UN has not possessed sufficient institutional expertise to properly exploit the maritime arena. Nevertheless, the Department of Peacekeeping Operations (DPKO) has begun to institutionalize maritime operations, allowing for their better use and for a greater understanding of the benefits they bring to extant and future UN PKOs.

This chapter begins by examining the most prominent cases of UN-led maritime operations within PKOs. Using these case studies, key trends and constraints on the use of maritime forces are then elicited. Finally, it examines how the UN has begun to develop and institutionalize the maritime elements of PKOs, concluding that maritime forces will have a role in future missions provided that adequate capabilities can be attained.

The record of naval peacekeeping

The involvement of navies in UN peacekeeping operations has been historically sparse. While gaining a large amount of experience in land operations, the UN has traditionally looked toward mandating external commands to implement resolutions that have a maritime component. Although UN-flagged ships were deployed off Palestine in 1947–8 and Western New Guinea in 1962, these operations were very much the exception. During the Korean War, some allied ships did fly the UN flag but were outside of UN control. In the 1990s, during the wars in the former Yugoslavia, various naval task forces under the North Atlantic Treaty Organization (NATO), the Western European Union (WEU), and national-level commands enforced a UN-mandated arms embargo in the Adriatic. While some of these vessels were prepared to assist UN forces on the ground, at no stage were they controlled by the UN. Other examples include operations in East Timor under the Australian-led International Force for East Timor (INTERFET) operation and even counter-piracy operations in the Gulf of Aden, which again are mandated by the UN but are implemented by national and multinational force commands.

In recent years there has been a noticeable upward trend in maritime operations being led by the UN. The vast majority of these are riverine operations, but a relatively large blue-water task force operating off the coast of Lebanon has demonstrated the UN's capacity for managing more advanced naval operations. This section examines both past and current missions in riverine and open-ocean contexts, and draws some key considerations regarding the implications or otherwise of UN-led maritime operations.

ONUCA: Gulf of Fonseca 1990 to 1992

The first use of maritime forces within a UN PKO chain of command occurred in the Gulf of Fonseca under the auspices of Chapter VI of the UN Charter: the UN Observer Group in Central America (ONUCA). The mission was mandated to verify the 1987 Guatemala Agreement between the governments of El Salvador, Guatemala, Costa Rica, Honduras, and Nicaragua.[4] The scope of this agreement required a large force of observers operating on the ground, in the air, and on the water. The maritime contingent was designated to operate in the Gulf of Fonseca, where El Salvador, Honduras, and Nicaragua all have coasts. The initial requirement of forces called for eight patrol boats, but the UN found it difficult to find a country willing to provide this maritime capability.[5] This difficulty was overcome when Argentina agreed to contribute four fast patrol boats (FPBs) along with 29 officers and troops.[6] These boats would carry UN observers and be under the command of the observer group's headquarters. Based in Honduras, the force patrolled the waters of all three countries bordering the gulf.[7] After beginning operations in late June 1990, the unit conducted 1,800 hours of patrols within five months.[8] It also showed signs of operational learning and the capacity to integrate with other elements of the mission, beginning joint patrols with aviation units to increase their operational effectiveness.[9]

When the mission ended, on 17 January 1992, the maritime unit had sailed more than 72,000 nautical miles, averaging a patrol time of nearly 12 hours per day.[10] While it is difficult to assess how effective the maritime unit was, being the first UN-led maritime PKO a number of points can be elicited. The boats were required to be painted white and—as this was an observer mission—be unarmed. While not particularly problematic for the small FPBs deployed, as one Argentine analyst pointed out this could be a substantial issue if the vessels had been larger or had integrated weapons systems.[11]

While the UN led the mission, the boats were each commanded by an Argentinean and an Argentine staff officer was the squadron commander ashore assigned to the UN headquarters. This elegant solution ensured UN command but alleviated the potential political problems of placing valuable naval assets (and thus by extension sovereign Argentinean territory) under UN control.[12] While being an observer mission, and not mandated to operate under combat conditions, the UNOCA maritime deployment is a useful example of the problems and potential for maritime forces within a PKO context. Many of the issues, such as command and control, the availability of forces, and the procedures for the use of vessels under UN PKOs have arisen in subsequent missions.

UNTAC: Cambodia 1992 to 1993

Following the 1 May 1991 ceasefire and the signing of the 23 October Paris Agreement, the UN Transitional Authority in Cambodia (UNTAC) was formed. The military aspect of this mission was tasked with the verification of the withdrawal of foreign forces, supervision of the ceasefire, weapons control, and mine clearance. While authorized under Chapter VI, the UNTAC mission was complicated by high levels of violence, leaving UN forces attempting to manage a situation without an appropriate mandate.

The mission's maritime component was tasked with patrolling the rivers and coast of Cambodia, ensuring the cessation of external military assistance to Cambodian belligerents and the cantonment, the regrouping, and, if needed, the demobilization of extant indigenous naval forces.[13] The mission did not require countries to contribute vessels but, instead utilized Cambodian vessels *in situ* to perform its operations thereby alleviating the pressure on troop-contributing countries (TCCs) to provide valuable assets.

The 376-person contingent was drawn from Uruguay, Great Britain, Canada, and the Philippines. It was placed directly under UN command and operated six sea patrol boats, nine river patrol boats, three landing craft, and 12 special boats.[14] Operating for just over a year and a half, it provided support for UN operations in Cambodia's littorals but did not encounter the levels of violence that UN forces ashore endured. Its most notable contribution was made in March 1993 when, following an outbreak of severe ethnic violence, it monitored the flight of over 20,000 ethnic Vietnamese to Vietnam via the Mekong River. Its presence provided passive protection to the refugees leaving the country, but importantly did not involve any use of force and therefore did not violate the mission's overall mandate.[15]

MONUC/MONUSCO: Congo 2001 to present

As of 2016, Uruguay has had maritime forces in the Democratic Republic of the Congo (DRC) for 15 years. Originally deployed under the UN Mission in the Democratic Republic of the Congo (MONUC), and then continued under the subsequent UN Organization Stabilization Mission in the Democratic Republic of the Congo (MONUSCO), the riverine force has over the course of its deployment altered its area of operations, force posture, and mission priorities as the in-country security situation and UN mandate changed. After being deployed in July 2001 to reopen the Congo River, a major artery for human and economic traffic, the unit faced challenges in the security situation in the area and the navigability of the river itself, which required the size of the unit to be doubled.[16]

Operating four armed fast patrol boats and a number of Zodiac rigid-hulled inflatable boats (RHIBs) in two companies, the contingent's mission centered on maintaining good order and security on the river and through the operation of barges and pushers, moving material, goods, and personnel to places that were not easily accessible by land.[17] These mission goals were intended to be impartial and in keeping with the initial traditional PKO mandate of MONUC. As the mission continued the unit began to transfer operations away from the Congo River to the Great Lakes Region where there was large-scale insecurity.[18] This transfer began before the transition to MONUSCO and the implementation of the more robust mandate.

It is evident that the unit's mission has gradually changed. In 2012, the riverine unit divided its forces between Lake Kivu and Lake Tanganyika, with the majority of capabilities deployed to the former.[19] This was done to address the increasing insecurity in the Great Lakes area and followed the chartering of a new vessel to specifically support the civilian protection element of the mandate.[20] Indeed, after these developments, the unit began joint, if limited, operations, with the National Armed Forces of the DRC (FARDC)[21] aimed at deterring illicit and armed activity in an area that borders the DRC, Burundi, Rwanda, and Tanzania.[22] Such endeavors have been constrained due to the low capabilities of the local forces.[23] At the time of writing in July 2016 the unit deploys three fast patrol boats and 10 Zodiac RHIBs, and has acquired a "mothership" to support the use of the latter on Lake Tanganyika due to the volatility of the area.[24]

While the riverine contingent is not part of the UN Force Intervention Brigade (FIB) created in 2013, it does act in support of it, providing technical assistance in an area where the water is of great geographical and economic import. Without significant retooling or re-equipping, the riverine unit was able to adjust to the more robust and nontraditional mandate of MONUSCO. Alongside dealing with the armed groups threatening the mission's mandate, the riverine forces also undertake missions to prevent smuggling, piracy, and illegal taxation by these actors.

UNMIL: Liberia 2003 to 2004

The initial stages of the UN Mission in Liberia (UNMIL) in 2003 saw the deployment of a Dutch amphibious vessel in support of UN troops on the ground. The vessel, which was commanded by a Dutch captain, fell under overall UN command once it entered Liberian waters. It undertook a number of missions, providing support for forces on the ground (including medical support) and transporting troops, equipment, and supplies to towns on the Liberian coast.[25] This brief mission demonstrates how naval vessels can contribute to UN PKOs by providing assistance to operations in areas of potential instability without impacting the mandate or core UN PKO principles and with a minimal footprint in relation to the local population.

MINUSTAH: Haiti 2008 to 2014

The deployment of maritime forces to Haiti under the UN Stabilization Mission in Haiti (MINUSTAH) marked the third contribution to a UN PKO made by the Uruguayan navy.[26] Patrolling an area larger than Haiti's land mass (over 30,000 sq. km), the 16 patrol boats and eight fast rubber boats of the maritime contingent were primarily tasked with assisting in the management of the country's borders and the reduction of illicit trafficking of drugs, people, and other contraband.[27] In performing these operations, they met the core mandate term of the mission: to secure a stable environment for Haitian development and assist in upholding the law. They did not require more a robust, specialized mandate or altered rules of engagement.

Arising from these missions, the unit also undertook to provide support for port security, search and rescue, humanitarian assistance, and limited logistical support.[28] Following the 2010 earthquake, the maritime force adjusted its operations so as to support international and local forces involved in humanitarian and disaster relief (HADR) while maintaining its core operations.[29] However, the difficulties in undertaking patrols of such a large ocean area with such limited craft were apparent. The UN viewed the contribution as being too small to effectively combat drug trafficking and further maritime force contributions were not forthcoming.[30] By 2012, possibly as a result of these difficulties, the maritime unit had been given a capacity-building role where the crews would provide the Haitian "Coast Guard with technical knowledge to improve its training and thereby increase its participation in patrolling Haiti's maritime borders."[31]

The maritime component of the mission was withdrawn in the summer of 2014. The Uruguayan force, despite its small size, had demonstrated one of the key contributions that maritime forces can provide—flexibility.[32] In the course of its operations, the force successfully interdicted vessels carrying illicit drugs, provided at-sea support for UN and nongovernmental organization (NGO) personnel ashore, and assisted in the electoral process by providing logistical support.

MINUSMA: Mali 2014 to present

The deployment of a riverine unit to the UN Multidimensional Integrated Stabilization Mission in Mali (MINUSMA) is a reflection of not only the robust nature of the mission's mandate but also the inland utility of naval units. The Bangladesh Navy unit deployed to its area of operations on the Niger River in April 2014.[33] The unit is equipped with nine vessels of various types, and is expected to carry out at least two patrols per day.[34] The flexibility of the riverine contingent allows it to carry out a multitude of functions, ideally suited to the large and multidimensional mandate set out for the mission. The Bangladesh Navy includes river security operations, reconnaissance, and armed protection to UN personnel as core missions.[35] This would suggest that they expect their riverine forces to support UN forces operating on the ground and even deter potential violence through the threat of force. The presence of deterrence within their operational parameters fits with the overall mission mandate outlined in Security Council Resolution 2164, which includes deterrence as one of the tools to ensure "security, stabilization, and protection of civilians."[36]

UNOCI: Côte d'Ivoire 2005 to present

The riverine element of the UN Operation in Côte d'Ivoire (UNOCI) mission is the smallest of the UN's maritime PKO components. As the Chapter VII mission in Côte d'Ivoire discovered that close coordination and force sharing with the French *Licorne* Force was difficult to manage and the situation on the ground required extra forces, the UN secretary-general recommended a broad reinforcement package for UNOCI.[37] Included in this was a 30 person small-boat operation tasked with assisting in the deployment and extraction of troops in the Abidjan region.

Deployed in late September 2005 as part of a wider contingent of Bangladeshi forces, the two high-speed boats, armed with both heavy and light machine guns, have been conducting patrols and search and rescue (SAR), and have provided transportation in the lagoons around Abidjan. The limited number and type of vessels, which have little ballistic protection capability, reduces their effectiveness and ability to operate in combat conditions.[38] Nevertheless, they are acting in a necessary support role to the ground forces, given the geography of the region. In 2014, the unit assisted an indigenous Côte d'Ivoire operation aimed at providing security over the December holiday period.[39]

UNIFIL MTF: Lebanon 2006 to present

The Israel–Hezbollah war in Lebanon in 2006 serves as an excellent example of the utility of naval power within a peacekeeping context. It demonstrates how national naval forces can act in the protection of civilians and the reinforcement of peacekeeping operations and is the first case of the UN taking charge of a large-scale, sustained blue-water maritime operation. As a direct result the UN DPKO has been forced into making organizational and doctrinal adjustments to accommodate the use of such levels of maritime power, which has had a consequent impact on how the maritime arena is viewed within the UN PKO community.

As the 2006 conflict in Lebanon intensified, navies from a number of countries conducted operations aimed at the evacuation of foreign nationals and the delivery of humanitarian aid. With the passage of Security Council Resolution 1701 on 11 August, significant pressure was applied to the UN to rapidly deploy extra peacekeeping forces to reinforce the existing UN Interim Force in Lebanon (UNIFIL) presence and meet the requirements of the ceasefire agreement. The need for such a rapid deployment of operationally ready troops was outside of what had been the regular experience for the UN, and as such Europe was asked to provide the initial deployment, especially the provision of mechanized troops.[40] Naval forces from Europe (namely France, Spain, and Italy) rapidly transitioned from relief and evacuation operations and through the use of their expeditionary amphibious capability deployed heavy mechanized forces.

Using the Italian contribution as an example, following successive evacuation and relief operations the Italian Navy deployed the first echelons of their Joint Landing Force on 2 September after leaving port in Italy on 30 August. There was a 22-day interval between the passage of Resolution 1701 and the arrival of the first contingent of effective reinforcements. The Italian operation, named *Leonte*, had organic air and support assets, and safely delivered almost 1,000 marines and their armor within two months. This Italian-commanded and controlled amphibious operation delivered UN capabilities quickly and effectively. Once deployed the Italian ground forces fell under UN command.[41]

The sight of UN vehicles arriving on potentially contested ground from nationally commanded ships provides a potent example of how UN PKO forces can be rapidly deployed once TCCs have the capability and geography allows. It also demonstrates the advantages of amphibious capabilities in areas where infrastructure is damaged and the delivery of equipment would be prohibitively expensive or dangerous by air.

Following the deployment of reinforcements for UNIFIL, the UN embarked on what was described by the secretary-general as, a "new challenge for a peacekeeping operation" in agreeing to deploy a Maritime Task Force (MTF) upon the request of then Lebanese prime minister Fouad Siniora. The MTF "would help prevent the unauthorized entry of arms or related material by sea into Lebanon, until such time that [Lebanon's] naval and security forces are able to fulfill such tasks on their own."[42] Although the request came through the Lebanese, which allowed for the easier deployment and legal legitimacy for foreign vessels operating in territorial waters, the reality was that the deployment of the MTF was a key component in convincing the Israelis to lift their naval blockade of Lebanon. Crucially this mission does not explicitly require the use of force and is for all intents and purposes a monitoring and sea-control operation.

The MTF operates under the UNIFIL command structure and as such is the first substantial blue-water naval operation within an official UN PKO context. Initially, however, the operation was conducted by a UN-mandated interim naval task force (MTF 425) composed of forces already operating in the area. Under the command of the Italian Navy, forces from Greece, France, and the United Kingdom participated. It should be noted that all of these forces were interoperable given their history of operational coordination under the auspices of NATO. This force began operations on 8 September 2006 and transferred responsibility for the mission to the UN MTF on 15 October.

The MTF was first led by a German naval contingent and consisted of naval vessels from Denmark, Greece, The Netherlands, Norway, Sweden, and Turkey, all of which are established naval powers.[43] It has two main roles, which were first prescribed in 2006 and have not changed. The first is to prevent the smuggling of illegal weaponry into Lebanese territory through the provision of a naval presence in the area. The second is the training/capacity building of the Lebanese naval and coast guard forces.

Under these specific mission designations, the MTF has an area of interest (AOI) of around 12,000 square miles and a 5,000 square mile area of maritime operations. This runs the length of the 110 nautical mile Lebanese coast, and extends to sea for 48 nautical miles.[44] The area of operations allows the MTF to monitor incoming commercial maritime traffic and then refer suspicious vessels to the Lebanese Navy or upon the request of Lebanese authorities, board vessels within Lebanese territorial waters. In having to refer such vessels to the Lebanese authorities and board them only in Lebanese territorial waters the MTF can maintain neutrality while remaining within the rules of engagement and UNIFIL's mandate.

The MTF's mandate further restricts it from being involved in disputes between Israel and Lebanon over maritime sovereignty and demarcation. The so-called "line of buoys" which delimits Israeli and Lebanese maritime sovereignty is a source of significant tension between the two sides. The MTF has no mandate to monitor this line but it remains a cause of concern.[45] It was reported by the UN secretary-general, that despite having no mandate to do so, the MTF maintains a presence in the southern part of the vicinity of maritime operations to "prevent tensions" in the vicinity of the line of buoys.[46]

By March 2007 the MTF had hailed over 3,000 vessels and referred 10 suspicious vessels to Lebanese vessels, and at the time of writing 63,000 ships had been interrogated, and 6,000 had been referred to the Lebanese authorities.[47] Perhaps as a signal of the ongoing success of the mission, no vessel intercepted so far has been found to be carrying illicit cargo.

The capacity-building side of the MTF's role is equally important, as, if the Lebanese forces become capable of carrying out their own maritime security operations, the MTF would not be under as much pressure to provide capabilities and would be eventually able to stand down. In order to carry out this role, the MTF carries out joint maritime interdiction and tactical exercises, runs various courses on seamanship and other maritime skills, and gives lectures on various maritime topics.[48] Over a four-month period in 2015 the MTF carried out 313 types of training and exercises with the Lebanese Navy.[49]

While training is one component, the other is the provision of equipment. A number of countries have donated vessels and importantly Germany provided six coastal radars to allow the Lebanese to monitor their own territorial waters.[50] Although capacity building is extremely important, it has been acknowledged that the Lebanese continue to be constrained by their lack of suitable vessels to carry out interdiction operations and thus the MTF remains vital in ensuring that Resolution 1701 is adhered to.[51]

UNMISS: South Sudan 2015 to present

The deployment of a riverine unit to the UN Mission in South Sudan (UNMISS) should be seen as a confluence of geographical necessity and a robust mandate that requires the protection of civilians in what is a very hostile environment. A 2012 report on UNMISS suggested a phased increase in riverine strength, initially only operating in low-threat environments and then a gradual ramping-up of capabilities.[52] While this initial effort failed due to the inability to find a TCC willing to supply such capabilities, a 2013 report further highlighted the importance of riverine capacity within the same terms as attack helicopters and unmanned aerial vehicles (UAV), suggesting that a failure to have such capabilities was hindering the mission's chances of success.[53] The importance of a maritime unit was again highlighted in 2014 when the secretary-general noted: "During the rainy season, the waterways of South Sudan become the main route for the transportation of both people and goods . . . the advent of the rainy season and fighting in various parts of the country are factors that make a strong case for UNMISS to have a riverine battalion as part of its military component."[54]

A 200-strong riverine tactical unit from Bangladesh was finally deployed on 24 June 2015. Its primary function is to provide protection for barges and other transportation vessels operating on the White Nile.[55] It is also tasked with missions similar to those of the riverine unit deployed to Mali, including fire support to ground forces, medical evacuation, and SAR.[56] As with other missions, the specific use of a maritime or riverine component does not create a special condition for the use of force. In this case the conditions on the ground, most notably the social and geographical prominence of the waterways in the area of operations, have driven the proposed deployment.

Trends

The upward swing in the deployment of riverine forces on peacekeeping operations has coincided with the increasing robustness of UN PKOs in general. As missions in the DRC and South Sudan demonstrate, for UN PKOs to be effective it is vital that their structures reflect the geographical and social realities of the area of operations, which in those cases have significant maritime aspects. Riverine unit deployments are seemingly now being included as part of a wider DPKO initiative to create forces more capable of carrying out their mandate, be it traditional or not.

The deployment of these forces does not directly challenge the core principles of UN peacekeeping. Consent, impartiality, and the non-use of force have all been challenged by recent UN missions, but with riverine deployments what is evident is that these forces operate within the same limits as ground forces. As of yet they have not required nor have they been given new or special mandates for their operations in any of the case studies presented. In cases where the mandate has become more robust, such as in Mali and the DRC, riverine forces' operations have changed as part of a package of operationally stronger forces. Their mobility and ability to penetrate areas not accessible by land make them ideal to act in support of units on the ground and in the implementation of mandates on rivers and waterways.

This support role is far removed from the original observation mandate of the ONUCA deployment; it is evident that riverine and littoral forces such as those deployed in Haiti have been involved in an enforcing/policing role rather than just an observational one. The focus on capacity building also suggests that these forces are now stepping in to replace or support indigenous capabilities. Maintaining maritime and riverine forces is difficult and expensive, and thus such specialized PKO capabilities are often required as many target states do not possess the capacity to sustain such capabilities. It is likely that in the future riverine and littoral forces will continue to be deployed in support of local authorities on the ground, assisting in the establishment and maintenance of law and order.

Open ocean contributions remain rare and the main example, the Maritime Task Force as part of UNIFIL, was a reaction to a specific set of circumstances. Its operational mandate does not specifically challenge core principles, in as much as the wider UNIFIL mandate did in relation to the use of force. Again it is difficult to separate the maritime component from the land component when examining these issues. The uniqueness of the deployment also suggests that blue-water operations are most likely to be pursued on a case by case basis and will be contingent on the UN overcoming some of the difficulties outlined below.

Difficulties

Despite the clear advantage of, and need for the deployment of maritime forces, problems exist in maintaining such operations within a UN PKO context. The central issue is one of supply. As the experience of the MTF suggests, the UN will struggle to maintain even limited maritime forces over a sustained period of time. Writing in 2009, the secretary-general reported that the MTF was not sustaining its force numbers and had been operating on a reduced basis. This led "to a reduction in training opportunities with the Lebanese navy, as maritime interdiction operations represent the primary task for the Task Force." The reduction in ship numbers delayed the one mission that could result in such a reduction being sustainable.[57] This was not an unusual state of affairs and it became apparent in 2010 that there was no TCC available to contribute a lead ship and take operational command of the MTF, forcing command to be transferred ashore.[58] A letter from the secretary-general reflected the seriousness of the situation: "In order for the UNIFIL Maritime Task Force to continue to carry out its dual-mandated role—to help the Lebanese Navy prevent the unauthorized entry of arms or related material by sea into Lebanon by carrying out maritime interdiction operations, and to provide training for the country's naval personnel—the necessary maritime assets and leadership must be forthcoming."[59]

While in the earlier phases of the operation the more established navies of Europe and NATO contributed forces, these navies have in recent years come under extreme pressure in terms of resources. Although European navies may be looking to sustain balanced, modern fleets they are often smaller in number than they were previously.[60] This has been caused by the realities of austerity, the impact of technology where multifunctionality has become the standard in modern ship design, and the numbers of operations and exercises navies are now being called upon to perform. And while these navies are modern, with vessels capable of a huge number of tasks, the reality is that numbers matter and that states are going to be reluctant to hand over significant and precious national assets for sustained periods of time to missions that do not directly impact their own security. This problem has been remedied to some extent by the inclusion of naval forces from what may be considered nontraditional naval powers.[61] Brazil and Bangladesh have become significant contributors. More advanced ship to task analysis has reduced the number of required vessels, further alleviating this problem.

Extending this issue to riverine operations, the same problem may emerge albeit on a slightly different level. The record of riverine operations demonstrates that only two countries, Uruguay and Bangladesh, have contributed substantial forces. If UN PKOs are going to increasingly look to utilize such capabilities, new sources of supply will need to be found. This may be difficult given the specialization of resources and training required for riverine operations. Such specialization also means that when deploying riverine or littoral forces on policing or more robust operations, which are increasingly becoming the norm, valuable national assets are potentially being endangered. This must raise the threshold for deployment approval in capitals across the world.

Essentially, the maritime sphere of operations is a complex one and the record of such operations suggests that if the UN is serious about more frequently utilizing naval power, it will have to engage closely with TCCs in order to ensure that the required capabilities are available. At the 2015 Leader's Summit on Peacekeeping only three countries, Bangladesh, Uruguay, and Ghana pledged to provide maritime or riverine forces for UN PKOs.[62] The struggle to find appropriate assets for maritime PKOs presents a substantial dilemma for the UN.

The issue of interoperability is more pronounced in maritime operations than it is for land operations.[63] This has been a considerable challenge for navies for a sustained period of time. As one prominent naval analyst points out, technological and psychological hurdles are the primary concern.[64] Will diverse technological capabilities hamper joint operations?[65] Will vessels accept commands of a foreign officer in a time of emergency or will they call home?[66] Or will maritime forces have enough time to integrate their operational procedures before the mission begins?

These problems have been observed within the MTF. The commander of UNIFIL, General Paolo Serra, noted in 2012 that rotational issues were hampering efficiency and institutional learning as vessels from different countries were being deployed for a range of periods, from one month to two years.[67] More importantly Serra noted that "the effectiveness of the maritime component depends on the clearly identified capabilities, equipment, and training. Due to the fact that troop contributors have different types of equipment and procedures in communications, the MTF has no common means for data exchange and uses commercial satellites as a primary means to meet minimum military requirements."[68] This was a problem highlighted by a Belgian commander of the MTF who, while acknowledging the skill and readiness of all units deployed, noted that the non-NATO/EU contingent could not communicate effectively for technological reasons, such as a lack of bandwidth or satellite communication (SATCOM) capability.[69] Within the mandate of the MTF, where the operations are relatively simple, such limitations may not have a substantial operational impact. However, future scenarios with more complex mandates will require a solution to the interoperability issue.

If the UN is to take on more complex maritime operations, it is important that such difficulties are addressed on both a technological and doctrinal level. This can be achieved through the exclusive use of forces that are capable of integrated operations, the acceptance that the UN should mandate but not lead such operations, or the development of standard operating procedures that can interact with existing and established naval doctrines.

Organizational learning and the future

One of the consequences of the reinforcement of UNIFIL in 2006 and the addition of capabilities not seen before in UN PKOs, including the MTF, was the creation of a Strategic Military Cell (SMC). This was designed to supplement the existing Military Division within the DPKO which was found to be "insufficient to meet the significant and immediate expansion of the force," thus the cell was structured like a military headquarters and staffed by members of the TCCs in Lebanon.[70] Importantly, the SMC included a Maritime Operations Branch. This was staffed by two officers and was tasked with monitoring the MTF, short-term strategic planning, and use of operational expertise on maritime issues.[71] Thus, for the first time, the DPKO had a maritime planning and staff capacity operating within its headquarters.

This would prove to have a significant impact on how the DPKO views the utilization of maritime capabilities. Within two years the UN reported on how the maritime component of the SMC had "been able to effectively address the absence of maritime planning and deployment expertise in the Secretariat."[72] The capability survived the end of the SMC as the UN sought to integrate many of the skills brought by such expertise into their formal organization.[73] This was in reaction to the changing circumstances of PKOs, which, even in 2008, were "more frequently required to operate in higher threat environments, in which all inclusive peace agreements and cease-fires are elusive."[74]

As a result, the Office of Military Affairs has created a position to advise and support existing and future maritime operations. Specific roles include the monitoring of deployments, planning and standardization and participation in predeployment, and mission assessments.[75] The importance of this posting should not be underestimated as since 2008 there has been a consistent inclusion of maritime operations within future PKO planning. The increasing robustness of mandates and the developing emphasis on missions such as the protection of civilians has placed new pressures on the DPKO to integrate new technologies and methods into PKO doctrines and procedures; the inclusion of maritime forces is an important element of this. As highlighted previously, in areas where the water is a dominant geographical and social feature, the UN PKO forces must have the ability to operate on it.

As various bodies within the UN recognized the role of maritime force within PKOs, the utility and impact of having dedicated staff officers became apparent, both in the increasing use of maritime assets but also the proposed use of navies in a new and diverse array of missions. An example of the influence the new maritime staff was having on force planning within the DPKO came in 2008, when the secretary-general suggested that the UN deploy a multinational maritime force off the coast of Somalia to support the African Union Mission in Somalia (AMISOM). This force was to be either part of or distinct from the existing counter-piracy elements already *in situ* off the Somali coast and would provide a sea-base for rapid response to operational needs on the ground.[76] While this force did not go ahead, as AMISOM was reinforced on the ground, it does suggest that the DPKO was thinking about naval deployments with greater clarity. Indeed, it is evident that the UN began to recognize the potential coercive signaling power that naval deployments possess.[77]

This widening of operational thinking became even more evident in the 2009 contingency planning for a possible UN PKO in Somalia, where naval forces, including supply, landing, and patrol vessels were part of the proposed operational requirements.[78] Latterly the UN has also taken on a liaison-type role as the DPKO has begun to act as an information-sharing and capacity-building hub for maritime anti-piracy operations. This is being undertaken by a team that included a military maritime officer, and it shows how far the DPKO has come in terms of understanding and attempting to undertake operations within the maritime sphere.[79]

There is now an acknowledgement that riverine and even naval forces are part of an array of capabilities that commanders in the field and the DPKO feel are necessary for their forces to meet their mandated tasks, especially in the protection of civilians.[80] This is reflected in the 2015 publication of the first UN PKO manuals for both riverine and maritime units.[81] Naval and riverine units were also included in the 2009 "Tables of Organization and Equipment," with detailed missions outlined for each type of unit, highlighting the multitude of tasks naval platforms can undertake. The development of a maritime component within the DPKO has laid the foundation for future naval and riverine involvement in PKOs, something that is evidently more important as the nature of such operations evolves.

Conclusion

The record of naval involvement in peacekeeping demonstrates that riverine and other maritime forces are increasingly being engaged in more robust forms of peacekeeping. This is a microcosm of a general trend in UN PKOs. Importantly there is an apparent recognition that peacekeeping forces require assets and capabilities suited to the mandated tasks and area of operations. Therefore, riverine forces in particular are now more consistently employed in regions where inland waterways are a prominent geographical or social feature. This involvement should not be seen, however, as specifically or uniquely having an impact on UN PKO principles. To date, UN maritime operations have fallen within the mandates of wider UN operations. Sometimes these mandates have been more robust, and the challenge and impact on UN principles arises from these mandates and not the employment of maritime forces.

The use of riverine forces in particular, but also littoral and blue-water capabilities, can be an important part of ensuring the successful implementation of a PKO's goals. In previous years, the UN has lacked the internal knowledge to effectively understand how navies could be used. The MTF and the consequent institutionalization of a maritime element within the Office of Military Affairs has altered this state of affairs. For the first time, the UN, when necessary has the means to effectively integrate maritime operations into peacekeeping. However, the reluctance of TCCs to contribute assets poses a significant problem. If this can be addressed, maritime units can be a valuable element in ensuring the effective implementation of more complex peacekeeping mandates in the future.

Notes

1 For the purposes of this chapter, the author uses the following UK Ministry of Defence definition of the maritime area: "The maritime operating area ranges from the deep waters of the open oceans to the more confined and often shallower waters of littoral regions, estuaries and rivers." See UK Ministry of Defence, Development, Concepts and Doctrine Centre, "British Maritime Doctrine," Joint Doctrine Publication 0–10, 2011, 1–7.

2 *Blue water* can also be defined as open ocean operations. See United States Navy, *Naval Operations Concept*, (Washington DC: Department of the Navy, 2010), 8. While the *littoral* is a contested definition, it is best thought of as being the area of land and its adjacent sea that can be influenced from the sea. See UK Ministry of Defence, "British Maritime Doctrine," 1–6.

3 In 2014, Ban Ki-moon set out some of the challenges facing UN PKOs, highlighting that the nature of the operations had fundamentally changed

and that peacekeeping would need to be more mobile, flexible, and adaptable. See UN secretary-general, "Remarks at Security Council Open Debate on Trends in United Nations Peacekeeping," 11 June 2014, www.un.org/apps/news/infocus/sgspeeches/statments_full.asp?statID=2251#.U6FObNFZpaQ.

4 UNOCA was created under UN Security Council Resolution 644, UN doc. S/RES/644, 7 November 1989. For the mandate and its extension see UN, Central America: ONUCA–Mandate, www.un.org/en/peacekeeping/missions/past/onucamandate.html.
5 Security Council, "UNOCA: Report of the Secretary General," UN doc. S/21274, 27 April 1990, 4.
6 Security Council, "UNOCA: Report of the Secretary General," UN doc. S/21909, 26 October 1990, 2.
7 Ibid.
8 Security Council, "UNOCA: Report of the Secretary General," UN doc. S/22543, 29 April 1991, 4.
9 Ibid.
10 Juan Carlos Neves, "The Argentine Navy and United Nations Peacekeeping Operations in the Gulf of Fonseca," *Naval War College Review* XLVII, no. 1 (1994): 35.
11 Ibid., 17–19.
12 Ibid., 39–40.
13 Security Council, "Report of the Secretary-General on Cambodia," UN doc. S/23613, 19 February 1992, 23.
14 Ibid., 19.
15 Security Council, "Fourth Progress Report of the Secretary-General on the United Nations Transitional Authority in Cambodia," UN doc. S/25719, 3 May 1993, 25.
16 Security Council, "Special Report of the Secretary-General on the United Nations Organization Mission in the Democratic Republic of Congo," UN doc. S/2002/1005, 10 September 2010, 9; National Navy of the Republic of Uruguay, "The National Navy and Peacekeeping Missions."
17 Ibid.
18 See MONUC Deployment Map November 2008, in Security Council, "Fourth Special Report of the Secretary-General on the United Nations Organization Mission in the Democratic Republic of the Congo," UN doc. S/2008/728, 21 November 2008, 22.
19 Security Council, "Report of the Secretary General on the United Nations Organization Stabilization Mission in the Democratic Republic of Congo," UN doc. S/2012/355, 23 May 2012, 14.
20 MONUSCO, "MONUSCO Charters Boat to Secure Traffic on Lake Tanganyika," 12 March 2012, http://monusco.unmissions.org/Default.aspx?ctl=Details&tabid=10662&mid=14594&ItemID=19126.
21 It must be assumed that such cooperation has taken place within the restrictions laid out in Resolution 1906, which limits cooperation and security sector reform with units which violate human rights. See Julie Reynaert, *MONUC/MONUSCO and Civilian Protection in the Kivus* (Antwerp: IPIS, 2011).
22 Security Council, "Report of the Secretary General on the United Nations Organization Stabilization Mission in the Democratic Republic of Congo," UN doc. S/2012/838, 14 November 2012, 13.

23 Oleg Bushuev, "UN PKO: Maritime/Riverine Security & Capacity Building," PowerPoint presentation, slide no. 14/23, www.slideserve.com/silvio/un-pko-maritime-riverine-security-capacity-building.

24 General Assembly, "Budget for the United Nations Organization Stabilization Mission in the Democratic Republic of the Congo for the period from 1 July 2015 to 30 June 2016," UN doc. A/69/797, 26 February 2015, 102–3.

25 Nederlands Instituut voor Militaire Historie, "United Nations Mission in Libera (UNMIL)," 01 May 2009, www.defensie.nl/binaries/defence/documents/reports/2009/05/01/united-nations-mission-in-liberia-unmil/united-nations-mission-in-liberia-unmil.pdf.

26 The maritime unit was known as URMAR within the Uruguayan navy. Uruguay agreed to provide a maritime force in September 2008. It became operational in January 2009.

27 Security Council, "Letter Dated 2 September 2008 from the Permanent Representative of Uruguay to the United Nations addressed to the President of the Security Council," UN doc. S/2008/640, 8 October 2008.

28 Uruguay Navy, The National Navy and Peace Missions (in Spanish), www.armada.gub.uy/Pagina/institucion/esmay/misiones-de-paz.html#1.

29 Ibid.

30 Security Council, "Letter Dated 30 December 2011 from the Chair of the Security Council Working Group on Peacekeeping Operations Addressed to the President of the Security Council," UN doc. S/2011/817, 30 December 2011, 7.

31 Security Council, 6789th Meeting of the Security Council, UN doc. S/PV.6789, 20 June 2012, 9.

32 Security Council, "Report of the Secretary-General on the United Nations Stabilization Mission in Haiti," UN doc. S/2014/162, 7 March 2014, 12.

33 General Assembly, "Report of the Secretary General: Budget for the United Nations Multidimensional Integrated Stabilization Mission in Mali for the Period from 1 July 2014 to 30 June 2015," UN doc. A/68/823, 28 March 2014, 79.

34 General Assembly, "Report of the Secretary General: Budget for the United Nations Multidimensional Integrated Stabilization Mission in Mali for the Period from 1 July 2015 to 30 June 2016," UN doc. A/69/784, 17 February 2015, 28; and Bangladesh Multinational Operations Directorate, *Newsletter Bangladesh Navy in UN Missions*, October 2015, 6.

35 Ibid.

36 Security Council Resolution 2164, UN doc. S/RES/2164, 25 June 2014, 6.

37 Security Council, "Third Progress Report of the Secretary-General on the United Nations Operation in Côte d'Ivoire," UN doc. S/2004/962, 9 December 2004, 15.

38 Bushuev, "UN PKO: Maritime/Riverine Security & Capacity Building," slide 15/23.

39 Bangladesh Multinational Operations Directorate, *Newsletter Bangladesh Navy in UN Missions*, 10.

40 Sharon Wiharta, "Peacekeeping: Keeping Pace with Changes in Conflict," *SIPRI Yearbook 2007: Armaments, Disarmament and International Security* (Oxford: Oxford University Press, 2007), 116.

41 This arrangement regarding command and control was replicated by the other nations delivering reinforcements from the sea.

42 Security Council, "Report of the Secretary-General on the Implementation of Security Council Resolution 1701 (2006)," UN doc. S/2006/730, 12 September 2006, 9–10.

43 United Nations, *United Nations Peace Operations Year in Review 2006* (New York: UN Dept. of Public Information, 2006), 6.

44 Guy Toremans, "Scoop for the Belgian Navy: First Time in Command of a Multinational Maritime Task Force,"*Naval Forces* II/2009 (2009): 107.

45 Security Council, "Report of the Secretary-General on the Implementation of Security Council Resolution 1701 (2006)," UN doc. S/2013/120, 27 February 2013.

46 Security Council, "Report of the Secretary-General on the Implementation of Security Council Resolution 1701 (2006)," UN doc. S/2016/189, 26 February 2016, 6.

47 UNIFIL, UNIFIL Maritime Task Force, http://unifil.unmissions.org/Defa ult.aspx?tabid=11584&language=en-US.

48 Bushuev, "UN PKO: Maritime/Riverine Security & Capacity Building," slide 4/23; and Joese Leondro, "Maritime Security Operation and UN Convention on the Law of the Sea Requirements and Capabilities the UN View," PowerPoint presentation, http://eu2013.ie/media/eupresidency/content/documents/maritimeseminarpresentations/REAR-ADMIRAL-LEANDRO-Session-IV-b.pdf.

49 Security Council, "Report of the Secretary-General on the Implementation of Security Council Resolution 1701 (2006)," UN doc. S/2015/475, 25 June 2015, 5.

50 *Jane's Navy International*, "Lebanon's Maritime Task Force Still Going Strong," 19 February 2010, 5.

51 Ibid., 6.

52 Security Council, "Report of the Secretary-General on South Sudan," UN doc. S/2012/820, 8 November 2012, 9–10.

53 Security Council, "Report of the Secretary-General on South Sudan," UN doc. S/2013/366, 29 June 2013, 7, 18.

54 Security Council, "Report of the Secretary-General on South Sudan," UN doc. S/2014/158, 6 March 2014.

55 General Assembly, "Budget Performance of the United Nations Mission in South Sudan for the Period from 1 July 2014 to June 2015," UN doc. A/70/599, 8 December 2015, 52.

56 Bangladesh Multinational Operations Directorate, *Newsletter Bangladesh Navy in UN Missions*, 8.

57 Security Council, "Tenth Report of the Secretary-General on Security Council Resolution 1701 (2006)," UN doc. S/2009/330, 29 June 2009, 14.

58 Security Council, "Thirteenth Report of the Secretary-General on Security Council Resolution 1701 (2006)," UN doc. S/2010/352, 1 July 2010, 12.

59 Security Council, "Letter Dated 11 August 2010 from the Secretary-General Addressed to the President of the Security Council," UN doc. S/2010/430, 12 August 2010, 4.

60 One analyst argues that all of the major European NATO navies have seen recent reductions in deployable vessels. See Bryan McGrath, "NATO at Sea: Trends in Allied Naval Power," *AEI Security Outlook 3*, September

2013, www.aei.org/files/2013/09/17/-national-security-outlook-no3-septem ber-2013_1420494099.pdf.

61 The list of nations that have contributed to the MTF: Bangladesh, Belgium, Brazil, Bulgaria, Denmark, France, Germany, Greece, Indonesia, Italy, The Netherlands, Norway, Spain, Sweden, and Turkey.

62 Leader's Summit on Peacekeeping, Pledges for Current and Future Missions, 28 September 2015, www.un.org/en/peacekeeping/operations/leader summit.html.

63 Ground forces can be assigned individual areas of responsibility more easily than naval forces.

64 Geoffrey Till, *Seapower: A Guide for the Twenty-First Century*, 2nd edn (London: Routledge, 2009), 278–9.

65 Ibid.

66 Ibid.

67 Security Council, 6789th Meeting of the Security Council, 5.

68 Ibid., 6.

69 Guy Toremans, "Scoop for the Belgian Navy": 107.

70 General Assembly, "Comprehensive Review of the Strategic Military Cell Report of the Secretary General," UN doc. A/61/883, 26 April 2007, 4.

71 Ibid., 7.

72 Security Council, "Comprehensive Review of the Strategic Military Cell," UN doc. A/62/744, 18 March 2008, 26.

73 In 2010, the Office of Military Affairs took over all of the functions including the management of the MTF from the now defunct SMC.

74 General Assembly, "Report on the Comprehensive Analysis of the Office of Military Affairs in the Department of Peacekeeping Operations Report of the Secretary General," UN doc. A/62/752, 17 March 2008, 4.

75 Ibid., 28.

76 Security Council, "Letter Dated 19 December 2008 from the Secretary-General to the President of the Security Council," UN doc. S/2008/804, 19 December 2008, 5.

77 Ibid.

78 Security Council, "Report of the Secretary-General on the Situation in Somalia," UN doc. S/2009/132, 9 March 2009, 11.

79 In the 2010 PKO budget a maritime military officer was included as part of the Somalia team. It is not clear from recent budgets that this position still exists but the team remains as the "focal point in military naval operations against piracy." See General Assembly, "Budget for the Support Account for Peacekeeping Operation for the Period from 1 July 2010 to 30 June 2011," UN doc. A/64/697, 5 March 2010, 41; and General Assembly, "Budget for the Support Account for Peacekeeping Operation for the Period from 1 July 2014 to 30 June 2015," UN doc. A/68/742, 10 February 2014, 36.

80 General Assembly, "Evaluation of the Implementation of Protection of Civilians Mandates in United Nations Peacekeeping Operations," UN doc. A/68/787, 7 March 2014, 16; and General Assembly, "Report of the Secretary-General: Overview of the United Nations Peacekeeping Operations: Budget Performance for the Period from 1 July 2012 to 30 June 2013 and Budget for the Period from 1 July 2014 to 30 June 2015," UN doc. A/68/731, 31 January 2014, 50.

81 See DPKO, "United Nations Peacekeeping Missions Military Maritime Task Force Manual," 1 September 2015, http://repository.un.org/handle/11176/387297; and DPKO, "United Nations Peacekeeping Missions Military Riverine Unit Manual," 1 September 2015, http://repository.un.org/handle/11176/387298.

11 New technologies and UN peacekeeping operations

John Karlsrud[1]

- Opportunities and challenges
- Surf, not turf
- Beware of techno-hubris
- New technologies do not equate with robust operations
- Conclusion

United Nations (UN) peace operations are beset with increasingly complex and intertwined challenges, ranging from symmetric and asymmetric threats, and organized crime and terrorism, to poor governance. Furthermore, missions are mandated to operate where there may not be a peace to keep, or to engage robustly with armed groups. External factors are also changing—the financial crisis is lingering on in many countries, and there is strong pressure on national governments to cut costs, including in UN peace operations.[2] Concurrently, over the past two years, we have seen an increase rather than decrease in UN peace operations; new missions have been fielded to South Sudan, Mali, and the Central African Republic (CAR), and the total number of military, police, and civilians in peace operations has reached more than 125,000.[3] In this context, Secretary-General Ban Ki-moon launched a comprehensive review of UN peace operations, which concluded in 2015. It followed a narrower review of technology and innovation in UN peacekeeping provided by a UN expert panel in February that year.[4] The panel, led by Assistant Secretary-General Jane Holl Lute, advised on how UN peacekeeping could "benefit from ongoing technological innovations in a systematic and integrated manner in the longer term."[5]

Indeed, the last decade has seen important technological advances. Information communication technologies (ICTs) underwent a seismic shift from traditional hardware to a convergence to mobile platforms for email and social media. Computing power continues to rise exponentially, and the cost of hardware has been on a steady decline, enabling cloud computing and the advent of "big data."[6] Importantly, it is not only developed countries which now feed this deluge of data; according to the UN Development Programme (UNDP), mobile phone ownership in developing countries already in 2012 accounted for 56 percent of the world's 5.4 billion subscriptions[7] and with smartphones becoming more affordable,[8] innovative use adapted to local context is flourishing. The UN International Telecommunications Union (ITU) has reported that 40.4 percent of the world's population now has access to the internet, with 32.4 percent living in the developing world,[9] a figure that is rising rapidly. Increasingly, affected populations in countries hosting peace operations are able to engage directly with online platforms, leveling the playing field and increasing the potential for engagement with authorities and external actors. This signals a profound change for the internal structure, management, and coordination of UN peace operations. I will return to this later in the chapter.

New technologies accentuate a number of interesting trends and dilemmas in UN peacekeeping. The first is the constant negotiation between Northern and Southern member states on their role in UN peacekeeping, by the fact that most of these technologies originate from Northern member states, although some, such as the crisis-mapping tool Ushahidi, originate from the Global South. New technologies can also be used as arguments for more intelligence- and technology-driven robust missions, although this is a somewhat implicit assumption that deserves to be unpacked and rejected. UN missions do not need new technologies to become more robust, but to be able to avail themselves of the newest technology and thus better implement their mandates. UN missions can also use these tools to help empower local populations to take part and have more ownership of the discussions of their countries' future—perhaps alleviating some of the democratic deficit that too commonly exists.[10]

The chapter proceeds as follows: First, I detail what opportunities and challenges that new technologies harbor for UN peacekeeping operations. Second, I look at the issue of partnerships, both within the UN and between the UN and other actors. I then move on to explore the concurrent developments with regards to robust missions and new technologies. Finally, I consider doctrinal implications of these technological advances in contemporary peace operations and conclude with some recommendations for how to move forward.

Opportunities and challenges

So, what can new technology do for UN peace operations? After many years of despair at the slow uptake of new technology in UN peacekeeping, new optimism emerged in 2013, as surveillance drones were deployed in the UN mission in the Democratic Republic of the Congo (DRC). Experiences from a decade of network-centric warfare in Iraq and Afghanistan are also slowly permeating into UN peacekeeping, through the gradual reengagement by Western countries through troop contributions and perhaps most importantly seconding of military staff to missions and the headquarters in New York. In this paradigm, all capabilities are tracked down to the individual level in real time, with rapid information flows enabling the right type and amount of force to be employed at the right level, at the right place and at the right time. Combined with crisis-mapping, presenting information visually rather than via text, we see the contours of potentially radically new ways of planning and executing peace operations. Some of these technologies are already being put to work—the use of surveillance drones in the DRC and crisis-mapping in Mali are two examples that this chapter looks at more closely.

Technology can help to improve situational awareness, force protection, and, most importantly, to better protect civilians at risk. It is possible today to track the movement of personnel and capabilities on all levels in real time—from individual trackers carried by each soldier, to vehicles and larger units. The UN Department of Peacekeeping Operations (DPKO) is already tracking civilian vehicles, but not in real time. While it may not be realistic to expect that the UN will be given the necessary resources to equip each soldier with track markers or that UN troops will acquire and employ precision-guided weapon systems in the near future, a range of other tracking technology is within reach and already being used in field missions. The UN Multidimensional Integrated Stabilization Mission in Mali (MINUSMA) is experimenting with the Ushahidi crisis-mapping platform to "geotag" reports of security incidents and other information and present these in real time maps.[11] Visual presentation of information is more intuitive and provides a much better tool for decision-makers at tactical, operational, and strategic levels than long-winded reports where patterns are easily missed. Information can be grouped in layers, according to the type and classification of the information.

UN peace operations can draw from a wide range of sources of information: Aside from their considerable presence of military troops, and police and civilian staff on the ground, this includes information from non-UN partners and open sources, as well as increasingly commercial satellite image providers. These can provide up-to-date images at low cost, enabling missions to monitor evolving situations on the ground. In Darfur, the Satellite Sentinel Project and the Enough Project hired DigitalGlobe, a commercial provider of satellite imagery, to take satellite pictures. The images were analyzed by experts at DigitalGlobe and volunteer technology communities (VTCs) supporting the Enough Project. The project showed that satellite images could be powerful tools to monitor violence on the ground, document human rights violations, and provide early warning of impending attacks. However, it also showed that the collection of information for humanitarian or human rights purposes can be vulnerable to misuse by hostile third parties.[12]

The rest of the UN system is gathering vast amounts of data on an everyday basis, and is looking at how it can improve its data collection for sustainable development. Secretary-General Ban Ki-moon set up Independent Expert Advisory Group on a Data Revolution for Sustainable Development (IEAG) in 2014, which has provided advice on how the UN can better make use of new technologies and the data deluge on a global level.[13]

UN peace operations can also engage and partner with VTCs, which are volunteer technologists that engage and support international organizations and nongovernmental organizations (NGOs) from a remote location digitally, usually during disasters, but also in conflict situations such as Libya. The engagement started in 2010 with thousands of VTCs responding to the earthquakes in Haiti and Chile, and flooding in Pakistan. Volunteers processed large volumes of information and, for example, plotted these into maps. Crisis-mappers and other volunteers are forming a new class of actors with their own set of advantages and challenges. They can bring a significant mass of intellectual power to bear in a crisis—and in Haiti during the 2010 earthquake they were able to turn a virtually blank spot on the map into the most accurately mapped place in the world in a matter of hours.[14] Being volunteers, VTCs can act much faster than multilateral organizations. They are also hard to replace: The sheer amount of human data processing means that this will remain outside the scope of the UN or other organizations to undertake. However, there have also been growing pains. While their intention to do good is praiseworthy, VTCs are seeking to professionalize their activities and establish codes of conduct and guidelines to ensure that unintended and negative consequences of involvement do not arise.[15]

In the DRC, peacekeepers have handed out cell phones to the local population as part of an effort to create community alert networks

(CANs), which can alert the UN Stabilization Mission in the Democratic Republic of the Congo (MONUSCO) when a situation is emerging, and the network can be used to run simple perception surveys. This enables real-time monitoring of evolving issues and improves the mission's ability to capture, understand, and integrate local perceptions into daily decision-making, and enhances its ability to protect civilians. Elva, a similar network set up by Saferworld and the Caucasus Research Resource Center in Georgia, is combined with a mapping tool, is used to map security incidents, infrastructure issues, and to request assistance in emergency situations.[16] However, while fairly simple to set up and run, these networks bring their own set of challenges, discussed below.

Since the Arab Spring, the world has become aware that social media, mobile technology, and "Web 2.0" technologies have great potential to engage populations in democratic dialogues, but also undeniable anti-democratic risks: "Social media are only platforms—they can serve as media outlets for repressive movements as well as democratic ones."[17] Nevertheless, these technologies present opportunities for peace operations to more strongly engage with local populations, opportunities that must be taken on board for peace operations to stay relevant to the people they are supposed to serve and to counter adversaries that currently are much more adept at the use of these tools than the UN. The UN has successfully used radio and other technologies for strategic communications to reach out to local populations, and although many missions actively communicate their activities through social media, there is still a large untapped potential for using social media and other tools to achieve missions' long-term objectives.

These technologies also accentuate the need to update the doctrinal framework guiding UN peace operations to reflect a changing operational environment. The UN has developed guidelines to better understand local perceptions, and there is also a critical need for mission leadership to take on board these lessons: "to take full advantage of opportunities to collect systematically and effectively analyse, information on local perceptions to enhance missions' situational awareness, inform confidence building, and support inclusive post-conflict governance."[18] While this is a good first step, the UN peace operations review should ensure that these messages also are reflected in the planning and funding of future missions.

Surf, not turf

As UN peace operations are becoming increasingly complex, both in terms of mandates and tools to implement them, they also work with a wide range of UN partners. To ensure good cooperation on implementing mandated tasks the UN needs to move away from separate lines of communication and internal turf fights. Intra-organizational cooperation is needed to make sure that all parts of the UN are able to access information critical to their operations and to support populations in need. One good recent initiative was the establishment of the UN Operations and Crisis Centre (UNOCC) in New York.[19]

At the same time, more and more information is available—causing a data deluge that makes it difficult to find an efficient way of accessing, sifting through, and analyzing relevant and actionable information. In UN peace operations, which are struggling with information overload and limited data transfer bandwidth, this is particularly challenging. As diverse platforms of information are converging and sometimes integrated and merged, a real-time understanding of the situation on the ground can become available for decision-makers at all levels. But this necessitates the requisite bandwidth between the field and UN headquarters in New York, and it is equally important to also have that bandwidth between mission headquarters and staff at the tactical level.[20] Many UN peace operations rely on satellite communication for their connection in the field and New York. With fiber cables increasingly connecting the African continent, the situation is slowly improving, but there is a clear need for more innovative solutions and significant investments to enable sufficient bandwidth and real-time communication between strategic, operational, and tactical levels in UN peace operations. In the short term, the UN could partner with global satellite providers, but in the longer term there is need for more fiber optic cables along the coasts of Africa and across the continent.

To enable rapid deployment of relevant expertise that would allow for precise data analysis and the deployment of advanced technologies, UN member states should consider the suggestion by the Expert Panel on Technology and Innovation in UN Peacekeeping to establish a mechanism to furnish the UN with civilian and technological expertise in the form of civilian contributing countries (CCCs) or technological expertise contributing countries (TechCCs), similar to the already existing arrangements for police and troop contributing countries (PCCs and TCCs).[21] This would be a practical follow-up of the civilian capacities reform initiative rolled out in 2009.[22] Member states could provide, for example, network engineers to set up efficient and secure communications at an early phase of mission deployment.

Inter-organizational cooperation also needs further strengthening. The integration of operations and crisis centers at the UN in the

UNOCC is matched by similar initiatives at the global level. The European Union (EU) has taken the initiative for collaboration between the crisis rooms of, among others, the UN, the North Atlantic Treaty Organization (NATO), and the Organization for Security and Co-operation in Europe (OSCE), as well as regional organizations such as the African Union and the League of Arab States,[23] but closer cooperation is needed. Organizations need to ensure interoperability and enable real-time exchange of data between, for example, the EU Situation Room and the UNOCC to make collaboration useful to decision-makers. However, concerns about sharing sensitive information remain and the UN is still perceived to be having difficulties with safeguarding sensitive information.

But the increasing convergence between information platforms also highlights difficult questions. How should UN peace operations cooperate with humanitarian actors? In the humanitarian field, common operational datasets (CODs) were developed by NGOs and the UN agencies under the leadership of the UN Office for the Coordination of Humanitarian Assistance (OCHA). The CODs ensure that common standards are followed during the collection and storage of information, and that there is an easy exchange of information between organizations in the UN system.[24] UN peace operations have access to this information, and increasing convergence between data platforms enables real-time exchange of information and swift decision-making. However, humanitarians will continue to insist on their neutrality, and are wary about sharing more sensitive information with peace operations, or using information gathered by, for example, surveillance drones in eastern DRC.[25] OCHA has already developed guidance for humanitarian workers on surveillance drones and new technologies, and here UN peace operations are still lagging behind.[26]

Cooperation with the private sector is increasing, but much more can be done. Leaders in information technology, such as Google and Microsoft, can and do help the UN in getting a grip on how to sort through the vast piles of data it gathers in more effective ways. Military components, civil affairs, human rights officers, and other civilians in the field send their written reports up the chain of command each day. How can this information be formatted, quantified, presented, and analyzed for longer-term trends? The suggestion of the UN expert panel to equip more military, police, and civilian peacekeepers with smart phones and tablets to enable real time and geo-tagged information and reporting should be heeded.[27] To be relevant and actionable for decision-makers, the data provided by local populations on the ground through social media, Twitter messages, and other forms of communication must be cross-checked in real-time with other sources to ensure veracity and validity. Digital "exhaust" can be useful to detect macro trends—group geo-tagging of mobile phones to detect population movement, using sudden spikes of remittance transfers to detect geographical locations where tension is looming[28]—and the secretary-general should find ways for the banking, telecoms, and remittances industries to share their data without revealing business secrets.

The UN is also deploying new systems for gathering information. In Mali, the All Sources Information Fusion Unit (ASIFU) is the first explicit intelligence unit in a UN peacekeeping mission. The surveillance drones—or unmanned aerial systems (UAS) in UN parlance—in the DRC have received much attention since their deployment in December 2013. So far, the drones have been used in operations of the Force Intervention Brigade and the *Forces Armées de la République Démocratique du Congo* (FARDC) against the M23 and *Forces démocratiques de libération du Rwanda* (FDLR) rebel groups, but also in identifying a sinking boat on Lake Kivu and aiding the UN mission in rescuing a number of civilians.

The surveillance drones in the DRC are not the first in a UN context: Drones have been used in the DRC since 2006, in Chad since 2009, and there has been extensive use of helicopter-based reconnaissance in the DRC and Mali. However, the UN has never before had an airborne surveillance program with centralized drafted rules and procedures such as the one we see advancing with the unmanned aerial vehicle (UAV) program. There is thus urgency to develop general and country-specific guidelines for the use of the surveillance drones, and the UN is in the process of finalizing these.[29]

MONUSCO has chosen the private contractor Selex to deploy the Falco UAV system to the eastern DRC; there are several drones in each system, and they fly at a medium altitude of 15,000 feet (c.4,500 meters), have night-flight capability, and have long endurance, meaning that they are able to stay in the air for up to 72 hours. The drones are surveillance platforms equipped with a high resolution camera for stills and video, as well as an infrared camera for night operations and bad weather, and a thermal camera to identify groups of people. They also have a synthetic aperture radar on board and create 2D or 3D images of the objects of interest on the ground, meaning that they can look through foliage, although not the triple foliage canopy that is common in the areas covered with rain forest in the eastern DRC. The drones are large enough to also include other payloads, such as signals intelligence equipment, distance measuring equipment, GPS, altimeters, and so forth.

Surveillance drones can enable the UN to radically improve its situational awareness—to survey large areas for troop and population movements, zoom in on emerging situations, and track the movement of particular groups—also at night and in deep forest. The conflict affected areas in the DRC are mainly in dense jungles, rough terrain, and in regions with poor infrastructure, making them difficult to access. UAVs may improve the security and safety of UN troops and civilian personnel, and allow for the pursuit of belligerent groups while avoiding unexpected confrontations and ambushes. If equipped with change detection software, the drones could also scan roads for improvised explosive devices (IEDs) and can identify possible disturbances to the ground surface.[30] Compared to previous airborne surveillance platforms used in the DRC, such as the helicopters, drones are expected to be much more cost-effective; and the helicopters and planes which have previously been used for surveillance may then be used for other purposes.

The UAVs also have other tactical uses, such as collecting information that may indicate emerging situations and potential violence, thereby enabling peacekeeping troops to position themselves in ample time between potentially conflicting groups and prevent attacks on civilian populations. The UN considers the deployment of drones in the DRC successful and wants to also add this capability to MINUSMA in Mali and its missions in South Sudan and the Central African Republic, but South Sudan has rejected the proposal.[31] In Mali, the UN is aiming to include longer-range UAVs, drawing upon their experience from the DRC.[32] With the inclusion of drones a number of difficult questions also emerge. How long should data be stored and who can require *post facto* access? Can the International Criminal Court (ICC) request the UN to share the data at a later date? Going forward, the UN must address these questions and develop the institutional framework not only on the mission level, but also on the global level.[33]

The OSCE has deployed two short-range drones to eastern Ukraine.[34] Some concerns, however, remain. Although the drones were chosen in part for their light footprint, they have been targeted by military-grade jamming equipment and attempts at shooting them down, and one of the drones crashed for unknown reasons in February 2015. These difficult conditions are severely limiting their effectiveness.[35]

Beware of techno-hubris

The current interest in the possibilities new technology provide should be complemented with a solid dose of skepticism. Unfortunately, more information does not necessarily lead to more or better action to protect civilians or troops, as witnessed in Bosnia, Rwanda, and more recently in the DRC during the limited action taken to protect civilians in Goma in November 2012.[36] In the end, this remains a question of political will, not ability. Surveillance drones and other tools can have a deterrent effect on potential perpetrators by making it clear that they are under observation, hopefully raising the bar for committing atrocities. However, they must be accompanied by a strong public-relations campaign informing the host population about the rationale for their deployment and the limits of what they can and cannot do. It is easy to imagine a situation where host populations will only be enraged by the continued inaction of the international community when provided with even better information of ongoing atrocities on the ground. So far, NGOs in eastern DRC argue that the local population has dubbed the drones "loud mosquitos" and that they have not been sufficiently informed about the function and purpose of the drones—not even knowing whether they are armed.[37]

To increase the accountability and effectiveness of aid, vulnerable and affected populations are under increasing pressure to share their personal information in order to receive support. NGOs, UN agencies, and others gathering this information are vulnerable to hostile actors seeking to access and use this information for their own ends. Satellite imagery is available for everyone, and phone data can easily be monitored. Ensuring privacy and gaining secure informed consent may seem like a privilege for better situated populations, quite literally. There is thus a critical need to stop at regular intervals and make sure that peace operations do not harm those that they intend to help. These challenges may also be encountered by affected populations engaging with peace operations. UN operations have set up community-alert networks in the DRC and aim to do the same in other missions. Civil affairs, political affairs, and other substantive sections engage with and gain information from a wide range of sources on a daily basis. The unintended consequences of storing this information on common platforms and merging it with other data must be examined closely to enable proper checks and balances to be built in.

Today, host populations risk being treated as second rate citizens—it is implicitly assumed by many international actors that the need to secure informed consent to obtain and use information is a luxury good that does not apply in situations of crisis. The local population participating in the community alert networks in eastern DRC can be the target of possible reprisals by hostile groups. Using crowdsourced information can have unintended and negative consequences through group or individual re-identification when combined with other information (known as the Mosaic-effect),[38] putting civilians in danger of persecution, torture, or death by hostile actors. MONUSCO has modified its approach to instead provide a hotline number for local populations to call to limit negative and unintended consequences.[39] The humanitarian principle of "do no harm" and the military principle of "reasonable chance of success" should be kept vigilantly in mind.

With the increasing digitalization of information and exponential capability of data storage, new questions emerge: For how long will information be stored? And can member states, the ICC, or NGOs ask for information collected by surveillance drones and use it in court? Will data be stored if it can reveal cases of UN inaction in the face of blatant violations of international law? Who will ensure the security of data collected in the longer run? The UN is already becoming the target of offensive cyber-attacks, which are primarily attempts to access sensitive information.[40]

Technology can enable remote control, and increase demands for accountability and local empowerment, but also lessen demands for accountability from the international community. In the calls for more and better technology there is an inherent danger of distancing ourselves from those we intend to help, and shifting accountability from helpers to receivers.

There may also be a partnership gap here. To enable reform and further progress, the role of traditional TCCs should be acknowledged. They must be consulted and listened to—in many cases these countries are the sources of innovative technology that has spurred economic and social development, for example the development of Ushahidi and mobile banking in Kenya. Their ownership is crucial to building a credible agenda advancing the technological evolution of peacekeeping operations, and to make sure that technological solutions are developed and adapted to the needs and existing capabilities on the ground.

In an environment of increased risks and complex threats, there is a real danger that technology will speed up a tendency of troops, civilians, and humanitarians to retreat to the safe walls of their compounds. As seen in the example of surveillance drones, increased knowledge creates increased responsibility. There is an urgent need to work against the "bunkerization" of UN peace operations, and to use technology and innovation to enable peace operations to match the increased knowledge that technology can provide with increased mobility and agility, and the requisite will to implement their mandates.

New technologies do not equate with robust operations

The objective that has been used when arguing for the inclusion of new technologies in UN peacekeeping has been to improve the safety, effectiveness, and situational awareness of peacekeeping operations. In much of the writing and comment that has emerged over the last few years, the term *new technologies* seems to be used as a euphemism for the inclusion of various tools for intelligence gathering and dissemination. While this is not entirely wrong, it also limits the understanding of what new technologies can bring to UN peacekeeping, as detailed earlier in the chapter.

UN peacekeeping needs intelligence capabilities in the shape of surveillance drones, community alert networks, partnerships with crisis-mappers and many other innovations that new technologies can bring. The UN Interim Force in Lebanon (UNIFIL) is a perfectly good example of a mission that has a lot of modern technologies and troop contributions from a range of Western states, while still being a traditional peacekeeping operation. However, among many actors there seems to be a connection made between the inclusion of modern military capabilities and the more robust version of peacekeeping, leaning towards peace enforcement. For some, MINUSMA may be seen as a laboratory for including some of the concepts and lessons learned from Afghanistan. It will be essential to support this process by providing the new TCCs arriving from Western states with a better understanding of the similarities and differences between NATO and UN missions, and the need to take a less combative stance in Mali.

With the Western capabilities MINUSMA is becoming more robust. But the robust posture may also have a self-fulfilling effect, drawing attention to the mission and increasing the chance of targeted attacks against the UN. When the al-Qaeda in the Maghreb and other armed groups realize what are the weakest spots in the UN presence, retaliatory attacks will most probably be targeted at the soft underbelly of the UN—the funds, programs, and agencies carrying out development and humanitarian work.[41] In this manner, new technologies can indirectly have an unfortunate impact on doctrinal development at the UN, pointing UN peacekeeping in a direction of offensive operations.

Instead, the UN should embrace new technologies as tools that can give voice to local populations, level the democratic deficit, and further positive change. Used correctly, new technologies can be of significant help to achieve the strategic objectives of UN peace operations. Zooming out, it is clear that there is a need to reflect the opportunities and risks of new technologies in the doctrinal framework of the UN.

They represent new tools and capabilities that military, police, and civilian components should take on board and utilize, bringing data to decision-makers on all levels.

Conclusion

Technological development rarely brings anything fundamentally new. What we see most of the time is incremental innovation—drones in UN peacekeeping are an extension of seeing, of the binocular, and currently not a weapon system, although this is a distinct possibility in the future.[42] However, on a more fundamental level the digital revolution we are in the midst of is a paradigm shift at the level of the Industrial Revolution, creating new opportunities, but also new challenges. Modern information and communications technologies have radically altered how we live and work in both hemispheres of the globe. Local voices can have global reach, most if not everything can be digitized and shared, and machine intelligence is slowly becoming more than a distant vision.

Concurrently, UN peace operations have received clear marching orders from member states to do more with less. However, the financial crisis was followed by an increase rather than decrease in the number of operations, further increasing the financial strain on member states. In the next few years, there will be significant pressure to cut costs. Innovation and technology can be helpful in this process, but resources must be directed to where the UN can make the most impact.

The discussion on technology and innovation in UN peace operations should thus enlarge the focus from cool gadgetry such as night-vision goggles, tracking of UN vehicles, and surveillance drones, to a more fundamental understanding of what tools and capabilities can make peace operations better at protecting civilians and implementing mandated tasks at the lowest cost. Some seem to think that acquiring new technology is a matter of choice, but including new technology and moving innovation is not a choice, it is the only way forward. When launching the surveillance drone capability for MONUSCO, Under-Secretary-General Hervé Ladsous said that UN peacekeeping finally "entered the 21st century."[43] Peace operations are also increasingly facing actors that are using advanced technology to commit organized crime, often in conjunction with armed groups.

The exit of Western troops from Afghanistan can create a new source of supply of troops and capabilities for the UN, premised on the ability of the UN and these countries to adapt and come to a compromise on command and control, where a sufficient amount of strategic mission assets such as helicopters and surveillance drones are directly under the control of the military component in high-risk environments. The return of the West can be mutually beneficial. The UN can offer Western member states theaters where troops can continue to deploy and maintain their capacities and capabilities, and UN peace operations can become an arena for sharing of experiences between traditional and new TCCs. These capacities will be in demand. However, new tools require new capacities—for example, analysis capacity is crucial. It is not a layman task to analyze satellite pictures and synthetic aperture radar data. There is thus a need to complement the focus on tools with a push to include relevant posts in the UN staffing table to ensure a long-term and sustainable approach. The push for more technology should also be balanced by due concern for possible negative unintended consequences, making sure to not increase the vulnerability of the populations that we intend to help. The doctrinal framework must be updated with these twin ambitions in mind, taking into consideration the potential that new technology can unleash while also using technology to increase the ability to protect and listen to local populations and avoiding any negative impact.

The UN is inherently geared for incremental and not revolutionary change, and there is a tendency of preparing for yesterday's and not tomorrow's challenges. With this in mind, the UN needs to set its sights on good enough solutions, striking a balance between available technology, cost effectiveness, and what is politically acceptable. What is within reach, and how should the UN get there?

Finally, the embrace of new technology should be interspersed with solid doses of realism and cultural sensitivity. No matter whether technological innovation is incremental or moves leaps and bounds, the objective must remain the same—to alleviate suffering and protect civilians in need, and increase the protection of UN troops and civilians in the field. In the midst of the technology frenzy it is sometimes easy to miss this simple, but central point.

Notes

1 An earlier version of this chapter was published as "Innovation and Technology in UN Peace Operations: Opportunities and Risks," in the Center on International Cooperation 2015 *Annual Review of Global Peace Operations 2014* (New York: Center on International Cooperation, New York University, 2015). The author would like to acknowledge the thoughtful comments and inputs made by Chiyuki Aoi, Richard Gowan, Alischa Kugel, and Calin Trenkov-Wermuth. All errors and omissions remain my own.

2 See Kristin B. Sandvik, Maria G. Jumbert, John Karlsrud and Mareile Kaufman, "Humanitarian Technology: A Critical Research Agenda," *International Review of the Red Cross* (2014): 1–24; and John Karlsrud, "Peacekeeping 4.0: Harnessing the Potential of Big Data, Social Media and Cyber Technology," in *Cyber Space and International Relations: Theory, Prospects and Challenges*, ed. Jan-Frederik Kremer and Benedikt Müller (Berlin: Springer, 2014), 141–60.

3 Some 122,729 in peacekeeping and 3,440 in special political and peacebuilding missions. For more details, see UN, Peacekeeping Fact Sheet, updated 31 December 31 2014, www.un.org/en/peacekeeping/resources/statistics/factsheet.shtml; UN DPA, United Nations Political and Peacebuilding Missions, updated 31 August 2014, www.un.org/wcm/webdav/site/undpa/shared/undpa/pdf/ppbm_Aug2014.pdf.pdf.

4 Expert Panel on Technology and Innovation in UN Peacekeeping, *Performance Peacekeeping: Final Report of the Expert Panel on Technology and Innovation in UN Peacekeeping* (New York: United Nations, 2015).

5 UN, "USGs Announce Expert Panel on Technology and Innovation in UN Peacekeeping," press release, 4 June 2014, www.un.org/en/peacekeeping/documents/Expert-Panel_Technology-Innovation_UNPeacekeeping.pdf.

6 *Big data* will here be defined as any large amount of structured, semi-structured, and unstructured data that can be mined for information.

7 UNDP, "Mobile Technologies and Empowerment: Enhancing Human Development through Participation and Innovation," New York, 2012, 12.

8 James Temperton, "Orange Klif: Hands on with Mozilla's £25 Smartphone." *Wired*, 3 March 2015, www.wired.co.uk/news/archive/2015-03/03/mozilla-orange-klif?utm_source=Adestra&utm_medium=email&utm_campaign=wired%20awake%204%20march.

9 ITU, "Key ICT Indicators for Developed and Developing Countries and the World (Totals and Penetration Rates)," 2014, www.itu.int/en/ITU-D/Statistics/Pages/stat/default.aspx.

10 Cedric de Coning, John Karlsrud, and Paul Troost, "Towards More People-Centric Peace Operations: From 'Extension of State Authority' to 'Strengthening Inclusive State-Society Relations,'" *Stability* 4, no. 1 (2015): 1–13.

11 Ushahidi is a web-based reporting system that utilizes crowdsourced data to formulate visual map information of a crisis on a real-time basis. The data can be provided via text messages, email, twitter and web-forms. "'Ushahidi,' which means 'testimony' in Swahili, was a website that was initially developed to map reports of violence in Kenya after the post-election fallout at the beginning of 2008." Ushahidi, Ushahidi's Mission, 2014.

12 Nathaniel Raymond, Caitlin Howarth, and Jonathan Hutson, "Crisis Mapping Needs an Ethical Compass," *GlobalBrief*, 6 February 2012, http://globalbrief.ca/blog/2012/02/06/crisis-mapping-needs-an-ethical-compass/.

13 UN, *A World that Counts: Mobilising the Data Revolution for Sustainable Development* (New York: United Nations, 2014).

14 Harvard Humanitarian Initiative, *Disaster Relief 2.0: The Future of Information Sharing in Humanitarian Emergencies* (Washington, DC: UN Foundation & Vodafone Foundation Technology Partnership, 2011), 30.

15 See also OCHA, "Humanitarianism in the Age of Cyber-warfare: Towards the Principled and Secure Use of Information in Humanitarian

Emergencies," New York, 2014; Arthur Mühlen-Schulte and John Karls-rud, "Quasi-Professionals in the Organisation of Transnational Crisis Mapping," in *Professions and Organizations in Transnational Governance*, ed. Leonard Seabrooke and Lasse F. Henriksen (Cambridge: Cambridge University Press, 2016).

16 For more, see Elva, Community Safety Network, 2014 www.elva.org/p rojects/community-safety-network/.

17 Karlsrud, "Peacekeeping 4.0," 15.

18 UN, "Guidelines: Understanding and Integrating Local Perceptions in UN Peacekeeping," New York, 30 June 2014. See also Niels N. Schia, Ingvild, M. Gjelsvik, and John Karlsrud, "What People Think Does Matter: Understanding and Integrating Local Perceptions into UN Peacekeeping," *Policy Brief* 13 (2013).

19 UNOCC includes the Secretariat organizations as well as the UN High Commissioner for Refugees and the UN Development Programme. Unfor-tunately, the UN Children's Fund (UNICEF) chose to remain outside the structure.

20 Bandwidth here refers to the amount of data that can be transferred to and from UN peace operations.

21 Expert Panel, *Performance Peacekeeping*.

22 Reflecting on the increasingly important role civilians are playing in peace operations supporting the development of institutions in countries ravaged by conflict, highlighted in the 2009 UN secretary-general's report "Peace-building in the Immediate Aftermath of Conflict," the secretary-general initiated a civilian capacity reform in 2010 by appointing an Independent Senior Advisory Group, led by former Under Secretary-General and head of DPKO Jean-Marie Guéhenno. The secretary-general started with the implementation of a number of steps to make more effective use of civilian capacities in 2011, after receiving the recommendations from the advisory group.

23 For more, see EU, "Towards a Global Network of Crisis Rooms," 2013, http://eu-un.europa.eu/articles/en/article_14331_en.htm.

24 Inter-Agency Standing Committee (IASC), "IASC Guidelines Common Operational Datasets (CODs) in Disaster Preparedness and Response," Geneva, 2010.

25 IRIN, "NGOs Against MONUSCO Drones for Humanitarian Work," 23 July 2014, www.irinnews.org/report/100391/ngos-against-monusco-drones-for-huma nitarian-work.

26 OCHA, "Humanitarianism in the Network Age," New York, 2013; Daniel Gilman, "Unmanned Aerial Vehicles in Humanitarian Response," *OCHA Policy and Studies Series, June 2014–10*; and Daniel Gilman and Leith Baker, "Humanitarianism in the Age of Cyber-warfare: Towards the Prin-cipled and Secure Use of Information in Humanitarian Emergencies," *OCHA Policy and Studies Series*, October 2014–11.

27 Expert Panel, *Performance Peacekeeping*, 61.

28 For more, see UN Global Pulse, About, 2014, www.unglobalpulse.org/a bout/faqs.

29 For more on this, see Frederik Rosén and John Karlsrud, "The MONUSCO UAVs: The Implications for Actions and Omissions," *Conflict Trends* 4, (2014): 42–8.

30 Selex ES, "SELEX Galileo's Falco Continues to Soar with 4th Export Customer and Falco EVO Runway Rollout," 2012, www.selex-es.com/docum ents/737448/5403990/body_9_July_12_SELEX_Galileo_Falco_continues_to_ soar_with_4th_export_customer_and_Falco_EVO_runway_rollout.pdf.
31 Somini Sengupta, "Unarmed Drones Aid U.N. Peacekeeping Missions in Africa," 2 July 2014, www.nytimes.com/2014/07/03/world/africa/unarm ed-drones-aid-un-peacekeepers-in-africa.html?_r=1.
32 Personal conversation with UN official, 17 February 2015. See also John Karlsrud and Adam Smith, "European Military Participation in MINUSMA: Experiences and Lessons-Learned," International Peace Institute, New York, 2015.
33 For more, see John Karlsrud and Frederik Rosén, "Lifting the Fog of War? Opportunities and Challenges of Drones in UN Peace Operations," in *The Rise of the Good Drone*, ed. Maria Gabrielsen Jumbert and Kristin Bergtora Sandvik (Surrey: Ashgate, 2015).
34 Deutsche Welle, "Drones for OSCE Truce Monitors Arrives in Ukraine," 6 October 2014, www.dw.de/drones-for-osce-truce-monitors-arrive-in-ukra ine/a-17978951.
35 Julian Borger, "Arming Ukraine Army May Escalate Conflict, West Warned," *The Guardian*, 8 February 2015, www.theguardian.com/world/ 2015/feb/08/arming-ukraine-army-escalate-conflict-ocse.
36 UN, "Evaluation of the Implementation and Results of Protection of Civilians Mandates in United Nations Peacekeeping Operations, UN doc. (2014) A/68/787, 7 March 2014, para. 25.
37 IRIN, "NGOs Against MONUSCO Drones for Humanitarian Work."
38 The *Mosaic-effect* describes the combining and cross-referencing of seemingly anonymous data with other accessible data sets in order to re-identify individuals. For more see, for example, the Engine Room, "Responsible Data: A Conceptual Framework," 2014 www.theengineroom.org/responsi ble-data-a-conceptual-framework/.
39 Expert Panel, *Performance Peacekeeping*, 74.
40 BBC News, "Governments, IOC and UN Hit by Massive Cyber-attack," 3 August 2011, www.bbc.com/news/technology-14387559.
41 For more, see John Karlsrud, "The UN at War: Examining the Consequences of Peace Enforcement Mandates for the UN Peacekeeping Operations in the CAR, the DRC and Mali," *Third World Quarterly* 36, no. 1 (2015): 47.
42 John Karlsrud and Frederik Rosén "In the Eye of the Beholder? UN and the Use of Drones to Protect Civilians," *Stability of Security and Development* 2, no. 2 (2013): 1–10.
43 UN Office of the Spokesperson, "Highlights of the Noon Briefing by Martin Nesirky, Spokesperson for Secretary-General Ban Ki-Moon, Monday, 5 August 2013," www.un.org/sg/spokesperson/highlights/index. asp?HighD=8/5/2013&d_month=8&d_year=2013.

12 Conclusion

Towards a United Nations stabilization doctrine—stabilization as an emerging UN practice

Chiyuki Aoi and Cedric de Coning

- Stabilization as a concept: Key features
- UN stabilization missions
- Demarcating and distinguishing peace operations and stabilization: Towards a new UN stabilization doctrine
- Conclusion

After the end of the Cold War, United Nations (UN) peace operations mainly as a result of the new focus on resolving internal conflicts, expanded to take on multidimensional mandates and tasks. During the first decade of this century, in response to the lessons learned from the failures in Somalia, Rwanda, and Bosnia-Herzegovina, the traditional principles of peacekeeping were revisited and a more flexible interpretation emerged that allowed the use of force, not only in self-defense, but also in defense of the mandate. This new interpretation of the use of force principle, combined with an emerging practice of deploying peacekeeping missions with a Chapter VII (enforcement) mandate, was meant to enable peacekeeping operations to better protect civilians.

The 9/11 attacks and the ensuing "War on Terror" also brought significant pressure to bear on the good offices role of the UN—to impartially arbitrate between all parties in a conflict, even those "beyond the pale." In the area of peace operations, this pressure has surfaced with the increased tendency of the UN Security Council to list terrorist groups and task UN peace operations with helping to protect a government and its people from these aggressors. The increasing trend of mandating missions to support the extension of state authority has also highlighted some of the inherent tensions that emerge when UN peacekeeping missions have to balance a protection of civilians mandate with a statebuilding mandate, especially when government security forces are implicated in acts of violence against the civilian population.

Furthermore, the Security Council is increasingly mandating bridging operations. The British intervention in Sierra Leone in 2000 showed that the combination of an external force mandated by the Security Council and a UN presence could stabilize a situation in the longer term. In recent years we have seen bridging operations being staged in the Central African Republic (CAR), the Democratic Republic of the Congo (DRC) and Mali, where European Union (EU), French, and African Union (AU) troops were able to stabilize the situation, with a subsequent transfer of authority to a UN operation. Often, the transfer of authority has preceded any peace agreement between the parties on the ground, but has mandated the UN to support the state in extending state authority, in practice making the UN a party to the conflicts that linger on.

UN peace operations are thus again in a period of flux that is testing its doctrinal limits. The Security Council is not directed by the UN Secretariat's peacekeeping doctrine. In reality, the peacekeeping mandates issued by the Security Council precede and inform new doctrinal developments. The mandates given for the peacekeeping missions in the CAR, DRC, and Mali may, for instance, require a doctrinal change that clarifies where stabilization fits into UN peacekeeping doctrine. As a result of these developments and pressures on the existing UN peacekeeping doctrine, the UN secretary-general in October 2014 nominated a high-level, independent panel to review UN peace operations. The panel, led by the former president of Timor-Leste (East Timor), José Ramos-Horta, submitted its report to the secretary-general in June 2015.[1] The secretary-general subsequently provided his own implementation report to the 2015 session of the General Assembly and Security Council.

The Ramos-Horta panel notes that UN peace operations have been increasingly called upon to deploy "in the midst of conflict as a crisis response tool to deter escalation, to contain conflict while protecting civilians and, at the same time, to attempt to restart or revive peace processes."[2] The panel characterizes these as "conflict management" missions, and differentiates them from ceasefire monitoring missions and peace implementation missions. The panel recognizes, however, that the Security Council and Secretariat have used the term stabilization for a number of missions, and it "believes the usage of this term by the United Nations requires clarification."[3]

As the panel observers, the UN has not yet formally defined the concept of *stabilization* in its official doctrine or terminology. However, there are now four UN missions that have the word in the name of the mission and that have such tasks in their mandate: those in the CAR, the DRC, Haiti, and Mali. Furthermore, the history of UN peace-keeping—from the Congo in the 1960s to the Balkans in the 1990s and contemporary operations—suggests that, in hindsight, there have indeed been other UN operations that we could now more properly reinterpret as stabilization rather than peacekeeping operations.

The analyses of contemporary cases in this book indicate that some of them may also be considered UN stabilization missions. However, we would warn against a conflation between the concepts of peace-keeping, stabilization, and counterinsurgency, and we will give a more detailed view of our understanding of the stabilization concept in a UN context later in this chapter. The purpose of this chapter is hence to consider how recent developments in stabilization concepts and prac-tices may relate to current UN peace operations, and how they inform the discussion to develop better doctrines and guidelines for UN action. The chapter first identifies key features of stabilization, based upon a qualitative review of already-developed concepts and doctrine of stabilization, building upon key representative historical cases. It then reviews those UN peace operations that currently have *stabiliza-tion* in their names and mandates to identify to what extent these could indeed be considered stabilization in contemporary doctrinal terms. Finally, the chapter considers how UN peace operations concepts and practice might merit from a conceptualization and definition of *stabi-lization* and a clearer demarcation between peacekeeping, stabilization, and counterinsurgency operations, and concludes with a recommenda-tion that the UN should not just include stabilization into existing peacekeeping doctrine, but rather add a new standalone UN stabiliza-tion doctrine that provides for the possibility of offensive mandates, where deemed necessary.

Stabilization as a concept: Key features

Stabilization is a main task for many international missions today, including those conducted by the North Atlantic Treaty Organization (NATO) and its member governments, the EU, the AU, and as this chapter argues, by the UN.[4] Indeed, the practice of stabilization is burgeoning, but to date there has been no common definition of either stability tasks or stabilization. As indicated in the review of national approaches to emergent peace operations issues in Part I of this volume, there is no common definition of *stabilization* shared among the per-manent members of the Security Council or large troop-contributing countries (TCCs). As discussed in Chapters 1 and 2, the United States and the United Kingdom lead in the doctrinal debates in the area of stabilization, but these two countries define and approach stabilization quite differently. Most other nations, notably the large UN TCCs, have not invested similar efforts in conceptualizing stabilization. Furthermore, none of the international or regional organizations mentioned above possess a formal doctrine on stabilization at the time of writing, although NATO is apparently in the process of developing one.[5] Nor have these organizations defined specific stabilization-related tasks and mandates.[6]

Given the fact that there is no universally accepted definition of *stabilization*, this chapter starts with examining some of the most influential national doctrines that have had impact internationally in NATO, the AU, the EU, the UN and other international and regional organizations, by virtue of their member governments sending troops or influencing their decision-making (for example, at the Security Council).[7] While it is possible and often helpful to perceive stabilization as a set of capabilities requiring resources, rosters, and integrated approaches,[8] for the purpose of this book, it is more useful to try to identify key *qualitative features* that characterize and at times distinguish stabilization from other forms of contemporary operations, including UN peacekeeping operations and peace support operations with its full spectrum.[9]

Key feature 1: Stabilization is essentially political (the primacy of a political purpose)

First of all, it should be noted that stabilization is essentially a *political* endeavor, where the end-state of stabilization assistance is the creation of a stable and legitimate state that institutionalizes paths towards political settlement of conflict.[10] As such, it is a form of statebuilding, without the preexisting condition of a stable political settlement. It hence involves by necessity a mix of civil-military and diplomatic actors, where the integration of these different actors, processes, and projects is essential. In order to ensure coherence among these different actors and processes, it is increasingly recognized that, as a key lesson learned from the past decade of engaging in various stabilization missions, assistance and projects must drive towards the achievement of the common goal—that is, to assist emerging or fragile states to achieve stability and legitimacy, with the ability to resolve disputes without resorting to violence, and the acceptance and buy-in of formal structures by local populations through building human and national security; fostering host government capacity and legitimacy; and stimulating economic and infrastructure development.[11] From this perspective, the liberal template of statebuilding assistance where a large number of projects across humanitarian, social, economic, and political sectors are accorded simultaneous focus is rather problematic; rather, prioritization of assistance needs to be made on the basis of the end-state, i.e., the creation of the stable and legitimate political order, which makes the statebuilding process essentially a political one.

It is often recognized, however, that the "end-state" or stable political order is something that is indefinable *a priori*; rather, the aim is to create a space or condition for a locally determined political arrangement to emerge and sustain itself. Hence stabilization differs from cases of peacebuilding assistance, where an agreed political process is in place; or peacekeeping, where a ceasefire or peace agreement is in place and where the parties to the agreement consent to the role of the peacekeeping mission (see below for further discussion).

Key feature 2: The lack of, or divided and fluid nature of, consent by strategic actors

One of the key characteristics that distinguishes stabilization from peacekeeping is the lack of, or divided and changeable nature of, consent from the local parties at the strategic level. Moreover, in stabilization, consent must be negotiated constantly in order to acquire or maintain it as the basis of the operation. It is often the case also that in stabilization, local parties—the population, societal actors, and the elites often linked with armed groups—are fragmented and are likely to be multifaceted in terms of allegiances to, and relations with, the state and governing authorities of concern. The complex nature of relations between the local population and elites to the state hence make the issue of consent for stabilization force even more complex.

As confirmed in both the reports of the Brahimi and Ramos-Horta panels on peace operations and defined in the 2008 Capstone Doctrine, the UN has an institutional preference for peacekeeping operations where consent at the strategic level is clearly given by all parties to the conflict. Indeed, the UN considers operations without such consent as "peace enforcement," and whilst the UN Security Council may authorize enforcement operations, the UN peacekeeping doctrine and both the Brahimi and Ramos-Horta panels reaffirm that such enforcement operations reside outside the purview of its peacekeeping functions and should ideally be undertaken by regional organizations like the African Union or coalitions of the willing that form *ad hoc* multinational forces for this purpose, such as the Australian-led International Force for East Timor (INTERFET), which began operating in 1999. The Ramos-Horta panel goes further to recommend that "extreme caution must guide any call for a UN peacekeeping operation to undertake enforcement tasks and that any such mandate task should be a time-limited, exceptional measure."[12] The Ramos-Horta panel was also at pains to specify that UN peacekeeping operations are not suited to engage in military counter-terrorism operations.[13]

The UN considers consent a precondition for effective peacekeeping operations, while acknowledging its fluctuating nature, and the 2008 Capstone Doctrine hence declares that the UN is not in the business of "creating" consent.[14] The tactical-level use of force, to protect civilians or to defend the mandate, however, is sanctioned, as long as such use of force is linked to an existing framework of political settlements and peace agreements.

This formulation is linear as peacekeeping is essentially linked to extant peace agreements. The Brahimi reform was very much about how to bring peacekeeping back from murky, grey-zone operations between war and peace to operations with a firm basis in existing peace agreements. The Ramos-Horta panel also reaffirms the crucial link between peacekeeping operations and peace agreements, but at the same time it recognizes that the UN will continue to find itself in conflict management situations. The panel notes that the "concepts, tools, mission structures and doctrine originally developed for peace implementation tasks may not be well suited for these settings."[15] UN peacekeeping doctrine is thus deeply linked to the notion that a pre-agreed ceasefire or peace agreement needs to be in place. The role of the mission is to help the parties to the conflict, that has now come together in a peace process, to "keep" the peace by facilitating the implementation of the agreement and acting as an impartial observer and guarantor of the process. The symbolism of UN peacekeeping—blue helmets and white vehicles—further reinforce the image of a non-fighting, transparent, and impartial force that is not a party to the conflict.

Stabilization, by contrast, operates in a context where a political settlement is lacking, hence neither peace agreements nor consent from the parties to the conflict can be assumed as a preexisting condition for operations. However, in most stabilization contexts the host government agrees to, if not welcomes, the stabilization mission and there is thus some form of consent from one party to the conflict, albeit often extremely fragile.

Stabilization usually entails close cooperation with government forces, for example, when training and supporting local security forces.

Consent, however, is never a clear-cut issue in stabilization; rather, in stabilization, consent is negotiated, and given by local parties who see merit in involving the international community in their attempts to consolidate or expand their power base. At times, the possibility cannot be denied that consent is acquired or maintained through a combination of diplomacy and coercion, if necessary. In addition, stabilization forces necessarily have to renegotiate and adapt their position when the population and key elites renegotiate their own positions *vis-à-vis* the state, shifting the conditions for political arrangements which the stabilization force is expected to support. If stabilization forces support government security forces, the relationship between stabilization forces and local elites and the populace necessarily becomes more complicated as allegiances among local power holders shift.

Key feature 3: Approaches to campaign authority

As a result of a stabilization force's complex relations with local consent, the campaign authority of stabilization missions differs from that in peacekeeping operations. In peacekeeping, consent is the legal foundation and backbone of the deployment of the operation, hence of its authority, and formal consent is complemented by other aspects of campaign authority such as the mandate, the way in which the mandate is implemented, and the way in which local expectations are met by peacekeepers.[16] In stabilization, campaign authority derived from the consent of the host government is not sufficient, as consent from the other parties to the conflict is likely to be lacking, divided, or fluid. Whilst all stabilization operations must necessarily have a clear basis in international law (in the form of Security Council authorization or by invitation from the host state), non-UN missions draw only the main parameters of their mandates from UN resolutions. The additional, often more important, direction is provided by those that undertake the operation. But a stabilization force's authority may be compromised or enhanced by the way it implements its mandates and the way it deals with local expectations, even to a greater degree than in UN peacekeeping contexts, for the overall political arrangement is either still being negotiated or non-existent. Moreover, a stabilization force's relations with the host state also influence the way campaign authority is exercised.

Stabilization missions' campaign authority has implications most notably for the use of force. Just as the use of force in UN peace operations is dependent upon, and linked to, strategic level consent, the use of force in stabilization is also linked to the campaign authority and the overall political arrangement that drives the mission. In the UN context, one important consideration is whether a mission is authorized to use force for "offensive" or "defensive" operations.[17] In UN peacekeeping operations, the use of force is authorized for self-defense, and since the 2008 Capstone Doctrine also in defense of the mandate. In addition, the Security Council may authorize the use of force to, for instance, protect civilians. These are all examples of defensive or protection tasks. However, in the case of the Force Intervention Brigade (FIB) in the DRC, as discussed in Chapter 9, the Security Council authorized the offensive use of force to forcefully disarm and neutralize the M23 and other rebel groups. This has raised the question as to the outer limits of peacekeeping. How far down the spectrum of use of force can a UN peacekeeping mission go before it is no longer peacekeeping, before it has crossed the threshold into enforcement and offensive operations? As we argue below, one way in which to address this question is to place UN missions that are authorized to use offensive force in a new category of UN peace operations, namely "UN stabilization missions."

In stabilization, the use of force is aimed at influencing the behavior of aggressors, so that they are deterred, contained, or even rendered unable to use violence, with the larger goal of encouraging them to pursue their grievances and interests as part of a peaceful negotiated political process. The use of offensive force in a stabilization context, however, still needs to be linked to the overall stabilization effort and the political end-state goal that entails. Very often this is expressed in the constraining principles of proportional or minimal necessary force, as excessive force is likely to have undesirable consequences on the perception by the parties to the conflict or the local population in general regarding the legitimacy of those who employ such force. Inability to project enough force, however, also lowers the credibility of the stabilization force, so there is an emphasis on projecting a credible capacity and will to use force, if stability should be challenged.

Key Feature 4: Stabilization is a process, not activities

There is a lack of clarity concerning whether stabilization refers to a "process"[18] towards a political goal, or a set of "activities" that are understood to be "non-traditional" by the military.[19] For example, in the US thinking, *stability tasks* are defined, and *stability* refers to, a building block of "full-spectrum operation." Hence stability becomes part of counterinsurgency and other operational themes. By contrast, the UK thinking denotes stabilization as a context, or an approach in its own right. Although stabilization is often interpreted to provide for a familiar platform on which to understand the specific tasks the military performs in stabilization, this approach is inherently problematic unless these tasks are clearly linked to the political goal of the stabilization effort.

In our view, stabilization is essentially a strategy, where the theory of change is to contain aggressors and spoilers and enforce stability so as to create a political space that is more conducive to moderates on all sides finding a political path out of the conflict. Stabilization is thus a means towards a political end-goal, hence it needs to be managed flexibly, with the understanding also that the process actually could go backwards and is likely to be fraught with uncertainty and unintended consequences. The reliance on the idea that stabilization is part of a set of linear activities also tends to put operations into rigid conceptual "boxes," thus reducing the room for adaptation and innovation.

Stabilization as a concept may share these common tenets, but the concept is essentially still ill-defined and fraught with disputes. Because it is simply unrealistic to expect that all differences in interpretations will be resolved, each agency or organization may have to continue to adopt its own concepts and methodologies for stabilization as needed. For instance, a UN stabilization concept will need to be contextualized and positioned with reference to existing UN concepts and doctrines on peacekeeping, peace enforcement, use of force, and so forth.

One serious issue when examining the stabilization terminology and concept is that there is a lack of clarity about the boundaries between counterinsurgency and stabilization, and stabilization and peacekeeping.[20] As regards the former, questions are asked regarding whether stabilization presupposes the existence of insurgency, or merely a state of destabilization and insecurity that threatens the viability of the state. A related issue is determining, in cases where a counterinsurgency doctrine already exists, whether a standalone stabilization doctrine is needed as well, as a counterinsurgency doctrine, by nature, covers operational-level or operational-strategic level guidance for practitioners. Principles are also similar in existing stabilization and counterinsurgency doctrines.[21] The standard interpretation is that where the threat to stability is an insurgency and a decision is made to counter it, stabilization then becomes counterinsurgency: Hence, counterinsurgency is a subset of a broader stabilization concept. We contend that both stabilization and counterinsurgency, if implemented comprehensively, will necessarily address a larger set of issues and dimensions that determine the political viability of the state and the sustainability of a political settlement. Stabilization will, however, imply broader political contingencies and will not always involve attempts to defeat insurgencies by isolating and neutralizing them.

In a similar vein, when the threat to stability is terrorism, stabilization could include elements of counter-terrorism. However, stabilization is not the same as counter-terrorism—which the Ramos-Horta panel excludes from the UN's tasks. Stabilization is rarely what counter-terrorism would imply, i.e., attempts to target terrorists.

Furthermore, there is confusion about the relationship or boundary between stabilization and peacekeeping. Although many governments formally take stabilization and peacekeeping as quite separate and distinct tasks, the issue arises because non-UN stabilization operations often overlap with peacekeeping operations in terms of tactical-level activities, phases, and at times narratives, despite differences in campaign authority. In the UN context, as discussed in more detail in the next session, the Security Council and Secretariat have started to use the stabilization concept and have introduced stabilization tasks in several UN peacekeeping missions, such as in the CAR, the DRC, and Mali. We are of the opinion, however, that to equate UN peacekeeping with stabilization where there is no political settlement, hence requiring different approach to force and campaign authority, appears especially misplaced.

To further complicate the confusion, some employ the term *stabilization* in the UN context as an overarching concept for "late peace-keeping" or "early peacebuilding," which integrates peacekeeping, peacebuilding, statebuilding, and peace consolidation in a post-conflict setting.[22] This interpretation may offer a clearly divergent understanding from the previously discussed key features of stabilization, and differs from the interpretation that places stabilization as an over-arching umbrella term that may include offensive tactics at the higher end of the force spectrum. For example, the Ramos-Horta panel situates what it terms conflict management missions at the opposite end of the spectrum, amidst ongoing conflicts, to help: "(i) deter escalation; (ii) contain conflict; (iii) protect civilians, and; (iv) attempt to start or revive a peace process."[23]

Such disagreements in interpretation and understanding are significant because differing interpretations will result in different preferences for the timing of engagement and the actual content of operations, as well as the way in which they are carried out. These differing interpretations can be identified between the mandate given by the Security Council and how the mandate is operationalized into tasks by the mission on the ground. At the field level, differing interpretations can emerge between the civilian and military components or even between different TCCs.[24]

In our view, stabilization has a range, which could cover, at the higher end of the spectrum, proactive protection of civilians, and protecting governments and political processes from aggressors, including with the offensive use of force where necessary to proactively degrade the capacity of the aggressors to use violence. At the lower end of the spectrum, stabilization can include defensive actions to protect civilians, governments, and political processes, which could transition into peacekeeping when a peace settlement is in place and stability has been sufficiently restored.

A further confusion with regard to the stabilization concept is the distinction between stabilization and peace enforcement. In the UN context, the upper end of the range of stabilization operations is often conflated with peace enforcement, i.e., when offensive force is used to contain or degrade aggressors. Peace enforcement is defined in the Capstone Doctrine as use of force conducted at the strategic level in the absence of local consent to restore peace, and is normally entrusted to member states or regional organizations and arrangements.[25] The UN peacekeeping doctrine leaves this out of the purview of actual peacekeeping. Despite this, as discussed in Chapter 9, the use of force in contemporary UN peacekeeping is escalating, and in the case of the FIB in the DRC, a UN peacekeeping mission was mandated by the Security Council to undertake offensive operations against explicitly mentioned armed groups. There is no basis for this type of use of force in the current UN peacekeeping doctrine. However, Chapter VII of the UN Charter provides for enforcement actions, and this is used by the Security Council to authorize all coercive actions, including sanctions, and actions by "coalitions of the willing" such as the 1991 Iraq War or the 2011 Libya campaign. The Security Council also invokes Chapter VII when it authorizes UN peacekeeping missions to use force to protect civilians, but this does not equate these missions with peace enforcement. Similarly, we argue that one cannot equate stabilization missions with peace enforcement, although there may be cases where the two overlap. All stabilization missions are not peace enforcement, and all peace enforcement missions are not stabilization missions. As discussed in the next section, we associate UN stabilization operations with a certain set of characteristics that distinguish them from some types of peace enforcement missions.

UN stabilization missions

The UN Multidimensional Integrated Stabilization Mission in the Central African Republic (MINUSCA), the UN Stabilization Mission in the Democratic Republic of the Congo (MONUSCO), and the UN Multidimensional Integrated Stabilization Mission in Mali (MINUSMA) reflect a new trend in all having stabilization in their names and mandated tasks. Whilst each of these missions have their own unique features, taken together they represent a new category of UN operations, which has to do with protecting civilians and governments, or governance structures, against an aggressor(s) or general destabilization, amidst ongoing violence, while at the same time being part of a larger process that seeks a political settlement for the conflict. The UN Stabilization Mission in Haiti (MINUSTAH) similarly has stabilization in its name and tasks, but seems to reflect a broader use of the term that does not fit well with how the concept is used in the other three UN missions mentioned above.

If we analyze the CAR, DRC, and Mali missions we can identify that the characteristics they have in common—which in essence match the key features of stabilization analyzed earlier—are as follows:

1 that they operate in the midst of an on-going conflict, and without a political solution or settlement that is sufficiently comprehensive to bring the conflict to an end;
2 that the aspired end-state of the intervention is the emergence of a stable and secure political settlement;
3 that their core tasks are to contribute to restoring and maintaining stability and security by helping to protect a government and its people from identified aggressors;
4 that they work in support of and alongside the local authorities and security forces who have the primary responsibility for protecting the government and its people; and
5 that they are expected to use force, including offensively when mandated and where necessary, to contain and degrade the capacity of the aggressors to pose a threat to the people, government, and international actors.

On the basis of these characteristics we define *UN stabilization missions* as operations that aim to help states in crisis to restore order and stability in the absence of a peace settlement, by using force and other means to help national and local authorities to contain aggressors (as identified in relevant Security Council resolutions) and to protect civilians, in the context of a larger peace process that seeks a lasting political solution to the crisis.

The central tension between the established UN peacekeeping principles of consent, impartiality, and the limited use of force, and these

UN stabilization missions is that the theory of change of the stabilization missions is to contribute to stability and security by containing identified aggressors and spoilers, while protecting the general population. In each of these missions the Security Council has identified specific aggressors that need to be contained—the M23 and others in the DRC, Al-Qaeda in the Islamic Maghreb (AQIM) and others in Mali, and Séléka and anti-Balaka in the CAR. Depending on the exact language of the mandate, containing these aggressors can include proactively degrading their capacity to use violence, and in the case of the mandate of the FIB in the DRC, the UN mission was authorized to neutralize the threat.

As analyzed in Chapter 9 by Kjeksrud and Vermeij, in the case of the FIB the mandate to undertake offensive operations goes beyond the established use of force principle, which has up to now always been framed in defensive terms. The UN Peacekeeping Capstone Doctrine of 2008 opened the door for the tactical use of force to contain spoilers and to defend the mandate. The use of force against pre-identified aggressors, and the use of offensive force, both mean that the Security Council has, in these stabilization missions, authorized the strategic use of force. Hence the authors of Chapter 9 argued that the mandate of the FIB crossed the boundary between peacekeeping and stabilization (or even "peace enforcement" in their parlance).

It should be noted also that these military operations went alongside assistance to promote political processes and governance structures that is aimed at preventing and managing further violent conflict, leading to peace consolidation. Whilst these stabilization missions are tasked with containing aggressors and creating a general climate of safety and stability, other initiatives are pursuing the political track, with what is regarded as the legitimate political actors. In most of these cases, the aggressors use long-standing tensions between those at the center of power and those on the periphery that feel marginalized and excluded, to mobilize opposition against the central government. There is thus a linkage with legitimate political debates, but the Security Council has singled out the identified aggressors because it sanctions the use of force to pursue political objectives. These stabilization missions are thus tasked to contain those aggressors that use violence to pursue their political objectives, whilst the UN more broadly, together with regional actors, supports and encourages the parties to the conflict to seek peaceful political solutions.

UN stabilization missions should thus not be misunderstood as seeking military or security solutions to these conflicts. They should rather be seen as part of a larger strategy to proactively shape the security environment, by containing the aggressors and improving the security situation for the civilian population, in order to create space for the political and peacebuilding actions that are aimed at seeking medium- to long-term political solutions. At the same time, increased security also enables humanitarian assistance to reach those in need and allows early recovery actions that can help to restore and improve the provision of basic services and civil administration.

Whilst the UN has developed comprehensive guidance on the issue of protection of civilians, it lacks any doctrinal thinking about stabilization, including guidance on how force can be proportionally applied to contain or degrade aggressors. Such a doctrine should cover the spectrum of operations, from defensive tactics to the use of proactive and offensive tactics (but that is usually carried out simultaneously). It should also consider what implications stabilization operations, and especially the use of offensive tactics, may have for civilian and humanitarian counterparts, both in the UN mission and engaged elsewhere in the UN or broader international assistance community. Furthermore, there have not been attempts at sufficiently considering the doctrinal implications of incorporating various capabilities, such as naval assets, as considered in this volume in Chapter 10, or technologies that allow for enhanced surveillance, intelligence gathering, and information sharing, as addressed in Chapter 11.

As the Ramos-Horta panel also urged, the UN has to clarify and define what it means when using the term *stabilization* in a UN peace operation context. It is the contention of this book that stabilization is distinct from peacekeeping, and also at times from peace enforcement. The UN also needs to make it explicit that stabilization itself is a broad concept that goes beyond the employment of military force to contain aggressors, and that requires a comprehensive and integrated approach to achieving stability. On that basis, the UN can start defining its own approach and role in stabilization.

Given the risks and costs associated with stabilization, it is natural for some to question whether the UN should be doing this kind of mission at all. The doctrine has consistently been that when enforcement or stabilization is necessary the Security Council should authorize a coalition of the willing or a multinational force (MNF) to secure and stabilize the situation, and once a peace agreement is in place and the violence has stopped, the UN can replace the MNF with a UN peacekeeping mission. A gap has now emerged between this established doctrine and the recent precedents in the CAR, the DRC, and Mali where the UN has deployed "peacekeeping" missions amidst ongoing conflicts with a stabilization mandate.

The AU and French missions that were first deployed in Mali and the CAR followed the MNF model, but these forces needed to be relieved because they were not self-sustainable. The UN ended up—as a last resort—being deployed into these situations, even though they were not yet sufficiently stable to warrant a peacekeeping mandate. Deploying missions into Mali and CAR with a stabilization mandate was thus not the result of a strategic choice based on UN doctrinal assessment of the comparative advantage of deploying stabilization vs. peacekeeping forces. In reality, the Security Council had no other option but to deploy UN operations, because the countries that would otherwise have had to fund these missions, i.e., France and those that would have funded the AU missions, deemed the costs too high. As these countries are also members of the Security Council and major financial contributors to UN peacekeeping, they were able to convince the UN that it should take the responsibility for these missions, regardless of the doctrinal concerns that the Secretariat and major TCCs may have had. As the Ramos-Horta panel recognized, the Security Council has the prerogative to authorize UN operations to undertake offensive operations, as it did in Somalia in 1993 and in the DRC in 2013.[26]

We believe this trend is likely to continue because in Africa the AU and sub-regions do not currently have access to predictable funding, and there are few other regional organizations that have the legitimacy and credibility to take on such a role, and in a changing and uncertain global order the UN is one of the few institutions that have the credibility and legitimacy to undertake such missions. Long-term conflict trends also suggest that there will continue to be a need for this kind of stability mission for the foreseeable future. It thus looks highly likely that the Security Council will find it necessary to mandate such missions again. If so, there is a glaring need to provide doctrinal guidance on how the UN should, and should not, act when given such mandates.

We thus agree with the Ramos-Horta panel that the UN is likely to continue to find itself facing these conflict management situations. In fact, we are of the view that these stabilization missions reflect a larger shift in the orientation of UN peacekeeping from conflict resolution to conflict management. In the early post–Cold War era UN peacekeeping was typically used to implement comprehensive peace agreements aimed at resolving civil wars. Over the last decade this has changed and UN peacekeeping has been increasingly used to manage conflicts, i.e., to contain aggressors and spoilers, and to protect civilians. Simultaneously, other UN tools and capacities, such as special envoys and Special Political Missions, or similar capacities of regional and sub-regional organizations, such as the African Union, the League of Arab States, the Economic Community of West African States (ECOWAS), or the Intergovernmental Authority on Development (IGAD), have been increasingly used to pursue the political track. In addition to the three UN stabilization missions discussed earlier, other UN peacekeeping missions, such as the AU/UN Hybrid Operation in Darfur (UNAMID) and, post-December 2013, the UN Mission in South Sudan (UNMISS), also reflect this broader trend where UN peace-keeping is limited to conflict management whilst others inside and outside the UN (IGAD in South Sudan, Algeria in Mali, etc.) are leading the effort to resolve the political conflict.

The Ramos-Horta panel has asked the UN to clarify its usage of the term stabilization, but it is our view that the UN needs to go further and doctrinally clarify the distinction between UN peacekeeping and UN stabilization missions. In the next section we argue that stabilization is not a form of peacekeeping, and thus cannot be accommodated within the UN peacekeeping doctrine. On this basis we argue that the UN should develop a UN stabilization doctrine that is distinct from and complimentary to the UN peacekeeping doctrine.

Demarcating and distinguishing peace operations and stabilization: Towards a new UN stabilization doctrine

If the UN is mandated to undertake stabilization operations, what are some of the key considerations that need to be taken into account? As the Ramos-Horta panel also noted, the typical UN peacekeeping mission, and the units, trained, prepared, and equipped to do consensual peacekeeping, are not suitable for the kind of conflict management tasks that stabilization missions require. When the UN is mandated to undertake stabilization missions, some of the following factors need to be taken into account:

- Under the understanding that stabilization is a long-term and comprehensive endeavor, a UN stabilization mission needs to be given a clear mandate that distinguishes it from others inside and outside the UN that may have complimentary responsibilities. The stabilization mission's tasks need to be linked to clear milestones and an overall comprehensive strategy. Such a focus generates the kind of political attention and strategic coherence that stabilization missions require to succeed. The Ramos-Horta panel notes that in situations where a UN operation is deployed "in parallel with a non-UN force . . . a clear division of labour and distinction of roles must guide their respective operations."[27]

- Not all TCCs have the will or capability to do offensive operations, which in the stabilization context might include actions aimed at degrading or even neutralizing aggressors. It may thus be better to work with a few TCCs that do have the capabilities and are willing to use it. This means that the FIB-model, where a special brigade or battle-group is created for a limited period around a specific objective, is a more realistic way to generate the kind of forces needed for stabilization operations. Mali presents another complimentary model, where nations with advanced technological capabilities can provide tactical intelligence and support capabilities to those forces that have the capacity to undertake offensive operations.
- If we associate UN peacekeeping with blue helmets and white vehicles, which symbolize the impartiality and transparency of an inter-positional force, then stabilization operations can be said to require a green posture. If your task is to degrade or even neutralize the capabilities of identified aggressors, then stabilization operations must be able to use stealth, attack with surprise, and may need special forces that can operate behind the lines to gather tactical intelligence.
- In most cases, only TCCs that have a direct interest at stake will be willing to deploy units to a mission where active combat is likely, because only they will be able to justify the increased cost in casualties and loss and damage to equipment, etc. However, using countries with a national interest at stake has both positive and negative consequences, and more effort would need to be devoted to monitor and manage the negative consequences, both at mission and higher political and strategic levels.

These factors, which are not meant to constitute an exhaustive list, remind us why stabilization operations, especially those with an authority to engage in offensive tactics, requires a different mind-set, approach, and set of capabilities than those employed in UN peacekeeping. A business-as-usual approach is likely to result in a serious mismatch between supply (UN peacekeeping) and demand (stabilization context), as the 2014/15 experiences of the UN mission in Mali shows. The mission's high casualty rate—with 68 fatalities from hostile action as of 31 May 2016—reflects that there is indeed a mismatch between the mandate, the operationalization of the mandate, and the resources made available to the mission in this process.

Stabilization operations that are deployed amidst conflict, and that are tasked with containing aggressors, should anticipate that the aggressors will test their resolve, and the mission should thus be ready to protect itself and other international actors associated with it. When the Security Council mandates a stabilization operation, such missions must be sufficiently resourced with troops, enablers, and appropriate support, as well as with leadership and decision-making processes, to enable them to successfully implement their mandate. There is a considerable risk, however, that the trend of the Security Council to mandate increasingly robust stabilization mandates will not be matched by the requisite resources or capabilities, nor doctrinal developments, to enable these operations to achieve their goals.

Whilst UN stabilization missions should be deployed as part of a larger comprehensive political strategy, the UN will need to take into account that the mission will be constrained in its ability to play a leading or prominent role in mediation and reconciliation, as its actions to contain aggressors may make it more likely to be seen as a party to the conflict by those actors and sectors of the population that are associated with the aggressors. Here we disagree with the Ramos-Horta panel that when a UN mission finds itself in a conflict management posture "it is indispensable that the United Nations play the lead or a leading role in the peace process."[28]

To some degree, the UN missions in Darfur and South Sudan, because their protection of civilians mandates are perceived by their host governments as partial, are already indicative of this implication, and as a result in both cases the missions themselves cannot play a prominent role in resolving the larger political disputes. However, they do both play important roles in creating the conditions that enable the political process.

We are of the opinion that all stabilization operations, because of their alignment with the government of the day that represents the state, are likely to be considered partial to some extent by some of the political actors and parts of the population, until a political settlement is in place and stability has been restored. Whilst UN stabilization operations should strive to present themselves as impartial when it comes to the political settlement, their mandate to act against certain identified aggressors implies that they cannot expect to be perceived as impartial by all the actors in the conflict. This has important consequences for the role the mission can play in political negotiations. It also has to be carefully considered in the support the mission provides to national authorities in statebuilding and the extension of state authority, including in security-sector reform, strengthening the rule of law, enhancing state-society relations, supporting elections, and strengthening governance and government services. We believe there is an inverse relationship between the level of force that needs to be used to achieve and maintain stability and the degree to which a UN stabilization mission will be perceived as an impartial mediator in a peace process. As stabilization operations slide towards the more robust end of the scale, the ability to provide good offices and mediate in the crisis will decrease as the UN is increasingly considered, and effectively is, a party to the conflict.

Therefore, we argue that stabilization operations require a new UN doctrine that distinguishes it from the existing peacekeeping doctrine and its core principles, identity, and approach. We do not believe that stabilization operations that meet the characteristics discussed earlier can be accommodated within UN peacekeeping doctrine. When the Security Council mandates the secretary-general to undertake stabilization operations, the UN should not have to do so using the existing peacekeeping doctrine and its blue helmet identity.

A new UN stabilization doctrine with a separate identity should be developed that provides guidance on the conditions that require stabilization and the criteria and benchmarks the UN should consider when deciding whether to deploy a stabilization or peacekeeping mission. Such a new doctrine should define clearly what stabilization means in the UN context, and how it differs from peacekeeping. It should also provide guidance on the kind of leadership tools, command and control, capabilities, mission support and logistics, and rules of engagement and equipment that would be required should the UN be tasked with a stabilization mandate.

A separate stabilization doctrine will help to protect the existing peacekeeping doctrine and identity it from being misapplied in contexts where it is not fit for purpose. It will also help the UN maintain credibility and legitimacy by ensuring that it has appropriate doctrine, equipment, and soldiers that are prepared for the type of task assigned to it by the Security Council.

In terms of core principles for stabilization missions, the UN needs to clarify what consent and impartiality mean in a stabilization context and how they may differ from the way these principles are applied in UN peacekeeping. Consent by the host government is likely to be a requirement for the UN in most cases, bar extreme mass atrocity crime scenarios, but consent from the other parties to the conflict is likely not to be a prerequisite, especially not from those associated with the aggressors such missions will be tasked to contain. However, wide consent is of course desirable and gaining consent, including through an impartial posture towards all the peaceful political entities, will be a benchmark for a transition to a UN peacekeeping operation, and should thus be embedded in the idea of "campaign authority."

The principles regarding the use of force will be important elements for a UN stabilization doctrine. As the proactive and offensive use of force concepts are new elements not previously dealt with in UN doctrine, they will need to be unpacked in detail, together with associated principles of proportionality and minimum necessary use of force. Such a doctrine will also need to provide guidance to UN forces acting in support of national security forces, including principles and procedures for vetting, accountability, and monitoring.

In addition to military action, the UN stabilization doctrine should also identify the role and contribution of the UN police as well as civilian components in stabilization contexts. Individual UN police officers and formed police units can play a significant role in building national capacity and in supporting and bolstering national police capacity. The "civil affairs" component can play an important role in support of enhancing state-society relations and extending state authority. The "public information" component will have an important role to play in providing information and countering the propaganda of the aggressors and their associates. The "political affairs" component will be central in analyzing the motives and behaviors of the identified aggressors and keeping the stabilization operations politically aligned with the larger political strategy of the UN and international community. More intense military action increases the risk of misconduct, and negative consequences for the civilian and humanitarian community, and units that have the competencies to monitor, mitigate, and advise the mission leadership on these aspects, and that can manage the liaison with the humanitarian community, will also be crucial for the success of such missions.

The adoption of a stabilization doctrine does not imply that the UN should seek to play an expanded role in stabilization contexts. The UN should maintain its preference not to do stabilization operations, and thus make it clear that it should only be tasked to undertake stabilization operations in exceptional cases and as a last resort. In order to avoid the exception becoming the rule, the UN should take steps to help ensure that others that are willing, such as the AU, are better able to do so in future: for instance, by funding AU operations, or helping to find more predictable sources of funding for AU operations, so that the UN is not forced into taking over stabilization operations from the AU for lack of resources, as it had to do in the CAR.

Another important aspect relates to the larger strategic coherence of the international effort. If a UN stabilization mission is only one element in a larger UN and international engagement, how is the larger UN and international effort coordinated? Who ensures overall coherence and alignment? What processes are in place to ensure that the different parts of the UN and internal system pull in the same direction, and are aligned to local political developments? Recent experiences in Afghanistan, Somalia, and elsewhere have demonstrated how difficult it is to achieve coherence among international and regional organizations such as the UN, the AU, NATO, the EU, and the World Bank, and how challenging it is to align their goals with the priorities and objectives of the national and local authorities.

Conclusion

The Ramos-Horta panel pointed to the need to better clarify what stabilization entails in a UN context. In this chapter we have made a first attempt to contribute to a deeper reflection on what stabilization means in the UN peace operations context, and have considered the diverging understandings that currently exist. We have argued that stabilization needs to be clearly defined to make sure that the UN and its partners are on the same page when future UN stabilization missions are mandated and deployed.

If we zoom further out, our modest ambition has been to contribute to a deeper discussion on UN doctrinal development by way of bringing to light and discussing key member states' positions on UN peacekeeping, as well as emerging practices from the field. Together with the Ramos-Horta report, we hope that this book can contribute to and stimulate further debate on UN doctrine for peace operations.

This debate is becoming increasingly important and relevant. After many years' decline, the number of conflicts has been on the rise over the last few years, so the relevance and need for UN peace operations will grow. At the same time, and in a period of turbulence in global governance, UN peace operations remain the most credible and legitimate international mechanism for conflict management and resolution. In addition, we are in a period characterized by financial austerity since the global financial crisis in 2008–9. In this larger context, UN peace operations will continue to be the preferred (and most cost-efficient) choice of the international community when it comes to dealing with conflicts and increasing transnational asymmetrical threats.

Notes

1 UN, "Uniting our Strengths for Peace: Politics, Partnerships and People," Report of the High-Level Independent Panel on Peace Operations, New York, 16 June 2015.

2 Ibid., 28.

3 Ibid., 29.

4 Sian Herbert notes that out of the 49 missions examined in his report, 30 use the words *stability* or *stabilization*. See Sian Herbert, "Stability and Stabilisation Approaches in Multinational Interventions," Helpdesk GSDRC Research Report, Applied Knowledge Services, www.gsdrc.org/docs/open/HDQ966.pdf.

5 NATO, "Political Guidance on Ways to Improve NATO's Involvement in Stabilisation and Reconstruction," Brussels, 2011.

6 For an academic review of such stabilization tasks, see Christian Dennys, *Military Intervention, Stabilisation and Peace: The Search for Stability* (London: Routledge, 2014).

7 The so-called P3 in the Security Council (France, the United Kingdom, and the United States) has through precedent taken responsibility for drafting most of the Security Council resolutions, and it is thus reasonable to link the emergence of the term *stabilization* in UN mandates to its prominence in the domestic doctrines and usage in these countries over the last decade.

8 NATO, "Political Guidance"; and Chiyuki Aoi and Yee-Kuang Heng, *Asia-Pacific Nations in International Peace Support and Stability Missions* (New York: Palgrave, 2014).

9 For an earlier academic attempt as such, see Chiyuki Aoi, *Legitimacy and the Use of Armed Force: Stability Missions in the Post-Cold War Era* (London: Routledge, 2011).

10 Note, as a prominent example, UK Ministry of Defence, Development, Concepts and Doctrine Center (DCDC), "Security and Stabilisation: The Military Contribution," Joint Doctrine Publication (JDP) 3-40, November 2009. This states that "stabilisation is the process that supports states which are entering, enduring or emerging from conflict in order to: prevent or reduce violence; protect the population and key infrastructure; promote political processes and governance structures which lead to a political settlement that institutionalises non-violent contests for power; and prepares for sustainable social and economic development," ibid., xv. See also Stabilisation Unit (a British cross-government unit), "The UK Government's Approach to Stabilisation (2014)," London, 2014, www.sclr.stabilisationunit.gov.uk/attachments/article/520/TheUKApproachtoStabilisationMay2014.pdf.

11 Ibid., 24.

12 UN, "Uniting our Strengths for Peace," 32.

13 Ibid., 31.

14 DPKO/DFS, "United Nations Peacekeeping Operations: Principles and Guidelines" (so-called "Capstone Doctrine"), United Nations, New York, 2008, www.un.org/en/peacekeeping/documents/capstone_eng.pdf.

15 UN, "Uniting our Strengths for Peace," 30.

16 UK Ministry of Defence, "Security and Stabilisation," 2–13; see also US Department of the Army, "Stability" doc. no. FM 3-07, 2014.

17 Cedric de Coning, "Do we need a UN Stabilisation Doctrine?" in *What Needs to Change in UN Peace Operations? An Expert Briefing Book Prepared for the High-Level Independent Panel on Peace Operations*, ed. Richard Gowan and Adam C. Smith (New York: New York University and International Peace Institute, 2014), 31–2.

18 Interview with official at UK Ministry of Defense, DCDC, 2009.
19 Note the US military definition of stability operation: Stability operations encompass "various military missions, tasks, and activities conducted outside the United States in coordination with other instruments of national power to maintain or reestablish a safe and secure environment, provide essential governmental services, emergency infrastructure reconstruction, and humanitarian relief (JP 3–0)," as cited in US Department of the Army, "Stability" and the subsequent passages on pages vi-vii of the same document.
20 See Samuel Griffin for a discussion about doctrinal boundaries: Samuel Griffin, "Iraq, Afghanistan and the Future of British Military Doctrine: from Counterinsurgency to Stabilisation," *International Affairs* 87, no. 2 (2011): 317–33.
21 See, for example, AFM; and Ministry of Defence, "Security and Stabilisation."
22 Robert Muggah, "The UN Turns to Stabilisation," *Global Observatory*, 5 December 2014.
23 UN, "Uniting our Strengths for Peace," 30.
24 John Karlsrud and Adam C. Smith (2015) *European Military Participation in MINUSMA: Experiences and Lessons-Learned.* New York: International Peace Institute.
25 DPKO/DFS, "United Nations Peacekeeping Operations" (Capstone Doctrine), 16–19.
26 UN, "Uniting our Strengths for Peace," 31.
27 Ibid., 32.
28 Ibid., 31.

Index

intelligence 1, 230, 272, 278, 282, 283, 301; consent and 16; intelligence unit 9, 14, 278; stabilisation 81; US 36; *see also* ASIFU; data/information
INTERFET (International Force for East Timor) 164, 196, 197, 250, 293
international law 119, 124, 281, 294; Russia 133, 135, 138, 148, 149
interoperability 3, 46, 262–3, 277
Iraq 3, 10, 146, 273, 298; NATO 7, 9, 147; UK 69, 77, 78, 81, 84, 85; US 35, 40, 52, 57
ITU (UN International Telecommunications Union) 272
Ivanov, Ivan 138

Japan 69, 153, 170

Karlsrud, John 1–30, 171, 211–26, 271–87
Kennedy, John F. 43, 44
Kjeksrud, Stian 27, 227–45, 300
Koenders, Bert 9
Kosovo 69, 77, 149, 190; consent 194, 204; EU 194–5; EULEX Kosovo 195; impartiality 193–4, 195, 204; independence 194–5; KFOR/NATO 39, 98, 100, 192, 193; mission that support the formation of new state/administration 21, 24, 26, 190, 191–5; sovereignty 190, 192–3; UN transitional civil administration 192–3, 194–5; *see also* UNMIK; Yugoslavia (former)

Ladsous, Hervé 231, 232, 237, 283
Latin America 153, 162–5, 166–7, 168, 170–1
League of Arab States 173, 277, 303
Lebanon 8, 91, 100, 101; Multinational Force mission 37; new technologies 282; *see also* UNIFIL
legitimacy 60, 61, 215; government 18, 61; peacekeeping mission 47, 51, 58, 61, 83, 90, 153, 308 (state-building 26, 200, 202, 205); stabilization 61; UN 90, 134–5, 205, 302, 306; *see also* impartiality

Liberia 7, 8, 13, 21, 23, 161; *see also* UNMIL
Libya 1, 99, 100, 298; China 118, 119; NATO 90, 136, 147, 223; regime change 118, 179; Russia 136; UN Security Council Resolution 1973: 118, 136, 179
Lilly, Damian 201
Liu Zhenmin 121–2
local ownership 19, 61, 218, 281
Lukin, Alexander 25, 132–51
Lute, Jane Holl 271

M23 (*Mouvement du 23 Mars*) 228, 234, 236, 238, 239, 278, 300; defeat 229, 230–1, 240; Rwanda/Uganda's support 229; use of force against 15, 240, 295; *see also* DRC
Mackinlay, John 72, 74
Mali 20, 161, 278; AFISMA 159, 167, 174, 232; ASIFU 9, 278; Barkhane Operation 99, 107, 231, 232; consent 17, 238; elections 232; France 90, 99, 100, 105, 107, 302; IED 231, 232, 233, 235, 236; impartiality 1, 2, 18, 27, 236, 237, 239 (*de facto* partiality 234–5); new technologies 273, 279, 282, 304; peace agreement, absence of 17; peace enforcement 167, 183; protection of civilians 8, 167, 232, 255; protection of government against insurgency 1, 2, 18, 22, 24, 27, 148, 231–3; robust peacekeeping 167–8, 282; Serval Operation 90, 99, 100, 107, 231, 232; stabilization 8–9, 11, 16–17, 20, 232, 240, 255, 290, 297, 299, 302, 304; terrorism 9, 17, 126, 160, 167–8, 169, 170, 231, 232, 235, 282, 300; UN peacekeeper, attacks on 1, 16, 28, 126, 170, 231–2, 234–5, 239, 282, 304; UN peacekeeping principles, challenges to 227, 233, 234–9; UN Security Council Resolution 2100: 107, 148, 165, 166, 170; UN Security Council Resolution 2164: 255; use of force 14–15, 16, 160, 227, 238–9; *see also* MINUSMA

Routledge Global Institutions Series

2 The UN Secretary-General and Secretariat (2005)
by Leon Gordenker (Princeton University)

1 The United Nations and Human Rights (2005)
A guide for a new era
by Julie A. Mertus (American University)

Books currently under contract include:

The Regional Development Banks
Lending with a regional flavor
by Jonathan R. Strand (University of Nevada)

Millennium Development Goals (MDGs)
For a people-centered development agenda?
by Sakiko Fukada-Parr (The New School)

The Bank for International Settlements
The politics of global financial supervision in the age of high finance
by Kevin Ozgercin (SUNY College at Old Westbury)

International Migration
by Khalid Koser (Geneva Centre for Security Policy)

The International Monetary Fund (2nd edition)
Politics of conditional lending
by James Raymond Vreeland (Georgetown University)

The UN Global Compact
by Catia Gregoratti (Lund University)

Institutions for Women's Rights
*by Charlotte Patton (York College, CUNY) and
Carolyn Stephenson (University of Hawaii)*

International Aid
by Paul Mosley (University of Sheffield)

Coping with Nuclear Weapons
by W. Pal Sidhu

Global Governance and China
The dragon's learning curve
edited by Scott Kennedy (Indiana University)

The Politics of Global Economic Surveillance
by Martin S. Edwards (Seton Hall University)

Mercy and Mercenaries
Humanitarian agencies and private security companies
by Peter Hoffman

Regional Organizations in the Middle East
by James Worrall (University of Leeds)

Reforming the UN Development System
The Politics of Incrementalism
by Silke Weinlich (Duisburg-Essen University)

The International Criminal Court
The Politics and practice of prosecuting atrocity crimes
by Martin Mennecke (University of Copenhagen)

BRICS
*by João Pontes Nogueira (Catholic University, Rio de Janeiro) and
Monica Herz (Catholic University, Rio de Janeiro)*

The European Union (2nd edition)
Clive Archer (Manchester Metropolitan University)

Protecting the Internally Displaced
Rhetoric and reality
Phil Orchard (University of Queensland)

For further information regarding the series, please contact:

Nicola Parkin, Editor, Politics & International Studies
Taylor & Francis
2 Park Square, Milton Park, Abingdon
Oxford OX14 4RN, UK
Nicola.parkin@tandf.co.uk
www.routledge.com